Memoirs o
Dalit Comm

Memoirs of a Dalit Communist

THE MANY WORLDS OF R.B. MORE

Edited, with an introduction, by ANUPAMA RAO

Translated by WANDANA SONALKAR

LeftWord

First published in January 2020 by
LeftWord Books
2254/2A Shadi Khampur
New Ranjit Nagar
New Delhi 110008
INDIA

LeftWord Books is the publishing division of
Naya Rasta Publishers Pvt. Ltd.

Marathi original © The Estate of R.B. More
English translation © Wandana Sonalkar, 2019
Introduction, and this volume, © Anupama Rao, 2019

First published in Marathi in 2003 as *Dalit va Communist Chalvalicha Sashakt Duva: Comrade R.B. More* ('Comrade R.B. More: A Powerful Link Between the Dalit and the Communist Movement') by Paryay Prakashan, 5/6 Rajgir Sadan, opp. Sion station, Mumbai 400022

leftword.com

ISBN 978-81-940778-0-0

Printed and bound by Chaman Enterprises, Delhi

CONTENTS

Note to Readers	11
Acknowledgements	13
Translator's Note	15
Ramchandra Babaji More and the Itineraries of Dalit Modernity by Anupama Rao	21
The Autobiography of Ramchandra Babaji More	49
The Biography of Ramchandra Babaji More by Satyendra More	109
Ancestors	109
The Historic First Tile-Roofed Two-Storey House Built by an Untouchable in India	111
Those Who Laid the Foundations of the Dalit Movement	112
Background of the Historic Mahad *Satyagraha*	122
More's First Meeting with Babasaheb	127
The First Opposition to Untouchability	128
The Caste Question	129
Dr. Babasaheb Ambedkar Absent at both Conferences on Untouchability in 1917–18	131
Montagu–Chelmsford Reforms and the Southborough Committee	132
Shahu Maharaj Initiates Dr. Babasaheb into the Movement	136
Founding of the Bahishkrit Hitakarini Sabha and the Colaba District Bahishkrit Parishad at Mahad	137
Establishment of the Mahar Samaj Seva Sangh	141

Implementation of the Bole Resolution in Dasgaon Before the Mahad *Satyagraha*	142
The Newspaper 'Bahishkrit Bharat' and More's Participation in Starting It	146
The Amaravati Temple *Satyagraha* and the Death of Balaram Ambedkar	148
Second *Satyagraha* Conference at Mahad—the Burning of the *Manusmriti*	149
Establishment of the Samaj Samata Sangh, or Association for Equality in Society	154
More's Work in the Farmers' Movement	157
The Simon Commission	161
More Joins the Communist Party	163
The First Dalit Communist	167
Having Left Babasaheb's Fold, More Remains Loyal to the Dalit Movement	168
Round Table Conference	172
Poona Pact	179
Comrade More's Work in the Trade Union Movement	184
The Kalaram Mandir *Satyagraha* at Nashik	191
More Becomes Active Again in the Peasant Association	195
Dedicated Dalit Comrades in the Communist Party	196
Independent Labour Party	202
More Turns Down the Offer of an Election Ticket	207
The Second World War—Congress and the Communists	209
The Stafford Cripps Mission and the Establishment of the Scheduled Castes Federation	213
More's Selection for the International Workers' Conference	216
Dalits Elect Com. Dange to the Legislative Assembly	220
More's Underground Life	221
Hardships of Life in the Movement	223
Defeat of Babasaheb in the Elections of 1952	230
Conversion to Buddhism	234
Babasaheb's Colleagues Also Join the Communist Party	235

The Ambedkar College at Mahad and More's Work in Education	239
More's Journalism	242
More and the Cultural World	246
The Communist Evaluation of the Caste Question	248
More's Activities in the Last Stage	255
The End and Last Respects	257
Glossary of People and Terms	261
Appendices	271
Appendix A	271
Appendix B	272
Index	281

The poet Tulsi Parab (1941–2016) introduced me to the public and political culture of a Bombay that once was. He brought that past to life through walks and conversations, and introduced me to people who continue to inspire.

I am heartbroken that this book did not see the light of day through his extended illness, even though it bears so many traces of what he taught me to see.

ANUPAMA RAO

NOTE TO READERS

For fidelity to the original, we give here some points of style that have been followed in the compilation of this volume.

Apart from emphasis, italics have been used for Marathi and Hindi words. Latin words are italicized, and so are non-English words used in literary criticism like '*Bildungsroman*'. The names of books, newspapers and magazines also appear in italics. While names of ancient texts such as the *Manusmriti* are italicized, corpuses such as the Vedas, Puranas, Dharmashastras, etc., appear in Roman. The first mention of an organization with a non-English name has been italicized in the translations.

We have used the spellings given by the translator/editor for all Marathi names. Exceptions to this rule are well-known, especially non-Marathi names, e.g. Diwan Bahadur Ramasamy Mudaliar, Asoka Mehta, Ajoy Ghosh, etc.; in such cases, the most commonly used spelling of their names has been used. Informal honorifics like 'buva' or 'dada' have been suffixed to the names, e.g. Gopalbuva, Madkebuva, Balaramdada, etc.

There are no footnotes in the Marathi original. Notes by the Translator are indicated with '—*Tr.*', while all other notes and captions for images have been inserted by the Editor.

Some Marathi terms have been explained in the text itself. The ones which haven't been have very specific contexts. A brief Glossary is provided.

Publisher

ACKNOWLEDGEMENTS

ANUPAMA RAO: I am grateful to Subodh More, without whom this book would have been impossible. No words can thank him adequately for his passion, enthusiasm, and commitment to this project over the last decade.

Thanks are due to the More family, especially Mrs. Devayani Satyendra More, for giving us permission to translate this unique work.

My grateful thanks to: Mahesh Bharathi, the late Sudhakar Borkar, Arjun Dangle, the late Namdeo Dhasal, Rohini Pandey, J.V. Pawar, Anil Sawadkar, Ramesh Shinde, the late Narayan Surve, Vijay Surwade, Prakash Vishwasrao and the staff at Bhupesh Gupta Bhavan, Mumbai, and to the Maharashtra State Archives at Elphinstone College.

S. Anand (of Navayana) played a vital, supportive role in discussing the project with me, and offering advice when the idea for the project first arose.

Peter Connor, at the Center for Translation Studies (Barnard) provided the grant, which kick-started the project.

Poorvi Bellur, Josue David Chavez, Sohini Chattopadhyay, and Anish Gawande helped me to imagine this book as a spatial map, and taught me in the process about collaborative work.

Surabhi Sharma and Ajay Noronha filmed interviews and helped to archive places associated with R.B. More's Bombay. I am particularly grateful to Surabhi Sharma, a fellow traveller and among my oldest friends. She has taught me much about the city as visual artefact over the past three decades.

I did some of my initial thinking about how to present R.B. More's work during a fellowship in Berlin at RE:WORK, also known as the IGK Work and Human Life Cycle in Global History. I am pleased to be able to publicly thank that special community, especially Andreas Eckert, Jurgen Kocha, and the indefatigable Félicitas Hentschke.

A very big thanks to Nazeef Mollah at LeftWord Books for his keen eye, and very fine editing. Sudhanva Deshpande and Vijay Prashad have supported this project from its inception. To them, a big thanks.

Wandana Sonalkar is more than a friend. She is family. I'm thankful for her companionship on this journey.

WANDANA SONALKAR: I would like to thank Anu Rao and Subodh More for their patience and dedication, for staying with me as my translation dragged on. This has been a long-drawn-out, but intense project. We came to Mumbai in 2013 when Tulsi was still well enough to delight in his return to the city. The work became another layer in life itself, something I shared with Tulsi, Ojas, Daryan, Madhura, and lately, little Riaan.

Working on the manuscript in Mumbai during the editing stage, I re-entered the world of R.B. More with the help of Subodh More, Anil Sawadkar, and others. This also opened up many layers of the legacy of Ambedkar and his co-workers in the anti-caste movement, as well as aspects of the present-day realities of caste and of resistance to it. Working with the editorial team at LeftWord Books was a joy. I must especially mention Nazeef Mollah, whose charm came through even as he was being thoroughly meticulous and professional.

I, too, value Anupama Rao's companionship on this journey.

TRANSLATOR'S NOTE

WANDANA SONALKAR

My approach to this translation was to deliver a readable text in English that retained some of the flow and flavour of the original.[1] However, in engaging with this text, many other concerns came up which had to be confronted. This had a lot to do with the peculiarity of the book, which has the Marathi title: *Comrade[2] R.B. More: A Powerful Link Between the Dalit and the Communist Movement*. The book is in two parts: the autobiography of R.B. More (RB), and a biography of More written by his son Satyendra R. More (SR). The autobiography of is short, since R.B. More died in 1972, without having completed the manuscript, and his son took up the story from where he left off.

My first reaction when I turned to translating the S.R. More text was that it had been *easier* to translate the father's memoir told in his own words. There was in the autobiographical first part a sense of immediacy, of the author being close to his own experience, which I read as innocence: there was a naturalness which brought literary pleasure in the act of translation. The son's biography of his father is weighed down by a sense of hagiographic and ideological purpose. There is much more jargon. At several junctures there are long lists of names of those who participated in a specific event, be it a political meeting or some other activity.

But when I returned to the text much later, to edit it, I realized that the difference between the two texts is more complex. There are continuities as well as differences between the two sections. In the interim some conversations made me aware of how the text (not very widely read in the original Marathi) was regarded by the Dalit community and by Communist Party members, even those who had not read it, because of R.B. More's identity as one who had both worked in Ambedkar's movement and joined the Communist Party: a certain underlying anxiety on both the 'sides'. Both the Dalits and the Communists wanted to claim More as their own, and yet were uncomfortable with his association with 'the other side'. Also, More's family felt that his contribution had not been fully appreciated by either side. A

---

[1] My main teacher in the niceties of the language was my late husband Tulsi Parab, who was a poet and had a deep and nuanced knowledge of Marathi.

[2] The word 'Comrade', or the abbreviated 'Com.', is used here, as elsewhere in the text, as a title, a respectful form of address for those who have declared their allegiance to communism.

colleague from Women's Studies[3] made another useful and insightful suggestion when I spoke about this translation at a faculty seminar at the Tata Institute of Social Sciences: that I pay attention to the psychological layers in the writing of a father's biography by his son.

First of all, we are struck by R.B. More's beginning: he tells us of his birth in 1903, and of the religious *jatra*, or procession, that took place in his native village of Ladawali that night. Though he was not a conscious presence on that occasion, he gives us a rich depiction of how Dalits and caste Hindus walk side by side, and how the untouchable Mahars have pride of place, because the gods that are celebrated in this festival are firstly the Mahars' gods, and then gods of the whole village. Untouchability is not much of a barrier among the farmers and agricultural labourers in the villages, at least in the Konkan region. There are numerous occasions when all castes come together to complete seasonal agricultural tasks. Even religious occasions do not separate them. It is political leaders who pulled out the four-*varna* system from the religious texts and made it into law; and the Peshwa regime in nineteenth-century Maharashtra that brought in rigid and humiliating practices underlining that people of certain castes were 'untouchable'.

RB's first encounters with the practice of untouchability come when he is made to sit separately from 'touchable' classmates at school. His writing style is to skilfully weave a fairly intricate account of the spread of education and a modern way of life among untouchables in the coastal Konkan region in the early twentieth century, with the personal story of a young untouchable boy's progress through school, while reminding us from time to time of the *systematic* social degradation imposed on his community as a whole. With remarkable literary economy, More has entwined many layers of personal experience with social analysis. This is what I encountered as 'ease' of translation, a feeling of contact with authenticity. The daily occurrences of the practice of untouchability in the big school at Mahad are set out without drama, with a gentle mockery at the absurdity of it.

As RB grows older, he is buffeted along by circumstance. A young man from the villages of Konkan is making his way in the cities of Bombay and Poona, armed only with his intelligence and his readiness to do any kind of work. He is determined to complete his education, though this is interrupted repeatedly. This is a remarkable account of working-class Bombay in the early twentieth century: the comradeship of hard labour and the uncertainty of finding work, and what is most fascinating, the rich cultural life of the workers. RB sings, and watches plays, eventually acting in them. We have a glimpse into the earlier cultural roots of the much more ideologically Communist Indian People's Theatre Association, which was formed in 1943. Dalits, especially Mahars, were singers, dancers, and actors in many traditional forms of stage performance, and this carried over into city life in various forms.

[3] Thanks to my former colleague, Asha Achuthan, for this point.

R.B. More's narrative ends with an account of his role in an important political event for the untouchables: the 1927 *satyagraha* where Dalits from the surrounding districts gathered to assert their right to use the water of the Chavdar lake, or public reservoir. He thought of his role in the Mahad *satyagraha* as an important contribution to the Ambedkarite movement, and also wrote a separate booklet on this subject.

The younger More also jumps to this event early in his narrative. SR inserts more names, and reiterates the claim that his father was the first to put forward the idea of inviting Dr. Ambedkar to Mahad, and to suggest a collective sampling of the reservoir water by untouchables as a *satyagraha*. In repetition, the claim becomes more audacious and contestable. RB, on the other hand, gives a simpler account of events and his own part in them without any exaggeration. New suggestions come forward in meetings; there is no claim that they originate with himself.

RB's main concern here is to emphasize the importance and the mechanics of mass mobilization for progressive struggles. Perhaps this was the main motivation behind his joining the Communist Party, as in several places (as he, as well as SR, tell us) he expresses the opinion that it was the *organizational weakness* of the Communists that led Ambedkar to build a separate movement for the emancipation of the untouchables. It seems R.B. More felt that, with the organizational success of the Mahad *satyagraha* behind him, he could contribute to the capacity of the Communist Party to organize Dalits and to take up their struggle against untouchability as part of their agenda.

Whereas RB saw his role as one of building bridges between the Communist movement and the Dalit movement, his son sees him as undervalued by both. This feeling of resentment is entirely absent from RB's autobiographical fragment and from his Mahad *satyagraha* booklet. A hagiographic style thus emerges out of family dynamics. Earlier, we have a brave declaration by the son of his father's position in the Communist Party: 'These were Communist activists who did not recognize a division between leader and activist, who had live relations with the people. This was the first generation of Communists, fired by the ideal of building a society based on people's power, selfless and soaked in the affection showered on them by the people. And More was one among them.' But in the later part of the text there are indications of some cracks. The story of separate water pitchers in the trade union office for Dalits and 'touchables' is an instance where More could influence everyday practice among the Communists.

Re-reading the text I had translated after a long interval made me more sympathetic to S.R. More. He is writing with several different concerns at once: to talk about Communist Party work in the face of state repression, of the dedication of Party workers; to underline especially the role of Dalit Party workers mobilized by RB (we thus have long lists of names in the text[4]); to bring out the politics

---

[4] This meticulous *naming* of co-workers and comrades is something I noted earlier while

behind the rift between the Dalits and the Communists which persists even today; to underline his father's extreme honesty and commitment. SR explains earnestly and in detail RB's actions attempting to link the Dalit and Communist movements. Difficult to translate and to read, yes, but the writing reflects the earnestness and tortuousness of RB's own life.[5]

R.B. More refused to take more than the bare minimum from the Party for his personal needs; his long periods of underground work and his total absorption in party work exacted a heavy toll on his family. There are moments in the text that reveal tensions between father and son. In most of his narrative, SR refers to himself as 'the present author' witnessing (and suffering) his father's life trajectory, but when he is attributing agency to himself, in his often frustrating efforts to get a schooling, or in his participation in the Party's cultural troupe, he uses the pronoun 'I'.

One might speculate on the father's reasons for inflicting such extreme deprivation on himself and his family. He was determined to be different from those opportunist Dalit activists who left Ambedkar's fold. Many of the Communist leaders who paid lip service to the Dalit cause but failed to make this a central part of the Party's agenda also bore casteist attitudes in their everyday comportment. RB's refusal of anything more than a below-subsistence level of financial support became an assertion of self-respect. There were, of course, exceptions, and the son scrupulously mentions the names of those who went out of their way to help the family, treated his mother with respect, and himself with affection.

RB bore all these privations lightly; the clue to this can be found in his own autobiographical account, where he describes himself as a fortunate and much-loved child, enjoying a carefree life filled with toil but not exploitation, where he rejoices in the proximity to nature and observes that all castes become equal when they are labouring side by side. He became aware of the evils of untouchability only when he started going to school, and was soon able to take part in the struggle against it. That is why he could bear poverty and homelessness for the sake of the cause he believed in and could impose such a life on his wife and children. His son, however, had to suffer extreme poverty at an age when he was too young to understand the reasons behind it. He saw the advantages his father had with a sound primary education even though he had to struggle for the right to schooling; and yet saw the same father allowing him to be removed from a school register because he couldn't pay the fees.

---

translating another text by members of the 'Ambedkar movement', *We Also Made History: Women in the Ambedkar Movement*, by Urmila Pawar and Meenakshi Moon.

[5] R.B. More's family also brought out another booklet documenting his correspondence with leaders of the Communist Party where he tried to make the leaders aware of the importance of caste in Indian society, and of the movement of Dalits as a part of the revolutionary struggle. We have reproduced this text in Appendix B.

The son's narrative is thus more than a hagiography written with sprinklings of Communist jargon. There is a complex dynamic between father and son. Because of S.R. More we see another side of R.B. More, Dalit activist and Communist organizer as he certainly was, but also a family man. In his own narrative, RB fails to protect his mother from the rapacious greed of relatives. In his son's story, he imposes extreme deprivations and tribulations on his family, who, after his death, are left searching for meaning and justification. The interweaving of all these strands makes for a complicated structure, sometimes dense, sometimes prolix, sometimes hagiographic, sometimes straining for a blunt honesty. The text as a whole offers unique material and many clues for historical research.

I hope that readers of this translation will find their own insights in what is a remarkable account of rural and urban workers' lives, of the real dynamics of a people's movement and the contradictions between contemporary movements inspired by different ideologies and politics. At the same time, we have the human story of a complex political actor, written by two hands. In first translating the text, and then coming back much later to prepare the final version, I have engaged with both the authors twice over and that is what I have attempted to convey in this note.

RAMCHANDRA BABAJI MORE

AND THE ITINERARIES OF DALIT MODERNITY

ANUPAMA RAO

The divide between struggles organized around caste as opposed to class, and between anti-caste activism and Left politics has occasioned intense debate and discussion. Both organize around a critique of inequality, and each struggles for social justice. Yet they have 'emerged as two very different radicalisms', to borrow from the feminist anthropologist Marilyn Strathern, writing in another context.[1] Caste has been viewed as a 'traditional', ascriptive category, while class is viewed as a political identity produced by the onset of modern, capitalist transformation, and the prevalence of culturally unmarked, free labour. Since developmentalism was an ideology shared by modernizers across the nineteenth and twentieth centuries more generally, including by Eastern and Western Communist parties alike, the relationship between caste and class was assumed to be one-way, with capitalist modernity enabling the remaking of caste into class.

This rare text, the Marathi-language autobiography of the important, if under-acknowledged, Dalit labour organizer Ramchandra Babaji More (1903–1972) suggests a more complex confrontation between caste and class in twentieth-century Bombay. More's life reflects the powerful ways in which the social experience of caste, class, and Bombay city combined to produce the historical conditions of possibility for a specifically urban Dalit modernity to take shape in early twentieth-century Bombay. It is this which allowed R.B. More to imagine social justice through a joint commitment to caste annihilation and the emancipation of labour. The account we have before us is thus as much a subaltern history of Bombay, as it is the autobiography of a Dalit Marxist: More's account tracks the story of a heterodox, utopian Marxism which was neither fully comfortable with the Ambedkar movement nor with the Communist Party, but which was quintessentially urban and enabled by Dalits' complex encounters with colonial urbanity.

ॐ

---

[1] Marilyn Strathern, 'An Awkward Relationship: The Case of Feminism and Anthropology', *Signs*, vol. 12, no. 2, Winter 1987, p. 289.

Directions for the Samadhi of Gopal Baba Walangkar, Raodhal.
Photo courtesy of Anupama Rao.

R.B. More was born in Ladawali in 1903, and grew up in the village of Dasgaon in Raigad district, in the Konkan. Dasgaon was close to Dapoli, which was famous for its long history of anti-caste activism. Military pensioners from the Mahar and Chambhar castes had purchased land in Dapoli to create a unique community of well-to-do, educated Dalits in the region.[2] Gopal Baba Walangkar, a radical Dalit thinker of the late nineteenth century resided there, and played an important role in organizing against caste injustice.[3] Walangkar was related to More's family by marriage, and he had educated members of More's extended family including More's maternal grand-uncle, Vitthal Joshi, who 'was literate in both the modern Marathi script and the Modi script', and who 'earned money by writing out mortgage papers and purchase papers (for land transactions) in the Modi script'. Walangkar's legacy was therefore palpable in the long tradition of Dalit education and anti-caste activism for which the region was known.

More describes his family as part of an educated, well-to-do elite: 'My father lived the life of a rich farmer for a short time; his maternal cousin built a two-storey house. My elder brother [he had died before More was born] got a job in the Education Department. He would ride his own horse from the market in Mahad

[2] Mahars and Chambhars in western India had a long history of colonial and pre-colonial military employment. Their experience of social mobility, through employment in the British Army (and access to schooling), was followed by subsequent exclusion from military service (1891) due to their status as 'untouchable' castes in the wake of the reorganization of the British Army, which privileged 'martial races'.

[3] Walangkar was a direct associate of the famous anti-caste thinker, Jotirao Phule (1827–1890), who was influenced by Christian Nonconformism and radical republican thought. An ex-military man, Walangkar famously petitioned the colonial state for government jobs for untouchables, and wrote against caste oppression. He was a nominated member of the Mahad Municipality, and widely known as a teacher and Dalit astrologer in Dapoli.

Samadhi of Gopal Baba Walangkar, first erected in 1904.
Photo courtesy of Anupama Rao.

and elsewhere. *There were eight to ten schoolteachers living in the untouchable colony in Mahad fifty years ago* [my italics].' However, More's father was cheated of his property and died early, leaving his wife to care for young Ramchandra and a sister. The family was humiliated by having to give up their own house and take up residence in a paternal uncle's outhouse for which they paid rent. To add insult to the injury, members of the 'big house' also pocket the money that More sends home from Bombay and Pune once he starts working.

More's early life was structured around the tension between his desire to complete his education, on the one hand, and the necessity of supporting his impoverished family on the other. A brilliant student, he received a coveted scholarship to attend Mahad's English high school, but he was unable to take advantage of this opportunity due to his caste identity. He writes of having exam papers flung at him while taking the high school entrance exam in Alibag 'for under-elevens' so that caste Hindus could avoid physical contact.[4] Though he stood first in the exams, and received a monthly scholarship of Rs. 5 to attend high school, More was prevented from joining the local English high school in Mahad. It took the intervention of upper-caste social reformers, who helped get an essay about his experience of school segregation published in the *Satya Prakash* ('Light of Truth'), for More to be allowed admission into the high school at Mahad.[5] He eventually passed the sixth class in Marathi, and the second class in English.[6] However, the experience of caste exclusion persisted: More later refused a chance to continue his education in the town of Tale because this would have meant sitting outside his high school classroom on a scaffold.

More turned to activism at a young age, when his daily experience of caste segregation was coupled with the powerful effect of ideas of social emancipation on his mind. Barred from sitting together with upper-caste students for drill and drawing at his high school, More began to wander the town and make contact with the community. He organized local Dalits who come together to create a tea shop which became a central meeting place and a rest stop for Dalits, who were otherwise prevented from using the town's public amenities, especially drinking water. From there More went on to play a key role as a local organizer in the movement for public access to water tanks and government property, which was the inspiration behind the famous Mahad water *satyagraha* of 1927 led by B.R. Ambedkar.

In fact, More was the main link between local struggles in the Konkan and Dalit politics in Bombay. More also played a central role in the emergence of civic

---

[4] Elsewhere I have argued that the verandah was a colonial technology of segregation that responded to new juridical demands for equal access, even as these were redefined to accommodate caste prejudice. Anupama Rao, *The Caste Question: Dalits and the Politics of Modern India*, Berkeley, CA: University of California Press, 2009, Chapter 1.

[5] It is possible that this public letter was read by reformers and by government officials, and that it was interpreted as a petition to the government about the misuse of government funds for education, since these were supposed to be available to students from all castes.

[6] More reminds us that the same Brahmin landlord who objected to his presence in the high school, V.V. Dharap, later filed a case against Ambedkar (and other Dalit activists) during the Mahad *satyagraha*, claiming that untouchables were excluded from the Chavdar tank by custom. For an account of the Mahad *satyagraha* which focuses on the legal case and B.R. Ambedkar's skilled reading of customary exclusion, see Rao, *The Caste Question*, Chapter 1.

associations (e.g. the Bahishkrit Hitakarini Sabha, or 'Association for the Welfare of Outcastes', and the Mahar Samaj Seva Sangh, or 'Association for Service to the Mahar Community'), the publication of Ambedkar's first newspaper, *Bahishkrit Bharat* ('Ostracized India'), and the circulation of popular cultural forms such as *tamashas* and (Ambedkari) *jalsas*, which were crucial to the rise of a Dalit public sphere. However, by 1930, More had ostensibly parted ways with the Ambedkar movement to become a trade unionist, labour organizer, and card-carrying member of the Communist Party. Though he was a lifelong member of the Party, More was a consistent critic of the Party's avoidance of the caste question: of caste's role in structuring hierarchical relations within the Party, and between the workers who were the target of its outreach.

More's decision to embrace Communism at the very moment when the Ambedkar movement succeeded in bringing national attention to the question of untouchability and organize around the demand for civic and political rights, remains enigmatic. It recalls the debate between rights and redistribution, and between the politics of identity (caste) versus political economy, which defines the conflict between Ambedkarites and Communists through a forgotten figure who tried to bridge that divide.

Text and Context

It is hard to see More's life on its own terms, as the story of an extraordinary individual's public, political life: his life is inextricable from the collective history of Dalit life, labour, and political activism in Bombay. More was a bridge between communities with different political ideologies, and he played a generative role in imagining a political utopia that transcended the divide between caste and class. This division, played out as a confrontation between Ambedkar and Indian Communists, is a history that is specific to Bombay (and to Dalit politics in Maharashtra). However, it also has deep and enduring relevance for how we understand India's political and intellectual history across the twentieth century, spanning British colonialism into decolonization and beyond.

The account of R.B. More's two lives—Ambedkarite and Communist—is narrated twice: first in his words, and then by his son, Satyendra. Together, their composite narrative illuminates the conflict between the promise of Marxist emancipation on the one hand, and Communists' reluctance to apprehend the complex roots of caste inequality, on the other. More's awkward position as a Dalit Communist committed to a radical critique of caste hierarchy *and* class emancipation became evident in the late interwar period, when Left and Ambedkarite politics parted ways, and episodic efforts at joint political action gave way to often violent conflict between the supporters of Ambedkar and Marx.[7] By looking

---

[7] Debates about Dalit Marxism would reappear in the 1970s and resuscitate earlier cleavages

behind and before that political collision, More's account asks whether the conflict between Marx and Ambedkar was necessary, and reminds the reader of a time when cultural nationalism, Communism, and Dalit politics had not yet developed as agonistic ideologies, each claiming the exclusive loyalty of its adherents. In fact, More's life serves a reminder that Marxism was indigenized through the encounter with caste radicalism, while Marxist accounts of (labour) exploitation played a crucial role in helping urban Dalits organize against the vicissitudes of working-class life.

Much Dalit writing today takes the form of *Bildungsroman*, with political awakening to caste humiliation functioning as a key moment in the formation of the adult Dalit self. More's narrative can be seen as an early precursor of the form. However, this would be both narrow and limited. Instead, this narrative of More's life illuminates the difficulty of reducing the complexly ramified life of a Dalit activist through available models of activist memoir, Dalit autobiography, or Communist history/hagiography and in the process underscores the inherent instability of self-narration, and its truth claims.

The text before us is complex and interesting. R.B. More stands at the head of a 'red family' that stretches across three generations, and each generation has had a hand in shaping his life's narrative. This social fact is remarkable when one recalls that someone like Nehru argued that Communism could not take hold in India; on the other hand, George F. Kennan could argue that the authoritarianism of Communism and of eastern cultures were compatible.[8] More dispels both myths by showing us how Bombay city enabled heterodox, everyday practices of Dalit critique, including that of Marxism.

More had to be persuaded to write his autobiography, and began writing it just before he died in 1972. His autobiography therefore ends in 1924, at the cusp of preparations for the historic Mahad *satyagraha*. It is his son, Satyendra, in fact, who provides a complete accounting of his father's political life. Besides his editorial work for the *Bahishkrit Bharat*, and writing for Dalit and Communist newspapers, More wrote little during his long activist years except for correspondence with the Communist Party's Central Committee on the centrality of caste to political organizing, and an extended note on Dalit politics for a seminar at the Gokhale

---

around the caste-class debate, though these debates were now largely oriented towards questions of language, representation, and aesthetic practice. For an account of Dalit politics in the period, and the role of the Dalit Panthers in challenging the *status quo*, see Rao, *The Caste Question*, Chapter 5.

[8] Nehru may have been thinking about the difficulty of converting the majority of Indians to communism, but the decisive steps are taken by a small number of people, often from a minority community. Yuri Slezkine has argued that the Jews, as an ostracized minority community in Europe, embraced communism because they had no historical past they could turn to for redemption; their hope was entirely in the future. Yuri Slezkine, *The Jewish Century*, Princeton: Princeton University Press, 2011.

Institute of Politics and Economics. He didn't offer an explicit accounting of why he was drawn to Communism, and he certainly didn't theorize the relationship between caste and class.[9]

Satyendra More writes in the recognizable genre of Communist hagiography, albeit with a twist. R.B. More's narrative does not carry the impress of properly 'political' categories of identity and identification: His account describes the peregrinations of an urban dandy, albeit an impoverished one, through the city of money and machines. However, the son claims the father for Communism, and addresses the in-between position of a Dalit Communist who was an Ambedkarite at heart, yet made a lifelong commitment to a party and political ideology that did not give him his due, and failed to recognize the significance of the caste question. Satyendra does this by underscoring More's personal sacrifices and selfless dedication, and by working within a recognizable narrative tradition that conflates activists' lives and Party history. He also does so through translation: local events are globally ramified through the mechanical use of Marxist terminology, and a resort to turgid description. What we lose in the process is the sense of political experiment that inflects R.B. More's text. Thus, Satyendra More's biography also reveals the perils of an Indian Marxism wedded to words and ideas that were—and are—yet to be made their own.

Despite this, R.B. More's political life resists easy assimilation. Satyendra More claimed his father for Communism, but he did so by emphasizing two things: R.B. More's decision to join the Party in 1930 while maintaining extensive contact with the Ambedkarite movement throughout his life; and More's persistent criticism of the Communist Party's evasion of caste. When read against itself, Satyendra More's act of memorialization is thus also a severe indictment of the exclusions that structure the divide between heterodox histories of political emancipation, on the one hand, and its subsequent 'flattening' and homogenization on the other.

More's grandson, Subodh, a Communist Party of India (Marxist) cultural activist and a tireless researcher in his own right, combined the Marathi autobiography, S.R. More's biography, and primary material (rare photographs, the covers of out-of-print journals) in order to better situate R.B. More in his many worlds. R.B. More emerges as a figure who bridges the worlds of Dalit protest and activism that predated him, and a key actor in shaping a modern, urban discourse of Dalit rights. Taken together, the autobiography and biography of R.B. More present us with *Dalit Bombay*: this narrative is about Bombay as much as it is about More, it is about the city Dalits produced, and which, in turn, produced

---

[9] More was one of the editors of *Bahishkrit Bharat*; ran a newspaper called *Avhan* ('Challenge'); wrote occasionally in *Janata* ('The People'), the publication that succeeded *Bahishkrit Bharat*, and which also carried the first translation of Marx's *Wage Labour and Capital*, and serialized Gorky's *Mother*; and relentlessly campaigned for Ambedkar's ideas through Communist organs such as *Yugantar*.

them. Subodh's account thus claims More for a Dalit Marxism that is expansively conceived. Subodh's curation of these two texts returns More to his context, to a Marxism that was essentially urban, and profoundly 'new'. Now, when the text is read against itself it supports the claim that R.B. More was not merely an activist, but an organic intellectual who imagined the future of Dalit Communism.

Indeed, what is unique and powerful about this account is that it tells us as much about the city that enabled new political formations as about the lives of Bombay's destitute and dispossessed: Bombay's distinctive urbanity is both a framing device and a key protagonist in shaping More's political worlds. R.B. More's narrative gains traction against the backdrop of a late colonial Bombay which saw the rise of popular nationalism, trade unionism, and worker protest, and which became a key site for incubating B.R. Ambedkar's political projects. In particular, More's account suggests an important role for Dalits in the development of a popular, or 'vernacular Marxism', and the cultural forms through which it circulated. By linking R.B. More's life with the successes and failures of the Ambedkar movement and the Communist Party as these transitioned from late colonial into post-colonial politics, we also get a bird's-eye view of the social structure and political ideologies that governed the daily life of Bombay's working poor.

Dalit Bombay

As is well known, Bombay's history is interlinked with the rise (and fall) of the region's cotton economy. The city's rise is directly linked with the American Civil War (and the problems faced by British industry in procuring Southern cotton), which led to the opening of colonial markets in Egypt and India to cotton export. The opening of the Suez Canal to steam shipping aided the effort. The impact of cotton demand on the subcontinent was twofold. First, the rich black soil of the Khandesh and Berar regions of western India was taken over by cotton. New technologies for rationalizing production and accelerating the circulation of Bombay cotton soon followed, creating new linkages between the rural hinterland and the city, and between Bombay and the British empire.[10] Second, the cotton economy of the late nineteenth century coincided with a broader commercialization of Indian agriculture and peasant production for global markets.

Production of cash crops for export, especially cotton, was not the primary

[10] Sandip Hazareesingh, 'Chasing commodities over the surface of the globe', Commodities of Empire Working Paper No. 1 (https://commoditiesofempire.blogs.sas.ac.uk/files/2016/03/WP01.pdf); Sven Beckert, *Empire of Cotton: A Global History*, New York: Knopf, 2014. Also of relevance is Walter Johnson, *River of Dark Dreams: Slavery and Empire in the Cotton Kingdom*, Cambridge, Boston: Harvard University Press, 2013. For an account of why American cotton did not 'take' in the cotton-growing districts of southern Maharashtra, see Sandip Hazareesingh, 'Cotton, climate and colonialism in Dharwar, western India, 1840–1880', *Journal of Historical Geography*, vol. 38, no. 1, 2012, pp. 1–17.

source of livelihood for most rural farmers, and re-investment of capital into agricultural production was largely non-existent. Nevertheless, the dependence of farmers on cash loans from village moneylenders for survival—and the payment of colonial revenue demand—indicates the extent to which social relations had been commodified. The fact that cultivators found themselves in a cycle of debt bondage in which they had little say over the sale of their crop yields suggests that they were no longer in control over their own labour.

With the end of the American Civil War, a sharp drop in demand for cotton on the global market ensued, and intersected with excessive colonial revenue demands. Famine, followed by the infamous Deccan Riots of 1877, was the result.[11] Rural dispossession was a major cause of migration to Bombay in the period.[12]

Dalit migration tallied with these broad transformations. In addition, Dalits' expulsion from the British Army (1891), which was reorganized to favour 'martial castes', meant that a key avenue of social mobility was now closed. Members of the Mahar caste formed the bulk of Dalits who came to Bombay seeking to escape exploitative caste relations, and to embrace new economic possibilities. By the turn of the nineteenth century—indeed between 1872 and 1881 alone—the number of Dalits in Bombay rose by some 66 per cent. Dalits worked on the railways, in textile mills, and colonial public works. The 1921 census noted that outcaste labour constituted 12 per cent of the total workforce.[13] Ratnagiri district, where More grew

---

[11] While the effects of the war demand for cotton led to an immiseration of western India's peasants, indigenous capitalists in Bombay had shifted capital to cotton mills, which could be converted to textiles for the domestic market following the opening of railroads in the middle of the century, rather than rely on subordinate positions in an international market dominated by European finance, and European shipping.

[12] Jairus Banaji's classic study of the Deccan moneylenders underscores the importance of debt (and rent-seeking) for the colonial economy, and by so doing also makes an important intervention in the Marxist 'transition' debate by challenging the *telos* that is assumed in the distinction between 'real', and 'formal' subsumption. Through an exhaustive case study of the impact of the commodification of agriculture on nineteenth-century Deccan, Banaji shows that the subjugation of Indian small peasantry to the usury capital of Marwari and Gujarati merchants, and to a nascent capitalist class emerging from the big peasantry in the Deccan was accomplished by repurposing prior modes of production such that they could perform in a different historical environment but serve the requirements of surplus extraction nonetheless. Essentially, peasant indebtedness to local moneylenders had alienated them from the means of production, and it could be argued that like the industrial proletariat, the peasant, too, was now working for a wage. Jairus Banaji, 'Capitalist Domination and the Small Peasantry-Deccan Districts in the Late Nineteenth Century', Economic & Political Weekly, vol. 12, no. 33–4, 20 August 1977 (republished in *Theory as History*, Chicago: Haymarket Books, 2011).

[13] The 1940 census indicated that 72.5% of these workers were concentrated in the ring-spinning department, where they constituted 39.5% of all adult male workers. In the comparatively higher-waged weaving shed, Dalits accounted for 0.6% of adult male workers.

up, and the Konkan more generally, saw extensive Dalit migration to Bombay.

LIFE AND LABOUR

Early studies of Bombay were characterized by a singular focus on the shop floor and worker politics. Scholars drew on such studies to emphasize the incomplete proletarianization (and partial urbanization) of a South Asian labour force. Instead, More's autobiography allows us to understand the transformations of caste sociality that were enabled by modern transport, urban institutions, and Dalits' employment in colonial public works. More describes his first visit to Bombay at the age of eleven thus:

> For the first time in my life I saw railway trains, motorboats, brightly shining electric lights in buildings and on the roads, cars, horse carriages, the rattling of trams, the sirens of ships and the textile factories, people wearing all kinds of different costumes, enormous hotels and restaurants serving drinks and food, bars for alcoholic drinks and toddy, markets selling meat, fish, vegetables and flowers, shops and markets selling clothes, shops selling silver and gold. I had this chance to see Bombay because I came for the examination at Alibag.

These technologies provided new openings, but Dalits simultaneously faced new forms of social exclusion and spatial segregation. (More's account of his struggles with getting an education is a powerful illustration of this point.)

More's description of his life resembles that of 'the aleatory population of precarious workers' described by the French labour historian, Jacques Rancière.[14] Indeed his teenage years—it is hard to be exact with dates, but it appears that More came to Bombay to find work at the age of fifteen, soon after he was married to a girl in the community whose family was related to Gopal Baba Walangkar—are characterized by the tension between a desire to complete his education and the demands of earning a living. More's entry into wage labour is episodic. He works at the Seaman's Lodge collecting money, as a porter on the docks, and finally finds steady work at an arsenal factory outside Pune when he goes there to finish his (incomplete) education, after tiring of his life of economic precarity in Bombay. He writes of seeing Babasaheb Ambedkar once in those years, and he is deeply moved by the death of Bal Gangadhar Tilak in 1920. (He leaves Pune and comes to Bombay to participate in Tilak's funeral procession, before he returns to Dasgaon after being away for nearly three years.)

'[T]here were no low-caste men in the weaving shed. . . . When a man applied for work his caste was enquired into. Caste, in fact, was a great consideration.' S.D. Saklatvala, *History of the Mill-Owners' Association, 1875–1930*, Oxford: British India Press, 1931.

[14] Jacques Rancière, *Proletarian Nights: The Workers' Dream in Nineteenth-Century France*, London: Verso, 2012, p. 147.

The vagaries of daily-wage work leads to extended periods of homelessness, when More is sleeping on park benches, or taking shelter with friends and relatives in their *chawls* (tenements). His married life, too, is marked by periods of economic uncertainty and precarious existence: unable to pay their rent, the family is put onto the streets, while he remains 'underground' due to the ban on the Communist Party during most of the late colonial period.

Satyendra More records an especially poignant account of the family sitting under Elphinstone Bridge on a handcart, which contains all of their belongings after they have been evicted from their home for non-payment of rent.[15] The upper-caste leadership of the Communist Party chances on the family in this desperate situation, and expresses sorrow at their visible poverty.

> [D.S.] Vaidya asked me [Datta Kelkar], 'Is not the woman sitting under the bridge the wife of R.B. More?' I know R.B. More very well. But I had never met his wife or seen her. Several beggars used to take shelter under that bridge. Why should R.B. More's wife be sitting there? As I was thinking thus, Vaidya cried out in a concerned tone, 'Hey, it is she.' We both approached her. Next to her there were two or three tin boxes, a sack with cooking pots, and a little boy. The lady told us, 'We had not paid the rent, had we? So the bailiff from the court threw us out. My husband has gone to look for another room. Until then I will wait here.' Vaidya could not hide the tears that came to his eyes.

This anecdote is important because it reveals the gulf separating the upper-caste Party leadership from their Dalitbahujan cadre. For Satyendra More, who relates this event at the end of numerous descriptions of the family's poverty and their inability to find stable housing, it is further proof of his father's extreme devotion to Communist politics.

R.B. More's own descriptions of labour overlap with his descriptions of life in the neighbourhood—from visiting *tamasha* performances and frequenting the *chawls* where these socially disreputable performers lived, to smoking *bhang* (cannabis), and stealing to survive. An interesting account features 'visiting' a restaurant where More and his friends order food, and rush out before they are made to pay. More is caught, however, and made to leave behind his clothes until he returns with the money to pay for the meal.

In More's narrative, precarity distinguishes Dalit life, which is defined by the prevalence of informal and episodic labour. More's anecdotes speak of seeking work, waiting to become a permanent employee, or switching between different daily-wage jobs that allow basic survival in the city. He writes of finding daily-wage

---

[15] The narrative of being 'put out on the road' is common. For instance Appa Ranpise, an organic intellectual who produced important accounts of Dalit cultural history, especially the crucial period between the 1930s and the 1960s, lived for a period on the road outside his room at the BDD *chawls* with his family when they were unable to pay the rent.

work in the docks, and then eventually being permanently employed at the Arsenal depot in Haji Bunder:

> I began to go to the docks to look for work. If one didn't find work, one could go near the ships and try and find something to eat. . . . Sometimes one could get work as a labourer on daily wages. If one stood in the queue for work, even if one wasn't selected as a labourer, one got one *anna* for attending the muster call. . . . The work of carrying sacks or chests filled with rice from the warehouse in those docks on one's head to the crane for loading on the ships was called 'stamping'. This work would become available sometimes, usually at night. . . . By standing in line, doing the work of 'stamping' when I got it, or doing coolie work for daily wages at the railway station, I could cover my expenses and pay for my board.

More's narrative is especially noteworthy for its accounts of daily life in Dalit and working-class neighbourhoods, where he describes the intersections between labour, leisure, and street culture as social fact. These anecdotes span the nearly two years that More spent in Bombay and Pune before returning to Dasgaon in 1920:

> All these friends smoked *beedis*, ate *paan* with tobacco, drank spirits and toddy and smoked hash and grass. They were the same ones who played one-string instruments, tambourines and drums and sang *bhajans* in the night. . . . All the people in the colony were scared of those friends of mine; nobody would dare to cross them. . . .
> Later on, because I knew English, some hawkers became my friends. They were well-known gangsters from that precinct. Even my friends of the Mariai temple were afraid of them. Since they were *pheriwallas* and hawkers from among the butchers in the market, they were fierce to look at and affectionate at heart. . . . [Because I roamed around the city with them] everybody began to say that I had been spoilt: that I had become a *mawali*. . . .
> . . . The kind of environment which I inhabited [in Pune] was one of *jogtins* and *muralis* dedicated to the gods, the licentious behaviour of the white soldiers and their friends, and the pitiable condition of the poor who worked in occupations related to the army.

More presents a social world teeming with figures for whom class exploitation, caste humiliation, and gendered violence exist as a social fact of daily life: the association between *Dalit* as a caste identity and *dalit-ness* as a general condition of abjection and destitution is fungible, and we see here a form of empathetic identification with the wretched and destitute lives that are an essential part of Bombay's landscape.

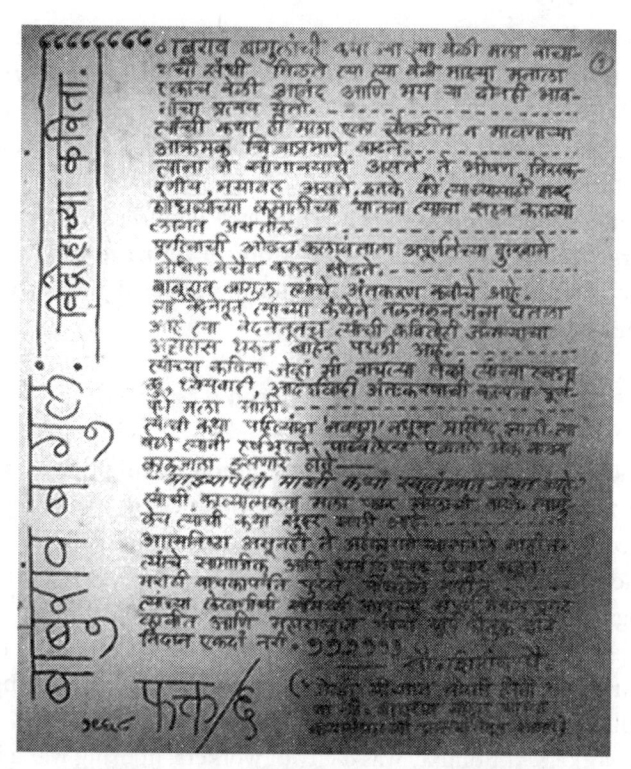

Extract from Bagul's *Jevha Mi Jat Chorli Hoti* ('When I Had Hidden My Caste') (1963), with the title 'Vidrohachya Kavita' ('Revolutionary Poetry') in the little magazine *Phaktha*, edited by Shirish Pai, 1968. Courtesy of Satish Kalsekar.

It is worth noting that when Germany-returned Gangadhar Adhikari translated the *Communist Manifesto* as the *Communist Jahirnama* (1931), class was described through its association with the social experience of hardship, and through the use of terms such as *kashta* (hard work), *daridrata* (impoverishment, destitution), *bekar* (unemployed, worthless), *bhukekangal* (pauperized). Class identity was also related to social forms such as the degraded Dalit classes, *dalit varga*, Pathans (popularly associated with the 'flesh trade', moneylending, extortion, and other parasitical activities that further impoverished working people), and the wild, rowdy *mawali*, identified with the communities of the hilly Sahyadri mountain range (and their traditions of banditry and guerrilla warfare). Each of these was imprecisely identified with class and constituted something like an excessively dispossessed multitude rather than a proletariat class *per se*.

Thus it is interesting to think about the affinities between More's description of urban subalterns, and their recurrence in descriptions of class as social heterogeneity, e.g. in the *Jahirnama*. We see it again in the famous writer, Baburao Bagul's depictions of slum life in *Maran Svast Hot Ahe* ('Death is Becoming Cheaper'). Bagul identified with Marxism, and his was a distinctive literary voice.

He presents the slum as a space teeming with visual difference: the mob, or the lumpen-proletariat here appear as so many life forms—deformed, drunk, violent, and violated, but also capable of giving 'care' to others who are equally dispossessed and downtrodden. Here the 'slum' achieves a sort of thick description and takes shape as a distinctive life form.

Since More's relationship to the city coincided with the city's early twentieth-century emergence, let us step back from More's own life to ask how the spatial politics of neighbourhoods and worker housing affected the infrastructure of activism in this period.

Poor Housing

Bombay's neighbourhoods reflect both the cultural mixing that was responsible for Bombay's famed cosmopolitanism, and the practices of spatial separation that had developed to demarcate communities by caste, region, and religion: spatial proximity and regulated social contact have long been two sides of the same coin in this demographically dense city. How did this come about?

By 1920, Bombay's population stood at a little over a million.[16] Eighteen per cent of labourers were employed in the city's mills, but industrial employment as a whole accounted for 30 per cent of the city's economy.[17] By 1925, the city had 148,000 mill workers. If Bombay was a city of workers, housing was a key issue for them. More's life story underscores the significance of housing and neighbourhood formation in the social lives of the working poor: *chawls* and, later, 'slums' such as

---

[16] Constraints of space prohibit a detailed discussion of colonial planning policy in the period. Suffice it to note that both the Bombay City Improvement Trust and the Bombay Development Directorate were understood as symbols of colonial authoritarianism set up to circumvent the Bombay Municipality, established in 1888, and whose constituency was extended to include ratepayers in the interwar period. Internal divisions within 'the state' are thus important for understanding the impasse of housing policy in the period. See Mariam Dossal, *Theatre of Conflict, City of Hope: Mumbai, 1660 to Present Times* (New Delhi: Oxford University Press, 2010) for a study of the connected politics of land, urban policy, and public works.

[17] In 1921, 85 mills employed 146,000 workers; six railway workshops employed 18,000 men; and three constructional dockyards employed 10,000 men. Figures from A.R. Burnett-Hurst, *Labour and Housing in Bombay: A Study in the Economic Conditions of the Wage-earning Classes in Bombay*, London: P.S. King and Son, Ltd., 1925. Burnett-Hurst's was an important independent survey into the life and labour of the industrial classes of Bombay, which was conducted between 1916 and 1919 with the support of the Ratan Tata Foundation of the University of London. A Dean of the Faculties of Commerce and Economics, at Allahabad, Burnett-Hurst had trained with the famous statistician A.L. Bowley. For important descriptions of the labour process in the mills and the docks, see R.K. Newman, *Workers and Unions in Bombay, 1918–1929: A Study of Organization in the Cotton Mills*, Canberra: Australian National University, 1981; and Rasiklal Cholia, *Dock Labourers in Bombay*, 1941.

BCIT's corrugated iron sheds.
Source: A.R. Burnett-Hurst, *Labour and Housing in Bombay:
A Study in the Economic Conditions of the Wage-earning Classes in Bombay.*

the Matunga Labour Camp were key loci of self-making for subaltern communities.

It should be recalled that this modern city was created as the consequence of a public health crisis of enormous magnitude. As is well known, the 1896 epidemic of the bubonic plague provided colonial administrators with an alibi for demolishing large swaths of central Bombay.[18] (The city also witnessed a large exodus at the time.) The plague allowed planners and government officials to undertake mass demolitions, followed by extensive experiments in urban governance and industrial housing. Unhygienic housing was razed; the Bombay City Improvement Trust (BCIT) was established to oversee construction of poor and working-class housing; and an important experiment in public-private partnership between state and indigenous capital to finance housing construction was undertaken.[19]

The result of social engineering was rather different on the ground, however. Demolitions led to a scarcity of worker housing because more homes were demolished than constructed after the plague.[20] A precedent was established for

[18] Prashant Kidambi, *The Making of an Indian Metropolis: Colonial Governance and Public Culture in Bombay, 1890–1920*, London: Ashgate, 2007. For a superb account of what might be termed a colonial sensorium, see Sandip Hazareesingh, *The Colonial City and the Challenge of Modernity: Urban Hegemonies and Civic Contestations in Bombay City 1900–1925*, Delhi: Orient Longman, 2007.

[19] In brief, the money to purchase land in working-class areas by government was realized through the sale of areas beyond the city's limit to individual investors who land-banked, and later used the land to erect middle-class housing colonies in the interwar period.

[20] In 1920, the Bombay City Improvement Trust claimed they had provided 21,387 tenements

the extensive use of 'eminent domain' for land acquisition. The *chawl*, which the eminent sociologist (and founder of Bombay University's Department of Sociology) Patrick Geddes described as a place for 'warehousing people', became the model for worker housing. The 1921 Industrial Disputes Committee observed: 'The heaviest burden which Labour has to bear in Bombay arises from the deficiency of housing accommodation and the low quality of much that is available.'[21] The report goes on to describe the extent to which tenants had to sublet their small rooms in order to pay rent. This was an issue that was noted in numerous studies focused on the high density of *chawl* life, and the questionable hygiene of its surroundings.

In working-class Bombay, the relationship between housing and homelessness was, thus, on a continuum: the street was a necessary extension of overcrowded, unhygienic housing. (More's own life of social precarity illustrates this point well.) Historian Rajnarayan Chandavarkar has drawn our attention to the structured informalities that governed the social life of labour in the period. Informal networks of patronage that crystallized within the secondary economy and the culture of the street involved intermediaries engaged in practices of rent-seeking: jobbers, rent collectors, local landlords, Pathan moneylenders, the proprietors of taverns and tea shops, brothels, gymnasia, and street-bosses of various kinds commonly known as *dadas*. Though it is underexplored in the historical literature (including by Chandavarkar), the politics of housing—struggles to secure housing, evade high rents, the episodic evictions that most of the working poor experienced, establishment of informal settlements, or 'slums', and struggles to secure tenurial claims—was an equally significant focal point for the working poor.

SPACES OF THOUGHT

The bulk of the *chawls* were built between 1922 and 1928 by the Bombay Development Directorate (BDD), which succeeded the BCIT in response to a wave of organized strike actions by textile labour. Thus, the BDD *chawls* had a distinct association with working-class protest, and they were major sites of Communist and Ambedkarite activism.

Chawls were between four and six stories tall. They were defined by their open gallery running the length of the building, common toilets on each floor stacked one above the other, and a *chula* (hearth) and *nahani* (drain, or washing area) in each room. Many *chawls* had stores or Irani cafés on the ground floor. Dalits often lived in tin sheds, created by hammering out kerosene tins after they were opened and fitted together, or in *zavlis*, huts made of dry leaves of coconut or date

---

as against the 4,428 tenements they had demolished. The demand for housing had grown exponentially by then, making these constructions a mere drop in the bucket given high demand.

[21] Kanji Dwarkadas, *Forty-five Years with Labour*, Bombay: Asia Publishing House, 1962, pp. 27–9.

palm. Built in long rows like warehouses, their roofs covered with rubbish, and a thin tin wall providing privacy between sheds, these places had no water, taps, or lavatories. 'In certain places such as the Matunga Labour Camp, tin sheds were officially constructed by the improvement trust and workers had to pay as much as Rs. 4 per month for one of them.'[22]

Given their human density, *chawls* were spaces of both desired and undesirable interaction. Water taps and toilets were important arenas of social conflict. Accidents were common: women's *saris* caught fire while cooking in ill-ventilated and poorly illuminated rooms, and men could be run over if they slept outdoors on the pavement, which they often did in order to make space for women and children inside the *chawls*.[23] Spaces in and around *chawls* were used for communal purposes. There were *khanavalis*, or canteens for single working-men, drink shops and gambling dens, and there was hawking on the streets. Community centres, reading rooms, and *vyayamshalas* (exercise halls) were created through residents' initiative. Two important studies of the 1940s by students trained in Bombay University's Sociology department described the activities of the Bhadekaru Sangh ('Tenant Union') organized by the Congress Socialists, which demanded lighting, water, and better infrastructure. The studies also noted the significant strength of Communists in the area.[24]

More conducted classes on Marxism and Leninism in this neighbourhood during the 1930s under the aegis of the Delisle Road Friends' Union. Indeed the localities of central Bombay—Byculla, Worli, Naigaon, Agripada, Bombay Central, and Delisle Road—were important areas of Dalit mass mobilization, especially for the Mahad water, and temple entry *satyagrahas* (1927–35). These areas had seen the growth of early Dalit-led or Dalit-focused associations such as the Bahishkrit Hitakarini Sabha, the Mahar Samaj Seva Sangh, the Depressed Classes Mission (which started separate Dalit schools in response to Dalit students' continued inability to enter mixed government or government-aided schools), the Bombay Mill-Hands Association (formed as early as 1890 by N.M. Lokhande), as well as Nonconformist missionary activity among the urban poor, activities of the non-denominational Prarthana Samaj, and so forth. The Friends' Union thus took shape in an area historically associated with anti-caste and anti-poor activism, but now focused on drawing Dalit youth into the working-class movement. Lal Chawl ('Red Tenement'), that is, Building No. 14 of the Delisle Road BDD *chawls*, was a meeting point for the Friends' Union. More conducted classes there together with

---

[22] G.R. Pradhan, *Untouchable Workers of Bombay City*, Bombay: Karnatak Publishing House, p. 17.

[23] Radha Kumar, 'City Lives: Workers' Housing and Rent in Bombay, 1911–47', *Economic & Political Weekly*, vol. 22, no. 30, 25 July 1987, PE47–56.

[24] See, for example, G.K. Gaonkar, *Socio-Cultural Study of the Labour Community in Greater Bombay with special reference to the BDD Chawls at Delisle Road*, Bombay: University of Bombay, Department of Sociology, 1958, Part Two, Chapter Five.

Zavli sheds.
Source: Burnett-Hurst, *Labour and Housing in Bombay*.

Sheds made from flattened-out kerosene tins—*chawls* in the background.
Source: Burnett-Hurst, *Labour and Housing in Bombay*.

S.V. Deshpande, and his friends Govind Tamhankar, Baburao Garud, and Bhargav Sonawane. More was also involved in creating a distinctive political Dalit culture in this area:[25] the first Ambedkar Jayanti, or public gathering on Ambedkar's birthday, was organized by him on the *maidan* of the BDD *chawls* on Delisle Road in 1933. Later, he would work with Comrade K.M. Salvi to organize in Matunga Labour Camp, where he came into contact with the famous Mang *shahir* (balladeer) Annabhau Sathe, and the writer Baburao Bagul.

Although he had spent most of his life in this neighbourhood, R.B. More moved to Goregaon around the year 1952. By then, urban expansion had produced an extended cityscape marked by efforts to shift the urban poor to newly emerging suburbs along the Central Railway line. Dalits had long associated the areas of central Bombay with Ambedkarite activism but, now, their imagination expanded to include the suburbs of Chembur, Ghatkopar, Vikhroli, and Ulhasnagar within their geography of 'Dalit Bombay'.

LEFT HISTORY, AMBEDKAR, AND DALIT POLITICS

Ambedkar's engagement with Marx is as significant as his encounters with Gandhi: both Marx and Gandhi were intimate agons. Yet Ambedkar's relationship with Marx has often been portrayed as one of rejection and refusal: Buddhist conversion (1956) preceded by evidence of longstanding antagonism between Ambedkarites and Communists is used to argue that theirs is an impossible relationship. The effort to downplay a complex history of alliance and agonism has as much to do with party politics as it does with differences of ideology; it was shaped by the uneasy alliance between Congress and the Communists regarding their perception of Ambedkar as anti-national; and it has consequence for lost possibilities of a heterodox, capaciously imagined Marxism that might have been produced in the encounter between Ambedkar and Marx, between caste and class. These issues frame Satyendra More's biography, which must contend with the question of *why* R.B. More became a Communist. They are also key for the political history of Maharashtra, which was the animating context of R.B. More's life.

Gail Omvedt reminds us of on an earlier phase of Ambedkar's activism in the 1930s, when he appeared receptive to Marxist analyses of the political economy of caste. Jayashree Gokhale, an important scholar of the contemporary Dalit

---

[25] The role of *tamashas*, and, later, the ubiquity of the Ambedkari *jalsa* requires extended discussion. Suffice it to note here that these central Bombay neighbourhoods were famous for those performative traditions. Appa Ranpise, an important archivist of Dalit literary and cultural history, writes that his father had begun performing in *jalsas* after migrating to Bombay. Ranpise writes about witnessing a performance of the Scheduled Caste Jalsa Mandal in Cement Chawl during an air raid in the middle of the Second World War. See Appa Ranpise, *Ambedkari Sahitya Sampradayache Samalochan* [An Evaluation of the Tradition of Ambedkari Literature], Bombay: Pranam Prakashan, 1999, 3rd ed.

Special Jayanti issue of *Janata* (1933), which explicitly calls up images of American slavery with its arresting photograph of a man clad in a *langoti*, or loincloth, kneeling to break free of his chains with the inscription, 'Hya gulamgirichya bedya mi asha todun taknar' ('I will break free from these chains of slavery').
Courtesy of Prakash Vishwasrao, *Dr. Babasahab Ambedkar*, Mumbai: Lok Vangmay, 2007.

movement, also argues that Marx's influence was evident in the model of caste-class unity on which the Independent Labour Party (1936–42) was based.[26] (The ILP was preceded by the formation of the Municipal Kamgar Sangh in 1935, which represented about five per cent of the fifteen thousand employees of the municipality. Efforts were also made to organize dockyard and railway workers in 1948.)

However, the political scientist Raosaheb Kasbe argues in his text, *Ambedkar Ani Marx* (1985), that there was an effective ban on revisiting this relationship between Ambedkar and Marx until the 1970s, when the Dalit Panthers re-opened the issue by challenging the *status quoism* of Dalit politics, and its cooption by Congress.[27] However, it should be recalled that the Republican Party of India (RPI), which was formed soon after Ambedkar's death in 1956, had built an alliance with the Praja Socialists, the Shetkari Kamgar Paksha (Peasants and Workers Party), and the Samyukta Maharashtra Samiti at its inception. RPI used the language of class and labour exploitation in an early manifesto, positioning Dalits as the vanguard of the exploited classes in their struggle for total emancipation. The RPI was also influenced by Dadasaheb Gaikwad, who was prominent in the Ambedkar movement since the Nashik *satyagraha* (1930–34), and worked closely with the Communists to organize *bhumiheen* (landless) *satyagrahas* in 1956, and 1964. However, Gaikwad was increasingly sidelined by urban, upwardly mobile Dalits led by B.C. Kamble, who took control of the Republican Party of India after Ambedkar's death.

Indeed, More's own life confirms this history of conflict and convergence: we see it vividly in More's efforts to maintain his identity as an Ambedkarite while functioning as a Communist Party organizer, and in his lifelong struggle to link the caste question with the labour question. His bimodal existence should come as no surprise. Bombay exerted a magnetic pull on Dalits and lower castes, but it was also a critical node for intellectuals and activists interested in global communism, and a key site for the Communist Party of India.[28] Yet, Ambedkar's engagement

---

[26] Jayashree Gokhale, *From Concessions to Confrontation: The Politics of an Indian Untouchable Community*, Bombay: Popular Prakashan, 1993; Gail Omvedt, *Dalits and the Democratic Revolution: Dr. Ambedkar and the Dalit Movement in Colonial India*, New Delhi: Sage, 1994.

[27] For an analysis of Dalit political culture and the Dalit Panthers, see Rao, *The Caste Question*, Chapter 3 (pp. 182–216).

[28] In 1921, M.N. Roy was sent to Tashkent by Lenin to head the Asiatic Bureau of the Comintern to train an army of Indian revolutionaries. The Indian Military School was closed in 1921, to be replaced by the University of the Toilers of the East. A number of *muhajireen* (lit., migrants, or, in this case, volunteers) who participated in the Khilafat movement were trained there. Some were among the thirteen members of the émigré Indian Communist Party—established in Tashkent in 1920—who came to the subcontinent in 1922 only to be arrested shortly after in the Peshawar Conspiracy Case. Meanwhile, M.N. Roy started publication of the *Vanguard of Indian Independence* by May 1922. He also began to communicate with the Maharashtrian Marxist, Shripad Amrit Dange, after reading Dange's

G. I. P. Rly. Depressed Class Workmen's Conference

MANMAD, Dist. NASIK.

12th & 13th FEBRUARY 1938.

Presidential Address

BY

Dr. B. R. AMBEDKAR

M. A., Ph. D., D. Sc., Barrister-at-Law,
M. L. A., J. P., Principal, Govt. Law College, Bombay

Ambedkar's presidential address (front page), 12 and 13 February 1938 G.I.P. Railway Depressed Class Workmen's Conference, Manmad.
Courtesy of Prakash Vishwasrao, *Dr. Babasahab Ambedkar.*

with the Communists was contentious. He struggled, during the 1930s and 1940s, to define Dalit politics in the region as he manoeuvred between the Maratha-led Congress, and the Communist Party. (After his death, the presence of the Shiv Sena radically altered the state's political landscape, and Dalits became prime targets of Sena violence.) On the national level, Ambedkar's representation to the Simon Commission (1928), followed by the historic Poona Pact (1932) would see him branded as an imperialist stooge, and castigated as anti-national. This was at a time when the Congress was increasingly moving leftwards starting with M.K. Gandhi and Jawaharlal Nehru's support for the accused in the Meerut Conspiracy Case, followed by the creation of the Congress Socialist Party (1934) as a caucus within the Indian National Congress. Anand Teltumbde further argues that 'even when they sympathized with the struggles of Dalits, the CPI never missed an opportunity to attack Ambedkar's leadership', and notes that the CPI often echoed the same criticism of Ambedkar that emanated from the Congress (i.e. that he was a British stooge), and denigrated Ambedkar for destroying the possibility of worker unity by introducing the caste question into the mix.[29] Thus, the discomfort surrounding

---

text, *Gandhi versus Lenin*. The two maintained a steady communication aided by the arrival of Charles Ashleigh of the British Communist Party in Bombay on 19 September 1922. Dange had started publication of *The Socialist* in the meantime. (The paper was started on 5 August 1922.)

Charles Ashleigh was joined in Bombay by Philip Spratt, who was asked in 1926 to journey to India (together with Ben Bradley and Lester Hutchinson) as a Comintern agent at the behest of Clemens Dutt, elder brother of R.P. Dutt, the well-known theorist of the British Communist Party, and author of *India Today* (1949). Spratt had been encouraged to launch regional Workers and Peasants Parties as a cover for building the nascent Communist Party of India. In Bombay, key members of the Workers and Peasants Parties managed to infiltrate the Girni Kamgar Union ('Textile Workers' Union') in 1928, just before the city's historic general strike of that year. By 1929, key Maharashtrian Marxists—G. Adhikari, S.A. Dange, S.V. Ghate, and S.S. Mirajkar—had been arrested in the Meerut Conspiracy Case on the charge of treason, together with Muzaffar Ahmed, P.C. Joshi, Philip Spratt, Shaukat Usmani, and others.

[29] Anand Teltumbde, introduction to *India and Communism*, by B.R. Ambedkar (New Delhi: LeftWord Books, 2017). Teltumbde's point about the similarity between Congress and (Indian) Communists' criticism of Ambedkar poses the broader question of how it is that Marxism came to function as a variant of nationalism. We might recall the debate between V.I. Lenin and M.N. Roy over 'The National and the Colonial Questions', with the latter asserting that eastern Marxism was compatible with anti-colonial struggles for self-determination. Sanjay Seth describes those debates and the ones which followed thus, '[A]nticolonialism in this perspective was more than merely bourgeois-democratic struggle, and socialism could be achieved through that political form. Thus did Marxism itself become a form of nationalism, not in practice and due to constraint, but as theory....' Sanjay Seth, *Marxist Theory and Nationalist Politics: The Case of Colonial India*, New Delhi: Sage, 1995, p. 229.

Ambedkar's relationship to Marx is a broader reflection of the difficulty that caste (and untouchability) posed for Indian Marxists.

Ambedkar's commitment to social democracy and the state notwithstanding, it is clear he had a rather complex relationship with the politics of labour, and therefore, with Marxist analyses of Indian social life. It is well known that he threatened to break the historic strike of 1928, which was organized by the Girni Kamgar Union, because the GKU refused to take heed of the division between textile mill workers, or to support the entry of Dalit workers in the weaving department.[30] However, it is also well known that Ambedkar played a critical role in the anti-*khot* agitation in the Konkan together with Communist leader S.V. Parulekar, and that he joined hands again with the Communists to lead the massive strike against the Industrial Disputes Act in 1938. Conflict between Ambedkarites and Communists was at an all-time high by 1942, when Ambedkar formed the Scheduled Castes Federation.[31] Writing about the conflict between Communists and activists of the Scheduled Castes Federation in 1945–46, Satyendra More writes:

[30] Interestingly, Satyendra More associates this period with R.B. More's growing awareness of, and interest in, Marxism. He writes, 'It was from 1928–29 that More was drawn towards understanding Marxism. In a way, one could say that Babasaheb himself urged More to understand Communist thinking. From the year 1928/29 onward, More began to attend the meetings on the Kamgar Maidan regularly.'

[31] Maratha Communist leaders in Bombay were receptive to issues of rural exploitation, e.g. the anti-*khot* (anti-landlord) agitation in the Konkan, which had a direct impact on *kunbi*-Marathas who constituted the bulk of Bombay's industrial workforce. As well, leaders in the Konkan such as the Anantrao Chitre, one of the leaders of the Mahad *satyagraha*, and Shamrao Parulekar, who later joined the Communist Party at R.B. More's urging, played an important role in organizing the peasantry against the *khoti* system. The examples should be balanced against an accounting of how a majoritarian, political Non-Brahminism interrupted and enlarged the field of Maharashtrian Marxism. In the aftermath of the Meerut Conspiracy Case (1928–32), Non-Brahmin leaders challenged Brahmin domination of the Communist Party and argued that they were the true representatives of the working classes. These contradictions within the movement broadly reflected the dual base of the movement, split as it was between industrial and agrarian labour.

As well, broader shifts were afoot at the level of high politics, which might help to explain the growing antagonism between Ambedkarites and Communists by the 1940s, not to mention Ambedkarites' resistance to Congress. Congress had won major victories across the Provinces after the historic elections of 1937, and planned to negotiate with the British on the terms of self-government as the party which represented the nation in waiting. However, important minority communities, e.g. Scheduled Castes, Sikhs, and Muslims challenged Congress's claim. For instance, Ambedkar shifted away from the caste-class model of his Independent Labour Party in the late 1930s to establish the All-India Scheduled Castes Federation in 1942 in order to negotiate with the British government about the rights of the Scheduled Castes. However, as is well known, the Cripps Mission and, later, the Cabinet Mission Plan neither factored the Scheduled Castes as a separate constituency nor recognized the Scheduled Castes Federation as their chosen representative in shaping the political landscape of independent India.

On one occasion, in Maharashtra, some anti-Communists who considered themselves faithful followers of Babasaheb launched attacks on Communists from the Dalit community. In Bombay these took place mainly in Delisle Road, Matunga Labour Camp and, to a lesser extent, in the BDD *chawls* at Naigaon.... Heads were broken and blood was spilt.... In the Cement Chawl in Delisle Road many Party members had their heads smashed. At the Matunga Labour Camp, Communists were dragged out of their homes and beaten. A staunch Communist like Hari Jadhav was tied to an electric pole and beaten up.

Indeed there are many examples of the fraught and unhappy relationship between Ambedkarites and Communists. However, the precise nature of Ambedkar's engagement with *Marx's thought* remains understudied. After all, the connection between Ambedkar and Marx has been represented as a matter of party affinity rather than of political philosophy, as a struggle between Ambedkarites and Communists. The more significant question, however, is what Marxism meant, and how it functioned as a 'structure of feeling' for making sense of everyday exploitation and the possibilities of social transformation. In brief, one should insist on the difference between *party politics*, on the one hand, and *Marxism as a form of thought keyed to human equality and emancipation*, on the other. And it is here, in the difference between them, that the insurgent potential and the fugitive life of Dalit Marxism are clarified.

Thus, if one were to ask what Marxism meant and how its potential for social and political emancipation was understood, we would do well to move to the domain of everyday life. Here we see that Marxism was understood, quite simply, as a way to make sense of modern contexts of exploitation in order to transform them. Furthermore, as regards the relationship between Marxism and anti-caste thought, we might argue that the latter already existed as a set of critical practices organized around images of destitution and dispossession, and the figures who perpetuated it, e.g. the cunning Brahmin priest, the moneylender, or the upper-caste bureaucrat in colonial institutions. I am suggesting that Marxism took up and redefined extant practices of anti-caste critique—e.g. the concern with historic dispossession, the focus on dignity and respect, and the demand to value work and labour. In the process, Marxist thought was rendered both more capacious and more specific.[32] Again, More's text provides a salutary reminder of this possibility, and of the lost worlds of Dalit Marxism.

---

[32] The primacy of labour—and the proletariat as the figure of a collective universality—is historically specific, even as it is interpretively over-determined. That is, the equation of the proletariat as the paradigmatic revolutionary subject is specific to the history of capitalism in the north Atlantic. Caste radicalism, which is a tradition that R.B. More had imbibed *before* he was introduced to Marxism, posed a challenge to Indian Communists: anti-caste thought asked what analysis might emerge when we prioritize the social experience of the Dalit in the place of the proletariat.

The question of what caste radicalism enabled and what Marxism precluded (and *vice versa*) recurs across R.B. More's autobiography, and the biography by his son, Satyendra More: its recurrence alerts us to the fraught, unresolved status of the question, and its affective significance. Early in his biography Satyendra More writes, 'Every person born in an untouchable caste has an inborn awareness that he must first struggle against untouchability; and so it was with More. He was looking for a leader who would not hurt the self-esteem and sense of self of the untouchables, who did not look at them with pity.' While R.B. More's brief autobiographical excerpt leaves us to imagine a more creative synergy between Ambedkar and Marx, Satyendra More organizes his account of the political history of the late colonial and early post-colonial periods around three main actors—the autonomous Dalit movement led by Ambedkar, Congress, and the Communist Party.

The political party is the main actor in Satyendra More's account. The reader is initially presented with an account of the Dalit movement which challenges standard Congress representations of caste politics as divisive, and Ambedkar as anti-national. The Communists are also criticized because they 'considered the Dalits to be part of the Hindu community, and were not aware of their separate existence. They considered the Congress to be their representatives. This was a lacuna in their thinking'. Later, Satyendra More mentions conflict within the Communist Party over the caste question. R.B. More submitted a special memorandum in 1953, which challenged the representation of Ambedkar as 'reformist', and 'separatist', and criticized the Communists for believing that caste could be annihilated solely through economic reform. The memorandum had an extended life undergoing revision in 1957, and again in 1964, and the 'visible impact of these three memoranda can be seen after More's death, after a gap of some 15 years, in Com. B.T. Ranadive's article on "Caste, Class and Property Relations", and in [E.M.S.] Namboodiripad's article "The Growing Unity of Democratic Forces against Caste Conflict"'. However, what is most noteworthy about Satyendra More's discussion of this special memorandum is his description of Party protocol governing dissent: 'Because there is great democratic freedom within the party, what has to be said should not be said outside the party.'

Satyendra More's account often reproduces an uncomfortable isomorphism between 'the Party' and 'politics', with accounts of internal debates in the Communist Party substituting for broader context, or richer analysis. Therefore, the minor narrative, which interrupts and undercuts his standard political history, is crucial. This is where Satyendra More stages a narrative of political redemption to challenge the charge of betrayal. He underscores the enormity of R.B. More's decision to join the Communist Party, remarking on the deep and continued fondness between Ambedkar and his father. He notes, 'Babasaheb was not angry with him, nor did he feel that More had betrayed him; on the contrary, he applauded him.' Who betrayed whom? How, indeed, does one manifest loyalty to an idea? What did it mean to be an Ambedkarite, a Communist, or a Dalit Communist? Satyendra More argues that although Dalit workers joined Communist trade unions, 'More was the only one to have been in the forefront of the Dalit movement and who left Babasaheb to join the Party. This was surely something for the Party to be proud of'. He attributes this to R.B. More's political education, which convinced him 'that the liberation not only of the Dalits but of all humanity could be achieved on the basis of Marx's philosophy of people's power'.

Ironically, when More informed him about his decision to join the Communist Party, Ambedkar is reported to have asked, 'I wonder whether the Communist Party in India, which belongs to Brahmins, will appreciate your dedication and honesty?'

☭

In her *Translator's Note*, Wandana Sonalkar makes the important point that R.B. More's act of self-impoverishment, his refusal to take anything more than subsistence-level support from the Party, was an act of self-respect. The child, Satyendra, experiences his father's voluntary impoverishment as a series of dispossessions, as so many evictions and exclusions. (We will recall that the family is often homeless, or at the mercy of compassionate *karyakartas* [activists], many associated with the Ambedkar movement, who find temporary lodgings for them in one or the other working-class *chawl*.) One could extend Sonalkar's point to ask whether R.B. More turned the Dalit's condition of a general (and generalizable) destitution into the occasion for political practice and social solidarity; we can ask whether he decided to make the difficult journey away from an affective, or identitarian relationship with Ambedkar in order to return to Ambedkar as a political philosopher who, like Marx, posed questions that return, repeat, and require creative resolution on the ground. That is, we might want to think of More's practice of cultivating a political self as an act of *disidentification* with the term 'Dalit' as an ascriptive identity, in order to embrace its radical, emancipatory potential.

The text that follows is about the life of a little-known Dalit Communist but it is also about Bombay's subaltern inhabitants, and the worlds they created through their work and their words. That world is also populated by men. It is as if women—who create families through marriage, support their activist husbands, run female-headed households, and engage in public, political action—are merely a backdrop to the narrative. Noting the overwhelmingly masculinist construction of the text shouldn't detract from reading it against the grain. Neither should it undercut the rarity of the text, and its importance as a sustained, if localized challenge to the categorial imperialism of Marxist thought and practice. In this Introduction, I have taken the inspiration of R.B. More to suggest some ways of approaching the everyday life of Maharashtrian Marxism and what this might tell us about the global itinerary of (universal) theories and concepts as these were imagined, engaged with, and put into practice by unknown, or under-acknowledged subaltern intellectuals.

THE AUTOBIOGRAPHY OF RAMCHANDRA BABAJI MORE

Comrade R.B. More had started writing his autobiography, but he died before he could complete it. So only the period up to 1927 is covered in his own writing. The detailed observations about the circumstances of his time that we find in this autobiography make it possible to bring More closer to his readers. Also, since he had spent so much effort in writing this account, it would be an injustice to him if his manuscript were not to be published just as it was. I am therefore publishing R.B. More's manuscript without any alteration.

—Satyendra More

☭

The first capital of the Marathi state in modern times was Raigad. It was in the village of Ladawali in the precinct of this same Raigad that I was born, at dawn on a Sunday on the second day of the lunar month, in the year 1903 CE. The night of the Chhabina of Viroba at Mahad was drawing to an end.[1]

The Chhabina of Viroba at Mahad is well known to all women and men in the region. It is a *jatra*, ordinary people call it a *jatra*. The first *jatra* takes place in the village of Nate which is in the foothills of Raigad district. It is called the *jatra* of the Khalnath of Nate. This *jatra* takes place before the *jatra* of Viroba. During the month of Chaitra, *jatras* in the name of all the gods are held one after the other, and at the end comes the *jatra* of the aged god of Goregaon. His palanquin is carried in front of all the others in the Chhabina of Viroba. And behind him come the palanquins of all the other gods: the god of Vinher, the gods of Poladpur, the Khalnath of Nate, the old Bhairibuva of Dasgaon. Along with them, brandishing their long poles of bamboo with red, green, yellow and white streamers tied to them, walk thousands of sturdy people of all castes, shouting out chants of *Harahar Mahadev*, forgetting all caste distinctions and untouchability.

The people who have come from their villages carrying poles or a palanquin are the elect of the village god, and the people with them are the folk of their village.

---

[1] The translator has utilized her discretion to make the text more readable, notably by breaking up running paragraphs that go into many pages. However, no changes have been made to the original text in translation.

Most of the elect are untouchables and most of the villagers accompanying them are caste Hindus. Some might find it strange to hear this. But, except for only a few villages, in the main the elect of the gods of the temples in the main area of all the villages are from among the Mahar people. Those who know of this custom will be convinced of the truth of what I am saying. When the *jatra* begins and the Chhabinas set out, then by whom, from whose mouth, according to whose will are the buffaloes and goats declared acceptable to them? Whose voice determines which way they turn, which omens they portend? In whose homes, on whose altars, do they find their place? Only in the homes of Mahars, not those of people of any other caste. Because these gods, especially Bhairi and Kalkai, are originally the Mahars' gods, and after that they are the gods of all the villagers. Before the Mahars converted to Buddhism, there was a practice among them of 'inviting' these gods for their marriages and other important functions. Among their marriage songs we have this one for example: 'Let us invite him / We wanted to invite the aged god of Goregaon'.

The reason I have talked about the Chhabina of Viroba and the different gods taking part in the *jatra* when I told of the time of my birth, is to make it clear that people do not distinguish between 'touchable' and untouchable on these occasions. The gods and goddesses of the non-Aryans and their annual festivals in the form of palanquin processions and *jatras* have existed from ancient times and they still go on today. This shows us one aspect of the feudal society, and shows that the common people do not wish to practise untouchability, even for religious reasons. In my view this is a fact of historical importance: only a few persons from the upper castes are responsible for untouchability. It is they who used false claims of ancient culture to weave four *sutras* based on four *varnas* and four *ashramas* or stages of life, to keep millions of Indians groping in ignorance and darkness for centuries on end.

And it is the social reformers, political leaders and so-called thinkers who, even though they understood the importance of the problem of untouchability, followed those persons from the upper castes, and beat the drum of the national independence struggle for years on end, with the result that untouchability did not end and the oppressed, exploited majority of the Indian people never attained real national independence. When we say today that our nation is independent, it means that it is no longer under the rule of foreign British rulers, but now it is dominated by our own landlords and capitalists. The real independence of India and the abolition of untouchability are not two separate tasks but two elements of the same endeavour. Because we have not held to this point of view, today we blow our trumpet about India being an independent country, while we see every village split apart by untouchability and two Indias in our one India: this is the reality of our nation. To hide this state of affairs from the world is like blindly imitating the cat who shuts her eyes when she drinks milk, thinking that no one can see her.

At the time of my birth my father was at Ladawali. He had come to Mahad the night before with the procession of the god Bhairi of Dasgaon, and from there to Ladawali after seeing to the completion of the Chhabina procession. My elder brother and sister were already married and they had died. And all the land, estate, and wealth that he had accumulated through his own efforts had been lost in the court cases filed against him by the Muslim *khot* moneylenders from around Dasgaon. From all points of view that was a bad period for him. In those days he was always sad and troubled. Seeing the face of his son would have given him little joy in these circumstances.

At Ladawali my grandmother and two maternal uncles lived in their own hut. There was always enough to eat in their house, they didn't have to worry about food. They grew several grains, pulses and oilseeds, like *nachani, vari, urad, hulga, til* and enough rice to last them a year. They would sell some of the grain to buy other things they needed. There was a *khot* in the village, but they never had to set foot on the doorstep of the *khot*'s *wada* to ask for anything. Instead, the *khot* would come to them to ask for mangoes and jackfruit. They used to call my grandmother *wadewali*, because her house was a *wada* for cattle, and she was the *wadewali*, the one who lived in a *wada*. Her father was a *joshi*; he had knowledge of the holy books and Puranas. She was able to recite stories from the Puranas. If there is an art of storytelling, then she was well-versed in that art. In my childhood, she told me many kinds of stories and kept me happy. She taught me good behaviour and good thoughts. Besides telling stories, she had mastered the art of singing songs too. She used to sing wedding songs, songs of the goddess Gauri, and songs to be sung at the time of doing collective work, and she would be invited to other villages by people wanting to hear her. She was also an excellent midwife. So people from all castes and faiths used to treat her with respect.

Bad times had come upon my parents even before I was born. But till I was eleven years old, that is, till my father's dying breath, he never allowed this hardship to touch me. I must have been about a year old when he started buying milk for me every day, and, until he died, he did not miss even one day. So anyone can imagine how much care he lavished on me in matters of food and drink, etcetera. Even though I lived at Dasgaon in my childhood because of my schooling, I made frequent trips to Ladawali. There my grandmother and maternal uncles provided abundant milk and milk products, eggs and chicken for me. My eldest uncle used to say, 'Our Ramchandra is born of the mongoose *jatak*, so he likes eggs and chicken very much.'

When I say that my father fell on hard times, I mean only that he lost the wealth that he had formerly enjoyed. At this time he became a poor farmer who had enough land to provide for himself. By working his own land, he could meet the needs of his family. This went on till I was eight or nine years old, and then, becoming the victim of a moneylender's treachery, he lost all his own land. This is how it happened: the moneylender sweet-talked him into signing a blank piece of paper, and then he wrote on it that my father had sold his land. Of course the moneylender became owner of that land, and my father, the former owner, became a mere tenant. Inevitably then, it was up to the landowner's whim whether he would allow my father to go on working the land as a tenant, and in the end the expected happened. One day the moneylender evicted my father from that land for good, and he was obliged to live the painful life of a landless labourer. This happened when my father's death was two or three years away. One cannot imagine what a devastating jolt this was for him.

When I was five or six years old I began to attend the Marathi school in Dasgaon.[2] At the time, in the entire Konkan region, there was no village Marathi school for Dalits other than the school in Dasgaon. With British rule came the telegraph machine, the railways and the factories of the capitalist world, a new working class emerged and new cities like Bombay came up. It was announced that education had been thrown open to all, but in Maharashtra, or at least in the Konkan, there were no facilities for the people of the untouchable community to get an education.

The last unit of the British government machinery was the white-skinned District Collector and Police Superintendent. The actual state machinery of the district was in his hands. Working under the District Collector were the *tehsil*-level Mamledar, Munsif and many other officers besides. But they were all of the Brahminical upper castes and classes. They carried out their personal and family duties following the rules of the *Manusmriti* faithfully, and with the treatment given to untouchables under the Peshwa regime always before their eyes. In those days the untouchables were not allowed to build stone houses or place tiles on their roofs, and they were not able to enjoy many of the rights of citizenship.

What this meant was that real power in the district belonged to the casteists, while the exploitative white foreigners themselves perpetuated untouchability. They used to blow their trumpet about the schools in villages being open to all. But in fact untouchable children were not allowed to sit in the class; they were unable to get an education. The few untouchable folk in the Konkan who managed to get an education in those days did it through being in the military. The children of military pensioners went to schools in cities like Pune, Bombay and Satara. The only village school giving an education to untouchable children was and is in Dasgaon: nowhere else. It was in this school in Dasgaon that my elder brother got educated and became a teacher and then died before I was born. Four of my father's maternal cousins studied in that school and became teachers. They were still working as teachers when I started going to school. Their monthly salary was seven rupees, and, later, eleven rupees.

---

[2] This school no longer exists, but another school named after R.B. More has been started in Dasgaon. See photographs of school, p. 241.—*Tr.*

The reason for Dasgaon and the Dasgaon school gaining such importance is that it was a port for small boats, surrounded by mountains with crags and cliffs, covered with terrifying dense forests inhabited by all kinds of wild animals including tigers. Together with Veer Dasgaon, the two villages had a large community of Mahar residents. Thus, there was brotherhood and a solid unity among them. On any occasion of a challenge, a hundred to two hundred men armed with sickles and axes would assemble in response to a single call.

In this village of united strength, the most important individual was my father's maternal uncle, of the same age as him, Vitthal Joshi. Astrology and interpreting the astronomical calendar was his ancestral occupation. Furthermore he was literate in both the modern Marathi script and the Modi script. He earned money by writing out mortgage papers and purchase papers (for land transactions) in the Modi script. Later on he also became a big forest contractor. His name was famous among the Mahar officers in the military. If retired officers and soldiers from the Dapoli military camp wished to travel to Pune, Bombay or any other military camp, they had to come through Dasgaon. When one had to go anywhere by boat or by a footpath, one had to come to Dasgaon. For them, and for Mahars travelling by foot, Joshi's house in Dasgaon was the place to stop over. In this house, visitors from outside were well taken care of. Dasgaon had become a point of transit joining the Dapoli military camp with Bombay. Dasgaon also became a place of retirement for military pensioners staying at Dapoli. With Dasgaon already having the strength of local unity, and with the support of high-ranked military officers who were also their brethren, nobody would dare to cross them, or have the nerve to take away the rights that they had attained. The (Mahar) people of Dasgaon broke the restrictions of religion and tradition to build large houses and wear fine clothes and ornaments. They obtained school education and acquired high government posts. The secret of all this lies in the account given above.

The reason why our school and our house gained such importance was merely that they had somehow lasted out, among the thousands of homes and hundreds of schools that were crushed in the abyss of untouchability. So in this native land of ours (the coastal Konkan region of Maharashtra), known as the residence of Chitpavan Brahmins or Kobras,[3] we suffered such torture because of untouchability, we were reduced to such a miserable condition, we were made to suffer such inhuman treatment, forced to lead such a degraded life, we were defeated and brought down to such a degree as can have no parallel in human history. The slavery that untouchability entails cannot be described by saying that the state made slaves of human beings. The practice of untouchability originated from a feeling of hatred and revenge. An emotion of class hatred lies behind it. It arises out of a class arrogance based on racist hatred. The followers of the Aryan

---

[3] Derogatory term for the caste of Konkanastha Brahmins, or Brahmins resident in the Konkan.—Tr.

religion nurtured it and made it flourish. The *varna* system is at its core. The *jati* system and the *varna* system have been adroitly combined to give untouchability a permanence, a power of sustaining itself. Brahmin is a *varna* and Brahmin is a *jati*. How can these two be separated from each other? As long as 'Brahmin' is in currency as the appellation of an individual or a group of individuals, so long will it be impossible for *varnas*, *jatis* and untouchability to disappear. The practice and sentiment of discrimination and hierarchy among the castes of the Hindu faith will never be eroded.

Many years before me, the elders of our family had gone to the village school, before other untouchables from the Konkan. Some readers may think this an exaggeration. Some may accuse me of self-praise. But it is the reality, and nobody can deny it or prove my statement wrong. My father lived the life of a rich farmer for a short time; his maternal cousin built a two-storey house. My elder brother got a job in the Education Department. He would ride his own horse from the market in Mahad and elsewhere. There were eight to ten schoolteachers living in the untouchable colony in Mahad fifty years ago. The credit for this and for the opportunity for improvement that some of us in Dasgaon obtained, lies with a great social reformer from the Mahar caste who rose to fame during the second half of the nineteenth century.

The name of this social reformer is Gopalbuva Walangkar.[4] He was a resident of the village Raodhal and a retired officer of the army. In those days, when persons who had passed the teachers' examination in the military school retired from service, they would be given prestigious government jobs. But once Gopalbuva returned after retiring from military service, he did not tie himself down to a government job again.

The British government, to stabilize its rule, had established military camps at various places in Maharashtra; so did it start such a camp at Dapoli in the Konkan. Later on, the camp's usefulness from a military point of view was finished. So persons retired from military service who had no other house, came to live here with their families. Since the Konkan was dominated by the Chitpavan Brahmins, the practice of untouchability was rampant there. Even a man's shadow was considered to be polluting there. In such circumstances, the (untouchable) people from villages all over the Konkan who had joined the military left their villages for good and took up residence in various camps. Naturally, they were present in large numbers in the Dapoli camp as it was in the Konkan. Babasaheb Ambedkar's

---

[4] Gopal Baba Walangkar (c. 1840–1900), retired from military service and settled at Dapoli in the Konkan area of Maharashtra. Around 1890 he founded the *Anarya Dosh Pariharak Mandal* ('Society for the Eradication of the Wrongs of the Non-Aryans') and wrote a petition opposing the decision of Lord Kitchener to discontinue the recruitment of Mahars into the army. Walangkar was a frequent contributor to the newspapers *Sudharak* ('Reformer') and *Dinabandhu* ('Friend of the Poor'). For more on Walangkar, see the Introduction to this translation.

दलितांची वृत्तपत्रें
[१८८८–१९६२]

लेखक
आ. श्री. ऊर्फ आप्पा रणपिसे
(महिमानगडकर)

प्रस्तावना लेखक—
ग. त्र्यं. तथा भाऊसाहेब माडखोलकर

आशिर्वाद — भदन्त आनंद कौशल्यायन
विद्यालंकार युनिव्हरसीटी
कोलंबो, सिलोन.

किंमत १ रु. ५० नये पैसे

Title page of Appa Ranpise's book on Dalit journalism.
Courtesy of Anupama Rao.

father Subhedar Ramji Ambedkar, as well as Gopal Baba Walangkar, lived there in the beginning. The pain of untouchability was always piercing their minds. In this country, even when the rule of the Mughals came, untouchability did not disappear. Then came the Peshwas. They carried the practice of untouchability to an extreme. And these two (Ambedkar Senior and Walangkar) were enraged that even the foreign white men did not use their power to abolish untouchability.

Dasgaon was a village on the road to Dapoli. Since it was dominated by Mahars, many persons retired from military service in other parts had come to live in Dasgaon. Since Walangkar knew this, he would often visit Dasgaon. He became friendly with the elders of our household and since his wife was related to our family, they left Dapoli and came to live in Raodhal. Later he became acquainted with the great leader of the Satyashodhak movement, Mahatma Jotirao Phule, and he became a leader and campaigner of the movement. The then Governor of the Bombay Presidency, noticing Walangkar's work as a social activist, appointed him a member of the Mahad Municipal Council, which had been recently started by his white officers. Gopal Baba Walangkar was the first man among the untouchables in all of India to be given such a prestigious post in the first days of the institutions of *swarajya*, or self-government. He was a teacher in the military school who was learned in English-language scholarship and whose erudition in Marathi-language knowledge was also vast. Since he was close to our family, for two years he taught my elder brother, four sons of my father's maternal uncle and one son from the Sawadkar family of Veer. He taught these six as a home tutor. Among those whom he taught was my father-in-law Tukaram Vitthal Hate Joshi, a schoolmaster in the pensioner school of the old days, and another was Subhedar Vishram Sawadkar. These two came into Babasaheb Ambedkar's movement after me. They recounted to me many of their memories of Gopal Baba.

Our school in Dasgaon is quite an old school. When I started going to school, it had only two teachers. The children attending the school were from those castes counted as *shudras*. Their surnames were not written down in the muster roll; their names appeared as so-and-so *bhoi* (fisherman), so-and-so *burud* (basket maker), so-and-so *sali* (weaver), so-and-so *patharat* (stone-worker), so-and-so *mahar*, so-and-so *parit* (washerman), *kumbhar* (potter), *gosavi* (nomadic community that traditionally lives by begging), *sonar* (goldsmith), *nhavi* (barber), *teli* (oil presser), etc. Since all the people of Dasgaon, other than the Mahars, belonged to the backward Hindu castes, having Brahmins as their religious gurus, they practised untouchability as a tradition. The pupils from 'touchable' and untouchable castes were made to sit separately. I would in actuality be touched every day, but the grown-ups did not quarrel over this.

The school was at a distance of a furlong from our colony. The way to the school during the monsoon was along the embankment bordering a field. If some grown-ups from another caste came face to face with the Mahar schoolchildren (who were a majority in the village) as they were coming and going along the embankment, the children would not get down from the embankment; rather they would compel the adults to climb down into the mud. And those poor caste Hindu people would get down into the mud and water, to avoid our polluting touch and also to avoid the possibility of disputes and quarrels. There was untouchability in Dasgaon, but it was not imposed on the untouchables by the caste Hindus. The Mahars had the honour of defending the non-cultivable land of the village; the Mahar people had the right over some village gods; economically they were not dependent on any other villagers, they were numerous enough to be able to hold their own against them—then who could treat them with contempt? In Dasgaon a weekly market for *sukati* or dried fish was held every Saturday. Untouchables and caste Hindus mingle freely in that market. Since there was a big forest in Dasgaon, untouchables and caste Hindus would set out together with spears and sticks to hunt boar and rabbits.

In the Konkan there is a practice of working cooperatively on fields of *nachani* (red millet) and *wari* (*coix barbata*). It is called *prasthan* or *kamgat*. For this work able-bodied men from two or three, or sometimes more villages would gather together. This was a useful way to find out which stalwart men lived in which village. Till the end of my childhood *kamgat* would take place every year and on that occasion untouchables and caste Hindus would sit next to each other, thigh to thigh. To sum up, the oppression experienced elsewhere because of untouchability did not come the way of us villagers of Dasgaon.

Of the two teachers of our school that I have mentioned above, one was a relative of our family. His name was Jayaram Vitthal Hate and the other was a Brahmin called Ramchandra Keshav Khare. He did not accept Brahminism and the dubious authority of the Vedas. He was a straight-thinking man and like his name Khare ('true'), a true teacher. In the school he did not practise untouchability at all. He was a favourite of all his pupils. When I was ill he visited our house once or twice, and sat down on the cot where I was sleeping to inquire after me affectionately. In 1914 he sent me to Alibag to appear for the high school scholarship examination for under-elevens that was held at the district centre. I passed in the first rank among more than two hundred students who appeared for the exam, and was awarded a government scholarship of five rupees a month. This was the great achievement of his teaching. In those days a schoolteacher's monthly salary was only eleven rupees, so one can see how much a monthly scholarship of five rupees meant.

The high school scholarship exam in Alibag district was going to be held in September 1914. A maternal cousin of my father, Tukaram Vitthal Joshi, took me to Tale just before this time. Tale is a large village in Mangaon *tehsil*, located at the foot of the fort there. Earlier, the government used to run Mahar schools in various places. In these schools students from the Mahar, Chambhar, and Mang castes would get an education. Towards the end the government started a Mahar school in Dasgaon, and that too in my home. But that was after I started attending the English school (from the fifth standard on) and after a dozen persons from our village had become schoolteachers.

Tale and Dasgaon are quite a distance apart. That was the first occasion for me to make such a long journey. When we reached Tale my uncle bought me a new outfit for going to Alibag and sent me back to Dasgaon. When I came to Dasgaon my father had fallen ill and was confined to his bed. When he saw me dressed for the first time in a white *dhoti* with a border and with a shirt, coat and cap, his eyes filled with tears and he was choked with emotion. My mother hugged me and, looking at my father on his deathbed and at me, started to wail with grief. I too began to cry. Several elders watching that pathetic scene were also filled with sorrow. At that moment, all my parents could do was to shower tears, which were tears both of joy and sadness, on me.

That was a critical moment in my life, one that I will never forget. Just a week later, death swooped down on my father and ended his life. My younger sister and brother had already fallen victim to the epidemic of smallpox. At the time of my father's death, we were a family of only four persons: my father, my mother, myself, and a four-month-old sister. At a time when my father was at death's door and my mother had just risen from childbed, there was not a morsel of food in our house. Why was a man who had a field with six ploughs, who had arranged the marriages of about twenty people from the Kunbi, Bhoi, and Muslim communities with his own money, reduced to such a condition at the moment of death? The real cause of this tragic situation was my father's extreme unselfishness and the usurious noose of the British imperialists.

Earlier my father had lived in a joint family with his maternal cousins. Later, to avoid quarrels arising from the division of the big house, my father entrusted the tall building to the four brothers and set up a separate household in a squat house next door. Even after he separated his household, he treated his cousins as if they were his own younger brothers. He helped them to set up house properly. They too never disobeyed Baba and treated him with respect like their own father. Now, when my father's death was a few days away, the family again became a joint household. When I returned from Tale, I took my food in the big house and meals for my parents also came from the big house. Even though I was so young, my mind was disturbed to see that the cooking fire in our house was not lit. What then must my parents have been feeling! My father barely ate something every day till Friday. Saturday was the day of his regular fast and he spent that day without food. On Sunday he didn't touch any food and then came Monday. This was the last Monday in the month of Shravan, and was a fast day for everyone in the house. Three-quarters of the day passed, and the time to break the fast arrived.

I had barely broken my fast and come to the upper floor when someone called out to me. I ran home as fast as I could and saw that a whole crowd of people had gathered around my father. One of them held me by the hand, sat me down by father's pillow and asked me to spoon milk from a bowl into his mouth. Others also touched his mouth with milk. But by now he was in the throes of death. His eyes were not blinking and his chest was heaving. Mother was sobbing quietly. Others were just managing to hold in their tears. Some wise elders were consoling people and asking them to stay calm. The sun was setting, and twilight had set in. In our house our usual hanging lamp had been lit. Two standing lamps were burning on each side of my father. It was at such a moment that my father departed for his long sleep. The house was devastated. On the next day handfuls of soil were thrown on his body. I was taken to the cremation ground with the corpse. I was then just eleven years old. This was the first time in my life that I had been to the cremation ground.

On the twelfth day after my father's death, my mother, my four-month-old sister and I left the house together in the morning. My uncle took my mother and sister to Ladawali and Namdeodada set out for Alibag with me. We took with us enough *bhakari* and *chatni* to last us for three days. Namdeodada was another maternal cousin of my father's and he too was a schoolmaster. He knew everything we needed to know about the journey: how long it would take to reach Alibag and by which route, and also when the examination was due to start and to end. In those days we had to complete the whole journey on foot. We started out from Dasgaon in the morning and made a night stop at Indapur. There were *dharamshalas* at several places. Travellers and persons of the *gosavi* caste and *fakirs* would make use of them. There was discrimination between 'touchables' and 'untouchables' in these *dharamshalas*. Except for Mahars, Chambhars and Mangs, everybody would stay together in these *dharamshalas*. These people would not allow Mahars and Chambhars to enter the *dharamshalas*. Rarely, if it was raining, they would be given some place in one corner. We learned of this and experienced it when we made a stop at Indapur. Before this I had never felt the anguish of untouchability. On the next day we set out onward from Indapur. Beyond Kolhad we came to the Sukeli Khind, or mountain pass. This *khind* was known to be frequented by robbers, and for fear of them, people passing through would travel in large groups. We passed through the Khind and made a second night stop at Nagothane. In the past there was a small motorboat for the crossing from Nagothane to Dharamtar. We went to Dharamtar and then travelled on foot till we arrived at Alibag. During this journey of three days, I had the bitter experience that because we belonged to the Mahar caste people scorned us, treated us with contempt, insulted us and oppressed us, and my heart was distressed.

Alibag was known throughout the Colaba district as a very orthodox and first-class misanthropic town. There even shadows were thought to be polluting. When we reached there we went to the home of a gentleman in the Mahar colony outside the town. Namdeodada gave him some money and asked him to make arrangements for our board and lodging, which he accordingly did. We had already found out the location of the building where the examination was to be held, and the date and time of the examination. We reached the examination hall one hour in advance on the scheduled day with the materials required for the examination. There I was asked which school I was from, my name and so on. It was not clear whether the person making these inquiries was a teacher or an official. We were still standing outside the examination hall. He was standing at the entrance and talking to us from a distance. Later he asked me to come in and gave me a seat near the door in a corner. The other boys who had come for the examination were seated inside; I alone was seated on the outside. The question paper was tossed to me from a distance and when I had finished writing my paper, I pushed it forward. It was picked up from there and taken away. All this was carried out with the utmost care to avoid touching me at any point.

When all the papers were done, we left Alibag and came to Bombay by boat. That year was the first time that I witnessed the Diwali festival in Bombay. In Bombay, a squat set of *chawls* had been built along the road leading to Carnac Bridge, between Musafirkhana and Crawford Market. This area of *chawls* was known as Family Lines. A large number of military pensioners and other Mahar people lived in these Family Lines. We went to stay with our relatives who lived there. Some other relatives were working in Cama Hospital. I would visit them from time to time.

For the first time in my life I saw railway trains, motorboats, brightly shining electric lights in buildings and on the roads, cars, horse carriages, the rattling of trams, the sirens of ships and the textile factories, people wearing all kinds of different costumes, enormous hotels and restaurants serving drinks and food, bars for alcoholic drinks and toddy, markets selling meat, fish, vegetables and flowers, shops and markets selling clothes, shops selling silver and gold. I had this chance to see Bombay because I came for the examination at Alibag. On this visit I stayed about fifteen days in Bombay and then returned to Dasgaon. The whole return journey was by motorboats on the sea and along creeks. So we were not touched by the fire of untouchability this time. From Bombay we took a big boat to Hareshwar and then we went to Dasgaon in small boats along the Bankot creek.

I had returned to Dasgaon but my house there was not open. There was a lock on the door. I began to be aware that I was fatherless, and I was eager to meet my mother as soon as I could. I spent one or two days in this condition when my uncle came to know that I had come back from Bombay and he came to Dasgaon to fetch me. I went with him to Ladawali. My mother embraced me and began to cry. My uncle and my grandmother comforted her. From then on my mother, my sister and I began to live at my uncle's place.

When I reached Ladawali I no longer needed any clothes. The clothes bought in Tale and those I had bought in Bombay were put away in a trunk. In Ladawali a loincloth and a shoulder-cloth sufficed for me. There were several boys of my age who looked after my uncle's cattle. I too began to go with them to tend his cows. My uncle had not compelled me to do this work, I did it willingly. I found it was great fun to run after the cattle, sing songs, play different games, and go to the river to bathe and swim. From Ladawali I often visited several villages near Raodhal. There I had the chance to hear many stories from the older people. One such story was about Rainak of Raigad. Here is a summary of it:

Before British rule, *desi* people ruled over Raigad fort. The commander of the army at Raigad fort was a Mahar named Rainak. All the administrative work of the fort was looked after by a clerk in the hereditary post of *karkhanis*. The English first captured Mahad which was the market town for Raigad, then took over the Chambhar colony, and then attacked the Raigad fort. Then Rainak ordered his army to fight against the foreign enemy and led the fight himself. The *karkhanis* did not like this. He surrendered to the British force and sent a message to Rainak saying that he should stop fighting against the British, surrender and hand over the keys of the fort to them. To which Rainak replied—'You may have betrayed the Raigad fort but Rainak will never betray the fort.' Saying this, he defended the fort for fifteen days. In the end, by using trickery the British forces set fire to the armaments store. They broke down Rainak's resistance and took him captive. Then according to the custom of the time, the British officers asked him to accept the post of officer in their army. But Rainak spurned the offer and behaved in a manner fitting to his courage and integrity. Upon which the Brahmins and other upper-caste *desi* officers who had been compromised by the British, and who were fired by caste hatred, demanded that Rainak be subjected to the *kadelot* punishment prevalent in the *Peshwa* regime. Accordingly, Rainak was given *kadelot* from the ramparts of the Raigad fort and the British flag was planted there, in the capital of king Shivaji the Chhatrapati. The large colony of the descendants of Rainak, the true defender of Raigad fort, in the area surrounding Queen Jijabai's palace, and the temple honouring the brave commander Rainak at the foot of the fort, stand today as evidence of this historic incident.

In our house at Dasgaon there were still pots and pans and other baggage belonging to us, and my mother kept her eye on them. Every month or two she would take me on a trip to Dasgaon and check what still remained and what had gone from our belongings. Whenever she discovered that rafters from the roof or materials for construction and carpentry work had disappeared, she would blame the people from the big house. They would treat me with affection and quarrel with my mother. Nobody paid heed to her protests and exhortations. While we were living in Ladawali, I once got a summons from Dasgaon. I went there and found that the school had informed us that I had passed with first rank in the examination at Alibag. The government had awarded me a scholarship of five rupees a month to attend the English school. Hearing this, the people from the big house made much of me. They seemed even fonder of me than before. I was also extremely happy to learn that from June I would be going to the English school in Mahad. I became impatient for the two months in between to pass so that I could go to the English school. The English school at Mahad had been established before I was born and was in a one-story building opposite the post and telegraph office. This building belonged to a well-known Brahmin family with the name of Dharap and had been leased out to the school. When the school opened in June I went and met the schoolmaster and asked him to put my name on the rolls. He took down my details and asked me to return after a week. When I went back after a week I was told that they were willing to take me into the school, but Dharap, who was the owner of the school building, had told them, 'If you admit a Mahar boy into the school I will not rent my building to you.' [The schoolmaster said]—'If I admit you in this situation, it will be like closing down the school. So we have to tell you that you should go to a city like Poona or Bombay to take your education. In Mahad it is not possible.'

Namdeodada was there with me. He tried on his part to persuade the headmaster. There were other teachers present with the headmaster, but they only nodded their heads to whatever the headmaster said, looked at me with contempt and asked me to leave. We came out of the school and took the road back to Dasgaon. The school had refused us. Now the question was, what to do next? But we could not find an answer just then. The next day Namdeodada went back to his school and I returned to Ladawali.

The rainy season had started. In the rainy season *irlas*, or basketwork capes, were woven for the women and *topas* or hats for the boys.[5] My uncle made a hat for me. I put it on my head and began to go to the fields to graze cattle. When the rain starts all the puddles fill up and streams of water start flowing down. When they meet the river the creeks fill up and begin to flow too. When the river overflows the fish from the creeks and puddles swim upstream to lay their eggs and spread all over the fields. These fish are called fish of the *walgan*. The young people of the village go to all ends to catch the fish of the *walgan*. This is because the fish is very rare and tasty. When people notice that the *walgan* has begun, they go out at all hours of the night using rods, nets and sticks to catch the fish of the *walgan*. This happens only once a year. So not everyone gets the chance to eat fish of the *walgan*. They are available every year in Ladawali. My uncle used to bring cooked fish of the *walgan* and millet *bhakari* to Dasgaon for us. That year we were in Ladawali ourselves so we had the chance to eat our fill of fish of the *walgan*. In that monsoon I went along with my uncle's children to catch crabs, mussels and fish from the fields. I also did small chores around the farm.

Before the Nagpanchami festival the transfer of rice seedlings and the sowing

[5] More has been refused admission to the Mahad school; his future is uncertain, but in the interim he takes pleasure in the monsoon and the experiences it brings.—*Tr.*

of *nagli* and *wari* would be complete. After that every night there would be singing and dancing in honour of the *Gauri*. I would lose myself completely in this singing and dancing. I was able to tell stories and also to read from the holy books. So the people of Ladawali would make much of me. All the people from my *mama*'s (maternal uncle's) colony would invite me to eat in their homes. I had uncles, grandmothers, aunts in every house. I did not know how the rainy season passed in that atmosphere of love and affection.

After that came the hot season. In the hot season we would go to the river to bathe. Next to the river there was Bhikoba's well and his fields.[6] I and the other children would sometimes go there to bring down mangoes from the trees and pick flowers when no one was looking. Everybody was afraid of Bhikoba. He was strict by nature but affectionate by temperament. One day, as I had put my clothes to dry on the sand and was sitting in the sun, he called me and asked me why I was not at school. So I informed him about the English school at Mahad and what the headmaster had said to me. He listened to me calmly and asked me to go. After this I spent some more months in the same activities.

Later one day he called me again and asked me to come to his *wada* on the next Sunday. Accordingly, I went there with my *mama* at the time he had specified and presented myself. In the seating area outside the *wada* there were two guests from Bombay seated on a rug. My *mama* had taken me to the *wada* and left me there. I was standing in front of the *wada*. The gentlemen asked me to come forward and sit on the rug. I went up and sat down, keeping some distance between me and them. They asked me several questions to get information about me. I answered their questions. They said that since I had won a government scholarship, the school at Mahad would have to admit me. After that they dictated some things for me to write down on a piece of paper. I wrote it down and when I went home I copied it on to a postcard and sent the card to an address that they had given me. Within a month I received a message from the school. I was called to the school; the matter I had written on the postcard had been published in a newspaper under my name. This was shown to me and I was asked, 'Did you write this?' I said yes. There was a great commotion among the teachers and pupils of the school. One said, 'Such a small boy and what nerve he has. He asks for the school's grant to be stopped!' From another came the remark, 'This is why we have to keep these people at a distance.' Some teachers and boys were glaring at me. After all this, the headmaster told me to come to school from Monday—'We have decided to put your name on the rolls of this school'.

I returned to Dasgaon and recounted what had happened. The teachers in

---

[6] Ramchandra 'Bhikoba' Dhodapkar, was the grandfather of the writer and anti-caste social reformer Keshav Sitaram, also known as Prabodhankar Thackeray, and great-grandfather of political cartoonist Bal Thackeray, who founded the Shiv Sena in 1966, based on a model of regional chauvinism that was virulently opposed to Dalits, Muslims, and South Indians.—*Tr.*

Dasgaon, and others, were very happy to hear it and congratulated me. I came to Ladawali, thanked Bhikoba and asked who his two guests were. He said, 'They are my brothers.' Then it was learned that one of them was a famous playwright of Maharashtra, Yashwant Narayan Tipnis. I could not find out exactly about the other. He was probably Govind Gopal Tipnis or Anant Vinayak Chitre. The Bhikoba that I was used to seeing in the garden at Gondal, and Bhikoba the agricultural expert and artist who organized the first historic agricultural conference at Mahad, were one and the same. When I came to know this I realized his true greatness. In my knowledge, he was the first social reformer in Maharashtra who had himself married outside his caste. When he married outside his caste in 1905 his relatives of the Chandraseniya Kayastha Prabhu caste excommunicated him. This person, who played a major part in securing admission for me in the school at Mahad was such a pioneering social reformer and activist of the previous generation. My admission in that school was the first-ever challenge to the orthodox and bigoted mindset of Mahad society. I must note here that the bigoted Dharap family that tried to bring obstacles in the way of my being admitted to the school was the same Dharap family that filed a suit in court to prevent untouchables from using the water of the Chavdar lake (where Dr. Ambedkar organized a *satyagraha* in 1927).

A lot of time had elapsed between my appearing for the exam in Alibag and my getting admitted to school. On the first day, as soon as I set foot in the school, a peon came and stood in front of me and asked me to follow him. We climbed the front steps and came to a platform, the peon went up the stairway to one side of the platform to reach the classroom. There I went and sat on a stool placed in one corner of the room. The boys in my class were sitting on a bench all together, with their backs to me. In front of them were the teacher's table and chair and a small cupboard. My stool was placed at such a spot that the pupils and teacher entering the classroom would not have to touch me. The danger of touching me presented itself only when I was entering or leaving the classroom. They had taken good care that their purity was not violated.

Not a single student of any caste other than the Brahmin, Gujar or Kayastha castes was attending that school when I started going. Among the Hindus there was no student from the Maratha or any such caste. And there was no Muslim either. After me two Muslim students were admitted, and after them one Maratha boy. From this one can see how education was at that time a monopoly of the Brahmin, Gujar and Kayastha castes. Untouchability was practised in the school. The teachers would not touch me and the students followed their example. There was a teacher named Dharap who used to say, 'As long as I live I will never touch you.' If one looked to clothes, my clothes were as good as, if not better, than those of other students. To tell the truth there was nothing inferior about me that might lead them to keep me at a distance or treat me with disrespect. Even so, I was treated with a searing contempt, and because of this I began to feel hatred for people of the upper classes and castes. When someone yelled 'Get away from me' at me as I was coming or going, I would reply, 'Get away yourself.'

Before I was admitted to the Mahad school I had been living in Ladawali, and after this too I stayed on at Ladawali and went daily to the school which was a mile or two away.

In the Mahar community widespread tales were told about the perfidious machinations of Brahmins and other upper castes, and so the whole community had become suspicious. When I started going to school in Mahad my mother gave me strict warnings. She would say, 'Don't eat anything that anyone gives you, don't drink their water,' and even, 'Don't eat so much as a *paan*, they might put anything inside it and take your life.' Our classes started at ten or eleven in the morning and went on up to five in the evening. From the time I had a meal at home and left for school in the morning till I returned home, I would not touch a morsel of food. The people of our community who came to the market in Mahad carrying loads of firewood were very curious to learn that I went to school with the children of Brahmins. Some of our relatives who came to the market would stop me on the road and ask about my well-being, and sometimes they would kiss me. The other middle-class people passing by would find this peculiar. They would make fun of these good people for this kind of behaviour or for their roughness. When I saw my innocent brethren being treated with such rudeness and contempt my heart would break and I would feel angry too.

Mahad is a small town in the Raigad valley next to the Chambhar fort. Two rivers flow past the town: one is the Savitri and the other the Gandhari river. Both these rivers are filled with salt water at high tide. So, neither of them had water that was good for drinking. In the town there are several wells belonging to rich people of different castes. They use the water from these wells. And those persons from the town or outside who do not get water from the wells use the water of the Chavdar lake, green with scum and bad-smelling as it is, after straining it for drinking. The municipality sold water from the Chavdar reservoir at one paisa a *handa* to the shopkeepers of the town. So the shopkeepers in the marketplace had their drinking water problems solved. The real problem arose for the poor people who came to the marketplace from far off. Among them all except the Mahars could quench their thirst by asking the shopkeepers for water or going to the Mahad lake. But the Mahar people were reduced to a pitiable state in this regard. My heart became heavily burdened when I saw the cruel derision I have described above, to which they were subjected by well-to-do passers-by, and their problems in getting water to drink. The people from the Raigad valley who came to Mahad, parched with thirst, would get water only when they came to the river at Ladawali or Kinjoli. Besides these people carrying loads of firewood, military pensioners also visited Mahad. They would have to stand in the sun outside the office to line up for their pensions. Among them were persons of the *hawaldar* and *jamadar* rank. These were educated people, and well-dressed, but they could not get water to drink anywhere in the marketplace.

In our school I could learn all my lessons, sitting at a distance from others, easily enough. But in the drawing and drill lessons all had to sit together. So, to avoid this, the teachers would not allow me in for these lessons. And of course, during those periods or in the midday recess I would wander out in the town and spend time talking to people seeing if there was anyone I knew. And from this came the idea of starting a tea shop in the place where carts were parked, to solve the problem of drinking water. It was to explain this idea to a few important people that I called a meeting in the Mahar *wada* in Mahad one day.

Mahar people from various villages in the Mahad precinct were present at the meeting. After discussion it was decided that a tea shop would be set up in a field near the wagon yard. A condition was to be imposed that the person running the tea shop would have to provide drinking water free of charge to our people. Accordingly, a pensioner gentleman named Mohoprekar set up the first tea shop. Two large clay urns of water were placed in the shop. The shop supplied tea at one paisa a cup and water was also made available. So people could drink water there and the person running the shop also earned a little money. I, however, was allowed to drink tea for free as many times as I wanted. As if I myself was the owner of that shop! The shop owner had to buy the water. But since he attracted more customers the expense was not too much for him.

Since people came to know that I had taken the lead in getting a hotel started so that people's drinking water problem would be solved, they felt great respect for me. I used to sit in that hotel and do various jobs for others, like writing their letters, writing out bail applications and other official letters, and so on. When I came to the school there was no place in the marketplace for us even to stand, and now the hotel became an office where we could discuss our problems and form new associations. When the rains approached, all the shops and stalls in the wagon yard were closed down. So our little tea shop also closed down. After the rains were over, Mohoprekar Joshi leased a small plot next to the bridge near the municipal market in the old market, and started a tea shop there. Since this site was in the middle of the marketplace, some of the caste Hindu shopkeepers tried to raise quarrels and fights. But now, because of the hotel in the wagon yard below, our people had become organized. The shopkeepers' efforts to stir up trouble had no chance against them. Now our opponents would just mutter about how the Kaliyug had come and Mahars had got above their station, and then fall quiet.

It was a matter of no small importance that, just a year after I started going to school, our people succeeded in starting a hotel right in the middle of the marketplace. The issue of my getting admission to the school in Mahad, and the permanent solution in a limited sense of the drinking water problem through the setting up of a hotel in Mahad, were both issues related to the core of the question of untouchability. In both these cases an assault had been made on the arrogance of the tradition-loving ultra-orthodox of Mahad, and they also challenged the prejudices of ordinary caste Hindus. My going to the Mahad school was, at least in Mahad, a victory for the movement against untouchability. Some of my schoolmates in Mahad and one or two teachers did not mind even if I touched them. In the marketplace there were many who did not consider me to be polluting.

At one time, the Satyashodhak movement had been quite influential in Mahad. One of the leaders of the Satyashodhak movement, Bhaskarrao Vithoji Jadhav was a resident of Mahad. The Tipnis and Potnis families (of the Kayastha caste) were supporters of the Satyashodhak movement. All these people were in favour of my going to school and of a hotel being started by a Mahar in the marketplace. They felt sympathy for me and for other Mahars. When there were no letter-writers in the marketplace other than Brahmin clerks, I would write letters for Mahar and Maratha people. So the tenants cultivating the fields belonging to the moneylenders of Mahad became close to me. When the water on the river banks rose too high the Maratha farmers of Karanjkhol would carry me on their shoulders up to Ladawali.

Our first hotel in the wagon yard ran only during the summer. Now this second hotel in the marketplace would run in all seasons. When the river water entered the marketplace the whole of the old market would be flooded. Then all the shops there would be closed for some days. Our hotel also closed down for a few days then. The site of the hotel was a plot owned by the municipality. But since we would get a lease on it each year the hotel became permanent. This was an *adda*, a gathering-place, for us in the marketplace. In the beginning nobody would stay there at night. But after some time some persons would stay there even at night.

About the time when I started going to the school in Mahad, hanging oil lamps—*lamandivas*—were going out of use and being replaced by kerosene tin lanterns. Standing oil lamps or *samais* were hardly seen any more. It was difficult to read and write at night by the light of the kerosene tin lamps or small glass lamps burning kerosene hung at a height. So at my uncle's house in Ladawali a tall kerosene lamp had been bought for me to study by. I would do my studies at night by the light of this lamp. Half the space in my uncle's house was for humans and half was for cattle. In the humans' half a woven cane screen had been placed to divide it into two. On one side there was the stove and other things, on the other side there were objects like a vessel for pounding rice, a grindstone, mortar, and so on. In this area there was a wooden box for my books and just nearby was placed in a corner a pile of fresh grass brought in for the milch cows and other animals. I used to sit there and study by the light of the lamp and I would sleep there too. At break of dawn, at the second cockcrow about four o'clock, the daughters-in-law in all the houses would get up to grind the flour and would sit at the grindstone singing songs. This was the time when I would get up, light the lamp, and start my studies. When I set off for school around eight or nine, I would not return home to Ladawali till half past seven or eight at night. This was because I had involved myself in lots of other things besides school. From the time I started going to school, I would go to Dasgaon every Saturday and on Monday I would go to school in Mahad from there—this was a settled routine.

In reality, what was the need for me to go to Dasgaon every Saturday when my mother and sister were at Ladawali? My mother was not happy about this. But the people from the big house in Dasgaon would call me there with a show of affection and I, out of diffidence, would not go against their word. Later, when I began to get my five rupee per month scholarship, that money would go to them. They would say, 'This is our brother's son and we have a right to his money.' So, the cost of my stay and my board was borne by my maternal uncle, while the money I received went to my father's maternal cousins. To bring about a change in this peculiar situation, my mother and I once went to stay at our house in Dasgaon. But even then things did not change. Instead, they quarrelled with my mother and made it difficult for her to stay there. Then we shut up the house and went back to live in Ladawali.

I was one of the bright students in my class. So some teachers would praise me and belittle my classmates. In the annual examination I got high marks in all subjects and passed, but in drawing and drill they would write on my report card that I had passed. That was downright false. Because the school would not allow me to sit in the class when the lessons for those subjects were going on, and in the results of the annual examination they would show that I had passed. If in the temple of Saraswati this kind of deceit is acceptable—to practise untouchability in fact and to make a show of not practising it—then it is better to leave to the imagination what happens elsewhere. In the Mahad school I passed the second English standard and standard six in Marathi. Then I began to study for the third standard. I was informed by the school that I would not get the scholarship money from then on. What happened to the three years' scholarship? The third year was probably counted as the time which was wasted before I was admitted to the school. While I was going to school the small expenditure that was required for my uniform, books and so on, was taken from my scholarship money. But if I was not getting the scholarship the question arose as to who would undertake that expense. Our people in Dasgaon who had taken a scholar's money were not willing to spend now, and my uncle was already hard-pressed to support us on his meagre income.

In this situation, my mother said, whatever happens we must go and live in our house in Dasgaon now. So one day we said our farewells to my grandmother and my uncle and departed with the intention of living permanently in Dasgaon. Uncle had given us enough grain to last for some days and he provided us with grain and other things from time to time. Now my going to school had ceased. I meant to go back to school after the May holidays, after buying books, etc. My father had never allowed my mother to go and work outside our home. She did all the work in the house, but she had not worked outside in the fields. But now after we returned to Dasgaon she started to go out to collect firewood, chop it into small pieces, then tie it up with plant fibres and bring it home, and finally make small bundles to sell in that village or the next village, and bring back food or money in exchange. This was the subsistence occupation of many poor persons in Dasgaon. The forest of Dasgaon was the only means of livelihood and sustenance for them. I too used to go with other children to collect twigs. Once when we had gone to the forest like this, a forest guard tried to catch three boys of my age and a young man, confiscate their sickles and take them to the police *chowkie*. So there was first an argument and then a fight with him. In all this the guard's head was injured. We picked up our sickles and ran home from there. A case was filed against us in the Mamledar's (magistrate's) court. We were issued a summons and court proceedings were initiated. A lawyer named Sathe was engaged to speak for us accused. After three or four months the verdict was declared and Accused no. 1, Bhagya Sakhya Mahar, the adult who had been with us, was sentenced to fifteen days rigorous imprisonment and we were given the alternative of a two-rupee fine or a week in jail. We paid two rupees each and got off. This was my very first conviction, when I was less than fifteen years old. It was said that one who had been convicted of a crime could not get a government job. So my mother and the people in the big house became anxious. They were afraid that, after being educated so far, I was going to waste it all.

When I had left school and was living in Dasgaon collecting firewood and doing odd jobs for the big house, a guest from Bombay came to the big house. He asked me how far I had studied, what I was doing, and so on and after this he told my four *dadas*—my father's maternal cousins—that if they sent Ramchandra (me) to Bombay he would secure for me a job as ticket collector with a monthly salary of forty-five rupees. At the time all these brothers were teachers in the Mahar school and they were earning eleven rupees a month. They reckoned: the four of us together earn four times eleven or forty-four rupees, and Ramchandra on his own is going to get a rupee more than that!—so they decided that they would send Ramchandra to Bombay to become a collector.

At the same time, they also decided to get me married. They said, 'We don't all four of us come together that often, and now that we are all here we must make some important decisions.' They discussed many things—which of them was to look after the house and the farm, how the instalments of the house loan were to be paid, who was to be married off that year, and so on. Their elder brother had a daughter who was of age. A man named Changdeo Khopadkar who worked as a clerk in Bombay had asked for her hand. This gentleman was a brother-in-law of the famous Gopal Baba Walangkar. He had come to Raodhal to get married. It had already been decided that the girl was to marry him. At the same time, it had been decided to get me married that same year. But where was the girl? 'If we find an outside girl we will lose contact with him. Besides, this is a boy who is going to bring in a good income. So we must find a girl from our family to marry him.' Since the one who gave his daughter in marriage would get his earnings, there was a bit of a fracas among them, and finally they fixed on Tukaramdada's daughter. So it was decided that three weddings in their family would be carried out on the same date and in the same *mandap*. This was to be the first wedding ceremony fitting to the big house, with all four brothers present. Neither I nor my mother were enthused to hear that my marriage had been arranged. My mind was distressed because I had had to leave school for lack of money, and my mother was always tense because of her widowhood and the trials she had to suffer. My marriage was taking place in this situation. What could we say other than—'Fine, let it happen'?

If the people from the big house taunted her on the subject of my marriage, she would say, peeved at the taunting, 'My boy is not yet old enough to be married. If you don't want to arrange his marriage don't do it, but don't bother me with claims of your generosity.' Of course, this business of her son, with no one to look after him, getting married, was in fact something that made her glad; and as for me, why should I not like the idea of getting married? To sum up, both my mother and I were in fact agreeable to the marriage, once they actually brought an acceptable proposal. We were happy that this marriage was taking place. The person whose daughter I was going to marry had great affection for my father. My father had tried hard to rescue him from the ill-treatment he was subjected to by his stepmother. And so he always remained grateful to my father. He was gratified that his daughter was to be married to the son of a man whom he called elder brother, my father. Since an old relationship that had worn thin was going to be revived through this marriage, some traditional customs were set aside for it. According to the old custom, the bride and groom should belong to different clans from both their mothers' and fathers' sides. Though the bride and groom in our marriage belonged to the same clan on our mothers' side, they were going ahead with the marriage. To put it in the language of our village folk, both bride and groom had the same *kothali*, or chamber, though the seeds were different.

When we got married, the bride Sita was six or seven years old and was just losing her milk teeth, while I was just getting my wisdom teeth. The elders of our family sent me to deliver invitations to our relatives in different villages, and I also had to carry out many small chores in preparation for the wedding. Seeing this, some elders were distressed and they said, 'Oh, it's an orphan getting married.' Our wedding took place with great ceremony. To tell the truth, it was like a dolls' wedding. In those days, even infants used to be married in their cradles. Our marriage was between persons of the same family. In our family I was the eldest among the children, so all the others called me *dada*, or elder brother. Even the girl who became my wife called me *dada* till she came of age. There was no occasion for the bride to feel shy of the groom here. From the day we were married we

Sitabai More, R.B. More's wife (L), with her mother.
Courtesy of Subodh More.

R.B. More with wife, Sitabai.
Courtesy of Subodh More.

both treated each other as equals, right down to today. This was an ideal for other couples to follow.

After the wedding the question of my education came up again. In the *khot* moneylender's village of Tale in Mangaon *tehsil* there was a big Marathi school and there one could study up to the third English class. There was a 'Mahar school' in the same village. My father-in-law was a teacher in that school. After the wedding he took me to Tale and began to make efforts to get me admission in the third English class in the big school. At first the director of that school flatly refused to admit me. Later, with mediation by some influential persons, he agreed to put my name down in the school register. To address the question of where to seat me, a plan was chalked out. This plan was as follows: adjoining the classroom where the third standard had classes was a window about two and a half to three feet high. A platform was to be erected outside this window. I was to ascend this platform with the help of a small ladder, so that I could face the class and be in communication with the teacher and my classmates, and could learn my lessons without touching other children in my class or in the school. Dada, my father-in-law, agreed to this plan and four workmen were hired at once to build the platform. They cut down branches from a *nanduki* tree in the school compound and under Dada's guidance built the platform in two days. After this, Dada took me to see the school, my classroom and the place where I was to sit. When I saw the whole setup I told Dada that I was not prepared to learn my lessons sitting on a stage outside the school building—'In the Mahad school they used to seat me separately outside the classroom, but at least the place was inside the school building. Here they are making me sit on a stage on the barren land behind the building; I don't like it at all'. Dada and some others tried hard to persuade me, but it was of no use. After two or three days Dada was convinced by me, and he cancelled the plan of sending me to that school. In Mahad I had to give up my education because of a lack of funds, and here in Tale, though there was no problem of funds, I had to leave the school because the problem of untouchability came in the way. To sum up, my educational progress came to a temporary halt because of economic and social difficulties.

When it had been decided not to send me to school, I was taken to Charai, a village near Tale, as a guest. My wife's grandfather lived there. His name was Putalaji and he owned land which had a yield of almost a thousand rupees. At that time he was the Police *patil* of the village. Even in the rainy season there were twenty to forty sheaves of rice remaining in his granary. Four or five big pots of milk would come to the house every day. He was that rich. His sons and daughters had come to Dasgaon for the wedding but he did not himself attend. We were taken to Charai to see him. He and his wife welcomed us and made much of us. From Charai we came to Tale and after some days I was sent to Dasgaon. During this trip to Tale I had been sent on a *jatra* with a robber. I wish here to say a little about that occasion.

In the Tale precinct at that time there was a well-known robber named Chandrya Kaatkari. He was much talked about. Rich people and government officials lived in fear of him. If anyone tormented the poor too much, he would teach them a lesson. He had a kind of hold over the *khot* moneylenders. The police could never lay their hands on him. Once he got tipped off that a certain police inspector was on his way to arrest him; he kept a watch on that inspector, and one day, when the inspector was out alone riding a horse, Chandrya stopped him and told him that he would tell him news of the notorious robber Chandrya if he would get down from his horse. Upon which he tied the inspector to a tree and rode off with the horse. This was a story told about him among the people. Many such legends were current among the folk of Tale. On rare occasions he would help out the poor by giving them money.

Putalya Mahar Patil of Charai, rich though he was, was one of his admirers and Chandrya used to visit him. Through him my father-in-law also became acquainted with Chandrya. He treated Dada with the greatest respect and even offered to give him money and jewellery. But Dada never took anything from him. On the contrary, he would try and persuade him to give up this life of wayside robbery and theft. To evade the reach of the police he moved around in semi-underground fashion. He sometimes came to Dada at night. I once told Dada that I wanted to see the village *jatra*. Sometime after this, Chandrya visited Dada just when there was a *jatra*, and he took me through the dense jungle to the village where the *jatra* was being held. The *jatra* site was next to a dense forest. When we were less than a mile from the *jatra*, he told me that he would wait in the jungle—'You go and see the *jatra* and then come and meet me here. We will go back to Tale together. Don't tell anyone who you are or who you came with'—I followed his instructions and he took me back to Tale before daybreak and handed me over to Dada. It was two or three days later that I learnt from Dada that the person who had carried me on his shoulders through the forest was a well-known robber of those parts. It was only when I became acquainted with Marxism as an adult that I understood why brave and decent people like Chandrya become robbers.

I had now returned to Dasgaon from Tale. After my marriage and on completing my trips to Tale and Charai, my life began to run on the same routine as it had earlier, when I left the school in Mahad and returned from Ladawali to Dasgaon. In the surroundings of Dasgaon I immersed myself in a variety of activities—singing marriage songs and songs in praise of the goddess Gauri, dancing, playing, going to the *akhada* to learn *patta* [a wooden sword used for sports], *bichava* [a short dagger] and *bondathi*, jumping on the wrestlers' pillar or *malkhamb*, watching *tamashas*, listening to stories and *kirtanas*, visiting villages to watch buffalo fights, going to *jatras*, doing *puja* and other rituals, keeping fasts, reading the scriptures, learning to recite *mantras*, and helping my mother in her work in the fields and byways. I used to do various small chores for the people of the big house and others.

If anyone asked me to run some errand, if it was something I could do I wouldn't say no. Some of the daughters-in-law would take advantage of my obliging nature, and, as they were pounding rice in the mortar, they would ask me to hold the pestle and I would hold it. The older women sometimes took pity on me and scolded them for this. There was a tavern in the village and grown-ups of our family would send me to fetch alcohol for them at all hours of the night. Since the owner of the tavern who sold alcohol was a man of our village, he thought nothing of selling drinks at any hour of the day or night or sending alcohol with young boys, even though all this was illegal. Every night two or three persons would send me to fetch alcohol, and I would go off without any fear of forest animals, scorpions and thorns or ghosts and spirits on the way. So that I should not refuse to do this work they would talk to me sweetly and even give me a little alcohol to drink to keep me happy. Because of this I too learnt to drink.

I was told by the families of two young men of Dasgaon who had studied up to the fourth Marathi class with me but were a little older than me, that they had gone to fight at the front. So I began to feel that I too should go and fight in the war. One day a recruiting officer came to the big house. He stayed for two days at our place. He asked my elder cousins about me. On hearing all about me, he said, 'Send Ramchandra with me so that he can take further education and he can become a big officer in the army.' I was prepared to go but the people in that house did not send me. Two days later, about two to three hundred army recruits from army camps at Khed, Chiplun and Mahad came to stay on the *maidan* next to the *dharamshala* at Dasgaon. They set up camp and then began to march to Bombay. The band went in front and behind it the soldiers dressed in their uniforms were stepping to the rhythm of the band. When they had gone beyond the mountain pass, I and two of my companions slipped away unseen by the grown-ups and began to walk behind them. After we had gone a mile or so, we were stopped and the soldiers went on ahead. We were disappointed and returned home. All these recruits into the army were of the Mahar caste. In 1891 the ban on Mahar soldiers had been lifted and Mahar Platoon 111 had been set up for the first time.[7] These recruits were from this platoon.

With no studies and no job, my time was being spent in useless activities like memorizing wedding songs, imitating the manners of the people of the nomadic *fakir, gosavi, gondhali, ghosi, bhaat* and *vaidu* communities. To add to this, a thorn entered my foot and caused a grave injury. Because of this I was confined to my bed, whimpering with pain, for months. Just as I recovered from this injury I was sent to Bombay for employment. This was my second trip to Bombay.

My relative tried to find a job for me. But because I was underage I could not find work. Some time back a Bombaywalla had assured me that he would find me

---

[7] See footnote 2 (p. 113) in Satyendra More's biography of R.B. More in the following section.

a job as a ticket collector. But now he was nowhere to be found. I could have got a job as an office boy, but I was not ready to do that work.

After coming to Bombay I had been staying with a distant relative in a *chawl* in Family Lines. We used to call his mother Akka. I and three or four others from Dasgaon were staying at Akka's place. They were all working somewhere or other and used to pay Akka for their food. It was four or five months since I had arrived and I had still not found a job. So I was not able to pay for my food. Nobody rebuked me, rather I was showered with affection. During this visit to Bombay I saw Dr. Ambedkar for the first time.

Seeing Dr. Ambedkar made me acutely aware of the importance of getting an education. I had to leave school halfway because there was no one to support me. If the years between had not been wasted, I too would have at least matriculated by now. Here I was, with neither education nor a job to my name. After my father died, my mother's brother looked after us for a while. So my mother did not have to toil too hard and I had a few years of school. Now my mother is slogging hard and here am I, roaming around Bombay. What a sorry state I am in! Such thoughts came to my mind from time to time.

I had made the acquaintance of several young men in Family Lines. I did not think it below me to smoke *beedis* with them, or to go to the toddy bars and drink toddy. There was a temple to the goddess Mariai there. The *pujari* in that temple had become my friend. While I went with him to the temple every day to sing *bhajans* and read books, I would also sometimes take puffs of marijuana from the chillum that he offered me. I had attained a skill in rendering the songs in a tuneful voice while keeping the beat on a one-stringed instrument, and because my Marathi was good I could read the books without faltering. The *bhajan* master and the persons reading the holy books would ask me to sit down and read the texts.

Most of the people living there earned their living doing some work connected with the army. There was also a large number who worked for the department stores Army and Navy and Whiteway & Laidlaw, the Hospital and the Medical Stores. They earned at most fifteen rupees a month. Just then someone told me about a job; it was for just a month and a half, a leave vacancy, but the wages were forty-five rupees. But one needed to speak in English, to be able to read and write, and also to have good clothes. The person who had told me about the job had promised the *sahib* in that job that he would bring a man who would meet these terms. One had to join service on the first. There were seven or eight days between. The main question was of the clothes; I had a *dhoti* and a coat. But this would not do among the European people; here one needed to have a coat and trousers. Finally, I managed with the help of a butler. On the assigned day I was taken and stood before the *sahib*.[8] The *sahib* took me to an office and showed

---

[8] Mahars were often employed as butlers by British officers, and businessmen.

me some books of printed tickets that looked like receipts. He explained to me where to write the date and signature, and made me sit down near a table with a drawer for the receipt-books and money. On the outer side of the table there was a window. The white sailors would stand outside the window, pay their money and take the tickets. All the persons receiving the tickets were white and they did not know Hindi or Marathi; likewise my English was not good, but still our work was not held up. When they came up to the window and said, 'one bed ticket' or 'four bar tickets', I would take the money and give them what they asked for and the job was done. To sum up, without much education and without any guarantee for the money, I got work as a seamen's cashier.

Akka and my relatives were happy to see that I had got a job. The place where I was working was a European seamen's office under control of the Navy. The office was located where the Maharashtra state legislature building stands today. From the point of view of us people, not only was the salary high but I earned extra income daily. There were lodgings for the seamen and a bar selling beer and other types of alcoholic drinks in that place. My task was to give them receipts for bed tickets and bar tickets and hand over the money collected to the officer. Bed tickets were for eight *annas*. Suppose a sailor paid one rupee for that ticket. I had been briefed by the person in whose place I was working that, if the man did not accept the eight *annas* I returned to him as change, I was to put the extra eight *annas* in my pocket instead of in the collection box. In this way I sometimes piled up as much as ten rupees in a single day, or at least five rupees per day.

Some particular friends of mine knew that I had a daily income. This extra money is not earned through toil, it is unholy money, it is a sin to keep it with you. So you must spend it. All these friends smoked *beedis*, ate *paan* with tobacco, drank spirits and toddy and smoked hash and grass. They were the same ones who played one-string instruments, tambourines and drums and sang *bhajans* in the night. When we had finished eating something in the restaurant we would go and sit in a toddy bar in the Dhobi Talao or Crawford Market area. We would beat on the benches and sing *qawwalis* and at dinner time we would go home swinging our arms. For about a week nobody at home knew that I had this daily income. Later on they came to know it, but they still didn't know how much it was. All the people in the colony were scared of those friends of mine; nobody would dare to cross them.

Later on, because I knew English, some hawkers became my friends. They were well-known gangsters from that precinct. Even my friends of the Mariai temple were afraid of them. Since they were *pheriwallas* and hawkers from among the butchers in the market, they were fierce to look at and affectionate at heart. If there was a *qawwali* or Ramleela programme somewhere far from the market area they would take me there and bring me home afterwards. My relatives and the other residents of Family Lines often warned me not to go with them. But I did not listen to them and carried on chatting with my friends, roaming around the city with them as before. So everybody began to say that I had been spoilt: that I had become a *mawali*.

I placed my first salary of forty-five rupees in Akka's hands and touched her feet. She was old but was constantly making trips outside her home every day. The boy whom we called her son was actually her deceased sister's son. As she was herself childless, she called this boy her son and satisfied all his demands. She arranged three marriages for him, and she gave all the money she earned to her maternal cousin in Dasgaon. It was through this cousin that I had come to her place in Bombay. I touched her feet. She was overcome, hugged me tightly and began to cry. She thought it a great thing that I brought my whole salary to her. I told her to take twenty rupees of it for my meals, five rupees to spend on herself, and to send the remaining twenty rupees to my home in Dasgaon. She sent on the twenty rupees, but the people in the big house in Dasgaon did not give the money to my mother.

Before I came to Bombay my house at Dasgaon had been rented out to the new Mahar school that had been started there. The teacher in that school was one of our family from the big house. Instead of giving the rent money to my mother, he pocketed it before it reached her. They put forward the same argument that they had made when they took my scholarship money earlier, to justify helping themselves to the rent. Because I was their brother the money I earned was theirs, my mother had no right to it at all. They did not give the money I sent from Bombay to my mother either. When I learned of this I realized clearly that I was indeed an orphan, and that the show of affection put up by the people in the big house had indeed come in my way, and afflicted my mother and sister. I thought to myself that as long as we had connections with the big house, even if I earned money it would not be of any use to my mother and sister. Instead of earning money that went to them I should go to Pune for further education. I remembered having read somewhere that Pune was a treasure-house of learning, and that came to mind now. My leave vacancy job with a large salary had ended and I was unemployed again.

I began to go to the docks to look for work. If one didn't find work, one could go near the ships and try and find something to eat. One could get dates, all kinds of dried fruits, sugar to eat on the ships. One could also get a full meal for two *pice*. Sometimes one could get work as a labourer on daily wages. If one stood in the queue for work, even if one wasn't selected as a labourer, one got one *anna* for attending the muster call. It was to the Alexandra Dock that I went most often. The work of carrying sacks or chests filled with rice from the warehouse in those docks on one's head to the crane for loading on the ships was called 'stamping'. This work would become available sometimes, usually at night. If the parcel or chest was small one was paid one *pai* for each trip, for a slightly larger one it was two *pice*, and for a double or larger-sized one was paid a paisa. If this coolie work was available at night I would work in the night and earn eight to ten paisas. From this I would

'Boy labour' unloading boxes.
Source: Burnett-Hurst, *Labour and Housing in Bombay*.

pay the *mithaiwalla*, eat some minced mutton and bread in a restaurant and take the remaining couple of *annas* to Akka. In those days the price of a month's board was only five rupees, and I would pay it in this manner. By standing in line, doing the work of 'stamping' when I got it, or doing coolie work for daily wages at the railway station, I could cover my expenses and pay for my board. Later I got work as a 'marker' in the Arsenal depot at Haji Bunder (dock). I had obtained this job for a salary of thirty rupees a month after months of being unemployed.

I used to go to work with other workers on the Port Trust steam train running from Carnac Bunder to Haji Bunder. Before this, I was not acquainted with Bombay city beyond Dhobi Talao, Crawford Market, Princess Dock, Alexandra Dock, Carnac Bunder, Bori Bunder, Museum and Colaba railway stations.

But when I started going to work at Haji Bunder I became familiar with some new areas of Bombay. The main among these were Grant Road and Foras Road. Later on I began to go to these areas more and more often. This was because three of my new-found companions were taking part in the Kamleshwar Drama Company that had just been started. When they asked me, I agreed most joyfully to act in this company. I had been fond of singing and dancing even before this.

Once during a ceremony at the school in Mahad, I had read out a prepared speech on the stage, and in the *tamasha* put up for the Holi festival at the Dasgaon school, I had played the leading role of Tatyabapu. So I was delighted to have a ready-made opportunity to take part in a play. The drama company had taken on rent a triangular-shaped room at the corner of the Batatyachi Chawl in Foras Road, on the second floor. A *tabla*, a harmonium and other musical instruments were kept there. Every evening after finishing work we would go to that 'theatre room'. The work we did was also quite comfortable: do work when it was there, otherwise relax. Our job was to place a stencil on the sacks of grain or other essential stuff needed by the army, and ink it over with a brush. This work went on about three or four days every week. First the coolie would bring the sacks to the shed and place them in a line. While this was being done we would be chatting among ourselves. Then the work of marking would begin. Since we markers were united we would decide among ourselves how much work to do and how much to leave for the next day. There were five of us working as markers in that shed. All of us, except for one, were 'theatrical'. After getting off from work we would go to the theatre room, and only later on go home: this was our regular daily routine. One could learn to play the *tabla* and the harmonium there, but I never picked up any of that. The director of the drama company was a fellow named Moreshwar. I don't know anything more about him, but it seemed he was most dedicated to the art. He staged a play called *Manovijay*—Victory of the Mind. In this play the six enemies of the Soul: Lust, Anger, Desire, Greed, Drink (addiction?) and Envy, were portrayed as characters in the play. Morality was another character in the play. I had to play a part of the main role of Lust which was not played by the leading actor, and the role of Morality was also given to me. Until the play was staged we would go every day to our theatre room to practise.

The Batatyachi Chawl where our theatre room was located was in the Safed Galli (literally, 'white lane'). This Safed Galli was a big centre of the prostitution business. All the *chawls* in that area were buzzing with prostitutes. Prostitutes lived in some of the rooms in Batatyachi Chawl and *tamasha* players and other people lived in the remaining rooms. The *tamasha* of the Shivasambha Kavalapurkar company was very famous in those days. I had seen their show once before I came to Bombay. I knew both the brothers and also the well-known *tamasha* singer-poet Bapu Pattherao and the dancer Pavali. These folk lived in rented rooms in the Batatyachi Chawl. This two-storey building had rooms with windows on the side facing the road and on the inner side there were verandas, stairs and the doors to the rooms. Our theatre room was in the farthest corner on the second floor. From the moment we entered the building till we reached our room we had to pass rooms belonging to prostitutes. The room occupied by the Shivasambha company was on the way, and we would stop to say hello before passing ahead. Some of the hookers would tease us and laugh and joke with us as we came and went. My friends would push me in their path; because I was the youngest they would make fun of me like this. Surrounded by such an atmosphere, I of course was very young but my older friends also kept a distance from the hookers and from alcohol.

In those days the main form of entertainment for common people was the *tamasha*. Theatrical plays had not become popular. Only very few people used to see plays then. Before then I myself had seen only one play. One of my relatives who had become a *sadhu* had once taken me to see the play *Raja Harishchandra* staged by the *Lalit Kaladarsh* or Patankar Theatre Company in the Bombay Theatre.⁹ This *sadhu* had earlier been a ruffian. He had taken part in the first Hindu–Muslim riot in 1898 and served a jail sentence. Later he began to read holy books and live the life of an ascetic. In Dasgaon, I had read several books in his company—*The Victory of Hari*, *The Victory of Ram*, *Bhagavat*, *Shivaleelamrit*, *Agamanigam*, and a book of stories from the *Mahabharata*. Besides this, I performed *puja* for two hours every day and meditated. I knew the *Pandurang Stotr* and the *Vyankatesh Stotr* by heart, as well as 101 *mantras*. He was the one who showed me this play. This was the first play I had seen in my life. It was at this time that I heard my first phonographic record: 'Why won't someone give me a ticket to Bombay?' In those days people referred to the phonograph as *bangadicha baaja*, the bangle player; it was a novelty. One sat before the phonograph and put the funnel to one's ear and listened to the song among various other sounds. This is how I heard my first recorded song.

As I stated earlier, my friends kept a distance from bad things. This was because they were educated and cultured. Their attraction to the art of theatre can be said to be a sign of their being cultured. This was their way of trying to rise from a lower class to a higher class. After the rehearsals of the play *Manovijay*, it was first staged in the Bombay Theatre. I was of course proud to have worked as an actor on the stage of such a famous theatre in Bombay at such a young age.

The money that I sent home when I was working in the Sailors' Home never reached my mother. This was repeated when I worked at Haji Bunder. I always felt that the environment in Bombay was not conducive to study, that I would be able to go on studying if I went to Pune. My mothers' relatives found it very strange that the people from the big house pocketed my money instead of giving it to my mother. But others would say, the people at the big house educated the boy, so why should they not take the money? In fact, the education that I got was not due to any expenditure from the big house. My primary education in the Marathi school was completed while my father was still alive, and my education in the English school was on the basis of my scholarship money and my maternal uncle's arrangements for my board and lodging. But in those days the little English education I had had was thought to be a great thing—'English education is the milk of the tigress'— and the undeserved credit for that went to the family of school teachers at the big house. 'Those school teacher relatives also arranged his marriage. So how does it matter if they take his money instead of giving it to his mother?' Who could stop the mouths of those who spoke like this? My condition was like that of someone who had been gagged and punched in the mouth.

After the play had been staged I made a firm decision in my mind to go to

---

⁹ 'Raja Harishchandra' was also the title of a Marathi film, said to be the first, produced in 1913.

Pune, and was waiting for my salary. I had told many of my friends that I didn't want to work here anymore, that I wanted to go somewhere else and study further. But I had told no one where I was going or when. From my earlier wages I used to keep five rupees to pay the milkman and the *mithaiwalla*, and give the remaining twenty-five to Akka. I decided that from this month's pay I would not give anything to Akka. On the day before my pay was due I wrote a letter to Akka and kept it in my pocket. In this I had written things like: I am going somewhere far away, don't worry about me, and so on. On pay day when I came home and was asked about it, I lied and said that I would be paid the next day. Then, when nobody was around, I put the letter and five rupees in the grain store and left the house. There were about twenty rupees in my pocket. It was about midnight. I went to Bori Bunder station and got on the train to Pune without buying a ticket, and got down in Pune before sunrise. Outside the station I went and sat in the garden meant for passengers travelling third class. There were several village folk, men and women, waiting to go to Bombay. I spent quite a long time watching their movements and listening to their talk and laughter. Then I had something to eat in a restaurant and took the road to Modi Khana. There was a woman I knew from Dasgaon in this Modi Khana. She had married a man called Abitkar who had retired from military service. Since Modi Khana was a colony of army pensioners and since the name Abitkar was well known there, I had no difficulty in finding their house. The woman's name was Kali ('Blackie').[10] She was of fair complexion, pleasant and naive. But since her name was Kali we used to call her Kalibai. Kalibai expressed her joy to see me and, according to the custom, she caressed me, cracked four fingers of each hand against my face, drew a handful of salt around me and threw it in the stove (to ward off evil spirits). Then she told the people in the house about my father and introduced me as his son. They did not know that I had come from Bombay and that I had been living in Bombay; they thought I had come from Dasgaon. Of course, they knew that to reach Pune from Dasgaon one had to come via Bombay.

If one had to go to Pune from Dasgaon there was another route. That was via the Madhya hill route near Raigad. In the past, people from the Raigad valley would carry wooden mortars and pestles and *kathavadis* or wooden trays for kneading dough on their heads and go on foot to sell them in Pune. But now that there were motorboats and trains, that route was more or less unused. In those days there were no motor cars of private or government ownership at all. In those days ordinary folk living in villages did not know the world beyond the *panchakroshi*—a distance of about five kilometres, or the maximum distance from which sounds can be heard. Some people would never leave their village to go to any other village. Even those people who came to live and work in Bombay or Pune from the

---

[10] In Marathi, 'Kala' or 'Kali' means black. The 'l' in these words is the guttural Marathi 'l', and so 'Kali' does not sound like the name of the goddess. Of course the goddess Kali is also dark-skinned.—*Tr.*

villages did not know anything beyond their village and their place of work and residence in Bombay or Pune. So my coming to Pune from Dasgaon was probably like my coming from England to Hindustan for them. When they asked me, 'How did you come so far?' I replied, 'I came to Pune to see the *tabut* (the medallion paraded by Muslims during the solemn observance of Moharram).' They took me literally at my word. Because there were just a few days left till the procession of the *tabut* of Moharram. In those days Diwali in Bombay, the *tabut* in Pune and Dussehra in Baroda were much talked about. People would come from far off to see these spectacles.

The Abitkar family looked after me well. Kalibai showered me with love like her own son. I was afraid that, if I told them I had come to Pune to study, these people would inform Dasgaon and my schoolteacher relatives would come and take me back to Bombay. So I didn't tell them anything about that. I had decided in my mind to stay with them as a guest for a few days, and then slip away from there. So while I was staying with them I tried to get to know more about Pune. But they did not know anything beyond army-related places; their knowledge was limited to the cantonment area of Pune. They told me some stories they had heard about the days of *Peshwa* rule. They said, 'We have nothing to do with Poona city. We hardly ever go there.' Even the children of the Modi Khana area did not go to school with children from the city. There were separate schools for these children in the vicinity. Just as in Bombay I had lived in the Family Lines meant for army people, so did I find myself among military people in Modi Khana. In the villages there were separate areas for our folk. I felt that even in Bombay and Pune there were separate colonies for us, but I did not at the time understand who had separated us in this way.

The *tabut* of Moharram came and went, and I decided to leave. Kalibai was about to tie up some bundles to take to Dasgaon, but I told her that I was going to Bombay to work, not to Dasgaon. One of her nephews came with me to the station and, even as I was saying no, he bought my ticket and seated me on the train. I was thinking how to escape him, but he did not budge until the train started to move. The train left the station and halted for some time at Khadki station. Seeing this I got down quickly on to the platform and came outside the station with the other people there. In my pocket there was a few rupees, and in my head thoughts going round and round—where to go now, what to do next.

When I came out of Khadki station I went and sat under a thorny *babhali* bush. Now I had left the boundaries of my childhood and entered the stage of youth. I was a young man seventeen or eighteen years old. Before this I had been directly or indirectly under somebody's supervision. I was near people who would praise or chastise my good and bad deeds. In Dasgaon and Ladawali there were my mother and father. Besides them, there were near relatives like my *mama* and my elder cousins. In Bombay there were Akka and others, and in Pune, if for just four or five days, there was Kalibai and the people of her family. But here, sitting under the thorny *babhali* bush, I was just an individual, under nobody's control and completely independent. The whole of my life after my father's death passed before my mind's eye. As I was thinking about my purpose in leaving Bombay, and how I would carry it out, another thought entered my mind. This was the idea that I should first go to Dehu and Alandi to take *darshan* of the *samadhis* of the saints Tukaram and Dnyaneshwar, and only afterwards do what I had to do.

When this notion entered my head I got up from the *babhali* bush and started walking towards the station again. There I asked people sitting outside the station about the road to Dehu and Alandi. There was a mature and knowledgeable person among them, who asked me where I had come from, why I had come here, and many such questions. Upon which I told him that I had come from Aadmavala, that my father had passed away, and that I was going to join the army after visiting Dehu and Alandi. I had read in my schoolbooks that Khadki was a large military station. That was how I thought up the fib I told him about my joining the army.

I don't remember now how many days I spent in the pilgrimage to Dehu–Alandi, or what I saw there. But I definitely remember having seen a temple of Tukaram at Dehu. When I returned from there I began to stay at a temple in the village of Dapodi near Khadki, through a temple *pujari* I had made friends with. In that temple there would be *bhajan* singing every night with *taal* and *mridanga*, in which I took part. Earlier I knew *bhajans* accompanied by a one-stringed instrument and *khanjeer*, or by *jhaanj* and *mridanga*. But I was not familiar with these *bhajans* which were sung with a lot of bodily exercise. In the temple at Dapodi I became acquainted with this style of *bhajan* singing and I also came into contact with some things that I should not have because of that temple. A temple is not in fact a place to stay. After one or two days the *pujari* showed me the door. But since I had no place to go I came and slept outside the temple at night. Seeing this, a man from the settlement near the temple took me to his house. I found the atmosphere in his house to be a bit strange. But I had no alternative but to stay there. From that house I started going to work in a canteen for white soldiers. This work was for daily wages. So every day some money would come into my hands. From this money I could pay the people I was staying with and have some left over for my small expenses. But I was fed up with both the work of taking tea to the white soldiers and the place I was staying at. I felt that, if I could get a job with a monthly salary I could find a better place to stay and also do something about my education. I was making efforts in that direction.

One day, a man in the canteen introduced me to a friend of his who worked in the Khadki arsenal. He pointed out to me who the main boss in the arsenal was, and informed me about how I could get to meet him. Accordingly, I came and stood at the gate of the arsenal at the time when the *sahib* was due to come there. When the *sahib* approached I said, 'Sir, I know English, I want work.' He said,

'Come on.' I walked on behind him. When we entered the gate he entrusted me to a sergeant and went off. The sergeant began to show his disapproval by raising his eyebrows at me. Then he said something. But because of my limited English and his incomprehensible accent I didn't understand what he said. Then he asked me my name. That much English I understood. I told him my name, which he wrote down, and then took me with him to a depot. There in a waterlogged place there were piles of wooden boxes filled with glassware. About twenty convicts from the Yerawada jail were standing there. The sergeant told me to instruct the prisoners to carry those boxes to a dry place at some distance. I made out what he was saying only from his expression and gestures, and explained what he was saying to the prisoners' warder in *bazaar* Hindi. With that the work of moving the chests began. The sergeant was pleased to see this and he praised me. That sergeant was a funny fellow. He was always saying something to me. He had guessed that I found it hard to understand him, and so he would repeat what he was saying and make gestures so that I could understand. He scolded me when I called him Sir. He would say, 'I am not Sir, Sir is not good.' At about three o'clock the warder asked permission for the prisoners to go back to the jail. The sergeant agreed, and the prisoners went away. Our work for that day was done.

The next day he told me what work I was to do and went off. I met other workers working in that depot. I made their acquaintance and in the recess I came to the gate. There was a watchman who would frisk each person going out before he let him go out of the gate. So he frisked me too. I came outside and came to Khadki Bazaar by a shortcut from the arsenal to the Khadki Bazaar. After spending quite a long time there I went back to Dapodi to the house where I was staying. At night my fellow workers in the canteen came and met me. I told them how I had managed to find work. They were surprised to hear it from me. They said, 'Nobody gets a job there outside their recruitment and without paying money, and we are amazed that you got yourself a job there.'

From the time I came to live in that house my going to the temple to sing *bhajans* had become less and less frequent, and after I took up the job in the arsenal I hardly even glanced at the temple. So that temple was gone. But after a few months I also lost the place to stay that I had got because of the temple, and I went to live in a *chawl* next to the Khadki Bazaar. A gentleman from the Konkan who had retired from the *khechar* (mule) section of the army was living in a rented room there with his wife from Pune. They had no children and they knew nothing about their native *gaon*, or village. I made their acquaintance and found out all I could learn about them. After I left the Modi Khana I took utmost care about one thing: to find out whatever I could about others, but never to reveal the true facts about myself. I behaved in this same manner with this couple. Then, seeing that I was educated, had a job and had nowhere to stay, they asked me to come and stay with them and I began to live in that *chawl*.

After I got the job in the arsenal I found a kind of stability. Since I had left Bombay, and especially after I left the Abitkars' home, I was full of hot air, like a calf. I was still in the same situation for some time after I started working at the arsenal. For a month or two I was doing the same kind of work at the arsenal as I had done on my first day. There would be different sergeants and different coolies to do the work of carrying loads. Sometimes there were prisoners doing this work, and sometimes coolies in military service. My job was to get the work done from them according to the sergeant's instructions. I had got a supervisor's post, above that of the coolies, just because I knew some English. But my pay was that of a coolie. Because of this job some soldiers became my friends. I would go to their camp after work to meet them, when they asked me to do so. Whenever I went to their camp I was treated to all kinds of food and drink and given cigarettes and other things. Later on, I will narrate how my friendship with these soldiers benefited me.

But here I want first to describe the other kinds of work that I did at the arsenal. After my work as a *mukadam* was finished I was given the job of a marker. But that work consisted of writing with a brush on parcels wrapped in sacking. In a couple of days I learned all about this work and began to do it with the other markers. Later I was promoted to working as a packer in the packing department. The work of a packer was a sort of clerical job. Besides, the goods in the store were in the packer's custody. The store in the arsenal had goods useful for the military. There was frisking at the gate to prevent these goods from being stolen, but even then all kinds of goods and material would be stolen. Some time after I started working as a packer I was given the job of voucher clerk and after some months I became a ledger clerk. All these jobs were carried out under the supervision of white officers. A ledger clerk, a voucher clerk and a dispatch clerk, they all got the same salary. All painted with the same brush! The difference between a coolie and a clerk was only in the hardness of their labour. A clerk did not have to put in as much bodily exertion as a coolie did. In fact both the jobs needed no intellect! The type of work I did went on changing quickly, but there was not much change in my life beyond work. The kind of environment which I inhabited since I left Kalibai's house in Modi Khana was one of *jogtins* and *muralis* dedicated to the gods, the licentious behaviour of the white soldiers and their friends, and the pitiable condition of the poor who worked in occupations related to the army. I felt suffocated living in these surroundings. But one thing was clear: I was aware that I was living in a foul kind of environment. And so I was always making efforts to get out of it. When a man living on his own is aware of the sin he is committing, he feels remorse when he is punished and makes efforts to come away from it. But if he is not aware, he feels no remorse even after he suffers punishment, and makes no efforts to turn away from that deed. When I left the unhealthy environment of Dapodi and went to live in Khadki, my life had turned in an appropriate direction.

Soon after I came to Khadki, I had to have a small surgical operation on my right leg. My Indian soldier friends arranged for me to get admitted to the Khadki Military Hospital to get this done. The operation on my leg was done in that hospital and my ailment was removed. I worked for two months after this operation. Then I learned about a night school that had been opened recently. This night school had been started by the Alegaonkar brothers who were followers of Lokmanya Tilak.[11] Its name was 'Alegaonkars' Night School'. As soon as I heard about this night school, I went there and registered my name. Since I was in a job I had no difficulty in paying the fees and meeting the expense of buying books. My admission to the night school was like a new life for me. It was a great joy for me that I had become a student again. Now a new routine began, of doing my job during the day and going to night school to gather knowledge. Some of the persons working with me at the arsenal had become my friends. Now to these were added friends from among the students of the Alegaonkars' school. Some of these friends liked to go and see *tamashas* and plays. Some loved to sing *bhajans*, some liked gambling and playing cards, while others had a liking for physical exercise, running and other sports. I spent what time I could with all of them and won their affection. Because of their company I picked up some bad habits. But I did not become addicted to them. The reading I had done earlier and the company of saintly persons had given me a meditative nature. Because of my youth I sometimes stepped out of line, but since I was in the habit of thinking about what I did, I would try hard to recover myself.

From the time I began to go to night school, I avoided spending too much time with my friends who were fond of *tamashas*, plays, cards, and gambling. Gradually, I became detached from all these things. But my friends were never angry with me for this. It never happened that I cut off an acquaintance, or when I had made friends with someone that I broke off with them. During my whole life I never had a personal quarrel with anybody. From childhood I had a liking for sports, for doing somersaults like an acrobat or a *bahurupi*, for running. The story that follows will illustrate how this came of use to me at times.

On one occasion word arrived at our school that there was going to be a 27-mile race. Those who took part in it successfully would gain fame and win prizes. On this some of us students talked it over among ourselves and it was decided that we would take part. So we decided to chalk out a circle with lime in an open ground with *babhali* bushes to practise running. We got ourselves informed about what clothes to wear while running, how to run and how to breathe, and then we

---

[11] The Alegaonkar brothers were working in the ammunitions factory at Khadki in Pune. Pandharinath Alegaonkar (Treasurer), Vishnupant Alegaonkar (Headmaster), Eknath Alegaonkar (Manager) and Mahadeo Alegaonkar (Superintendent) founded the Khadki Education Society in Pune in 1913, as they saw illiteracy of the workers as a cause of their exploitation. The Alegaonkar School that is mentioned here was the first school started by this Society.—Tr.

got up at four every morning to practise running in the place we had decided on. We set the clock before we started running. Usually it takes about six minutes to run a mile. On the first day we practised running for ten minutes, on the second for twelve minutes, then fifteen and twenty, on an increasing scale. Six minutes a mile meant that in an hour we ran about ten miles. In this way we accustomed ourselves to run for two and a half hours each day. In other words, we used to run twenty-five miles each day. In these two and a half hours we used to run from Khadki to Chinchwad and then back again to our ground in Khadki. We had started our practice with the aim of taking part in the twenty-seven mile race. For this we should have run thirty miles every day. But we did not go beyond twenty-five miles a day. And besides, the date for submitting entries for the race had already passed. So we gave up this business we had started, of running every day. I must say it was a matter of great gratification that we could easily cover a distance of twenty-five miles in two and a half hours. These days, city folk and village folk do not travel by foot very often. So this will not mean much to them. But we can explain it this way: a person can walk at most twenty-five miles in one day. So I was easily covering in two and a half hours the distance that a person can travel on foot in one day.

When I returned from Khadki to Dasgaon I became a pupil of the school at Mahad again. Then I would go from Dasgaon to Mahad or from Mahad to Dasgaon in half an hour. Later, during the agitation against the *khoti* system in the Konkan and during the working-class protest against capitalist imperialism in Bombay, I easily walked any number of miles each day.[12] Because of the habit of running I had no problem with walking any distance, and I never got tired however much I walked. The practice of running and walking was a great help in keeping me healthy.

While I was in Khadki another important event of my life took place. Some of my friends had set up a *bhajan* group. The manager of a particular temple had invited this *bhajan* group to perform at the Datta festival. Accordingly, this *bhajan* group arrived at the festival site at the time agreed upon, with their *taal* and *mridanga*. But the group had to sit outside the temple to sing. Some of the young

---

[12] The *khoti* system was a form of the *zamindari* system of land settlement implemented by the British in the Konkan. The traditional landlords, or *khots*, who were mainly Brahmins or Muslims, were given the right to collect taxes from the peasants. This resulted in extreme exploitation of the Konkan peasantry. Ambedkar launched a movement against the *khoti* system in 1937, moving a bill in the Legislative Assembly and later organizing a protest march to the Bombay Council Hall. Earlier, in 1922, S.K. Bole had introduced a motion in the Bombay legislature to abolish *khoti*. Sitaram Keshav Bole (1869–1961) was born in a well-off Bhandari (toddy tapper) caste family in Bombay. Later, he became a follower of Satyashodhak ideology. Bole met B.R. Ambedkar for the first time in 1907, when the latter was honoured for becoming the first Mahar to pass matriculation. Bole was elected to the Bombay Legislative Council from the Non-Brahmin Party in 1920. S.K. Bole also introduced, in 1923, a bill to open to the untouchable classes all public watering places, wells and *dharamshalas* which were built and maintained out of public funds.

men in that group found it insulting that, when their group was in no way inferior to the other *bhajan* groups, they were made to sit outside instead of mixing with others inside the temple. The next day they met me in the arsenal and we talked about this. Then one of them suggested that I write about this in *Satya Prakash*, and I most happily agreed to do so. It is important to note here that I had never in my life seen *Satya Prakash* or any other newspaper till then. As I remember, the name that these young men had given their group was 'Datta Prasadik Bhajan Mandal'. As my friends had suggested, I wrote out this story in easily readable Marathi, and gave it to them. In a week or so the whole story was published in *Satya Prakash* with the byline 'Ghamare'. My friends brought a copy of that issue to me. When I saw what I had written printed in a newspaper for the first time in my life, I read it over and over again greedily. This article bringing the injustice of untouchability to light was my first step in the world of journalism. This was an event of the first half of 1920. *Satya Prakash* was a newspaper of the Satyashodhak movement. I read it for the first time on that occasion. Later I read other newspapers of the Satyashodhak movement and other literature of the movement like *Gulamgiri* ('Slavery', by Mahatma Jotiba Phule) and *Dashavatar Pradipika*.[13]

In the Alegaonkars' school my name had been entered for the fourth form. From there I entered the fifth form. In that school they used the word 'form' instead of 'standard'. In Mahad I had passed the second standard and entered the third, but I had not completed the course for the third standard. I was satisfied that in this situation, the school in Khadki, without looking to certificates, had taken me into the fourth on the basis of a test. I had come to Pune because I was drawn to education, but my life there was an ordeal. To study along with doing a job one needs a congenial environment. In the home of the Abitkars, staying with Kalibai, I could perhaps have studied and done a job as well, but in trying to avoid everybody I lost my own way. I was spinning round and round like a kite with no moorings. Now I began to miss my mother and other relatives. My existence in Pune and Khadki seemed like two different worlds to me.

I had a distant relative in Lonavala. He lived there with his wife and children and worked as a clerk in the railway goods depot. I decided in my mind to visit him and ask about my people at home. So in one trip to Lonavala I found out, from a distance, where he worked and where he lived. In the next trip I arrived at his door. He had not come home from work. His wife was at home. She recognized me and

---

[13] The *Satyashodak Samaj* ('Truth-Seeking Society') was founded in 1873 by Jotirao Govindrao Phule (1827–1891) and his followers. The Samaj engaged in a vigorous polemic against caste and Brahminism, and sought to build a broad coalition of Dalits and Non-Brahmins comprised of a coalition of agrarian labourers, farmers, and landed gentry, united against priestly superstition and capitalist exploitation. The Samaj was actively engaged in producing an everyday counterculture that challenged the ritual and bureaucratic predominance of Brahmins. Phule's famous text, *Gulamgiri* ('Slavery'), written in 1873 suggests a comparison between caste exploitation and Atlantic world slavery.

said, 'Where have you been? Your mother is half dead from worrying about you.' Then she asked me to have a wash and set a meal before me. I said I would eat only after the man of the house returned. She told me, 'He will come home late, and if he has been drinking, he will be angry with you. So it is better that you finish your dinner now.' So I finished my meal and sat talking with her, to get more news of home. 'Aai and Pithubai are fine. Your mother is in good health, but she always talks of you and cries. I have only just returned from Dasgaon.'

As she was talking to me, Shirkavale More entered. Seeing this sturdy retired person of military bearing, I was subdued for a moment. Ramibai said, 'See, here's our Ramchandra.' He expressed his pleasure, and after he finished his meal he sat me down beside him and asked how I was. I told him I was working at the arsenal and attending the night school. Then he told me that he had met some of our folk in Bombay and they had told him that I had gone off in a group of *sadhus*, or holy men. But he had replied that such an educated boy would never go off with *sadhus*. 'So I was proved right after all. Now you go to sleep, we will talk in the morning.' So saying, he asked Ramibai to make my bed. I then undressed and went to bed. Those people also retired for the night.

As I lay in bed many waves of thought passed through my mind. So many days after I had left home, I was still penniless. If I stayed on with these people they would pester me with all kinds of questions in the morning. So I decided it was better for me to go away from there, and then I went to sleep. At four in the morning, I lifted the latch of the door without letting anyone hear me, and stepped out of the house. At the nearby railway station I caught the shuttle to Pune and reached Khadki. Then I went to work as usual. I was sure that Shirkavale would write to Dasgaon and tell my family where I was. So, before someone from Dasgaon or Bombay came to take me away, I felt it would be wise to return on my own. I now began to think in that direction. If I were to go it would be better to go during Diwali. There were about two months to go for Diwali. To ensure that I didn't forget anything important when I left, as soon as I got my wages I paid off my fees and collected the fifth form certificate from the Alegaonkars' school. Thinking that I should save whatever money I could, I stopped buying new clothes.

Just then news of an important event reached me: the death of Lokmanya Tilak. To learn more about this I went to Alegaonkars' school with a few friends. There we were informed that a special train had been arranged for those who wanted to take part in Lokmanya Tilak's funeral procession. Then I thought to myself—I had decided to go in Diwali, but Diwali was still far off. And anyway, what great difference would my going for Diwali make? I had decided to go after all, so why wait till Diwali? Besides, I should not waste the opportunity to join the funeral procession of a great Indian leader. I should think of this as a coincidence favouring my return to Bombay. OK then, I should just go—so I began to collect my things and went and sat in the special bogey at Pune station. The end of my sojourn in Pune and Khadki and my return to Bombay marked the end of one chapter of my life and my journey to the next chapter.

Arriving in Bombay I was able to witness the unprecedented event of Tilak's funeral procession. But I could still not put an end to the troubled and uncertain pattern of my life. Sardar Griha, the place from which the procession set off, was just a small distance from the Family Lines where I had been staying before I left Bombay. In fact I should have gone to Akka's place as soon as I alighted from the train, and deposited the money I had brought from Pune and my school certificate with her. But I did not manage to do this. At least after the procession it was essential for me to meet some of my relatives. But it is worth noting here, from my example, that a person's wrongheadedness can sometimes be responsible for his degeneration. What happened was that after the funeral procession was over, I was suddenly taken by the desire to see a play. The thought never even crossed my mind that I had just arrived in Bombay and I needed to meet my relatives first; plays I could see at any time. As the idea of seeing a play entered my mind, my feet moved in the direction of the playhouse. Since the play was about to begin, I forgot about dinner, ate some tea and bread quickly and got into a seat in the theatre. The play started at nine p.m. and ended past midnight. After that, I walked as far as Bori Bunder and sat down in the Bhatia Gardens near there around one-thirty. In the gardens some people were sleeping, some were sitting on benches and some were walking around here and there. I decided to spend the night sitting there rather than waking my relatives at that time of night. At about three o'clock sleep overcame me and I took off my coat and cap, folded them as a pillow under my head and lay down on the grass. In a short time I was fast asleep. When I woke up at five-thirty I found that someone had made off with all my things. I had nothing left but the shirt and dhoti I was wearing. My eccentric behaviour had really got me into trouble. I had stepped from the frying pan into the fire, but it was all my own fault.

Since I was not new to Bombay I was still confident that I would find a way out of this. So, without thinking too much about what had happened, I took the road to the docks. I went to an illiterate supervisor and agreed to write down the names of the dockhands for him for any wages he was willing to give me. I folded my *dhoti* to make it into a *lungi*. Now this *lungi* and shirt were my daily outfit and the gardens where I had been robbed were my nightly sleeping place. I began a life of daytime in the docks and night-time in the garden. I became acquainted with the people in the gardens who lived by stealing, and came to be known as one of them. In those days one could get a *bhakari* and a piece of pumpkin for two *pice* at the roadside near the docks, and a full meal for one *anna* on the ships. At night I would attend singing and dancing sessions and wander around, then at an unearthly hour I would get up and go to the docks and look for work on daily wages. I used the public latrines and washed myself or took a bath at the taps nearby. I washed my clothes at the same tap and sat wearing just a loincloth till they dried. On the days when I found work, I would get my wages in hand in the evening. From this I would go to a restaurant and eat *dal, roti,* vegetables and rice or sometimes mutton. But I had to be careful that I had enough money left over for breakfast in the morning. Sometimes I could not get work for as long as four days. At such times I would barely eat something and that too with the help of my friends at work. My friends too were like me. We helped each other as friends and accomplices.

A peculiar incident took place one day. It happened that I and a friend of mine had gone without eating for two days. We cooked up the scheme of going to restaurant and eating our fill. To do this, one of us would place the order for whatever we wanted to eat. After we finished our meal he would go off on the excuse of eating *paan* and not come back. The other would sit there for a while and then leave. If the restaurant-owner stopped him he would say, I did not give the order; take the money from the one who ordered the food. We thought that the restaurant-owner would be fooled by this trick and we would have a meal for free. In the end we really put this scheme into practice and went and ate in a restaurant. At the end of the meal the one who had ordered the meal went off and I remained behind. Then when I started to leave the owner asked me for money. I said, 'I didn't give the order.' He replied, 'Whoever may have placed the order, you ate here and you have to pay.' I said, 'I don't have any money just now, I'll pay tomorrow.' He said he would hand me over to the police. I said, 'Do it.' He then said, 'No, anyway the police won't get me my money. So you take off your clothes and take them back when you pay me tomorrow.' In the end, after arguing with him for some time I left the hotel at one a.m. wearing only a loincloth. I spent the night shivering with cold and in the morning I went to one of the ships and took the work of unloading coal from the ship's hold. I spent five days in that condition on the ship and on the sixth day I took my wages and alighted. I went to the restaurant that night and paid my dues, then put on the clothes I had left there and came out. I had eked out six days in Bombay somehow, wearing only a loincloth and sleeping on a ship. I had brought such a situation upon myself from my thoughtlessness. This was the greatest punishment I had suffered in my life. It demonstrates how an inconstant nature can get a person into trouble. After that I stopped attending the musical sessions at night and also stopped staying in the Bhatia Gardens.

I remembered how I wrongheadedly went to the theatre when I came to Bombay instead of going to my relatives, and then strayed on the wrong path and suffered. I was now determined to come out of all this. I would not spend the money I earned on inessential things; I would not spend time with my friends who were on the wrong path themselves. I would save at least enough money to buy a jacket, a cap and *chappals*, and then as soon as possible I would go and stay with the people I knew. I started a new routine of working on the ships or the docks during the day and sleeping on a nearby pavement at night. When I had saved enough money I bought myself clothes one day, got a haircut in the saloon and then went to a public bath in the Hamamkhana area for a wash before I put on my new clothes. Then I went to visit one of my relatives who lived in the Cement Chawl in Parel. He was happy to see me after such a long time. At night, after dinner, I went to bed there. In the morning I had my first hot-water bath in days, had breakfast and then went upstairs to try and meet Ambedkar Saheb.[14] But by that time he had left for London. I met his elder brother Balaramdada in the evening and asked him to guide me regarding my further studies. This was the first occasion on which I spoke with him directly. He treated me with great affection and asked me to come and meet him again in a few days. Of course, I spent those two or three days staying with this same relative. I met Balaramdada once again. Then he told me that nothing could be arranged immediately, he would think about it later. The next day I went back to the place in Bombay from which I had earlier left the city, the Family Lines near Crawford Market. Then I caught a ship that stopped overnight in Dasgaon.

My mother felt as though I had been reborn. My only sister was then seven years old. During my absence she had been married to one of my schoolmates. Just like my wedding, her marriage was like a dolls' wedding. She had been present for my wedding, but I was not present for hers. This was a matter of great sorrow for my mother. Now when she saw us brother and sister together, she was overcome with emotion and streams of tears were flowing from her eyes. My sister was my mother's very breath. Seeing my mother crying she too began to cry, and then of course I too could not hold in my tears. Our other relatives who had gathered there comforted my mother and asked how I was. My homecoming this time became the subject of talk in every house, because it was well known that persons from that village community from several generations, who had vanished like me, never came back again. How was it that I had returned? From this it appears that many persons of our community, not just from our villages but from other villages, often left their village and vanished. Could it be that this migration was an attempt at an individual's escape from untouchability?

When I returned to Dasgaon I found that my home had become a school. Our house had been rented out to a Mahar school and my mother was living in a small shed next to the big house and living on the wages of her labour. One of my father's maternal cousins was the teacher in that school and he did not even give the rent to my mother. About the time I returned, he had been awarded a contract for cutting forest timber in the village of Talegaon on the Dharamtar–Mahabaleshwar road. For this he needed the help of someone like me. My arrival solved a problem for him. He at once met the Deputy Inspector in the Schools Department and got me an appointment as stand-in teacher in the school at Dasgaon. Two things resulted

---

[14] In Satyendra More's biography, we learn that B.R. Ambedkar was living in the Cement Chawl at Poybawadi in Parel. His rooms would have been upstairs on the first floor.

from this. Firstly, he was free to do his work as a forest contractor and, secondly, I became a teacher in the school in my own home. The fact that not only had I survived and returned home, but I had also got a job as teacher in my own house, was a matter of great happiness for my mother, above all. She thought that her days of deprivation were over, but that did not happen. Because I was caught in the deceitful net of false affection that the people at the big house cast over me, and I still did not have the courage to break out of it. I behaved just as those people asked me to behave. They, rather than my mother, exerted their authority over me. I had to hand over my salary to them. However, I did not give the rent money to them but to my mother. They made a noise about this at first, but I did not listen to them. So I began to hand over three rupees a month as rent and two rupees for sweeping and cleaning the rooms daily to my mother. Besides this, I spared whatever money I could out of my pay, for basic needs, to give my mother. In those days one could buy a *mann* measure of rice for a rupee and other things were also cheap. So my mother got some relief. Now, whether I went on working as a teacher or not, five rupees a month would come into my mother's hands. My return to Dasgaon secured this much for my mother.

I had not gone to Bombay and Pune with the intention of making money. My objective was education. I felt bad because my education was incomplete. The question of how to take my studies further made me restless. That was why I went to Pune. I got into all kinds of trouble because of this and in the end I found myself a night school and even began to study there. But because of my stupidity I left that halfway and went to Bombay, and now I had returned to Dasgaon. The teaching job I had in Dasgaon was temporary. When it was over I had a thought of going to the school in Mahad again, and I told my mother this. Aai thought it a good idea.

While I was away in Khadki and Pune another important event had taken place in Ladawali. In Ladawali and the villages around there had been an epidemic of cholera. Hundreds of people had died just in Ladawali. In the space of two days about thirty people had died. My grandmother, my mother's eldest brother and his wife died on the same day. Only my youngest uncle survived. Since this unfortunate incident occurred in Ladawali there was nobody to look after my uncle's fields and his cattle. When the cholera epidemic had subsided my youngest uncle got married, on my mother's advice. After that my mother, my sister, my youngest uncle (*mama*) and his wife began to live together. When I returned from Bombay and Pune, Aai was in Dasgaon, but she had only just come there two months earlier after a quarrel with her brother. My uncle made frequent trips to Dasgaon and tried to convince her to come back to Ladawali, and she too was thinking of going back there. Because of my return just then her plan of going to Ladawali was postponed. Now when I talked about going back to school in Mahad she was all for the idea. After my father passed away I, Aai and my sister were living with my maternal uncle when I attended the school in Mahad. At the time our staying in Ladawali was out of my need. But now it was my uncle who needed us to stay with him, because he was in need of my mother's protection. Besides, we had rented out our house to the school in Dasgaon and the rent would also help him. Once we had fixed on the idea of my going back to school in Mahad, my mother went to live with her brother in Ladawali and I began to stay with the people in the big house. Of my six-month vacancy job, two or three months had passed and a few months remained. At such a time I had a great opportunity for myself individually, but from ignorance I was not able to take advantage of it.

This was how it happened—the person in whose place I was working as a teacher was dealing with people as a jungle contractor. He had to get a stamp of government approval to cut down timber from the forest and sell it. The authority to grant this approval rested with the European Conservator. Once, when this Conservator was in Dasgaon, our contractor took me to see him. I talked to him about the stamp in English. Later he asked about me and promised to get me an appointment as probationer Ranger in the Forest Office. He told me to work for six months in a centre at Wada near Poladpur. After that he would send me to do a course in Ajmer. Then, he said, I would become a regular Ranger with a horse, an office at the *tehsil* place and four round guards working under me. 'If you agree to what I have said, come and tell me so tomorrow and I will give you a written appointment order.'

In those days an Indian was rarely given an important post like that of a Ranger in the Civil Service. I was being offered the job even though I didn't have the necessary educational qualifications. That was because I had relatives in the Mahar regiment, and this Conservator had been connected to the Mahar and other army regiments. So this was a rare opportunity for me. But when the people in the big house and our neighbours sat down together at night to think about this offer, except for me and one or two other persons everyone was of the opinion that I should not take this job. What they said was that this was the Forest Office after all. Nobody could tell when I might be murdered there. Others will not like it (that I had such an important post). They will conspire to bring you down in any way they can and later will say they had nothing to do with it. Even though we are under British rule, our people are not taken into government service anywhere except in the army. Even an ordinary policeman's job is not given to our people. Even guards in the Forest Office are usually not from among our people. In view of all this, I should not take this job—this was everybody's opinion. Some said, 'Even if it is a golden dagger, should one pierce it in one's own heart?' On one side there was this resistance from my family, and on the other my fervent desire to study further, and so I let a good opportunity pass.

If I had accepted this job offer, I would have been much talked about as the first untouchable in the Bombay Presidency to be a candidate for a post as high as a Ranger in a Civil Service job in the government. And later I could have become a Divisional Officer, but that did not happen. That period of my life was a time that gave my life its direction. That was a time that pushed me to kick away the golden handcuffs of a job in the government, and stimulated me to stand at the forefront of the battle for freedom of my class and all the people. I have always felt a kind of righteous satisfaction in this.

When my term as a teacher in the leave vacancy was over, I changed from being a teacher to a student. My name was entered in the school at Mahad once again in the fifth English class. This was yet another turn that my life had taken.

Student, cowherd, farm labourer, worker, coolie, porter, marker, packer, clerk, teacher and now a student again; these were the transitions in my occupational life. Even as a child I came into contact with diverse things in the province of the spiritual and the cultural. Reading holy books, worshipping the gods, studying horoscopes, fasting, singing *bhajans* accompanied by the *ektari* and the *mridanga*, singing songs at weddings and at the *Gauri* festival, telling tales, taking part personally in *kirtanas*, *tamashas* and plays, all this came easily to me. When I came to the school in Mahad now, it was as a knowledgeable student, a student with experience.

That was a period of great social, political and economic events brought about by the first imperialist world war. The untouchables and those classes crushed by social inequity were building their own organizations. In the cities there were workers' strikes and struggles, and the winds of political movements were beginning to blow around us. My return to the school at Mahad had come after an interval of three or four years. During this time momentous events had taken place in the world. Great changes had taken place. But the practice of untouchability in the school at Mahad had not changed at all.

My classes took place in the same classroom as they had been held before, and just as they used to seat me separately then, so did they seat me separately now. It was a historic event in the movement for the abolition of untouchability that because of this English school at Mahad, I myself and the injustice of untouchability received publicity in the newspapers as early as 1914–15. Untouchability has been practised in India for hundreds of years. But since it is an injustice, a kind of oppression, a form of slavery, the enemies of the untouchables have always taken care that it should not be spoken of, that it should not be openly discussed. The actuality that students with a love of learning had the doors of a school closed against them was published in a newspaper sixty years ago because I was not given admission to that school, and in this way the social injustice of untouchability came to be publicly discussed. One might say that this public discussion in an older time was the trumpet call for the historic movement that later, in 1927, built up under Babasaheb Ambedkar's leadership to fight for the self-esteem, identity and independence of the untouchables.

Humans have enslaved humans, humans have decided that humans are untouchable, humans have exploited and oppressed human beings, humans have chained humans in colonial rule. Of course those who are enslaved must fight against slavery. That is why they must agitate. Those who have been declared as untouchable must fight against the practice of untouchability and they must agitate. Those who have been exploited and oppressed must fight against exploitation. Those who are colonized must struggle against colonialism, they must agitate, and so the reality is that the real war of the untouchables against the practice of untouchability, the real agitation against untouchability began in Mahad under the leadership of Ambedkar. In this context it is extremely important to mention that, soon after the British government embarked on the establishment of self-government bodies in this country in 1864, a representative from those considered untouchable, Gopal Baba Walangkar, was given membership of the municipal body at Mahad, in 1884. This will give the reader an idea of the central importance that Mahad held in the struggle for liberation of the millions of people who had been considered untouchable in India.

As mentioned above, I had entered the school at Mahad for the second time as a student who was wiser than before. I had by now a general idea of the relations between the people and the government, of the different strata among the people and their problems, of religious, social, economic and political differences. I was sharply aware of the problem of untouchability. This time I moved around fearlessly in the school and in the market at Mahad. My earlier diffidence had now completely disappeared. I now had the guts to answer any questions that were put to me according to my ability. After I was admitted to the school in Mahad for the first time, a restaurant had been started in the marketplace to solve the problem I, and my brethren coming from the villages, faced in getting drinking water. That restaurant was still running when I returned. It used to be closed during the rains and open in the hot seasons; but because it was far from the untouchable colony nobody stayed there at night. But now there were more customers visiting the restaurant. There had been a very large inflow of ex-soldiers in that vicinity. This was due to the disbanding and breaking up of the 111th Mahar regiment after the war was over. These unemployed soldiers were now earning their subsistence through farming or through manual labour. Because of their military occupation and their having travelled widely, they were bold and courageous. Because of my knowledge of Marathi and English, my thoughts on various subjects and my feeling for the interests of the common people, the knowledgeable visitors to the restaurant from villages all over felt great respect for me and gave me all kinds of information. Some people from villages near Mahad would make it a point to come and sit there every day. From morning till evening the place would be crowded with people and there would always be a discussion going on some topic or other. I used to be in the restaurant every day when I came to Mahad from Ladawali in the morning after breakfast. Then, during the drawing and drill classes when the school gave me time off to avoid my touch, I would again be in the restaurant. The same after school:

Group photo of Mahad *karyakartas*, including B.R. Ambedkar and R.B. More.
Courtesy of Subodh More, who was provided a copy by Vijay Surwade.

again I would be in the restaurant. So all in all I spent a lot of my time there.

During this time I could gather information from persons coming from villages from all over, just by sitting there. That restaurant had become a virtual information centre for a circle of about sixty square miles around Mahad. Raigad, Pratapgad and the villages of the valley come within that circle. So I gathered proper information about what kind of relations the people in this circle had with each other, and whether the Mahar folk were on terms of equality with people of other castes, or were subservient towards them. So I learned that even though the Mahars were in a minority in these villages, they did not bend before the people of the other castes. Because of the custom of untouchability, untouchables and caste Hindus kept a distance from each other. But they did not hate each other. When they went on a hunt, everyone set out together, armed with spears and axes. At such times they would not differentiate among untouchables and other castes. In these villages there are large numbers of poor peasants from all castes. They cannot earn enough for their subsistence in the village. So they are all forced to head for the city. In every house there is at least one adult male who has joined the army or is working in a mill in the city. Since both untouchables and other castes are in the same life situation they relate to each other as equals. It is a handful of people from the upper classes with their orthodox thinking who are responsible for the sense of otherness that has grown between the untouchables and the caste Hindu poor in the villages. When I understood this reality my thoughts received a stimulus.

Because of that restaurant in Mahad I came to understand the prehistory of the Mahar peoples of that whole area, their characteristics, their good and bad points, their cultural heritage, their love for their motherland. This organized community is a great force in Maharashtra. It has the capacity to bring about social and political change. This too I realized, and then the work of making this community aware about local issues began. The importance that Mahad has assumed in the movement for the liberation or freedom of the untouchables can be traced back to that restaurant. The first reverberations of the Chavdar lake movement and of Ambedkar's great deeds began from here.[15]

The Hindu and Muslim rulers who rose to power after the *varna* system based on discrimination among castes in India, and untouchability, its essence, had come into existence, tied up the untouchables with the chains of slavery. The British imperialists wrested state power from the hands of these Hindu and Muslim rulers and established their rule over all of India. They took on themselves the monopoly of exploiting and stripping the people of the whole of India. Of course along with the exploitation of all the people they also exploited the untouchables. But by giving the untouchables the new label of 'Depressed Classes' the British gave them a place in Indian political life. The Hindu and Muslim rulers had also treated the Hindu and Muslim people as slaves. But even so, under their rule, the untouchables were never given the same place in society as the Hindu and Muslim common people. For them the people were divided among Hindus and Muslims only. But the British, be it for their own selfish political ends, brought the untouchables as a third section of society, alongside the Hindus and the Muslims, on to the political horizon. During the Montagu–Chelmsford reforms the untouchables were designated as the Depressed Classes. During later reforms they were referred to as the Scheduled Castes. The educational and job-related facilities or concessions that the untouchables receive even today are given to them as Scheduled Castes. This is the objective reality. Before this they did not enjoy any of the fundamental rights of citizenship.

From the times of unregulated state power, there have existed the relationships between king and subject, between rulers and *raiyats* or peasants. Of course in India, the untouchable people were segregated away from their settlements by the subjects and the peasants themselves, were denied the use of public places meant for the use of the subject peoples and of wells, lakes, *dharamshalas*, etc., and were living the life of slaves of these subject peoples. They say that slavery ended the world over in 1861.[16] But we can say that the slavery that was inherent in the Indian

---

[15] Chavdar lake movement, the first *satyagraha* to access the water of the Chavdar reservoir in Mahad by untouchables was led by Ambedkar in March 1927, demanding implementation of the 1923 legislation initiated by S.K. Bole, which gave Dalits access to public water facilities. This is dealt with in more detail in Satyendra More's biography.

[16] The British abolished the slave trade in 1807, and abolished slavery in 1833.

चवदार तळ्याचा सत्याग्रह

डॉ. आंबेडकरांच्या नेतृत्वाखालील
दलितवर्गांच्या चळवळीचा मानदंड—

महाडच्या
दोन ऐतिहासिक परिषदा

लेखक
आर. बी. मोरे
(प्रमुख संघटक : महाड सत्याग्रह)

Front cover of R.B. More's book on the Mahad *satyagraha*.
Courtesy of Anil Sawadkar.

practice of untouchability ended only when the Indian Constitution declared that untouchability had been abolished. This means that the Indian ruling class, by way of the Constitution, has agreed to grant to the untouchable peoples the same rights, more or less, that are granted to the rest of the Indian people. And all Indians have no alternative but to accept the bitter truth that the beginning of all this was made by the British rulers.

I have given the above background in order to explain why so much time had to elapse, until the dawn of the twentieth century, before the struggle for the fundamental rights of citizenship for the untouchables could begin in Mahad. The untouchable people of the Mahad vicinity, long oppressed by the chains of untouchability, were struggling to liberate themselves from these bonds. The activity of driving forward that struggle went on in the restaurant in Mahad. This restaurant had become a meeting-place and a platform for the Mahar people of about two hundred villages in the Mahad *tapa*, or section, the Nate *tapa*, the Birwad *tapa*, the Vinhere *tapa* and the Tudil *tapa*, five *tapas* in all. The usefulness of this from the point of view of ideological awakening and organization cannot be imagined. The people were angered that they had to face insults at every turn because of untouchability, that others treated them with contempt. They had also become convinced that they should give up eating the inedible (that is, carrion meat), change their filthy living habits, and resist injustice; they had now started to put all this into practice.

The untouchables felt proud of me as a knowledgeable student of the English school in Mahad, a sturdy-chested young man who raised his voice openly against the injustice of untouchability that we all suffered, and my word carried weight with them. In the past untouchable persons were shouted at and sometimes even beaten in the open marketplace in Mahad. But if such a thing happened now, eight or ten youths armed with sticks would come running from the restaurant to help them, and if needed help would arrive in larger numbers. So now these other people, Hindus and Muslims, understood that the untouchable folk, especially those of the Mahar community, were becoming aware and getting organized. It would be wise not to cross their path.

Some of the Brahmins and Gujars in the marketplace would ask me mockingly, are you going to become a *mamledar* or a lawyer? To which I would reply, 'Never mind about me, but there are many persons in our community who are educated far beyond your expectations, who have acquired M.A., Ph.D., D.Sc. degrees or are barristers-at-law.' They would not believe me when they heard this. They were not at all ready to accept that persons from the Mahar caste could attain such high academic degrees. They would say to me that at most someone might become an LL.B., but nothing higher than that. To tell the truth, what they said was right at that time; because in those days an individual who was so highly educated would be a rarity even among Brahmins. But I had determined in my mind that I would bring Dr. Ambedkar to Mahad so that these persons' eyes would be opened, and I began to draw up plans for moving in that direction.

At one point a landlord named Deshmukh closed down that restaurant owned by Mohoprekar, as part of an action taken against Mohoprekar, who was his tenant. But I defeated the landlord's action: I took over the restaurant myself, put up a board saying 'R.B. More's Rest House', and then got it going again. This caused me to be much talked about. My success in teaching a well-known landlord a lesson won me the affection of other poor people besides the untouchables. Because of that restaurant in Mahad, every untouchable person coming to the market in the town was able to move about without fear. He spoke out against untouchability. The poor caste Hindus did not hate him for this or bear any anger towards him; on the contrary, they felt a kind of curiosity about the courageous behaviour of the untouchables. I myself was a schoolboy coming to Mahad every day from a nearby village, in a situation where the untouchable settlements were some distance from the school, so that I could not get a drink of water in the marketplace. Hundreds of untouchables coming there from the vicinity of Raigad were in the same position. So the opening of a restaurant in the marketplace in Mahad solved my problem and that of a few others for the time being. But the drinking-water problem of large numbers of men and women was not solved at all. So this was a problem concerning people's needs which remained a smouldering issue in Mahad.

Just then the year 1923 dawned. That year S.K. Bole moved a resolution in the Bombay Legislative Council to open up public wells, reservoirs, *dharamshalas*, drinking-water stands, etc. to untouchables, and the British rulers brought some glitter to their image by passing it.[17] Then the government passed the Bill on to government institutions and semi-government bodies like municipal councils for implementation. At this time a number of institutions came forward, posturing as backers of this government Bill, to claim that theirs was a progressive body, and to try and win the government's favour for some advantage of their own. Some talkative reformers among them even gave verbal assurances that they supported the Bill. But in reality not a single such body dared to implement the Bill. They did not even have the courage or honesty to spread the word in support of the Bill. To tell the truth, leaving aside a handful of educated persons like me among the untouchables who had a liking for public activity, nobody wanted to have anything to do with the Bill.

One day after the Bill had been passed, I organized a small meeting in the Maharwada or Mahar colony with some military pensioners visiting the marketplace and some of my friends, where I told them about this Bill which had been passed by the government. Besides me, there was another outspoken person present, an elderly man named Maruti Agavane. He had lost one arm and ran a shoe shop

---

[17] Resolution no. 4770 of 4 August 1923. For a discussion of juridical ideas of public access that animated the Mahad and temple entry *satyagrahas*, see Rao, *The Caste Question*, Chapter 2.

in the marketplace in Mahad. His thinking was inclined towards the Satyashodhak Samaj, and he always expressed great affection for me. In that meeting he gave a call to take up the water question. These people of the Chambhar (cobbler) caste from the Deccan plateau used to run their shops in Mahad for eight months of the year, and go home to their villages for the four months during the monsoon. In that meeting we made a decision of historic importance: to hold a conference of the Colaba District Outcastes' Association in Mahad under the chairmanship of Dr. Bhimrao Ramji Ambedkar. The heads of caste *panchayats* were entrusted with the responsibility of collecting three rupees a head from each and every village, to cover the expenses of holding the conference. Now a new air of enthusiasm sprang up among the untouchable youth in the marketplace. Everywhere there was talk about the prospect of Ambedkar Saheb coming to Mahad for a big gathering.

Later, in 1924, in the month of May, I went to Bombay and met Ambedkar Saheb. The people of the Social Service League had given him a room on the first floor above the Damodar Hall in Parel.[18] When he returned from England after appearing for the bar examinations, this room was the first office that he set up. When I went to meet him, Shivram Sambhaji Gaikwad was with me. We first met Anantrao Chitre of the Social Service League and then met Ambedkar and told him what we had to tell him. The presence of Chitre made things easy for me. He (Ambedkar) inquired about where I lived, what I did, how far I had studied and so on, and expressed his satisfaction. He then said to me, 'You don't know what people of the Konkan are like. They are very obstinate. They will always say, what we do is as it should be. They will say, who is this Christ-lover coming here telling us what to do? And they won't listen to me.' To which I answered, 'Saheb, they listen to me so they will certainly listen to you.' In the end he said, 'I have no time just now. Come back during the Diwali vacations and we will see what we can do.' Then I went back to Chitre who was in the next room. He asked me how I intended to collect money for the conference, and I told him that the people from villages all over would raise a little money. He then promised to help us in the financing and so we chalked out a plan. The plan was to put up a play and use the income from that for the conference. He was so impressed by the idea of a conference being held in Mahad under Doctor Saheb's chairmanship that he called me the very next day and finalized the plans for the play.

The Social Service League worked in the working-class vicinity under the leadership of the Servants of India Society, which had been established by Mr.

---

[18] The Social Service League was founded in 1911 by N.M. Joshi. Joshi was an important member of the Servants of India Society, which was founded by Gopal Krishna Gokhale. He also founded the All India Trade Union Congress, together with Lala Lajpat Rai. The League undertook relief work and welfare programmes for the poor. Anantrao Chitre and A.V. Tipnis, who played an important role in the Mahad *satyagraha*, were prominent members of the Social Service League.

[Gopal Krishna] Gokhale. One could say that this Society had laid the foundations of the cooperative movement in the working-class area of Bombay about fifty years earlier. The Social Service League began its work by way of setting up a cooperative credit society at Elphinstone Road, a cooperative printing press and a cooperative theatre company. Kadam was the leader of this cooperative theatre company. *Sant Tukaram* was the first play they had rehearsed. They promised to dedicate the takings of the first performance of this play to our conference in Mahad. We had secured a free performance of this play solely on the word of Chitre and Kadam. But who was to carry out the responsibility of selling the tickets? The play was to be performed in the Damodar Hall, and this hall was owned by the Social Service League. So we were to get the hall also for free. We only had to arrange for the sale of tickets. I felt that Balaram Ambedkar (Bhimrao's elder brother) could help us out in this, and so I went to see him and asked for his help. He too was very happy to learn that a conference was to be held in Mahad. He promised that he would come to Mahad for the conference, but he did not undertake the responsibility of selling tickets. He said, 'Our people do not watch plays, they go to see *tamashas*. So I cannot do anything for you in this regard.' On which I told him, 'If you give me the names of some of your acquaintances, I will go and meet them.'

He then gave me the name and address of Sambhaji Tukaram Gaikwad. At the time he was working as foreman in a French motorcar company, and he earned a salary of two hundred rupees. In those days a workman or a clerk hardly earned twenty to twenty-five rupees a month. He was a dedicated social worker of the time from the Mahar community. That was the first time I had met him. When he heard that I had received my Marathi and English education in the villages and when he heard about our plans for the conference, he was overcome with emotion. But when it came to the question of selling tickets, he flatly refused to sell the tickets himself or to get someone else to sell them, pointing to the people's bad habits and addictions.[19]

Balaram Ambedkar and Sambhaji Gaikwad were at the time the only two people I knew in the whole of Bombay who had a concern for social activity, excepting Dr. Ambedkar himself. Since both of them had turned me down, I was very disappointed. Then I went to meet three friends of mine who lived in the servants' quarters of St. George Hospital in the Fort area. I told them about all this business of selling tickets for the play. All three of them were working as uniformed guards or peons. Two of them were barely literate and the third had passed the fourth standard examination in Marathi school. With the help of these friends I

---

[19] S.T. Gaikwad's refusal to sell tickets for the play was based on his belief that the people were not used to seeing plays, they preferred *tamashas* and would spend their money on 'bad habits and addictions'. He did not want to engage with these problems, perhaps because he belonged to a higher income class. But in the end R.B. More succeeded in selling cheap tickets to his fellow workers, though he was unable to stop gatecrashers.—*Tr.*

Felicitation of Tukaram Gaikwad, with Ambedkar and R.B. More (second from left). Courtesy of Mahesh Bharati.

managed to sell some four-*anna* tickets and about twenty eight-*anna* and ten-*anna* tickets. And on the actual day of the performance these three came with me to the Damodar Hall to see to the other arrangements. I seated the one who was most educated at the ticket window to sell tickets, and gave the job of checking the tickets of people entering the theatre to the other two. Since the hall had four or five entrances, these two were not able to do their job properly. A large number of freeloading spectators eluded them and they filled up the hall.

When the play started Doctor Saheb was sitting in his office seeing to some work. I went to him and pleaded that he should request Balaramdada or someone else to give thanks before the play ended to the Manoranjan Theatre Company and to Chitre and Kadam for donating this show to us. He said, why do you need anybody else, you can thank them yourself. So I had no alternative but to propose a vote of thanks myself. After the last act of the play was over, the curtain was brought down and a table and chair placed on the stage, where I seated myself. After a while the curtain was raised and I stood up. There was a clamour of applause. I placed my hands on the table to steady myself and gave thanks in a few words speaking slowly, as if I was giving dictation to a class of schoolchildren. This was the first speech I had made before an audience of the educated of Bombay, on the dais of a public hall.

Nineteen twenty-four can be noted as a year that gave a great push forward to the untouchables' struggle for self-respect, independence and liberation. It was the year when it was decided to hold a convention of the Colaba District Outcastes'

R.B. More seated two places from B.R. Ambedkar, on his left, Siddharth College. Courtesy of Anil Sawadkar.

Association in Mahad and this decision was conveyed to the designated chairman of the convention, Dr. Ambedkar; then this was publicly announced in the Damodar Thackersey Hall in Bombay, and given wide publicity. The even greater importance of that year is that it was then that Dr. Ambedkar, having gained high academic degrees from European and American universities, returned to India after the completion of his educational programme and in the same year dedicated himself to public action with the establishment of the Bahishkrit Hitakarini Sabha ('Association for the Welfare of Outcastes').

I knew Dr. Ambedkar from before, but the occasion when I went to meet him to speak about the convention was unparalleled. That year I not only became known to him but I became a close acquaintance and devotee.

I had become one of those who revered his leadership. In those days, whether in Mahad or any other rural area, because of the contact with industrial cities like Bombay and because of the availability of new means of transport like the railways and motorboats, it had become difficult to practise untouchability as had been done earlier. The British rulers took advantage of these developments, and affecting to be great promoters of social reform, in 1923, they declared some public places to be open to untouchables. It was taking this background into account that I was able to bring about awareness among the untouchable folk with the help of some untouchable youth. It was decided to hold the convention in Mahad in 1924. But in fact it actually came about only in 1927. The intervening three years were important from the point of view of raising public awareness in Mahad. I therefore

A sample of R.B. More's handwriting (obituary for Shamrao Parulekar).
Courtesy of Subodh More.

Ramchandra Babaji More (1 March 1903 – 11 May 1972).
Courtesy of Subodh More.

wish to write about some important events that took place in this period.

The objective situation was becoming favourable for the abolition of untouchability, but special efforts were being made to sustain the practice. For example, about this time a private passenger bus service had started operating on the Mahad–Dharamtar–Bombay road. But the owners did not carry untouchable passengers. I wrote out a collective application protesting against this and sent it to the District Collector. He took note of the application and sent it for implementation to the Deputy Superintendent of Police. The D.S.P. wrote me a letter, assuring me that this injustice would be ended. The D.S.P. at the time was a European. I received the letter from him while I was still a student at the school in Mahad and, because of this, there was a great commotion among the teachers and other people in the Mahad market. The police inspector in Mahad called the bus owners and warned them about this; then he told me to let him know the names of any of these bus proprietors who prevented untouchable passengers from travelling on their buses, and promised to take action against them. Then I informed the untouchable people of what had happened, and they began to use this bus service for their travel. Because of this incident a great curiosity was aroused among the untouchable people, and they began to regard me as one of their leaders.

[Incomplete]

THE BIOGRAPHY OF RAMCHANDRA BABAJI MORE

SATYENDRA MORE[1]

Ancestors

Comrade R.B. More aka Ramchandra Babaji More was born on 1 March 1903 in his maternal uncle's village Ladawali, in Mahad *tehsil*, Raigad district (formerly Colaba district) in the Mahar caste (then considered to be untouchable).

Com. R.B. More's native village was Loner in the Mangaon *tehsil* in Raigad district, on the Bombay–Goa road (this is where the Dr. Babasaheb Ambedkar Technical University is now located). His grandfather was Shivram who was then known as Shivnak. Shivram's brother was Tanaji, then known as Taknak. Both brothers lived in the Maharwada in Loner, where they had no access to water nor did they have any land to cultivate. Extreme poverty was their lot. Tired of this situation, both the brothers set out with their wives and children, doing the work of breaking stones needed for road construction on the way, until they reached the Khandala mountains. While they were working there, a contractor got hold of Tanaji and, enticing him with the prospect of higher wages, asked him to come to work in cane fields in Mauritius for three years. Shivram refused because he was afraid to leave his native land. In the end Tanaji with his wife and children left Shivram's family behind and got onto a boat to Mauritius as partly bonded labourers, partly slaves. There Tanaji and his family found that they had stepped

---

[1] Unlike R.B. More's autobiography, Satyendra More's biography is broken up into titled sections so the Translator has not, on the whole, interfered with the original formatting. We have also kept the original section titles. However, long paragraphs have been broken up for ease of reading in a few instances. We have used parentheses to clarify the referent here, a pronoun or a partial proper name that might confuse the reader.

The reader should be warned that the text contains some historical inaccuracies. We have footnoted in those cases where the information and the dates are radically wrong but we have largely left S.R. More's narrative, analysis and polemic as they are. The account of preparations for the 1927 Mahad *satyagraha*, especially the names of participants and dates was cross-checked against the senior (R.B.) More's booklet on this topic.

In the section entitled 'Defeat of Babasaheb in the Elections of 1952', the Translator has made changes to clarify any confusion, cross-checked the number of votes won by each candidate and shortened the author's analysis of the reasons for Ambedkar's defeat. Anupama Rao has also remarked on S.R. More's interpretation of events in her Introduction.

out of the frying pan into the fire, as they were stuck as slaves in Mauritius and remain there to this day.

The people in Mauritius who are known as Maharashtrians are almost all from Raigad district in the Konkan and are all from the caste formerly known as Mahars. It is because of this that they have the suffix 'nak' attached to their names. This is a peculiarity of the names of Mahars from the Konkan. So Babasaheb Ambedkar's grandfather's name in the army was registered as Malnak Mahar. After these people settled in Mauritius their mother tongue changed gradually from Marathi to French. They still use the odd Marathi word, but their language is no longer Marathi. In the Konkan, girls' names often carry the suffix 'bai'. The former minister Sheilabai Bappoo of Mauritius is solid proof of this. In this way Comrade RB had a family link with Mauritius.

When the two brothers had separated in this way, Shivram set out on the return journey and reached Loner again sometime in the third or fourth decade of the nineteenth century. When he reached there he found that most of his relatives had left the village and gone their own ways. And so Shivram set out again from halt to halt, until he reached his maternal cousin Vitthal Anand Hate's home in Dasgaon, *tehsil* Mahad, district Colaba (Raigad), together with his wife and son Raghu.

Vitthal Joshi, aka Vitthal Hate, had received his education from the early Dalit leader of Maharashtra, Gopal Baba Walangkar, who had enrolled in the army as a soldier during British rule. He got this opportunity solely because of the geographical location of Dasgaon. Dasgaon is a village on the through road from Bombay to Goa. Also, since Dasgaon is a port town, a ship coming from Bombay would first stop at Dasgaon. Because of this, Dalit soldiers from the Mandangad and Dapoli *tehsils* of Ratnagiri district (Dapoli being Babasaheb's *tehsil*) and the Mahad *tehsil* in Colaba district would alight at Dasgaon before they proceeded to their own villages. They would stay in the Maharwada in Dasgaon.

In those days Dalit soldiers entering the army were illiterate, but as soon as they enrolled they would be given education in Marathi and English. They would be compulsorily taught all the school subjects like History, Mathematics, Science, Geography, and so on. Not only this, but they would be made to appear for all the examinations of the Normal School right up to matriculation level. The British considered this to be a necessity for their purposes at the time. And so these Dalit soldiers became well educated. But the Dalit people of the town were completely illiterate. The Mahars of Dasgaon learnt how to read and write from the soldiers of the Mahar regiment.

Vitthal Anand Joshi, aka Vitthal Hate, devoted his full attention to his learning and so made greater progress than the others. So he first took up the work of sitting outside the court in Mahad writing out pleas and applications for Dalits. Over time he became highly skilled at this. So other folk besides the Dalits began to come to him to get their applications written. From this he earned a good amount and became wealthy, so that he was well known not just in the Maharwada in Dasgaon but throughout the Mahad *tehsil*. Because he looked up people's horoscopes, he became known as 'Joshi'.

And that was how Shivram took up residence in Dasgaon and eventually broke all links with the village Loner in Mangaon *tehsil*.

The Historic First Tile-Roofed Two-Storey House Built by an Untouchable in India

When Shivram first came to Dasgaon his son Raghu was five or six years old, and his wife was pregnant. She died in childbirth, but her infant son was born safely. He was given the name Babaji; this was R.B. More's father. Vitthal Hate Joshi's sister took care of Babaji. Vitthal Joshi undertook his later bringing-up and taught him some elementary lessons. He devoted himself to farming and became a support for Vitthal Joshi in later life.

Vitthal Joshi later bought a piece of forest land in the forest near Dasgaon and began to think of building a two-storey house, or *maadi*, using teak wood from that land. The work of building the house was started. When it was complete, Vitthal Joshi Hate appointed a Brahmin to perform *puja* and carry out the rituals, and on 3 September 1888 he occupied the house. In those days, not only in Maharashtra but all over India, untouchables were prohibited by Hindus following the *varna* system from using a tile-roofed house or utensils made of copper and brass. So the building of this big house was the first such act of defiance by an untouchable in Maharashtra. The orthodox were enraged. But as Vitthal Joshi was economically well off and educated, and because he enjoyed wide social prestige in the town and the *taluka*, the orthodox were not able to take any action against him. So the Brahmin who had performed the house-entry *puja* and rituals for Joshi in return for the payment of *dakshina* (or, shall we say, from a greed for lucre), was boycotted by the entire Brahmin community of Dasgaon. But they were not satisfied with the imposition of boycott. The Brahmins were itching to punish Vitthal Joshi for having broken the tradition, the rules and *dharma* of the *varna* system. But because of British rule and the prestige commanded by Joshi they could not do anything. In the end the orthodox caste-minded people lodged a false complaint that Vitthal Joshi had used not just wood from his own land for building his house but that he had also cut down trees from government forest land. On this occasion, R.B. More's father Babaji took on himself the responsibility of ensuring that Vitthal Joshi was not arrested. He had to serve a three-year prison sentence. When R.B. More learned the truth about what his father had to suffer because of the false accusations of the orthodox upper castes, his mind was filled with even more revulsion for the traditions and customs of the Hindu religion.

Vitthal Hate Joshi's friend and witness to the building of his house, Gopalbuva

Walangkar, wrote an article about this on 23 October 1888 and sent it for publication in the newspapers, but it was not published. Later, on 1 August 1889, he published a booklet on the subject with the title *Destruction of Caste Pollution*. (This booklet was discovered by Rosalind O'Hanlon, the British scholar from the School of Oriental and African Studies, University of London, who had come to the University of Pune for her research.)

Although More's father had served a prison sentence for his involvement in the building of this historic two-storey house, out of self-respect he built himself a small hut-like house in front of that edifice, and continued his visits to the big house as before. The British had started a Marathi school in Dasgaon about the time when Babaji's first son Lakshman was born. Vitthal Joshi of the two-storey house saw to Lakshman's education up to the seventh standard in that school. So Lakshman became the first Dalit schoolmaster in the Konkan. This should be noted in the history of the Dalit movement. As a teacher, he used to ride a horse to the village Tudil. He earned a salary of seven rupees a month. B.S. Hate has written a novel, *Yugavidhan*, based on his life and with the background of the Chavdar lake *satyagraha* in Mahad.

Those Who Laid the Foundations of the Dalit Movement

Gopalbuva Walangkar had continuous intimate relations with this historic building in Dasgaon, and with Vitthal Anand Hate (Joshi)'s entire family. Even though Gopalbuva Walangkar's village was Walang in the Mahad *tehsil*, his ancestors had settled in the village Raodhal across the creek. It was from there that they were recruited as soldiers in the British army. According to the practice at that time, they were given an education once they entered the army, and only then did they enter service as soldiers. Thus, Walangkar had passed the last examination of the Normal School in the army, which was equivalent to matriculation. He was a social activist by nature. So, whenever he came to Raodhal on vacation, he would teach the local Dalits to read and write before he returned.

Besides doing social work outside the army, Walangkar also organized Dalit soldiers in the army to perform service for Dalit civilians. Not only this; during this time he also started an intense study of Hindu religious texts and the Puranas, in order to understand how untouchability originated and how the Dalits could be made free of it. But when he read the explanation that Dalits were treated so because of 'sins committed by them in their earlier births', he developed a kind of disgust for the Hindu faith. As he was undergoing a mental conflict of this kind, he came to know about the work of Jotiba Phule. So, while he was still in the army, he went to Pune to meet Phule and take his guidance; he then made plans for expanding his efforts to promote the struggle for liberation of Dalits.

In 1886 he retired from the military having reached the post of *hawaldar*.

After he retired, instead of returning to his village Raodhal, he took up residence in Dapoli Cantonment, in Dapoli *tehsil*, an area developed by the British, where arrangements had been made for Dalits to acquire school education. Many Dalits who had retired from the army were living there then. The illiterate folk used to refer to Dapoli Camp in the Ratnagiri district as Dapoli 'Kaap'.

After coming to live in Dapoli, Walangkar formed a separate organization of the untouchables and began to work for the abolition of untouchability. He felt it necessary to form such an association so that as many untouchables as possible could be drawn into this work. He started an association which he called the *Anarya Dosh Parihar Mandal*, or 'Anarya Society for the Removal of (Social) Ills'. He considered himself to be a non-Aryan, and declared that the untouchables must act to improve themselves; in this spirit he began the work of social reform in his community.

Thus, Gopal Krishna Walangkar established the Anarya Dosh Parihar Mandal as the first socio-political class organization of the Dalits in this country. This was a precursor to the independent movement of untouchables led by Dr. Ambedkar. This organization took up Dalit issues in the public domain. In 1891, the British regime put an end to military recruitment of Dalits. This was because it was in 1891 that the British initiated their first package of reforms, and intended to appease the non-Dalits by bringing them into the government. This was a policy made to win over the caste Hindu majority. That is why they took the despicable step of ending Dalit military recruitment. Up to this time the Dalits naively supposed that the British were ethical and would bring about the liberation of the untouchables. But whatever they had done (for the benefit of the untouchables) was for opportunistic reasons.[2]

In 1891, while Babasaheb's father held the rank of *subhedar* in the army, before he retired in 1894, the British government brought an end to recruitment of Dalits into the army. They announced a new policy of not allowing Dalits to enter the army as new recruits, while those already in service would be entertained only until 1896. In response to this, Dalit soldiers first sent written applications to the government, while the first militant protests by Dalits in the military were led by Dulbhya Subhedar.[3] He had a good command of the English language, and so he played a major role in sending written applications to the government. In short, the first person who can be mentioned as a leader among the Dalits from Maharashtra who were in military service was Dulbhya Subhedar. Dr. Ambedkar's father, Ramji

[2] R.B. More's text suggests, wrongly, that Mahars were taken back into the British Army in 1891 (p. 74).

[3] It is not clear whether the Dulbhya Bahadur referred to here is in fact Subhedar Bahadur Gangaram Krishnaji Bhatankar, who was active in the protest against the decision to stop recruitment of Mahars into the British army. In 1903 Shivram Janba Kamble organized a conference of Mahars at Saswad near Pune at which persons from 51 villages attended. Subhedar Bahadur Bhatankar presided over this conference.

Maloji, also helped Dulbhya Subhedar in conducting this correspondence, since he too had a good command of English. Later on Walangkar took up this issue through his Anarya Dosh Parihar Mandal. To this end, he submitted an application to the government in 1893 with the help of Justice Mahadev Govind Ranade. In 1899, Walangkar submitted a set of questions to the Congress party on the issue of untouchability. In this he demanded that the Congress should indeed follow a policy of working for political reforms. When, in 1898, Sir Herbert Risley began a study of Hindu religious rites and customs, he sent a letter to Walangkar's Anarya Dosh Parihar Mandal to seek information on the customs of Hindu Dalits. It becomes clear from this that Walangkar's Society was the first recognized organization of Dalits at the time.

The activists of this Society not only worked to overcome difficulties faced by the Dalits; they also tried to bring about awareness through their writings. Much of Walangkar's writing was published in the periodical *Dinabandhu* during this period. Later the British nominated him as an honourable Member of the Mahad Municipal Council. In 1900 he passed away in his native village Raodhal.[4]

The torch of independent struggle by the Dalits, which had been lit by Walangkar, was taken up by Shivram Janba Kamble of Pune. Like Walangkar, he took guidance from Jotirao Phule, and set up a movement for the abolition of untouchability among the Dalits. Kamble had not been educated in the military like Walangkar. He spent a large part of his life from boyhood working as a 'man-of-all-work' in the house of a European. At the time he had no knowledge of reading and writing. In 1885, when he was ten years old, he learned the alphabet from some of his literate labourer friends. He began to read whatever books in Marathi he could get hold of. He went on to read newspaper articles and books by Rajaram Shastri, Lokhitavadi, Baba Padamji, Agarkar and Mahatma Phule. Based on this, he built up an independent movement of the untouchables.

While he was doing this, his first published article appeared in *Maratha Dinabandhu* in 1902. This fired his enthusiasm and he began to write regularly in newspapers on the welfare of the untouchables. On 25 November 1902 he organized a meeting of Dalits from 51 villages in Saswad near Pune. He gave a public account of the tribulations of the Dalits and made the people aware of the need for social equality and political rights. He brought with him a written application which was a political manifesto of the Dalits. In this application he appealed to the British government saying that the Dalits were citizens just like

---

[4] *Dinabandhu* ('Friend of the Poor') was a weekly started in Pune in 1877 by Jotirao Phule and K.P. Bhalekar, to further the work of the Satyashodhak Samaj. In 1880 the trade union leader, and founder of the Bombay Mill-Hands Association (1890), Narayan Meghaji Lokhande (1848–1897), took over as editor. Since Lokhande is known as a pioneer in taking up the specific grievances of Dalit and Muslim workers, it is not surprising that Walangkar became a regular contributor.

those from the caste Hindu community. He therefore demanded that the ban on military recruitment of untouchables be lifted with immediate effect. So also they should be given jobs in the police. He mentioned several other issues: e.g. the education of Dalit boys and girls was the government's responsibility and it should make the necessary arrangements for this. Kamble obtained the signatures or thumb prints of 1,588 Mahars who were present at this meeting. Later, the letter was sent to the government. This was the historic first letter sent by Dalit citizens to the British government! Kamble sent copies of this letter to the British Parliament, to newspapers and to noted individuals within the country. But the British government did not want to risk losing the support of the non-Dalits, their cooperation in government and the peace ensured by keeping the Dalits suppressed.

In pre-British times, the Dalits had suffered the rule of others for generations. The British had made overtures to the Dalits while they were establishing their rule. It was not surprising that the Dalits had thought them to be friends. But the hollowness of their Dalit-friendly policy became clear in 1891. And yet, when the Dalits sent applications to the British, they would remind the rulers about the help they had given to them. Shivram Janba Kamble also followed this policy and even Dr. Babasaheb Ambedkar was not far behind in this. To what a wretched condition had the Dalits been reduced by the Indian social order! The Dalits could not possibly have gathered the strength to conduct a frontal struggle for their rights, and if they had, they would not have gained the support of the non-Dalits. Lacking a pragmatic understanding of this situation, all progressives including the Communists have condemned Dalit leaders for being puppets of the imperialists and servile to the British masters. In any case, Kamble's application found its way to the waste paper bin.

The British ignored Shivram Janba Kamble's written application, but he did not stop there. He informed the social reformer [Gopal Ganesh] Agarkar about what had happened. He then wrote a critical essay in Agarkar's *Sudharak* entitled 'The Mahars' application, the Government and Our Society'. Other newspapers also criticized the government for not giving a sympathetic hearing to this application. But Lokmanya Tilak's *Kesari* was silent on the issue. Although the call for reform based on justice and rights had been raised, Tilak chose to turn a blind eye. The issue became the subject of a social movement and many non-Dalits made this cause their own. A process of meeting a felt social and political need began here.

Kamble's activities expanded with time. In 1902, a Mahar gentleman named Govind Wullud Mukunda dipped his bucket into a public reservoir and drank from it. The news spread like wildfire, and the religious conservatives filed a complaint against him in court under Clause 277 of the Indian Penal Code. The news reached all the Mahars in Maharashtra. They sent applications to the British government supporting the action. But the government did not want to invite the anger of the non-untouchables, and ignored the applications completely. After this, the Mahars collected funds and decided to fight the case in court. The case came up before the magistrate of Ahmednagar district, Bapu Hari Godbole. He sentenced the accused to two weeks in jail and fined him eight rupees. After this the Ahmednagar District Collector Sir Richard brought the case to the Bombay High Court. The High Court revoked the sentence and declared Govind Wullud Mukunda to be free of guilt. Kamble wrote about this court case in his booklet *Suchipatra* ['Newsletter']. Using the booklet he made the case a lesson regarding the rights of Dalits. It was as a result of this and other such agitations that in 1923 S.K. Bole's Bill opening public reservoirs and *dharamshalas* to Dalits was placed before the Bombay Legislative Council and passed. The historic Mahad *satyagraha* and the rise of Dr. Ambedkar's leadership also drew strength from this.

While this struggle was going on, Kamble felt the need to establish an association of untouchables, just as Walangkar had done with the Anarya Dosh Parihar Mandal. Accordingly, in 1904 he started an association which he named the *Shri Shankar Prasadik Somavanshiya Hitachintak Mitra Samaj* ['Shri Shankar Society of Friends and Well-wishers of the Somavanshiyas']. He also started the first public library for Dalits, called the *Shri Satchidanand Vachangriha* ['Shri Satchidananda Reading Room'], aiming to cultivate the habit of reading among the untouchables.

Kamble also took part in social movements led by caste Hindus against untouchability, based on the belief that if untouchability were to be abolished for the sake of social integration, not only Dalits but others should also take part. He would attend meetings organized by caste Hindus on diverse social issues. Lokmanya Tilak was the main speaker at one such meeting held in front of the Ray Market in Pune to oppose the consumption of alcohol. Kamble was present in the audience at this meeting. He wished to speak in the meeting, and so he sent a note to the chairman saying that he belonged to the Dalit class and that he wished to speak in support of the organizers. The chairman passed the note to Tilak, who agreed, and Kamble was called to the stage. Tilak asked him to sit beside him and introduce himself. Many newspapers praised Tilak for his courage and for acting appropriately in this instance. But Tilak did not have the strength to become a Mahatma Phule and his praiseworthy behaviour was restricted to this occasion.

When news of Kamble's activity in leading a movement for the liberation of Dalits reached His Highness Chhatrapati Shahu Maharaj of Kolhapur, the prince was very happy.[5] He had already started working for the abolition of untouch-

---

[5] His Highness Chhatrapati Shahu Maharaj of Kolhapur, also known as Rajarshi Shahu Maharaj (1874–1922). He belonged to the Bhosle dynasty of Marathas, and was Raja (1894–1900) and Maharaja (1900–1922) of the Indian princely state of Kolhapur. He was a patron of the Satyashodhak Samaj founded by Jotiba Phule but later joined the Arya Samaj. His efforts for social reform are unique for that period in India—many of his progressive acts were initiated as early as 1902. They include ensuring education for the lower castes including Dalits, reservations for lower castes in jobs, prohibition of child marriage, and

ability before this. The Maharaj invited him to Kolhapur on 11 September 1908. He asked him about his work and the difficulties he faced, praised him and treated him with respect, and gave encouragement for his future work.

Reading and writing were a passion for Kamble. When he realized that he needed a journal to sustain the struggle, he started a monthly named *Somavanshiya Mitra* ['Friend of the Somavanshiyas'], the first issue of which came out on 1 July 1908. Through this magazine he intended primarily to start a campaign against undesirable practices among the Mahars. Also, he wanted to give voice to the educational, religious, social and economic problems facing the Dalits. Among the Mahars there was the evil custom of dedicating young boys and girls to the gods. Young girls, *muralis* and *jogtins*, were left to the goddess and were not allowed to marry after they reached puberty; instead they were prostituted in the open market in the name of the goddess. Kamble started a campaign in his magazine against this practice. As a result, many *muralis* and *jogtins* rebelled and gained their liberty. Kamble was the initiator of such movements in Maharashtra, and he also worked for the abolition of untouchability.

But even though the untouchable community was the class at the bottom of the hierarchy constructed by the Hindu religion, it still stood by the disgusting and debasing customs imposed on it. One would pretend to be deeply religious and put on the airs of someone who had reached an exalted position. Upper-caste people considered Dalits to be inferior, but the funny thing was that they also considered each other to be inferior. People would behave as if they were Brahmins even though they had been born in a caste deemed to be the lowest, and they would treat others as being lowly. Such castes also, like the Brahmins, build fences around themselves. Kamble launched a fight against such evils among the Dalits. Kamble sought to end practices like dedicating *muralis*, *jogtins* and *potrajs* to the gods and criticized their lack of courage and mental weakness. But people saw these efforts as an attack on their way of life. The Hindu religion had inculcated such servility in them that this was now as if in their blood; the Mahars rebelled against Kamble and closed down his magazine for good.

Contemporary with the militant struggle of Shivram Janba Kamble for the liberation of the untouchables, Subhedar Bahadur Gangaram Krishnaji Bhatankar had retired from military service.[6] In recognition of the courage he had displayed

---

even a decree against domestic violence against women. He met Ambedkar for the first time in 1917 and continued to associate with him until the end of his life.

[6] The Bhatankar and the Sawadkar families play an important role in the history of Dalit activism in the region. Marriage into Gopal Baba Walangkar's family connects them with each other, and with More's family. Thus, what we see here are links (through intermarriage) between military Mahars, which produced an educated and politically engaged elite.

Rao Bahadur Subhedar Gangaram Krishnaji Bhatankar was decorated during the Second Afghan War with a title and received a generous pension of Rs. 600/annum in perpetuity. Gangaram Bhatankar served as the first honorary Judge from the Mahar community. His

during his service, he was honoured with the title of Subhedar Bahadur and given a *jagir*, a sizeable land grant in Panvel *tehsil*, district Raigad. Besides this he was given land to build a large house for himself. But Bhatankar was not the kind of person to live only for himself; he wanted other untouchables to improve their lives as well. So, he requested the government to grant land in Panvel so that other retired soldiers could also build houses. Many benefited from this including Dr. Ambedkar's maternal uncle Murbadkar. Bhatankar helped many families. The residential colony was at first outside the town. It was known as the Subhedarwada.

Since Gangaram Bhatankar had been honoured with the title of Subhedar Bahadur, he was also given the powers of a bench magistrate. His court sat every Tuesday morning in the *mamledar* office. When Bhatankar entered the court on his first day, there was a large mat spread underneath the table and chairs. On the second Tuesday the clerks had removed it, and they were throwing the papers meant to be handed over to the magistrate on to the table, from a distance. This was a man who had spent his life in military service, so this angered him. He complained to the Collector. The clerks were immediately reprimanded by the higher authority. Bhatankar himself ordered all the staff to attend the court in full dress, wearing a *dhoti*, shirt, coat and hat. They all practised untouchability so they had to bathe after they returned home, and wash all their clothes. So, they were always angry with Bhatankar.

Subhedar Bhatankar was influenced by Gopalbuva Walangkar ever since he entered the army. He took up his legacy and worked to spread awareness among the Dalits, especially the Dalits of the Konkan region. In his personal behaviour Bhatankar carried himself with great self-respect. He was a pensioner, who had to collect his military pension from the treasury. Once, when he had gone to the treasury for his pension, the Mamledar threw the bag containing his pension at him. This awakened his self-respect, and, without thought for the consequences, he threw the bag back at the Mamledar and asked him to behave himself.

---

son, Y.G. Bhatankar, was a nominated member of the Panvel Municipality for sixteen years. Another son, R.G. Bhatankar, was elected as an MLA of the Independent Labour Party from Thane district in 1937. S.D. Tamhanekar, *Jhunjar Nete: Jagannathrao Bhatankar: Alpa Charitra*, Parel, Mumbai.

Gangaram Bhagoji Sawadkar (b. 1865) died in Turkey during the First World War, and was buried there. His wife was Gopal Baba Walangkar's brother's daughter. Gangaram's son, Subhedar Vishram Sawadkar (1889–1939) was a leading member of the Mahar Samaj Seva Sangh, and features prominently among the leaders of the Mahad *satyagraha*. He was also a member of Ambedkar's Independent Labour Party. Vishram's first wife was Gopal Baba Walangkar's grand-daughter. Vishram's son, Kashinath, was the owner of the Bharat Bhushan Printing Press, which was renamed the Buddha Bhushan Printing Press in 1956. Kashinath was an elected member of the Bombay Municipality.

These details are the result of extended personal communication between Anupama Rao and Anil Sawadkar since 2011.

> **RECORD OF GENERATIONS**
>
> **HEREDITARY SERVICES:** (of No.20074 - I.O. Subedar, Yashwant Gangaram Bhatankar, Ex-District Godown Inspector and Distributive Supervising Officer, Tahsil, Panvel.)
>
> On Father's Side:
>
> Great Great Grand Father Subedar Jiwnak
> Great Great Grand Father Subedar Major Raghnak Jiwnak.
> Great Grand Father Subedar Bapnak Raghnak.
> Grand Father Subedar Krishnak Bapnak.
>
> *4th *Services of *Bombay *each over *Rifles. *30 years.
>
> 19th Bombay Infy. — Service 32 years.
>
> Father Subedar Bahadur & Jagirdar Gangaram Krishnaji Bhatankar, 19th Bombay Infy. 21 years Service.
>
> Pensioned (Compulsarily retired) 7-12-1895 (Re-organisation).
> Jagirdar - 23-11-1901, Rs.600/- yearly for 3 generations.
>
> Awarded title of Bahadur: 20th December 1901.
>
> WAR SERVICES: Afghan War 1878-80.
> Defence & Battle of Kandhar - 1.9.1880, Medal & Clasp.
>
> CIVIL APPOINTMENTS: Famine Relief Duty Mamlatdar In Hoosangabad District 27-3-1900
> 2nd Class Hony. Magistrate Tahsil - Panvel (Dist.Kolaba) - 3.6.1901 to 29.1.1914.
> Municipal Councilar - Tahsil Panvel. 8-6-1901 to 29-4-1914.
>
> Uncle Subedar Ganpat Krishnaji Bhatankar (Head Clerk) 119th Infantry retired after 40 years service.
> Brother Ram Krishna Gangaram Bhatankar (living) Ex-M.L.A., Dist. Local Board Member - Kolaba Dist. & Municipal Councilar, Tahsil Panvel.
>
> Mother's father Subedar Sarnak Jiwnak came from 6th Bombay Infy. as a Colour Havr. in 1817 when the regiment raised at Dapoli.
> Service 30 years - 19th Bombay Infy.
> Uncle: Subedar Ramnak Ganganak (he was also native Adjutant).
> Killed in Ankai & Tankai near Aatpura. He was brought to the notice of Commanding Officer for Gallantry & Good Behaviour at the storming of Mooltan (Record of service of the 19th Bombay Infantry).
>
> Subedar Saknak Ramnak, 30 years service, Jemadar Kakhnak Ramnak 25 years service, *His son Jemdar Arjnak Lakhnak 19 years service. (All were in 6th Bombay Infantry.)
>
> * Their father was SUBEDAR MAJOR RAMNAK GHANGNAK in 6th Bombay Infantry - Service over 30 years.

This 'Record of Generations' shows that Yashwant Gangaram Bhatankar's family were in the employ of the British Army on both the maternal and the paternal sides for five generations preceding him. The document takes note of Gangaram Krishnaji Bhatankar's considerable achievements. These military records, carried by Mahar soldiers in army-issue iron trunks, function as *vamshavalis*, or family genealogies.
Courtesy of Anil Sawadkar.

> : 2 :
>
> Subedar Dharamanak Ramnak 34 years service. | 6th
> Subedar Jannak Ramnak 32½ years service. | Bombay
> Jemadar Saknak Ramnak 32 years service. | Infantry.
> Subedar Raghnak 32½ years service.
>
> * * * * *
>
> Extract from Regimental Order, by Colonel F.W.V. Leckie
> Commandant 19th Bombay Infantry, Mhow 7th December 1895.
>
> No.2126. Under instructions from Bombay Command Headquarters Subedar Gangaram Krishnaji having completed 21 years service, is removed to the Pension Establishment from this date.
>
> It is with great regret that the Commandant thus loses the services of this excellent Native Officer, whose retirement is alone necessiated by the new scheme of re-organisation of the Bombay Army.
>
> He is the descendent of a long line of Native Officers on both sides of his family who have performed good service to the Government and he himself has established an excellent record, having obtained his commission as JEMADAR within THIRTEEN YEARS of his enlistment. He held the responsible appointment of Native Adjutant and was subsequently pensioned.
>
> Both as a Non-commissioned Officer and Native Officer he has held various positions of trust and importance in the regiment.
>
> He was best shot in the regiment in the years 1883 and 1884 and has been included for many years past in the various teams which have won prizes for rifle and revolver shooting.
>
> The company under his command was the best shooting the year 1892 and 1894 and stands first now, in the current course.
>
> He is in possession of a first class certificate of Education in English, also in Musketry (special mention).
>
> Transport and Army Signalling.
>
> True Extract.
> Sd/- H.E. Louis. Lieut.
> Adjutant 19th Bombay Infantry.
>
> * * * *
>
> Extract from Regimental Order by Colonel J.G. Watts Commandant 19th Regiment Bombay Infantry, Deesa 31st January 1896.
>
> No.10: In publishing the following extract of the Controller's Pension circular by which Subedar Krishnak Bapna is pensioned at the higher rate of pension of 50 Rupees a month, the Commandant desires to place on records his appreciation of the services of this deserving and excellent old officer.
>
> Subedar Krishnak Bapnak belongs to a family of soldiers. His Grandfather was Subedar Major of the 4th Bombay Rifles and his father a Subedar of the same regiment.

Page 2 of the 'Record of Generations'.

Another story is that he had once gone to the town of Tale in Mangaon district to buy some cloth. His proud bearing and his dress led the shopkeeper to think he was a caste Hindu, but when he glanced outside his shop he saw the Dalits of Tale standing there. The shopkeeper then asked, 'Saheb, those Mahar people standing outside, have they come with you?' Bhatankar replied, 'Yes, they are my

> : 3 :
>
> Subedar Krishnak Bapnak leaves two excellent sons in the regiment to continue the good services which their father, grandfather have rendered to the State.
>
> In bidding farewell to Subedar Krishnak Bapnak the Commandant wishes many years of health and happiness to enjoy his well earned pension.
>
> True extract.
> Sd/- x x Lieut.
> Offg. Adjutant 19th Regiment Bombay Infantry.
>
> * * * *
>
> Extract from Regimental order, by Lieut-Col. C.R.
> Phillips, Commandant 19th Bombay Infantry,
> Malakand, 13th January 1902.
>
> ......
>
> No.69 REWARDS:
>
> The following general order dated Simla the 20th December 1901 is published for information.
>
> No.1147. The Governor General in Council is pleased to notify that the title "BAHADUR" is conferred on the undermentioned native officers under the resolution of the Government of India in the Military Department. No.867-B dated the 27th February 1893.
>
> Pensioned Subedar Gangnak Krishnak late of the 19th Bombay Infantry.
>
> x x x x

Page 3 of the 'Record of Generations'.

relatives.' The shopkeeper then asked him to make his purchases outside the shop. Bhatankar was angry and completed his purchases inside the shop. This was his personal rebellion against untouchability, unusual in those times.

The reputation of Subhedar Bhatankar had reached Shivram Janba Kamble. Kamble had decided to hold a meeting at Jejuri near Pune to expand the range of his movement. Having decided to bring Bhatankar to address this meeting, Kamble went to Panvel and met Bhatankar. Kamble requested Bhatankar to chair the meeting. He accepted, and on 5 April 1910 the second *Somavanshiya Parishad* [council] was held at Jejuri, presided over by Bhatankar.

Among the resolutions moved and passed in this meeting were suggestions for improving the conditions of the untouchables. All these Resolutions were then sent to the Provincial government in Bombay and the Central government. Neither the Provincial nor the Central government had the power to reverse the policy adopted in 1891 and to risk the wrath of caste Hindus by acting for the welfare of the Dalits. Even then, Kamble decided to inform the Minister for British India[7] and Members of Parliament. He sent the Resolutions to the then Minister for India, the Earl of Crewe, on 14 December 1910. Together with the Resolutions he sent an account of the countless Mahar soldiers who had fought with courage and some of whom had attained high ranks in the army: Second Grenadier, Sixth Bombay Infantry, Ramnak Namnak and others from 20 battalions of the Bombay Province who had made great sacrifices during the establishment of the British regime. But the British government did not give up its despicable opportunistic policy.

Vitthal Ramji Shinde had betrayed the untouchables by sending an abbreviated list of demands on their behalf to the Southborough Committee. A conference had been organized at Nagpur by the Depressed Classes Mission on 30–31 May and 1 June 1911, presided over by Shahu Maharaj of Kolhapur, to condemn this betrayal. Shivram Janba Kamble was present together with Dr. Ambedkar at this conference, and he too expressed his opposition to the misleading policies of Mr. Shinde. Later on Kamble was present at the Parvati Temple *satyagraha*. Shivram Janba Kamble died in 1948.

Background of the Historic Mahad Satyagraha

Before the coming of the British regime, the untouchable community was completely deprived of education. With the establishment of British rule, the colonial powers opened the doors of English education first to the Brahmins, then Non-Brahmins and finally to the Dalits. The education given to untouchables who joined the army did not follow that order; so untouchables in the army were the first to get educated. And it was because of the awareness generated by this that the Dalits in the army took up the task of giving civic education to other Dalits. Also, those people of other castes in some parts of the country who felt sympathy for the Dalits were helpless under the feudal regime. But the liberal capitalist ideology brought by the British gave them strength, and they too started separate schools for the Dalits. Even if some of these were closed down later, the fact that they were started in the first place is significant. Mahatma Phule and Savitribai started the

---

[7] Satyendra More means the Secretary of State for India when he uses this term.

> The Conference of the Deccan Mahars
> 1878, Cantonment, Poona,
> Bombay Presidency,
> INDIA.
>
> Poona, 14th November, 1910.
>
> To
> The Right Honourable
> **The EARL OF CREWE,**
> K. G., P. C., M. A., F. S. A.,
> Secretary of State for India,
> LONDON.
>
> HUMBLY SHEWETH,
>
> We, the Mahar inhabitants of India, residing in the Bombay Presidency, have experienced the vitalising influence of the general awakening of our Indian people, and long to participate in the new privileges which have been granted by our illustrious Emperor and King to the people of our country, in accordance with the declarations of our late Empress, Queen Victoria the Good, in the celebrated Proclamation of 1858. We do not aspire to high political privileges and positions, since we are not educationally qualified for them, but humbly seek employment in the lowest grades of the Public Service, in the ranks of Police Sepoys and of soldiers in the Indian Army.
>
> 2. We are making no new demands; we do not claim employment in services in which we have not been engaged before. Indeed, some few of our people do still hold positions in the Police Force, and have acquitted themselves most honourably. So also have our people been employed in the Indian Army from the very commencement of the British Raj in our country, and they have risen to the highest positions by their valour and good conduct.
>
> 3. But the present changes in the Indian Army have been most prejudicial to the interests of our people. We have been excluded from the Military Service entirely, for reasons unknown to us. If the Maratha Kunbis (cultivators) have been admitted into the Army, why should not Maratha Mahars (i. e., petty peasants) be allowed the same privilege? We rendered valuable service, as we have observed above, in the capacity of soldiers in times past, and we humbly claim the right of rendering the same service at present.
>
> 4. If the other castes of the Hindus should object to our enlistment in the same Regiments with them, for reasons of unjust sectionalism, we would request that separate regiments of our people might be created, or separate companies of our people might be attached to Muhammadan Regiments. The Muhammadans, by reason of their religion and social organization, are superior to the Hindus, both socially and morally, and are capable of recognising our manhood and the justice of our claims, to enjoy equal rights of citizenship with them, under the auspices of the British Raj. And we confidently expect justice and generosity from the

1910 Petition from Shivram Janba Kamble to the Earl of Crewe for Mahars' reinstatement into the British Army. Note the names of Mahar non-commissioned officers provided to establish the community's long association with the Army.
Courtesy of Gangadhar Pantawane.

first school for girls in Pune in 1848. The *Prarthana Samaj* started some schools in Bombay in 1855. Some night schools were set up. And a wealthy member of the Prarthana Samaj started a school for untouchables at Byculla in 1899, at his own expense.

> there the many names of Mahars who fell wounded or dead fighting bravely side by side with Europeans and with Indians who were not outcastes. I regret that one avenue to honourable work has been closed to these people."
>
> 8. And surely the hundreds of Mahar Non-Commissioned Officers of the Old British Army could not have held their positions with efficiency and honor unless they were competent "to exercise authority and manage men". The former Englishman was not so much under the dominance of the Brahminical institution of caste as the present, and he found brave men like himself among all the people that he approached with faith and sympathy. The Mahar has all the elements in his nature which the other castes and races of this great country possess, and under the kindly influence of British justice and British sympathy they can be awakened and developed as they have been in their brethren of the so-called higher classes. Are not the Brahman, the Muhammadan and the Parsi holding the highest positions under the Administration with success, simply because they have been courageously trusted?
>
> We would give here a list of a few of the Mahar Non-Commissioned Officers that served in the Indian Army in olden times, to demonstrate in a clear and tangible form the justice of our claim.
>
> 1ST GR. BOMBAY INFANTRY.
> Subedar Ragnak Mahadnak.   Subedar Dhondnak
>   Do.   Parasnak   Jamedar Gannak Parasnak
>
> 2ND GR. BOMBAY INFANTRY.
> Subedar Major Dharmnak Sabnak   Jamedar Bhagnak Gangnak
> Subedar Ittnak   Do.   Shivnak Goonnak
>   Do. Harnak Bhagnak   Do.   Bhagnak
>   Do. Ragnak Deonak   Do.   Ittnak
>
> 4TH BOMBAY RIFLES.
> Subedar Shivnak Changnak   Jamedar Gangnak Roopnak
>   Do. Shivnak Pandnak   Do.   Sudanak Ramnak
>   Do. Sudanak   Do.   Kootnak Dulnak
>   Do. Jivank   Do.   Krishnnak
>   Do. Ragank Jivnak   Do.   Shivnak
>   Do. Bapnak Ragnak
>
> 5TH BOMBAY LIGHT INFANTRY.
> Subedar Changnak Ramnak
>
> 6TH BOMBAY INFANTRY.
> Subedar Major Ramnak Namnak   Subedar Dharmnak Ramnak
>   Subedar Major Sakhanak   Do   Ramnak Mahadnak
>   Do   Jannak Ramnak   Jamadar Sakhanak Ramnak
>   Do   Ragnak Namnak   Do   Arjoonnak Laknak
>   Do   Laknak Ramnak
>
> 7TH BOMBAY INFANTRY.
> Subedar Ramnak Malnak   Subedar Gavornak Dadnak
>   Do Deonak Changnak   Do   Mahadnak Malnak
>
> 8TH BOMBAY INFANTRY.
> Subedar Major Changnak   Subedar Sudaknak
>   Subedar Goondnak Ittnak   Do   Dharmnak Ittnak
>
> 9TH BOMBAY INFANTRY.
> Subedar Major and Sardhar Bahadur Jamedar Laknak Bhiknak
>   Ittnak Bhiknak   Do   Saknak Bhitnak
>   Subedar Changnak Goondnak   Do   Ittnak
>
> 10TH BOMBAY INFANTRY.
>   Subedar Laknak

Page 3 of the 1910 petition.

The British brought a capitalist social system, and wherever this system was influential, the doors of education were opened up for Dalits in urban life. Before this, the only education Dalits acquired was given to them compulsorily when they were in military service. Thus, Babasaheb's father Ramji, who attained the post of *subhedar* in the army, got the opportunity to complete his schooling up to matriculation. And

12TH BOMBAY INFANTRY.

Subedar Major and Bahadur Gangnak Sajannak | Subedar Kesnak Gondnak

13TH BOMBAY INFANTRY.

Subedar Dharmnak Deonak | Jamadar Tannak

14TH BOMBAY INFANTRY.

Subedar Hirnak | Jamedar Laknak Sonnak
| Do

15TH BOMBAY INFANTRY.

Subedar Ittnak Laknak | Jamedar Dharmnak
Jamedar Arjoonnak Deonak |

17TH BOMBAY INFANTRY.

Subedar Bhiknak Jannak | Subedar Gannak Balnak
Do. Roopnak | Do. Kannak
Do. Babnak Changnak | Do. Mannak
Do. Gannak Mannak | Jamedar Gangnak Gannak
Do. Gonnak Gannak |

18TH BOMBAY INFANTRY.

Subedar Bhivnak Gonnak

19TH BOMBAY INFANTRY.

Subedar Bahadur Gangaram Krishnaji | Subedar Gowarnak Kalnak
Subedar Ramnak Luknak | Jamedar Soannak Toolnak
Do. Krishnnak Bapnak | Do. Kalnak
Do. Samnak Javanak | Do. Ittnak
Do. Ramnak Gangnak (Gallantry service at Multan) | Do Laknak
Do. Ittnak Malharnak | Do. Jannak
Do. Somnak Shankarnak | Do. Pandnak
Do. Bhagnak Ramnak |

20TH BOMBAY INFANTRY.

Subedar Major Ramnak Changnak | Subedar Soannak Hirnak (Talwar Bahadur
Subedar Laknak Harnak (Talwar Br.) | Do. Saknak

21ST MARINE.

Subedar Major Dahivadkar | Subedar Jannak, Balnak
Subedar Sudaknak Kamalnak | Jamedar Balnak Kalnak
Do. Deonak Gundnak | Do. Jannak Gannak
Do. Jainak Harnak | Do. Gondnak Ramnak
Subedar Ramnak Babnak | Do. Babnak Ramnak
Do. Doolabnak | Do. Narayan
Do. Kamalnak | Do. Sayagaumkar (Sappers and Miners) Order of Merit.
Do. Shivnak Hirnak |

24TH BOMBAY INFANTRY.

Subedar Yasnak Dadnak

26TH BOMBAY INFANTRY.

Subedar Deonak Malnak

28TH BOMBAY INFANTRY.

Subedar Mannak Yasnak | Jamedar Amritnak

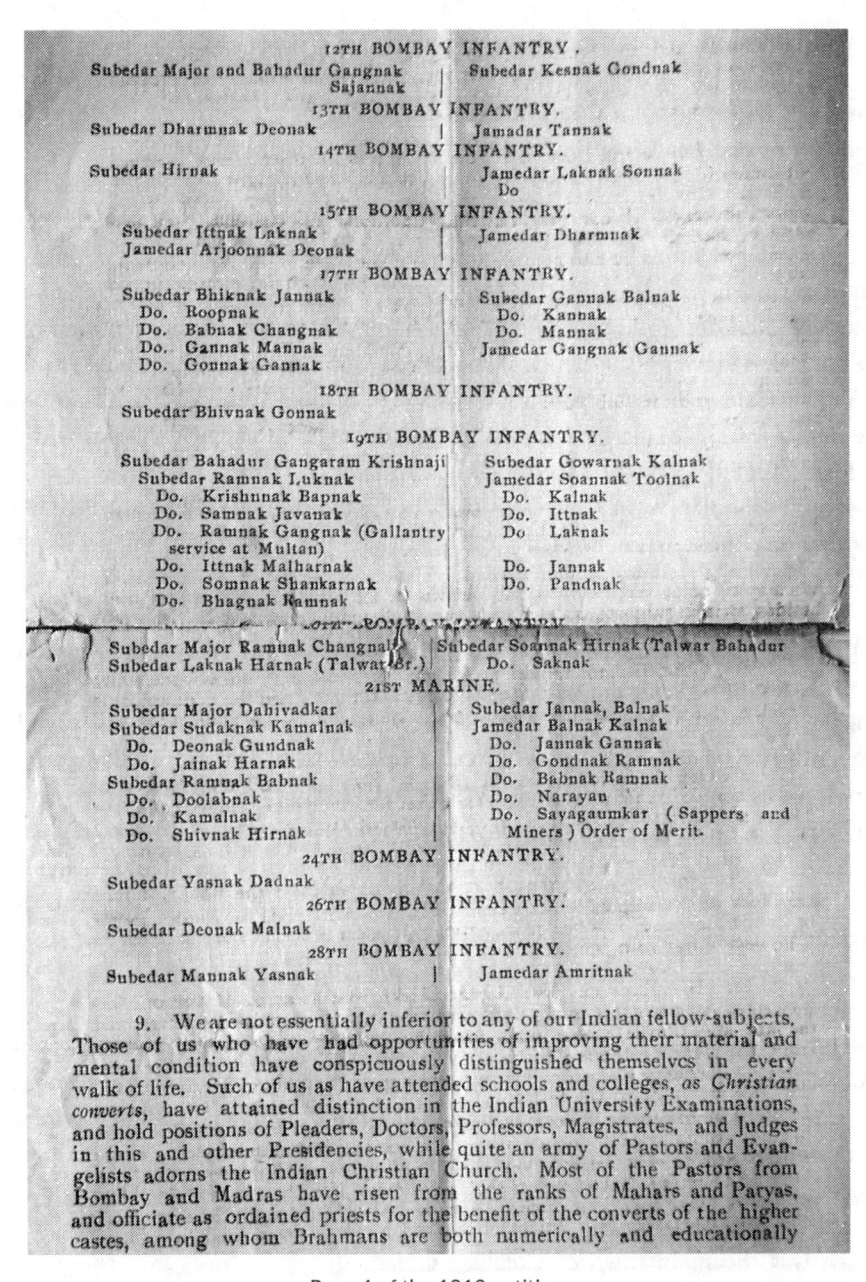

9. We are not essentially inferior to any of our Indian fellow-subjects. Those of us who have had opportunities of improving their material and mental condition have conspicuously distinguished themselves in every walk of life. Such of us as have attended schools and colleges, as *Christian converts*, have attained distinction in the Indian University Examinations, and hold positions of Pleaders, Doctors, Professors, Magistrates, and Judges in this and other Presidencies, while quite an army of Pastors and Evangelists adorns the Indian Christian Church. Most of the Pastors from Bombay and Madras have risen from the ranks of Mahars and Paryas, and officiate as ordained priests for the benefit of the converts of the higher castes, among whom Brahmans are both numerically and educationally

Page 4 of the 1910 petition.

so he realized the importance of education and enrolled Babasaheb and his elder brother Balaramdada in school and supported their education.

In More's case, his village Dasgaon was on the Bombay–Goa highway. Dasgaon, at a distance of six miles from Mahad, had undergone the greatest degree of capitalist development after Mahad, and had become the centre for about 15 to

20 villages around. The weekly Saturday market there has a history going back to ancient times. The British government had opened a post and telegraph office in Dasgaon. The geographical location of Dasgaon had resulted in a Marathi school being set up there in the seventh decade of the nineteenth century.

It was because he attained education that Vitthal Anand Hate, builder of the two-storey house mentioned earlier, had brought More's brother Lakshman to Dasgaon, got him admitted to the Marathi school there, and had seen to his schooling up to the seventh standard. Later, he also educated his sons Gopal, Tukaram, Namdeo and Jayaram up to the seventh standard. Other children from the backward classes also attended that school, but none of them learned as much as Vitthal Hate Joshi's children. That was a sign of those times. Vitthal Hate Joshi the *maadiwalla*, like Ambedkar's father, was himself educated; that was why his children studied up to the seventh class. In Mahad too there was an English and a Marathi school, but very few Dalit or Bahujan children would be enrolled. And even among those who enrolled, not one reached the seventh standard like the children we have mentioned in Dasgaon.

The British government's policy at that time was to spread education. Thus, as there were children in Dasgaon from Dalit families who had studied up to the seventh, the government appointed them as teachers in various villages all over Colaba district. But when they saw that other children would not come to school to learn from a Mahar teacher, they started separate 'Mahar schools'. Hate's sons were appointed as schoolmasters in these Mahar schools. So Dasgaon produced the first generation of Dalit (Mahar) schoolteachers in the whole of the Konkan region. A situation favourable to the spread of education was slowly coming into existence.

It was about this time that More's father's first wife and his son from her, Lakshman Master, both died relatively young. So he got married for the second time, to the daughter of a certain Dhotre from Ladawali village near Mahad. More was born to her in the year 1903 in Ladawali.

When More was five or six years old his father enrolled him in the Marathi school at Dasgaon. Ramchandra Keshav Khare and More's father's maternal cousin Jayaram Vitthal Hate were his teachers in the Marathi school in Dasgaon. Khare was a Brahmin, but he had acquired the strength to deny untouchability. These two paid special attention to More as a student. They prepared him for the fourth standard scholarship examination in 1913–14. The examination was to be held in Alibag, which was the main town of Colaba (Raigad) district. More's maternal cousin Namdeo Vitthal Hate, the schoolteacher, was entrusted with the responsibility of taking More to Alibag. While More was preparing for the examination, his father Babaji fell ill and passed away. At the time More was just ten years old and his youngest sister Pithu was four months old. More's other brothers and sisters had died earlier during an epidemic of cholera.[8]

---

[8] Cholera appears to have been endemic to the north Konkan region in the early years of the

Even in these unfavourable circumstances, More prepared for the examination and passed with good marks. But he was denied admission in the next class in the high school merely because he was an untouchable; and it was from here that his opposition to injustice began.

More's First Meeting with Babasaheb

The first time More had the chance to be in Babasaheb's presence was in his childhood. Babasaheb had completed his M.A. and Ph.D. from Columbia University, and his M.Sc. from London University. He had completed just one year preparing to be a barrister-at-law, when he obtained permission for a four-year break before he returned to India in 1917. He was compelled to do this because his request for just one year's scholarship had been turned down by the Maharaja of Baroda. So he was unhappy and was not in a state of mind to be felicitated by anyone. But, even at that time, there was not a single Dalit untouchable in society who had acquired M.A. and Ph.D. degrees in Economics. So it was a matter of pride for the Dalits to felicitate Babasaheb. They pressed him, but he gave a staunch refusal. So a meeting of the Brigade Panchayat was organized at the Family Lines near where the Phule Market is today, by those army soldiers and officers who had settled in Bombay.

Since Babasaheb's father was a retired *subhedar* of the army, he himself and later both his elder son Balaram and his younger son Bhimrao were members of the brigade caste *panchayat* by tradition. The Panchayat used this connection to call the meeting in the Family Lines. Babasaheb did not wish to go to the meeting and mix with people, but Balaramdada explained matters to him and managed to persuade him, so that he agreed to attend. So, it had been announced that Babasaheb was to attend the meeting.

Even before Babasaheb and his brother Balaramdada reached the place, a large number of people, hoping for an opportunity to see Babasaheb and hear him speak had formed a crowd waiting for him in the *chawl* compound. One of More's relatives had brought him along and he was among that crowd. More had come to Bombay for the Diwali holidays and to look for work.

Babasaheb came and sat in the sitting room in the place kept for him. More's relative, who was with him, seated both of themselves in a spot from which they could be seen by Babasaheb. Then Balaramdada began to introduce some persons sitting near him: this is a *subhedar* from such-and-such regiment, this is a *hawaldar* from such-and-such regiment, and this is so-and-so's son, this is so-and-so's brother. While these introductions were going on, Babasaheb recounted some memories of

---

twentieth century, according to British medical reports (L. Rogers, *Incidence and Spread of Cholera in India*, 1928). In fact, this region has been identified as the area in the Bombay Presidency most prone to cholera throughout the year, because of its high humidity.—*Tr.*

his childhood and laughed; and others also laughed at his humour and his wit, and seeing them, More laughed from time to time. Someone asked him, teasingly: 'Eh, boy, why are you laughing?' On which laughter broke out generally, and everyone's attention was directed to More. Then Balaramdada asked More's relative about the boy. He introduced young More to Bhimrao and Balaramdada as the grandson of Vitthal Anand Hate-Joshi, *maadiwalla* of Dasgaon, who was studying in the third English class at the high school in Mahad. Then Balaramdada pointed to More and said something about him to Bhimrao, who looked at him and smiled. At the time, More was just thirteen or fourteen years old. After the preliminary introductions were over, the agenda of the meeting was taken up. Several persons made speeches in the next one hour, but Bhimrao did not utter a single word till the end. It was as if he had decided to be present only as an observer. This was the first occasion More had of seeing and hearing Babasaheb.

After this, More returned to Dasgaon. In Bombay, Babasaheb was in search of a job so that he could complete his education. He got a job as a professor in Sydenham College, and began to build his savings. Some days later, More came back to Bombay from Dasgaon, again to look for work. Trying to meet Babasaheb through a friend, he arrived at the Cement Chawl in Parel Poybawadi where he lived. Babasaheb listened to his account of obstacles in his education, and treated him with affection. As he was leaving, he gave More a book of maps as a gift. Up to this time, More regarded Babasaheb as a learned man among his kin, and felt respect for him. But More openly admitted that, at the time, he did not have enough understanding to realize that Babasaheb was much more than that. And so did More's first face-to-face meeting with Babasaheb take place!

The First Opposition to Untouchability

Every person born in an untouchable caste has an inborn awareness that he must first struggle against untouchability; and so it was with More. He was looking for a leader who would not hurt the self-esteem and sense of self of the untouchables, who did not look at them with pity. This person should have the position that untouchability is a disease affecting our nation, and that one needs to free the nation from this disease. That is, he was looking for a leader who had embraced the cause of abolition of the caste system. More saw such a leader in Babasaheb and he was more convinced by him than by Mahatma Gandhi. This was because Gandhiji viewed the untouchables with pity. If one asked an untouchable person of Dr. Ambedkar's time or earlier, whether he wanted national independence first or social equality and freedom from social slavery, his answer would be that he first sought social freedom. Freedom from the slavery that had compelled him for hundreds and hundreds of years to suffer contempt and live a life worse than a cat or dog would come before freedom from the foreign rule of a hundred and fifty years. And was there anything wrong in this answer? If you imagine that you have been born in an untouchable caste and think about it honestly, you would find this response quite reasonable. This was the answer that Dr. Ambedkar gave when he met Lala Lajpat Rai in Columbia University in 1915.

More also determined, while he was in Mahad, that his life goal was the abolition of untouchability. To this end he began to spread awareness among the Dalit people and to organize them. He realized that this was not an aim that he could accomplish on his own. He decided in his mind that he would follow Dr. Babasaheb Ambedkar, and, while still a student during 1917 to 1920, he began to inform himself about Babasaheb's activities during his stay in India, and to study them.

If untouchability was to be abolished, it was not enough to form an association of Mahars alone. It was necessary to build unity among all untouchable castes, just as Babasaheb had done. In 1918, when a Dalit was to be nominated in a reserved seat in the Bombay Municipal Corporation, Babasaheb suggested the name of P. Baloo (Palwankar), an individual of the Chambhar caste and the first cricketer from his caste, rather than a Mahar. (P. Baloo later became an opponent of Babasaheb.) When the Mahars protested against this, Babasaheb told them, act as if you are his elder brothers. Similarly, at the time of the Mahad *satyagraha*, More organized the Chambhars of Mahad.

In Mahad More would expound before the Dalits on Babasaheb's collaboration with Shahu Maharaj at the conference at Mangaon in Kolhapur district, or the later conference in Nagpur. He had memorized Babasaheb's historic deposition before the Southborough Committee, even before Babasaheb came to Mahad for the *satyagraha*. Thus, More, having chosen Babasaheb as his leader, studied various aspects of his work, and, like Babasaheb, dedicated himself to the objective of annihilating caste.

The Caste Question

When More met Babasaheb Ambedkar for the first time he was about thirteen years old. Even at that age he had suffered the blows of being treated as untouchable, and so he was mature beyond his years. He felt proud to meet a man who had suffered the same pain, but had become such a great man.

In those days a person born in an untouchable caste who suffered the indignities of untouchability would be plagued by the question of how this practice originated and how it would end. When Ambedkar was asked to write an independent essay at Columbia University he first started writing on Sambhaji (the Maratha prince and son of Shivaji), but then he decided to study the problem of caste, which had caused him suffering. He discussed the topic with some scholars, but found their views to be childish in the extreme. Some even understood *varna* as skin colour.

Earlier, it was Dr. Babasaheb's position that untouchability was a part of the four-*varna* or *chaturvarna* system, and that this burden of *chaturvarna* could never be cast off. But even while he was at Columbia University and while he was studying in Europe, he was influenced by scholars such as Seligman who was his teacher, from whom he became acquainted with Marxist thought and the concept of class.[9] And so, at the age of 26, he presented a paper on 'The Caste System in India' on 9 May 1916 before the anthropologist Dr. A.A. Goldenweiser at an anthropology seminar. He used the concept of class in expounding on this question before an English audience. He was even then influenced by Marx's thought.[10]

Dr. Babasaheb Ambedkar compared the caste system to a multi-storeyed building with no staircase. One who is born on one of the floors can never change his floor. He put forward the image that the four *varnas* Brahmins, Kshatriyas, Vaishyas and Shudras are born on different floors, with the Shudras, whose numbers are 70 to 75 per cent, occupying the lowest floor, and since there is no staircase they cannot ascend to a higher floor. The Brahmin priestly class on the topmost floor has, according to Dr. Ambedkar, built a fence around itself to protect its superiority. To maintain their own purity and greatness they do not allow others to enter, and place restrictions on themselves. These restricted classes are, Babasaheb says, equivalent to caste or *jati*. *Marx has termed caste a distinctive feature of the Asiatic mode of production and social formation.* The classes which formed in other countries were horizontally, not vertically, aligned and so they can change through their own deeds, but this is not possible in the Hindu religion. Babasaheb used Marx's concept of class as the basis of his exposition.

In this way [Ambedkar] began to collect the resources for the annihilation of caste even while he was in America. When More met Babasaheb for the first time in 1917, he was entirely ignorant of his thoughts on the caste system and of his scholarship.

Babasaheb's analysis of the caste system and untouchability in later years was based on these thoughts. It is a fact that nobody else has made such a deep study of this question up to now. But he took the religious books as the main source of this study. In fact it would be possible to make a causal analysis of the origin of untouchability using a Marxist methodology. Many Marxist thinkers have made attempts to do this, and some such efforts go on, but they have met with little success. It is important to note that Babasaheb displayed a research effort and persistence in pursuit of this question which is superior to that of others.

---

[9] Edwin Robert Anderson Seligman (1861–1939) is best known as the initiator of global progressive public finance. He was Professor, Political Economy, at Columbia University between 1885 and 1933.

[10] At best, 'Castes in India: Their Mechanism, Genesis and Development' can be viewed as an effort to bridge the ideas of Marx and Weber. It would be quite a stretch to suggest that Seligman was a Marxist, or that Ambedkar's 1916 text was Marxist in its orientation.

Dr. Babasaheb Ambedkar Absent at both Conferences on Untouchability in 1917–18

Dr. Babasaheb Ambedkar looked at the question of caste and untouchability as an issue of human rights, and he did not wish to solve it from a position of 'taking pity'. This was why Babasaheb had differences of opinion between 1917 and 1920 with non-untouchable social reformers like Sir Narayan Chandavarkar and Vitthal Ramji Shinde who considered themselves trustees of the untouchables. So, he avoided participating in programmes where he would appear with them in public. On 11 November 1917 there was going to be a felicitation of Dr. Babasaheb Ambedkar in a ceremony to be presided over by Sir Narayan Chandavarkar [Hindu reformer and early member of the Indian National Congress] on the open ground in front of twelve *maadis* in Madanpura in Bombay and he was to be presented with a purse. Also, resolutions concerned with the political rights of the untouchables were to be moved in this meeting, and a delegation was to be chosen to meet the Minister for India Montagu and the Viceroy Lord Chelmsford to present the demands for political rights. But Dr. Ambedkar deliberately did not attend the meeting, even though he was to be felicitated, because Chandavarkar's point of view was one of pity for the untouchables, and Ambedkar did not approve of the untouchables' issues being framed in the wrong manner.

Similarly, the first Conference for the Abolition of Untouchability was held on the large ground of the French Bridge in Bombay on 23–24 March 1918, with the Maharaja of Baroda, Sayajirao Gaikwad, presiding. The chairman of the welcome committee was Sir Narayanrao Chandavarkar, and among the speakers were Bipin Chandra Pal, Lokmanya Tilak, Barrister [M.R.] Jayakar, Hon. Khaparde, Vitthalbhai Patel and others. Rabindranath Tagore, Mahatma Gandhi, the Shankaracharya of the Karveer Peeth and others had sent telegrams and messages. Dr. Ambedkar remained deliberately absent at this important meeting too. This was because the approach of all the above to the question of untouchability did not think of the untouchables' sense of self, but took up an attitude of pity.

While speaking in support of a motion that the monarchs of princely states should help the cause of the untouchables at this conference, Babasaheb's well-wisher Keluskar stunned the audience into silence by telling the story of how even the Maharaja of Baroda had not been able to provide residence to Babasaheb in his state, and how he had given in to pressure from the servants of the princely state and the orthodox public.[11] Chandavarkar then tried to push the truth of the matter under the carpet. Lokmanya Tilak made a speech declaring that 'I am not

---

[11] Krishnaji Arjun Keluskar was a well-known Marathi writer and social reformer. Keluskar presented Ambedkar with a biography of the Buddha during the felicitation ceremony that was held in 1907 when he completed his matriculation examination. The function was chaired by S.K. Bole.—*Tr.*

against the untouchables, untouchability is a custom and it must be abolished', but he refused to sign a manifesto signed by 380 of those present at the conference that carried the undertaking '*I will not practise untouchability and I will break the system of caste*'. Not only this, but Tilak's newspaper *Kesari* did not publish even a summary report of this conference. Babasaheb did not have faith in such hollow speechifying social reformers and those who took up political leadership but took care not to offend the orthodox, and that was why he did not attend this conference.

Even though the Communist Party did not exist at that time, there was consensus among the Communists that untouchability must be abolished. But their criterion was firstly opposition to British imperialism, and to their policy of aggravating casteist forces. Also, the Communist thinkers of the time had the mistaken belief that the Congress party was honest on the Dalit issue. The reality was that the Congress party was in the grip of feudal ideology. So the Communists' belief that the Dalits could confidently rely on the Congress was wrong. Tilak had refused to sign an avowal that he would not practise untouchability. When we examine the whole situation of that time, we see that Ambedkar's position regarding the Congress was correct. History has proved him right.

MONTAGU–CHELMSFORD REFORMS AND THE SOUTHBOROUGH COMMITTEE

After his India tour Montagu returned to England and presented the findings of his tour in the British Parliament. After that, it was decided to send out a Franchise Committee with Lord Southborough as its chairman, with the power to decide who would be eligible to vote, and what criteria should be applied in this regard.

The process of assimilating the Indian people into the state administration and according them political rights began in 1891. But in that year Dalits were deprived of some of their rights; it was in that very year that the British dissolved the Mahar regiment, and Gopalbuva Walangkar had to raise his voice in protest against the decision. In 1901 the 'Morley–Minto Reforms' were enacted to widen the scope of the political rights granted to Indians in 1891. Muslims and Anglo-Indians were granted political rights, but the Dalits were again completely overlooked. At that time Babasaheb had felt that it was necessary for him to bring up the issue of political rights for the Dalits, else he would be neglecting his duty. Because at the time the leaders of the Depressed Classes Mission, Vitthal Ramji Shinde and others, were not willing to see the question of the Dalits as a separate issue in this context. They saw the issue in terms of compassion for the Dalits and were willing to leave it to the goodwill of the Congress and the British. So Ambedkar refused to go along with them and demanded that, as a member of the Depressed Classes and a professor in Sydenham College, he should be allowed to present a petition to the

Southborough Committee and also appear as a witness. His demand was granted and on 27 January 1919 Babasaheb Ambedkar presented an independent petition to the Committee and also testified as a witness.

In this petition he pointed out that when the Imperial Legislative Council at the Central level and the State Legislative Councils at the Provincial level were constituted so as to bring the Indian people into the state administration, care had been taken to give scope to Hindus, Muslims, Christians, Parsis, Jews and all the different religions, and also to the *zamindar* and *jagirdar* classes. Only those property-owners who paid taxes had the right to vote on these Councils. So, of course the Dalits had no right to vote. Secondly, since the Dalits were considered to be an indivisible part of the Hindu community, the Hindus also got advantage from their numbers in the population. It was caste Hindus who demanded their due weight as representatives of the Dalits. So Ambedkar made the demand in his written petition that the Dalits should be separated from the rest of the Hindus, and that they should be recognized as having a separate existence, so that they could be granted nine seats in the Bombay Legislative Council according to their numbers in the population. Thus, since Dalits comprised eight per cent of the population, they should have eight seats in the Provincial Legislative Council of Bombay and one seat on the Imperial Legislative Council. He also demanded that, in view of the Dalits' economic condition, the property criterion for franchise should be relaxed for them.

The Congress party considered this demand to be of a casteist nature. The position of the Congress was that it was acceptable to divide the right to vote on the basis of community or religion for the Muslims and Christians, but to give this right to the Dalits would be divisive. In Dr. Ambedkar's view this was a matter to be decided by the Dalits for themselves. He stated in his testimony that to give this a casteist colour was tantamount to an effort to deny the Dalits the right to vote. He told the Committee how, when Dadabhai Naoroji had moved a resolution criticizing the government on the question of Dalits' rights, several persons claiming to be sympathizers of the cause of the Dalits criticized him and did not allow the resolution to be passed, thus causing Dadabhai to lose face. He also told the Committee how one legislator Khaparde who was a member of the higher council at the time, wrote an article declaring that 'those who were trying to bring about the uplift of the untouchables were made to be fools'. Ambedkar put forward this evidence and forcefully argued that to leave the question of the Dalits to the goodwill of the Congress would indeed be an injustice.

He also asserted that associations like the Depressed Classes Mission who were reluctant to give Dalits the right to vote and held instead that the government should nominate one or two Dalits out of compassion, which would place them under permanent obligation, had an attitude of pity towards the Dalits. Ambedkar clearly stated that the Committee should not regard such a society (the Depressed

Classes Mission) as representing the Dalits, as it had until then not taken a single Dalit on its executive.

He also spelt out in his petition how the above-mentioned nine seats should be filled, pointing out that there were at that time 25 untouchable persons who were educated and capable. The Southborough Committee was only empowered to make recommendations. It was ultimately up to the government to decide who should be given the right to vote and how many seats. But Dr. Babasaheb Ambedkar's exposition was so comprehensive and solid that the Committee was convinced that the Dalits had a separate existence and that, if a policy of taking care of their demands was not followed, there might in future be a danger to the regime from the Dalit classes. So, it recommended that these demands be accepted. Within the new capitalist mode of production and the economic development it brought, the Dalit people were becoming awakened. Realizing this, the government, aiming to keep them under control, granted them the right to vote for the first time by giving them seats on the Legislative Council.

The Communist intellectuals' opinion about these Montagu–Chelmsford reforms was that this was a carrot dangled before the Dalits and an example of the 'divide and rule' politics played by the British. They were looking at the issue only in political terms. They did not think of the social situation and the reality underlying this problem. They too considered the Dalits to be part of the Hindu community, and were not aware of their separate existence. They considered the Congress to be their representatives. This was a lacuna in their thinking.

In actuality, all these reforms came about only because there was a people's movement coming up to press for them. It is true that a separate force of Dalits could not have emerged at that time. But they wanted the right to decide for themselves what they wanted and what they did not want. The forces that were in the arena then were not capable (of deciding what the Dalits wanted) and their approach was one of pitying the Dalits. So, because Dr. Ambedkar, who himself was born in the Dalit class, thus presented his studied view of the whole issue before the government, the Dalits accepted him as their only leader; and an independent movement of the Dalits also arose as a need of the times. After this, during the period 1919–20, Babasaheb with help from Shahu Maharaj took part in Dalit conventions at Kolhapur and Nagpur, and so the foundation for a future independent Dalit movement was laid.

[R.B.] More was not aware of all these aspects during the early part of his political life. Not just he, but most ordinary Dalits had not really become aware of the actuality, as they should have been. More humbly admits this in his booklet entitled *Two Historic Conferences at Mahad*.

अखिलभारतीय बहिष्कृत-समाज-परिषद्.

(नागपूर, ता. ३० मे १९२०).

अध्यक्ष—श्रीमन्महाराज शाहू छत्रपति सरकार करवीर यांचें भाषण.

माझी योग्यता नसतां व माझे अनुमतीची जरूरी न ठेवतां मोठ्या बंधुप्रेमानें व सच्चेनें आपण मला आपला समजून आजच्या कॉनफरन्सचा अध्यक्ष नेमिलें, याजवद्दल मला मोठा अभिमान वाटतो.

कांहीं वर्षांपूर्वी माझ्या खोट्या समजुतीनें मी आपणाकडे बंधुप्रेमानें पाहत नव्हतों. आतां माझी चूक मला समजून आली आहे, व यापुढें तुमचेवर माझें बंधूसारखें प्रेम राहील अशी मला खात्री वाटते, हें उघडपणें सांगण्यास मला मोठा अभिमान वाटतो. वास्तविक पाहतां आजच्यासारख्या बहुमानास मी विद्येनें योग्य नसतां आपण मला अध्यक्षाचा मान दिला याबद्दल मी आपला फार आभारी आहे.

आपलें काय साधण्यासाठां दुसऱ्यास पाहिजे तितकी मांठवण यावयाची, त्यांची मनधरणी करावयाची, मी तुमच्या उद्धारासाठीं प्रयत्न करतों असें खोटेंच सांगावयाचें, वगैरे प्रकारांनीं अज्ञ लोकांस फसवून त्यांच्यावर आपली छाप बसवावयाची असे कांहीं स्वार्थसाधू लोक आहेत. अशा लोकांसारखें वागून आपणाला तोंडवश पाडून माझा स्वार्थ साधण्याची दुर्बुद्धि ईश्वरानें मला देऊं नये, अशी माझी त्याजवळ प्रार्थना आहे.

आज आपण येथें सर्व हिंदुस्थानांतील अस्पृश्य वर्गांपैकीं पुढारी मंडळी जमलेले आहां. अस्पृश्य हा शब्द कोणाही माणसाला लावणें हें फार निंद्य आहे. सर्व या शब्दाचा तुमच्या संबंधानें उपयोग करितात म्हणून मी त्याचा उपयोग केला आहे. तुम्ही अस्पृश्य नाहीं. तुम्हांस अस्पृश्य मानणाऱ्या पुष्कळ लोकांपेक्षां जास्त बुद्धिमान, जास्त पराक्रमी, जास्त सुविचारी, जास्त स्वार्थत्यागी, असे तुम्ही हिंदी राष्ट्राचे घटकावयव आहांत. मी तुम्हाला अस्पृश्य समजत नाहीं. आपण निदान बरोबरीचीं भावंडें आहोंत, आमचे हक्क समसमान तरी खास आहेतच, अशी भावना धरून आपणास पुढील कामास लागलें पाहिजे. या सत्कार्यांत जे उपद्व्याप करितात त्यांची लबाडी ओळखण्या इतकी समज हल्लीं जनतेस खास आलेली आहे.

मला आज सर्वांत मागासलेले देशबंधूंनीं या कॉनफरन्सचा अध्यक्ष होण्यास बोलाविलें आहे. वास्तविक पहातां मी कोणाचा पुढारी नाहीं; व पुढारी होऊंही इच्छित नाहीं मला पुढारी समजून माझ्या मागें कोणी येऊं लागल्यास त्यास आपण माझ्यामागें येऊं नका असें नम्रतापूर्वक सांगतों, व होईल तितका या बाबतींत प्रतिबंध करितों. हा प्रतिबंध मी अगदीं प्रथमपासूनच म्हणजे घराच्या बाहेर पडण्यापूर्वी माजघरांतच करितों; कारण तशी

Speech by Shahu Maharaj (1920); first page.
Courtesy of Anupama Rao, from the collection of the late Vasant Moon.

Shahu Maharaj Initiates Dr. Babasaheb into the Movement

Even though Dr. Babasaheb Ambedkar had returned to India leaving his education incomplete, his fame had spread all over Maharashtra. At the time, he was the only person among the Dalits who had reached such a high level of education! Besides, his study of the Dalit question also was profound. This was not merely as a scholar, but a social need of the time and a responsibility that history had placed on his shoulders. His reputation had reached the ears of Shahu Maharaj, who thus wanted to meet Dr. Babasaheb Ambedkar, and to show him how, in his princely state, untouchables and other Non-Brahmins had been given the right to education and to jobs, and how they had made progress. Also, Shahu wanted to discuss with him (Ambedkar) how his education could be used for the benefit of Indian society. But this did not happen until the year 1920.

After he met the Southborough Committee in 1919, Dr. Ambedkar began to feel the need to build a separate organization of Dalits, so that they could raise their voices. Associations like the Depressed Classes Mission were working for the interests of Dalits, and they were, thus, being organized in this context, but with a loss of identity. Therefore, Mr. Vitthal Ramji Shinde, on behalf of the DC Mission, had asked for representation of Dalits not in accordance with their population, but in a few token numbers only. It was not possible to base an independent organization of Dalits on such reformist activities. And Babasaheb was to return to London to complete his unfinished studies. But he wished to at least start a newspaper immediately. To this end, some Dalit leaders met Shahu Maharaj on Dr. Ambedkar's behalf and asked him for help in starting a newspaper. The Maharaj immediately wrote a cheque for two thousand five hundred rupees in the name of *Mooknayak*—Leader of the Mute—the name which had been designated for the newspaper. The first issue came out on 31 January 1920. Babasaheb had set up an office at 14 Hararwalla Building, Dr. Batliwalla Road, Poybawadi, Parel, Bombay, for this monthly magazine.

After starting this magazine Shahu Maharaj organized a conference of Dalits at Kagal in the Kolhapur state on 21 and 22 March 1920. In this conference Shahu Maharaj stated, 'Outcaste people of my state, I heartily congratulate you for having sought out your own leader. I am certain that Dr. Ambedkar will not rest until you have been liberated. Not only this, the day will come when he will be a leader of all of India. This is what my divine inner voice tells me.' In his speech Dr. Ambedkar said,

As soon as Shahu Maharaj ascended the throne of the Kolhapur state in 1894, he started schools, colleges and boarding houses for the *bahujan* (the term roughly means 'majority of the people', and has been used by the Non-Brahmin castes to refer to themselves) community who had been deprived of education. In these institutions opportunities were opened up for all: Marathas, Jains,

Lingayats, Shimpis, backward castes, Muslims and Dalits. Furthermore, these people, who had earlier been employed only as soldiers and peons, spear-bearers, cleaners and sweepers, were taken on in higher posts according to their education. In India such an experiment has not been carried out by the British, nor did any of the princes undertake such a thing in their states.

He ended his speech saying, 'So is Shahu Maharaj a true descendant of Shivaji Maharaj, and we are proud of him.' After the conference Shahu Maharaj himself, together with the *sardars* and title-bearers, dined together with the untouchable activists. In this way Shahu Maharaj initiated Babasaheb into social activism. Later, Shahu Maharaj became such a close friend of Babasaheb that he would visit him, like any commoner, in Parel, Poybawadi or in the BIT *chawls*. Since he knew that Babasaheb was about to return to London for further education, Shahu Maharaj organized the first All-India Outcaste Community Conference on 30–31 May and 1 June 1920. Chhatrapati Shahu Maharaj presided over the conference. Representatives from all over India attended the conference. In all 14 resolutions were passed. Through all these Resolutions the future direction of Dr. Babasaheb Ambedkar's movement was chalked out with the help of Chhatrapati Shahu Maharaj. After this, on 5 July 1920, Dr. Ambedkar embarked on his voyage to London for higher studies at his own cost, on the ship *City of Exeter*.

While he was pursuing his studies there, on 6 May 1922, Chhatrapati Shahu Maharaj passed away. As soon as he heard the news, Dr. Ambedkar dispatched a telegram to Rajaram Maharaj from London. In it he wrote,

> I was jolted by the death of Shahu Maharaj, his passing has divested me of a special friend. The untouchable class has lost a great benefactor; it has lost the greatest supporter of its interests. His death has caused me great sorrow, I do not know how to console you and the Maharani in this great grief that has come upon you. I share in this great grief that has come to you.

From the time he first met Babasaheb in 1917, having been [away] in Pune for his studies between 1917 and 1920, and until he returned to Bombay, More had no idea at all of these developments in Ambedkar's movement.

Founding of the Bahishkrit Hitakarini Sabha and the Colaba District Bahishkrit Parishad at Mahad

On 3 April 1923, Babasaheb Ambedkar returned to India as a barrister, having completed his university education. Without wasting any time in starting his practice, he applied for a license in June 1923 and received it on 5 July 1923. After this, with the help of his former teacher at Elphinstone school, the workers' organizer and dedicated member of the Servants of India Society, Narayan Malhar Joshi, he rented a room on the first floor of the Damodar Hall building in Parel, and set up an office there. This was where he started his legal practice. It was from this office that, with the help of Kamlakant Chitre, he sent his essay *The Problem of the Rupee* to London University [i.e. the London School of Economics], and from here that he turned his attention to starting a movement for the liberation of Dalits.

The movement for the liberation of Dalits is actually a movement for the liberation of the whole of Indian society. Realizing that it would not be enough for only Dalits to launch such a movement, he sought the involvement of non-Dalits as well, and on 9 March 1924 he called a meeting in which both Dalits and non-Dalits took part. In this meeting he announced the formation of the *Bahishkrit Hitakarini Sabha*, or 'Association for the Welfare of Outcastes'. Later, after discussions and consultations, on 20 July 1924 he publicly pronounced the principles and objectives of this association.

The president of this association was Dr. Sir Chimanlal Harilal Setalvad; Mayor Nissim Rustumji Jeenwalla, G.K. Nariman, Dr. R.P. Paranjpe, Dr. V.P. Chavan, and Bal Gangadhar Kher were vice-presidents; Dr. Ambedkar himself was chairman of the Executive Council, the secretary Sitaram Namdeo Shivtarkar and treasurer Nivrutti Jadhav. Among the members were several Dalits such as Samant Nanaji Marwadi, Zinabhai Moolji Rathod, Mahadev Ambaji Kamble, Sambhaji Tukaram Gaikwad and others. Among the trustees also there were Dalits and non-Dalits. The motto of the association was: 'Study, Organize and Struggle'. Babasaheb's office on the first floor of the Damodar Hall was the office of the association. Narayan Malhar Joshi and the Social Service League run by the Servants of India Society of which he was a member, and others like Anant Vinayak Chitre and Bapusaheb Sahasrabuddhe were all supporters of the cause espoused by Babasaheb.

Before Dr. Babasaheb Ambedkar established the above-mentioned 'Bahishkrit Hitakarini Sabha', Sitaram Keshav Bole had on 4 August 1923 moved a resolution in the Bombay Legislative Council that demanded the opening up of public wells, lakes, watering-places, courts, offices, and clinics to the untouchables. After a wide-ranging discussion, the resolution was passed and orders for its implementation were publicly announced. At the time More was a student in Mahad. When he read these orders More was very happy and he was completely preoccupied by the thought of how they could be implemented in Mahad. He remembered Dr. Babasaheb Ambedkar, and became obsessed with the idea of bringing him to Mahad to open up the Chavdar reservoir. At the time the issue of the Chavdar reservoir in Mahad had not presented itself to Dr. Babasaheb Ambedkar, nor was Anantrao Chitre aware that there was a reservoir worth staging a *satyagraha* for in Mahad. But this was not the case with More. From the time that More had come to study in Mahad in 1914–15, he thought about solving the problem of water faced by untouchable visitors to Mahad, and with this objective he started a restaurant there. He organized the untouchable people of the entire Mahad division around this restaurant.

Taking advantage of this, he built up Mahad as a place suitable for a *satyagraha*. And because More had so much confidence in this, just as the 'Bahishkrit Hitakarini Sabha' was being formed, in May 1924, without asking Babasaheb or the 'Bahishkrit Hitakarini Sabha', More organized a meeting in the Maharwada in Mahad. To this meeting he called Babu More, head of the Mahar caste *panch* of the villages around Mahad; Raya More, Krishnabuva Kinjalolikar, Jamadar Chapadekar, Ramji Asagikar, Tukaram Wargharkar, and Ramji Shirgavkar. He also called owners of shops selling leather *chappals*; persons of the Chambhar caste from the Deccan like Maruti Agavane of Satara, who used to set up shop in Mahad during the eight months of the hot season. He explained to those present what Bole's resolution meant. He then proposed that Dr. Babasaheb Ambedkar, who had reached the acme of education, should be invited to Mahad, and a huge gathering held to honour him and also to solve the water problem.

The meeting was completely convinced by More's proposal. The people assured him that they would raise the money needed to organize this convention from all the surrounding villages. But the responsibility of persuading Babasaheb to come was left to More himself. More accepted the responsibility and went to Bombay. At first, he thought that, since he was acquainted with Babasaheb Ambedkar, he should go directly to meet him. At the time More was barely twenty-one or twenty-two years old. So his reputable friends in Bombay advised him that, if he went alone to meet Babasaheb he would not make much of an impression. Instead, he should first meet the elderly social reformer Sambhaji Tukaram Gaikwad and inform him about the decision taken in the meeting at Mahad. Since Gaikwad was also from Colaba district, he was at once taken by the idea. Then More, along with Gaikwad, went to meet Babasaheb and he listened to what the young man had to say and told him that he would let him know about the decision on the Mahad meeting.

On that occasion Anantrao aka Bhai Chitre was with Babasaheb. Chitre too had come from the area near Poladpur and Mahad. He liked More's idea of holding a conference very much. Then Chitre took More aside and talked to him to assess whether or not this convention could be made a success. When More told him that three rupees would be collected from every village in the Mahad precinct, making Rs. 120/- in all, he was happy and he told More that he would himself help out with funds. Chitre recognized More to be an excellent organizer. He promised to give him his cooperation.

But More did not rest with this. In order to demonstrate what he could do and how he could make the convention a success, he met the manager of the Sahakari Manoranjan Theatre Company and secured a charitable performance of the play *Sant Tukaram*.[12] The play was performed for the Mahad convention as early as

[12] The Damodar Hall, where this performance was held, was the headquarters of the Social

1924 in the Damodar Hall in Bombay. Babasaheb, Chitre and other estimable persons were present for the performance. During the intermission More made a speech and explained the importance of the convention. The show did not make much profit, but Babasaheb too was convinced that More was a born activist who would not rest till he reached his goal. But Babasaheb did not give him a date for the convention.

In the days that followed, More would come to Bombay during every summer and Diwali vacation to press Babasaheb about the convention. In the end Babasaheb was convinced in his mind about the demand to hold a convention in Mahad. But since More was just a youth and because Babasaheb had no experience of whether the Dalit people would be able independently to organize such a convention, he asked Chitre to first make a survey of the situation in Mahad and of the issues faced by the Dalits, before he made his decision.

Chitre made plans for his visit according to Babasaheb's instructions. More went back to Mahad the very next day and informed all the local activists that Anantrao Chitre was coming to make a preliminary assessment on Babasaheb's behalf. All the activists set to work to prepare for the meeting with Chitre. The meeting finally took place at the end of 1925, in the Maharwada in Mahad. All the Dalit activists from the Mahad precinct were present at the meeting. Also most of their fellow villagers had come along in large numbers. The main matter placed before this meeting was that of holding a convention in Mahad under Dr. Babasaheb Ambedkar's chairmanship. But because of some unavoidable difficulties, Anantrao Chitre was unable to attend. But on Babasaheb's advice he had sent another of his trusted colleagues, Kamlakant Chitre, who then chaired the meeting.

Other esteemed persons such as Subhedar Vishram G. Sawadkar of Veer village in the Mahad *tehsil* were also present at the meeting. All the activists present gave an assurance that they would bring Dalits from all the villages of Colaba district and also collect funds from them. Subhedar Sawadkar himself announced in the meeting that he would ensure that funds did not fall short, that he would make the necessary arrangements himself. While speaking about the Bole resolution, Chitre informed the audience that another of Babasaheb's devotees, Surendranath Govind Tipnis, was chairman of the Mahad Municipal Council, and that he had already in 1924 chaired a meeting in which he had ensured that a resolution for the implementation of the Bole declaration was passed. Kamlakant Chitre then informed Babasaheb about all this: the legal provisions, the organizational capacity for collecting people for the convention, and the financial support given by the local people.

Service League, founded in 1911 by trade union leader Narayan Malhar Joshi (1879–1955). Holding charitable performances was a usual activity at this venue.

Establishment of the Mahar Samaj Seva Sangh

Even as preparations for the Mahad Depressed Classes Convention were being made in the Konkan, the senior social worker from the Konkan, Dadasaheb aka Sambhaji Tukaram Gaikwad took the lead in the establishment of an association with the long name, *Bahishkrit Aikya-Samvardhak Mahar Samaj Seva Sangh*—or 'Mahar Community Social Service Association for Promoting Unity among the Outcastes'—in Bombay at the Malabar Hill residence of the leading activist of the Mahad Satyagraha Association, Keshavrao Govind Adrekar. The aim of the association—which was meant to bring together young men of the community who would selflessly engage in social work—was to awaken those young men of the Mahar community who were employed in the Bombay–Thane region about the planned convention, to inform them about the movement to eradicate untouchability and other socio-political movements, to work against old customs, traditions and superstitions, to end vices like drinking alcohol, to publish literature, and to start libraries and schools in order to spread a love of learning. Later, in October, this over-lengthy name was changed to *Mahar Samaj Seva Sangh*, or 'Association for Service to the Mahar Community'.

Even though this name was apparently caste-based, referring to the Mahar caste, the association's basic objective was to bring about unity among the depressed classes and to work for equality. So that no one should accuse the association of casteism, the secretary of the association wrote an explanation of the seemingly casteist name of the association in his review of its work over five years from its foundation up to 11 October 1931: 'This association of the (Mahar) caste has been formed not for the preservation of caste, but to make the caste egalitarian. It will not be improper to make this clarification here.' This reveals how conscious social activists of that time were, and how clear they were about their objectives. The first president of this association was Dadasaheb Gaikwad's son Bhikaji Sambhaji Gaikwad, the general secretary Ramchandra Babaji More, and the treasurer Keshavrao Govind Adrekar. The association's main workers were Changdeo Narayan Mohite, Shankar Lakshman Wadawalkar, Pandurang Mahadev Salvi, Tanaji Mahadev Gudekar. The president of the Mahar Samaj Seva Sangh, Bhikaji Sambhaji Gaikwad, the untouchable leader, Bhanudas Kamble, and Chambhar caste leader P.N. Rajbhoj were so badly injured in the Mahad *satyagraha* that they had to be taken to hospital.

Branches of the association were established in various parts of Bombay like Naigaon–Dadar, Delisle Road, Agripada, Bhaucha Dhakka, St. George Hospital and Chandanwadi–Marine Lines, and office-bearers were also selected. The association also set up ten to twelve day schools for untouchable boys and girls, and three or four night schools for those who were employed.

The above-named activists of the Mahar Samaj Seva Sangh had a large role to play in organizing a plethora of meetings in preparation for the Mahad convention to be held in March—in Ratnagiri, Dabhol, Khed, Dapoli, Mahad, Mangaon, Rohe, Pen and other places—and making people aware of the planned *satyagraha*. Several of these workers took leave from work to spread the word. Because of their work, the first Colaba District Depressed Class Conference was successfully held on 19 and 20 March 1927. Several activists, including More, were holding meetings in villages all over the Konkan and they also mounted a strong publicity campaign in Bombay. It was because of this that the convention really became successful. But this has not been adequately noted by anyone, with the exception of Com. R.B. More and other activists of the Konkan. Many have given the credit of ensuring the success of the convention to the Bahishkrit Hitakarini Sabha and to non-Dalit, caste Hindu social reformers. But the actual facts were different. The Mahar Samaj Seva Sangh not only spread awareness among the untouchables, but it organized several lecture series in Bombay and invited several non-Dalit speakers to spread social consciousness on topics like the national question, the workers' movement, the problems of women, etc.

Implementation of the Bole Resolution in Dasgaon before the Mahad *Satyagraha*

The 1923 Bole resolution which was the stimulus for the Mahad *satyagraha* was first publicly implemented in the villages of Dasgaon and Goregaon near Mahad. This resolution of the year 1923 was welcomed by progressive-thinking non-Dalits as much as it was by the untouchables. Goregaon is a village with a marketplace in the Mangaon *tehsil* of Colaba district. The famous workers' leader N.M. Joshi came from there. Many of the Kayastha Prabhus and Brahmins of this village had inherited the legacy of N.M. Joshi's progressive thinking. So these people brought together the Mahars and Chambhars of the village in 1926, explained the Bole resolution to them, and called on them to make use of the public reservoir and wells in the village.

Since this was a village with a market, education had spread to some extent among the Dalits. They discussed the water issue among themselves, and, under the leadership of the local Chambhar politician Ramchandra Chandorkar, they courageously decided to drink from the reservoir and wells. Accordingly, Ramchandra Chandorkar jumped into the reservoir; upon which the other villagers were enraged and, when the news spread to the Marathas and other non-Dalits, they collectively attacked the Mahars and Chambhars, damaged their property and beat them up. Then news of this incident reached the police. The police merely arrived, looked on and left. Then the Mahars and the Chambhar leader Chandorkar informed the Mahar Samaj Seva Sangh in Bombay. The association held protest meetings in Bombay and collected funds to help the victims in Goregaon. More himself visited Goregaon to distribute these collected funds and to make an on-the-spot survey of the incident. He had earlier become acquainted with Ramchandra Chandorkar in Bombay. He heard all about the attack from Chandorkar. Then he held a meeting of the Dalits and distributed the money he had brought with him. More did not confine the issue to Goregaon village, but decided in his mind to implement the Bole resolution wherever possible in Colaba district. He took Chandorkar along with him to his own village Dasgaon and decided to implement the resolution there.

In Dasgaon there is a large public reservoir and a public well named the Crawford well. More, on behalf of the Mahar Samaj Seva Sangh, decided that the untouchables of Dasgaon would drink the water of this reservoir and well to put the Bole resolution into practice. Accordingly, he called a public meeting on the ground in front of the Dasgaon *dharamshala* on 4 December 1926. Pamphlets publicly announcing this programme were also distributed. The chairman of the meeting was a progressive gentleman by the name of Adarkar. About two to three hundred persons from the villages of Veer, Goregaon, Vahur, Dasgaon and Sape and others attended the meeting. Because the police had come to know about the meeting, the Mamledar and the police constable of Mahad were also present. More informed the meeting about the Bole resolution. Then, with him in the lead, all the Dalits drank the water of the lake and the Crawford well. Not a single caste Hindu of the village raised any objection to this. More's friend Ramji Babaji Potdar, from the Sonar caste, who worked as a teacher in the village school and held progressive views, played an active part in this programme. Because he drank water from the well along with the Dalits, the non-untouchable backward castes of the village boycotted him for three months. The barber refused to shave him or cut his hair. Later, however, the boycott was lifted.

This was a publicly announced action in the real sense that took place before the Chavdar lake *satyagraha* in Mahad. The people of this region collectively resisted all prohibitions and customs to drink the water, and thus, the 1923 Bole resolution was implemented in Maharashtra for the first time. The impact of this event was felt all over the Colaba and Ratnagiri districts; the people were infused with new energy and began preparations for the Colaba District Depressed Class Conference of 19–20 March 1927 with vigour. It was because of this action that the Dalits of the Konkan were filled with confidence and awakened to consciousness.

After this incident, Babasaheb felt that a convention in Mahad would be successful. Despite all their efforts over two or three years, the activists had not been able to get him to give them a date. But after this event and seeing the energetic preparations that were going on in Mahad, Bhai Anantrao Chitre in January 1927 wrote the following letter to Babasaheb's colleague in Bombay, Bapusaheb Sahasrabuddhe,[13] and let him know that it was everyone's wish that Dr. Ambedkar

---

[13] Gangadhar Nilkanth aka Bapusaheb Sahasrabuddhe was a long-time Brahmin associate of

should agree to preside over this convention. Later, Dr. Babasaheb informed Sahasrabuddhe of his willingness to attend the convention. The two letters related to this are given below:

Mahad, January 1927

Dear Bapusaheb,

The efforts to organize a conference of the untouchables at Mahad are in full swing. Enthusiastic untouchable youths like Subhedar Sawadkar and Ramchandra More are roaming from village to village awakening the people. It is everybody's wish that Dr. Ambedkar should agree to preside over the conference. He should be requested on our behalf; I am sure he will not disregard the request of our touchable and untouchable friends.

Anantrao Chitre

Bombay, February 1927

Dear Anantrao,

After great effort we have secured a promise to preside over the Mahad meeting from Babasaheb....

G.N. Sahasrabuddhe

Once Babasaheb's agreement for the convention had been attained, the activists were filled with enthusiasm. It was the wish of all the activists, including More, that some of the caste Hindu leaders from the city should attend the convention along with Babasaheb. On Babasaheb's bidding, More visited the then famous social reformer, the advocate Trivedi, at his residence in Bombay and requested him to come to the convention. But he avoided attending the conference on the excuse of other work. In the end, only two caste Hindu leaders promised to come and actually attended. One was Gangadhar Nilkanth aka Bapu Sahasrabuddhe, known to be a Brahmin follower of the social reformer Gopal Ganesh Agarkar, and a major supporter of the Social Service League and the Cooperative movement. The other was Anantrao Vinayakrao Chitre or Bhai Chitre. On the invitation card for the convention, only the names of Dr. Bhimrao Ramji Ambedkar as the chairman and those of Bhai Chitre and Bapusaheb Sahasrabuddhe as speakers were printed. This was the first and last printed pamphlet issued to publicize the convention. The pamphlet was sent to all newspapers, but not a single one showed the goodwill to publish it.

The responsibility of bringing Babasaheb and other leaders to Mahad for the conference rested with More. All of them set out from Bombay in a private car and reached the Dak Bungalow at Mahad at 12 noon. The following leaders had

---

Dr. Ambedkar. He was present at the Mahad *satyagraha* and in fact moved the resolution to burn copies of the *Manusmriti*.

come with Babasaheb from Bombay: Sitaram Namdeo Shivtarkar, Bapusaheb Sahasrabuddhe, Bhai Chitre, Balaram Ramji Ambedkar, Ganpat Mahadev Jadhav aka Madkebuva, Wakhrikar Gaikwad, Devji Dagduji Dolas, Sitaram Kalu Hate and Dattatray Mahadev Chitre. From Pune there were Shantaram Tipnis, Pandurang Nathuji Rajbhoj and others. Bhaurao Gaikwad from Nashik and others were not among them. The conference was mainly attended by people from the Konkan.

On that day Mahad town was festive with untouchable folk. Surbanana Tipnis from Mahad was also working for the success of the convention. On the 19th there was a steady stream of people; by the afternoon more than five thousand had reached Mahad. Excepting the people from Bombay, every person held a stick in his hand. In those days a person of the Mahar caste never left his home without such a stick in his hand. Especially when they set out from their village to another village, they had to carry a stick like this.[14]

Everyone knows that when an illiterate person has to sign a document, his or her thumb print is taken in place of a signature. But in the past, in villages in this region of Maharashtra, the signature mark depended on one's caste. For example a *kunbi* or cultivator used a plough sign, a porter used a palanquin, a *chambhar* or cobbler used an awl sign, and the *mahar*'s sign was a stick. So the huge crowd at the Mahad conference was a stick-wielding crowd. So, when Babasaheb came on stage in the auditorium of the Vireshwar Theatre the people, instead of clapping, raised their sticks to honour him. In his booklet on the Mahad conference More has described what a pleasing and thrilling sight it was to see more than five thousand sticks raised in the air at once.

More introduced the guests at the convention. After this, Babasaheb delivered a historic speech. In his speech he called on the people to throw off all traditional restrictions and live as human beings. He took due note of the social work that Gopalbuva Walangkar had carried out. Because of his speech, the people gained a new vision and their self-confidence was strengthened. Bhai Chitre, Bapu Sahasrabuddhe and the chairman of the local organizing committee (the 'welcome committee'), Sambhaji Tukaram Gaikwad, also addressed the audience at the convention. Several resolutions were adopted in this conference; among them was the important resolution to implement the Bole decision to open up public lakes, wells and *dharamshalas* to all citizens. Accordingly, on the next day Bhai Chitre called on all representatives to go and drink the water of the Chavdar lake in order to implement this resolution. And thousands of people, led by Babasaheb, took out a procession to the Chavdar lake and, breaking the centuries-old religious taboo, drank the water of the Chavdar lake.

This action had strong repercussions among the traditional caste Hindus of

---

[14] Mahars were village servants, guards of the village boundary, and delivered messages and announcements of important events likes births and deaths across villages. They traditionally carried a stick.

Mahad, and they spread the rumour that the Dalit people were going to enter the Vireshwar Temple and pollute it. So the caste Hindus of the town came out on the streets armed with sticks and badly beat up many of the representatives who had come for the convention. The president of the Mahar Samaj Seva Sangh, Bhikaji Sambhaji Gaikwad, the untouchable leader, Bhanudas Kamble, and Chambhar caste leader P.N. Rajbhoj were so badly injured that they had to be taken to hospital. The shops and houses of Chambhars and other Dalits were burnt down, and there was a lot of breakage of property. Not just the men but young and old women, and children were also beaten up. On the next day all the newspapers reported this incident prominently and this had reverberations all over the world. The struggle of the untouchables for their own independent liberation really started from Mahad. The fame of this convention and Babasaheb's name spread far and wide. And it was from this convention that More, as main organizer of the convention, emerged as a leader.

The Newspaper 'Bahishkrit Bharat' and More's Participation in Starting It

We have given an account above of how the Mahad *Satyagraha* Conference of 19 and 20 March 1927 and the Chavdar lake *satyagraha* were a great success. But a great visionary like Dr. Babasaheb Ambedkar had realized how historic an event it was and how it had the capacity to give a new direction to the social system. He had also recognized More's honesty, his growing natural gifts as an activist, and his organizational skill, as well as the modesty that went with it. Also understanding More's love of learning, his excellent knowledge of language and his writing skills, Babasaheb had taken him into his home to stay for six months before the conference, in 1926. More took Babasaheb's help in preparing for the conference. He would leave Bombay only with Babasaheb's permission to go to Colaba district for publicity. Babasaheb also realized that if a convention was to be held, and a movement to be launched, a newspaper was a necessity.

The journal *Mooknayak* started with the help of Shahu Maharaj had long since folded up. Now, when a convention was to be held in Mahad, there was a need for a newspaper to make propaganda for it—and the name *Mooknayak* would not do now. The Dalit people were now no longer mute as they had been in 1920. The nation *Bharat* in which they now lived was forbidden to them. This had to be brought home to everybody—it was with this thought firm in his mind that Ambedkar decided in 1926 itself on 'Bahishkrit Bharat' as the name for his newspaper. So it was decided to seek fresh permission for 'Bahishkrit Bharat'. Knowing that this would not happen immediately, that the procedure would take three to four months, he set to work to obtain permission. He started this work through More and the permission was granted before the date of the conference.

Front page of *Bahishkrit Bharat*, 3 April 1927.
Courtesy of Prakash Vishwasrao, *Dr. Babasahab Ambedkar*.

When Babasaheb returned to Bombay after the Chavdar lake *satyagraha* of 19 and 20 March, he brought More along with him. The first issue of the fortnightly magazine *Bahishkrit Bharat* was to be published on 3 April 1927. It was to carry Dr. Babasaheb Ambedkar's position on the historic *satyagraha* at Mahad, the summary account of the conference written by More himself, and some documents of the historic *satyagraha*. Also, other columns had to be written. The whole task, and also the printing, was to be completed within eight to ten days. So Babasaheb told More to stay in the Rahim Building, which was to be the journal's office until the first issue came out. And Babasaheb also stayed there with More on the last four to five days. Thus, his reliance on More was complete. And so did Babasaheb publish the first issue of *Bahishkrit Bharat* only with More's assistance.

After this first issue, More and Babasaheb began to live and work together constantly. Even when Babasaheb was not present, More stayed in the *Bahishkrit Bharat* office twenty-four hours a day and after doing all kinds of jobs including writing, reading proofs, overseeing the printing, etc., he would go and have his meals at Baba's residence. But when the date of publication approached, Babasaheb too would not go home. He too would sit with More and write all night. More would join two benches together and spread a mat over them. Babasaheb would sleep there while More spent several consecutive nights writing. In the evening both would eat the tiffin sent over from Babasaheb's house. In the morning both would take a bath at the tap, then go downstairs to the Irani restaurant to have bread and butter. After this Babasaheb would go to the High Court by tram, while More would return to the office to work. Thus, More enjoyed a close proximity to Babasaheb.

In those days, the two young activists, Dr. Babasaheb Ambedkar's biographer Changdeo B. Khairmode and Shankar Wadawalkar also stayed in the *Bahishkrit Bharat* office along with More. In September 1927, while these activists were chatting with More, Khairmode came up with the suggestion that, as Dr. Ambedkar's fame had spread far and wide after the first Mahad conference, and as it was likely to spread even further in future, he should be given an honorific title, just as Tilak was called 'Lokmanya' and Gandhi was called 'Mahatma'. In the conversation several others also expressed their opinion on this. Khairmode suggested that Ambedkar be called 'Babasaheb' and Ramabai be called 'Aaisaheb'. On this, Ramchandra Babaji More said that both the titles were appropriate and made a long speech about it. After this everyone agreed to both these titles. So that the titles would become popular, Khairmode, Wadawalkar and More began to use them whenever they spoke in meetings. Ambedkar's biographer C.B. Khairmode has stated clearly in Volume 2 of his biography that More and Wadawalkar had a large share in popularizing these titles.

The Amaravati Temple *Satyagraha* and the Death of Balaram Ambedkar

Even as preparations for the second Mahad *satyagraha* were going on, the movement for the Amaravati Temple entry in the Berar Province also began. Among the movements for social equality and in opposition to untouchability of the beginning of the twentieth century, the temple entry movement had an important place. Progressive persons among the caste Hindus took the lead in this movement. They would launch agitations and take the untouchables along with them. T.K. Madhavan, the young, educated journalist from the Ezhava caste in Kerala, had been taking the lead in this movement since 1918. He was a member of the state council in the princely state of Travancore in South India. He had even moved a Bill that untouchability should be abolished by law. A *satyagraha* was held in Vaikom in the Travancore state on 30 March 1924 to open up the Sri Mahadeva Temple there. In this the senior South Indian social reformer, Ramasamy Naicker (Periyar), T.K. Madhavan, Keshav Menon, Madhavan Nayar, Velappan Nayar and others took the lead. Later, a *satyagraha* took place at the famous Guruvayur Temple in the South, in which the senior Communist leader A.K. Gopalan also took part.

It was during this period, in 1925, before the Mahad *satyagraha*, that Madhavrao Govind Meshram demanded that the ancient shrine of Ambadevi in Amaravati be opened for Dalits. He wrote applications and made pleas, but the temple management ignored him. After this Dadasaheb Patil, Dr. Punjabrao Deshmukh and others who were associated with the Satyashodhak movement took up the untouchables' demand and on 26 July 1927 a huge meeting was held in Amaravati. In this meeting it was announced that a *satyagraha* would be held for temple entry. On 13 and 14 November a conference was held with Dr. Babasaheb Ambedkar in the chair, to prepare for the *satyagraha*, and it was announced that if the question was not resolved by 15 February 1928, a *satyagraha* action would be taken. While the conference was in progress, a telegram arrived on 14 November 1927 informing Dr. Babasaheb Ambedkar that his elder brother Balaramdada had passed away. Even so, Babasaheb with great courage continued the work of the conference, taking only a ten-minute break. After this a condolence resolution was passed.

While Babasaheb was away in Amaravati for the conference, he had asked More to remain in Bombay to look after the work of the journal *Bahishkrit Bharat*. Since More was staying at Babasaheb's residence at the time, it was he who brought out a leaflet to inform social and political activists about the death, and he also made the arrangements for the funeral procession. More and others paid their respects at the cremation ground, and at last the funeral pyre was lit. At a sorrowful time like this, More did not allow Babasaheb's friends and relations to feel Babasaheb's absence. And in the next issue of *Bahishkrit Bharat* More, using the pen name 'Student', wrote an article honouring the memory of the late Balaramdada Ambedkar. This was how much More had become a part of Babasaheb's family by then.

Second *Satyagraha* Conference at Mahad —The Burning of the *Manusmriti*

The first 'Colaba District Outcastes' Conference' at Mahad and its struggle on the water question was different from the temple entry movement of South India. It was the first struggle of the untouchables in India related to a material issue and to the identity and self-esteem of the Dalits. Its impact was felt not only in Maharashtra, but all over the world.

The second Mahad conference aimed mainly to assert the right to the water of the Chavdar lake, and to establish the rights of humanity and of equality by its implementation. This conference took place on 25 December 1927. In the first conference, most of the people present were from Colaba, Ratnagiri, and Thane and Pune districts. The rest of the Dalit community in Maharashtra did not know much about this conference. However, the news of the second conference was spread all over Maharashtra by the fortnightly journal *Bahishkrit Bharat*. The responsibility of arranging for and organizing this conference once again lay on More's shoulders. Since it was not possible to reach Mahad by motor car, the following route was decided on: from Bhaucha Dhakka in Bombay to the port of Hareshwar and from Hareshwar to Dasgaon port, thence to Mahad.

At the first Mahad conference the untouchable people and their activists had been badly beaten up by the orthodox of the town. So More and others decided that they would go to the second conference prepared for a confrontation. Accordingly, they mobilized a squad that they called the *Ambedkar Seva Dal*—or Ambedkar Service League—comprising ward boys and coolies of St. George Hospital, and young labourers living in *chawls* in Parel, Byculla, Agripada and Naigaon in Bombay. They took the help of Dalit activists retired from the army to set up this squad. In doing this, they received tremendous cooperation from the various branches of the Mahar Samaj Seva Sangh. After the second Mahad Conference was over, More, with Dr. Babasaheb Ambedkar's permission, changed the name from Ambedkar Seva Dal to *Samata Sainik Dal*—League of Soldiers for Equality. In short, the founder of today's Samata Sainik Dal was More himself.[15]

On 24 December 1927, as Dr. Babasaheb Ambedkar reached Bhaucha Dhakka in Bombay to embark for Mahad by boat, this squad of volunteers saluted him in military fashion with the sound of bugles. Later, everybody went and sat in the boat. When Dadasaheb Sambhaji Tukaram Gaikwad informed Babasaheb that all this had been organized by More, Babasaheb made much of him. More especially inquired after all those travelling by boat via Bombay who had come from outside the Konkan. Among these, More noticed that Bhaurao aka Dadasaheb Gaikwad was different from the others, and he gave Babasaheb more details about him. In the evening the boat reached the port of Hareshwar. There, through the efforts of Pandurang Babaji Jadhav and Dharmabuva Ostekar, enthusiastic activists of the Mahar Samaj Seva Sangh, hundreds of Dalits from the region of Shrivardhan and Janjira gave Babasaheb a hearty welcome. In the morning they departed by another boat going to Bankot via Dasgaon. In the afternoon the boat touched the pier at the port of Dasgaon. Hundreds of volunteers wearing badges of the local organizing committee for the conference greeted Babasaheb at the harbour.

Even before Babasaheb reached Dasgaon, the Deputy Superintendent of Police together with his team was waiting at the Dasgaon harbour. He handed over to

---

[15] The Samata Sainik Dal was formed in 1927 to protect Dalits from physical attack and intimidation. It was a highly disciplined force. Members wore a uniform that recalled the Mahars' military past.

Samata Sainik Dal.
Courtesy of Anil Sawadkar.

Babasaheb a letter from the Colaba District Collector stating that the Chavdar lake *satyagraha* had been officially banned, and the D.S.P. requested Babasaheb to accompany him to Mahad in his car, to meet the Collector. Entrusting to More the responsibility of taking the *satyagrahis* in a procession from Dasgaon to Mahad, Babasaheb set off for Mahad with Sahasrabuddhe.

Although the first convention had asserted its rights by drinking the water of the Chavdar lake, some orthodox local people afflicted by Brahminism had 'purified' it using cows' urine, and claimed in court that the lake was not public but privately owned. So the court granted a temporary stay. Babasaheb and the other *satyagrahis* had come to Mahad prepared to defy the stay order, and to go to jail if necessary.

On returning from meeting the Collector, Babasaheb gave the speech that he had specially prepared for the convention. Saying that *'this convention has been assembled to make a ceremonial start to the new age of equality that has dawned in this land of Bharat'*, he compared it to the French Revolution of 1789. Then he passed a resolution asserting basic rights, and other motions. Among them was the important resolution to burn the *Manusmriti*, the Hindu religious text which upheld inequality and treated *shudras* and women with contempt. This resolution was moved by Babasaheb's colleague from the Brahmin caste, Gangadhar Nilkanth Sahasrabuddhe, and it was seconded by P.N. Rajbhoj and Thorat. The said resolution read as follows:

> With a view to the *Manusmriti*, which insults the *shudra* castes, hampers their progress, and, by destroying their self-confidence and strength, perpetuates their social, political and economic slavery, and comparing it with the principles laid down in the declaration of the birthright of the Hindus of whom the above castes are a part, this conference is of the firm opinion that the said religious book is not fit to be called such, and in order to express this opinion it is undertaking the burning of this book which is destructive of the people and shows contempt for humanity.

After moving this resolution, Babasaheb called on the representatives at the conference to come to the pyre that had been assembled in the conference marquee, and to burn this book which was a stain on the face of humanity. For the first time in Maharashtra, the *Manusmriti* was burnt in front of such a large gathering of people. This action was carried out on the evening of 25 December and, with it, the day's proceedings were concluded. The burning of the *Manusmriti* had wide repercussions among the public. Several newspapers and the supporters of orthodox views criticized Babasaheb, and he roundly answered this criticism in the pages of the fortnightly journal *Bahishkrit Bharat*.

After the proceedings of the conference were over for the day, Babasaheb gathered together all the main activists and discussed with them whether they should carry out the *satyagraha* and court arrest. Babasaheb said, 'If we carry out the *satyagraha* the government will send me to jail too, but I have come here in readiness to go to prison. Now we must consider the views of others who are present here and decide whether or not we are to carry out the *satyagraha*.' Hearing this, there was agitation in the crowd. Shivtarkar said, 'Doctor, if you go to jail the people will be left helpless.[16] There will be no other leader and the government and the orthodox caste Hindus will take advantage of this to crush us. So I think we should call off the *satyagraha*.' On which More at once declared, 'This *satyagraha* cannot be called off.'

Some of the teachers and government servants who had come for the conference gave various reasons to express their feeling that the *satyagraha* should not be held. And some suggested that the *satyagraha* should be conducted, but that Babasaheb should not take part. But the majority, in which farmers, agricultural labourers and workers numbered, were of the opinion that the *satyagraha* should go ahead. After midnight the contents of a pamphlet containing a pledge were worked out. In it was written, 'I am prepared to carry out the *satyagraha* and to go to jail, struggle, and die if need be.' By four in the morning three thousand persons had signed the pledge or given their thumb prints. After it was seen that almost everyone had shown readiness to go ahead, the collection of signatures was stopped. Babasaheb was awake all night. At seven in the morning he gave More a letter to the Collector.

---

[16] Literally, 'robbed of their salt'.—*Tr.*

In this he had requested the Collector to come to the meeting and put forward the government's view. The Collector told More that he would come to the meeting, and More conveyed this to Babasaheb.

The work of the conference resumed the next day at nine a.m. Babasaheb informed the people assembled about the talks he had had with the Collector the previous day regarding the ban order on the Chavdar lake *satyagraha* that caste Hindus of the town had obtained from the court, and the case they had filed in the Diwani court. Then Babasaheb himself moved the resolution to carry out the *satyagraha*. He also told the people what the legal consequences of the *satyagraha* would be, and asked the representatives at the conference to publicly state their opinions. Twelve persons spoke in favour of the resolution and eight spoke against. While this was going on, Keshavrao Jedhe and Dinkarrao Jawalkar, both leaders of the Non-Brahmin movement, entered the conference marquee. They both expressed their support on behalf of the Maratha community. These proceedings went on till five in the evening. Just as they were winding up, the District Collector Mr. Hood arrived at the entrance to the conference. Subhedar Radhoram Ghatge went to meet him, and, as Babasaheb had instructed, brought him on to the dais. Babasaheb greeted him by shaking hands with him. He asked the Collector to tell the people what his colleagues had to say. The District Collector spoke in Marathi, saying, 'The Government does not recognize distinctions between "touchable" and untouchable. We accept your right to draw water from public lakes. But the Hindu people have asserted a claim in court that the Chavdar lake is not public property but private. Until this matter is decided in court, you should not perform a *satyagraha*.' Most of the persons who made speeches after this expressed their opinions in favour of conducting the *satyagraha*, while only four spoke against.

Now the responsibility of taking the final decision fell to Babasaheb. He firstly congratulated the people for their courageous attitude and their readiness for sacrifice. He said,

We have begun this struggle for the sake of our fundamental rights and for equality. You are the vanguard soldiers of this fight. Our organizational strength is tremendous, and we should demonstrate this to our opponents.

Our opponents have made the false assertion in court that the Chavdar lake is not public but private. But the court has not yet upheld their claim. I have confidence that the court will decide in our favour. We have a greater capability of fighting for our rights than our opponents have. This has now been proved. When it has been proved that of two wrestlers who have entered the arena, one has a greater strength than the other, there is no need for one to strike the other. So let us not carry out the *satyagraha* today and let us conserve our strength and capacity. Not to perform the *satyagraha* today does not mean that we are giving up the struggle. We have to fight many struggles in the future.

This decision of Babasaheb was an appropriate one, given his practical assessment of the organizational strength of the Dalits at the time.

History has proved that decision to be extremely far-seeing and correct. In the end the orthodox lost their case in court and that reservoir has now become open for all Dalits. The conference had been hugely successful; about twenty-five to thirty thousand people were present, and it was because of this conference that the Dalits came to a new self-realization and they began to raise their voice against injustice. During this conference, Babasaheb called a separate meeting of the women and made them conscious of their rights. He also gave separate guidance to the Chambhar community of the village. After the conference Babasaheb had a little time to spare and he visited the historic Raigad fort with More and other activists before returning to Bombay.[17]

Establishment of the Samaj Samata Sangh, or Association for Equality in Society

While the preparations for the second Mahad conference were going on, Babasaheb, in consultation with Dalit and non-Dalit activists of the Bahishkrit Hitakarini Sabha established the *Samaj Samata Sangh*,[18] or Association for Equality in Society in Bombay on 4 September 1927. More too had an active role to play in this. It was decided that the objective of the Samaj Samata Sangh was: to establish equality mainly meant to assimilate Dalits into Indian society, to build an Indian society in the real sense, and to raise its united strength against exploitation. The independence that India aimed to gain should not be only for Hindus and Muslims, but also for Dalits, to establish equality in society so that independence would be given its (true) meaning.

To broaden the activities of the Samaj Samata Sangh and to give it publicity, Babasaheb started the periodical *Samata* ['Equality'] in 1928 with D.V. Naik as its editor. Mr. Palyeyashastri and B.V. aka Mama Warerkar held *mantra*-chanting programmes and *pujas* at several places where they strung a *janavi* around the necks of some Dalits (in defiance of the custom that the *janavi* or sacred thread was to be worn only by upper-caste males). In those days Mama Warerkar ran a weekly

---

[17] Ambedkar's visit to Raigad fort commemorated the Mahar military past. A popular cultural account notes that Rainak Mahar defended Fort Raigad against British attack in 1773, and refused to switch allegiance after his leader was defeated. (This account appears in the translation of R.B. More's autobiography on page 61.) The British also valorized Mahar bravery by inscribing the names of twenty-two Mahar soldiers on the 'victory pillar' at Koregaon after the Battle of Koregaon, which occurred on 1 January 1818.

[18] The members of the Samaj Samata Sangh included G.N. Sahasrabuddhe, R.D. Kavali, P.P. Tamhane, D.V. Naik, N.V. Khandke, G.R. Pradhan, B.V. Pradhan, R.N. Bhaindarkar, D.V. Pradhan and B.R. Pradhan. After *Mooknayak* and *Bahishkrit Bharat*, Ambedkar started the journal *Samata* as the mouthpiece of this organization.—*Tr.*

called *Duniya* [or 'World', in Hindi]. He made it a point to carry news of activities of this kind. Similarly, in the movement led by the Satyashodhak Samaj, it had been decided not to have marriage rituals performed by Brahmins, but by activists of their own movement. Thus, on the same lines, the Sangh spread the consciousness among Dalits that they could have their marriage rituals conducted by persons from the untouchable castes.

Babasaheb decided to take a prominent part in the public celebrations of the Ganesh festival and that the Samaj Samata Sangh would launch an agitation demanding that untouchables should be included both in the festivities and the organizing committee for the public celebrations.[19] Babasaheb initiated talks in this regard. But the festival committee informed him that untouchables could not take part. So, the Sangh held demonstrations in front of the spectator area after the Ganesh idol had been set up. More and Sambhaji Tukaram Gaikwad also took part in these demonstrations as part of the Mahar Samaj Seva Sangh. This spread consciousness among the people. By spreading consciousness of this kind through his movement, Babasaheb showed that his movement was not just a movement of Dalits, but of all Hindus and all Indians, and by involving the Dalits in activities of the national movement, he roused national consciousness in them and tried to break down the fences that had been built up among different castes.

The work of spreading the activities of the Samaj Samata Sangh by setting up branches all over Bombay was going on. Even though Tilak was one of the foremost leaders of the national movement, untouchables were allowed to enter his house only up to a certain point. He was a supporter of the Hindu faith and of the *chaturvarna* system. Even though Mahatma Gandhi did not practise untouchability, he supported the system of *chaturvarna*, and he would state this openly. But the capitalism brought by the British delivered a jolt to the practice of untouchability in Tilak's own home after his death. Both of Tilak's sons, Ramchandra and Shridhar, were special friends of Dr. Babasaheb Ambedkar. Whenever the brothers came to Bombay they would not return to Pune without meeting Dr. Ambedkar. Whenever Babasaheb went to Pune they would try and get him to visit their residence in the Gaikwad Wada.

Shridhar Pant was much attracted to the social movement. He often spoke to Babasaheb about his wish that a branch of the Samaj Samata Sangh should be started in Pune and that its office should be set up in his home. But the brothers then had a case against the 'Kesari' trust going on in court. So Babasaheb advised Shridhar Pant that he should take part in the agitational activities of the Sangh only after the case had been decided. He agreed to this. Shridhar Pant was of an

---

[19] Public celebrations with a public installation of the image of the deity had been initiated by Bal Gangadhar Tilak. For more detail on the *Ganeshotsav* and competing Maratha efforts to celebrate Shivaji Jayanti, as well as the effect of such public festivals in remaking the Non-Brahmin public sphere in Western India, see Rao, *The Caste Question*, Chapter 1.

open and frank disposition and was soft-hearted. On 25 May 1928, he committed suicide by throwing himself under the Poona Mail near Bhamburdi station. He had disclosed his intention to do so only in a letter written to Babasaheb in Bombay, in which he said that he had no alternative but to take this step.

Lokmanya Tilak had purposely avoided publishing an advertisement of the first issue of Babasaheb Ambedkar's *Mooknayak* even after the copy had been set up. Even so, Babasaheb used to send *Mooknayak* to him, but Tilak never acknowledged receiving the copies, nor did he show the courtesy of sending him his paper in return. However, his son tried to make up for this by allying himself with Babasaheb's movement.

In May 1928 More took the lead in organizing a convention at Dapoli (in the Konkan) to inform people about the *satyagraha* conference in Mahad. More than five thousand people of the Dalit community were present for this conference. In this conference Hindu supporters of social reform presented them with *janavas*. The famous playwright Mama Warerkar took part in this act of presenting Dalits with *janavas*. But Warerkar told More not to announce his name in public. (This was told to the present author by R.B. More when he was still alive.) When both of them were returning together from Dapoli, Warerkar told More that if his name had been announced, he would be harassed by all kinds of unnecessary things like boycotts. [R.B.] More told me that Warerkar had expressed these fears to him at the time. More had tried to hold a farmers' convention on this occasion, but he was not successful in this.

The capitalist social system brought by the British gave a big jolt to untouchability and helped in spreading progressive ideas, and from this emerged several social reformers in caste Hindu society, and even revolutionary leaders like Mahatma Jotirao Phule who found the changing material conditions suitable for fostering the struggle for social change. The flag of equality which Mahatma Jotirao Phule raised on his shoulders was later taken up by Babasaheb and he began the struggle to establish equality in India. The Samaj Samata Sangh had been established to forward this same objective.

In order to carry on the movement to break the custom of discrimination by caste, the Samaj Samata Sangh in those days held 'inter-dining' functions where members of different castes took meals together, and tried to promote mixed marriages. The (material) conditions were becoming favourable for such marriages. More took the lead in arranging the marriage of his sister-in-law Yamuna Hate with a caste Hindu activist from the Mahad *satyagraha*, Kamalakar Kashinath Tipnis, which set an example. The marriage took place in the Damodar Hall in Parel in Bombay. It was conducted in a style that was progressive for those days: that is, the Vedic rituals were performed, but the priest was not a Brahmin but Prabodhankar Thackeray. But it is distressing to note that Shankar Wadawalkar, More's friend and an early educated activist of Babasaheb's independent movement, who was staying in Babasaheb's house with More, opposed this marriage and brought some youths to the wedding ceremony to disrupt it. They threw balls of paper on to the stage. So Prabodhankar Thackeray showered rice over the couple and was escorted out of the hall by More.

The newspapers also took note of this wedding ceremony. A photograph of the wedding was printed in the Bombay newspaper *Lokmanya*. Even with what happened, the society was slowly being awakened (to the possibility of social change). Yamuna Hate and Kamalakar Tipnis later became Babasaheb's senior followers and special friends.

Anantrao Chitre arranged the marriage of his daughter Sarojini with D.G. Jadhav, an educated youth from the Dalit community. And from then on, such marriages started taking place. Later, Shankar Wadawalkar's own daughter was married to a boy from the Koli (*adivasi*) community. But it is true that most of those who called themselves progressive were not able to break out of the cocoon of caste around them. It must be noted, however, that Babasaheb and his activists had translated their ideas into deeds and taken the initiative in marrying outside their caste.

More's Work in the Farmers' Movement

The Mahad *satyagraha* movement was conducted in order to bring about self-respect, consciousness of identity among Dalits and social awareness among non-Dalits. And the direction in which Dr. Ambedkar's thoughts turned when he established the Samaj Samata Sangh was that of widening the scope of the independent Dalit movement to the whole of Indian society, and to this end to bring in progressive thinking youth, and to foster their innate capacities as a real force in the struggle for independence.

More too was thinking on these lines after the Mahad *satyagraha*. If the Dalits' demand for equality was to be fulfilled, then, since those with whom they wanted equality were also backward, the struggle against untouchability could not be independently carried on by untouchables alone, but it had to bring enlightenment to the non-Dalits in order to dispel their backwardness too. For this, the common problems of both the groups had to be taken up for action. More fixed on this position firmly in his mind. For this, one would have to build an organization of cultivators and agricultural labourers in their capacity as workers, and at the same time fight against the untouchability that had its roots in the feudal age, and against the British, who, while they bring capitalism, also perpetuate old and new economic relations, that is, against imperialism. In short, he adopted the objective of fighting simultaneously against imperialism, capitalism and feudalism. Then he had discussions with Bhai Chitre on this subject. Bhai Chitre was also at that time inclined in the same direction. He gave More his tacit approval.

More then told Chitre that from then on he would be working to organize peasants and agricultural labourers. An independent movement of Dalits could achieve the task of destroying untouchability up to a certain extent under capitalism. But until the Dalit as untouchable and as an exploited toiling class did not find liberation, the black mark of untouchability would never be erased in the true sense. For that to happen, the movement of untouchables must move ahead taking up the issues facing workers and peasants. Bhai Chitre also agreed with what he was saying and More began his work along this path.

In the end, who is the Dalit? He is neither a capitalist nor a landlord, he is a worker like all other workers. He is a cultivator, an agricultural labourer, a factory worker, a casual labourer. Today he is treated as untouchable. But his fellow workers are also farmers and farm labourers. The problems they face as a class cannot be solved unless they unite on class lines. So it is also a need for the Dalit movement to organize caste Hindus and untouchable farmers on class lines. That is why Babasaheb began to organize farmers' conventions as soon as the Mahad conference was over.

Babasaheb's position on the work of annihilating untouchability was precisely this: that the movement for the social liberation of the untouchables and the movement of workers and peasants against exploitation should go hand in hand. Following this, Babasaheb tried to organize a farmers' movement against the *khoti* system in the Konkan, taking along with him Anantrao Chitre, Shamrao Parulekar, Nanasaheb Tipnis, Narayan Nagu Patil (father of Prabhakar and Datta Patil of the Peasants and Workers Party), and also Sambhaji Tukaram Gaikwad, C.N. Mohite, R.B. More, Shivram Gopal Jadhav, Pandoba Salve, Tanaji Mahadev Gudekar, Keshav Govind Adrekar, Shivrambuva Musadkar and other Dalit activists.

On 13 April 1929 the second convention of the Ratnagiri district Bahishkrit Parishad was organized at Chiplun on the initiative of More and Parulekar. On the second day of the convention, More held a conference of farmers against the *khoti* system. Besides Mahars, farmers and farm workers from the Kunbi and Maratha castes also took part. This historic conference put forward the demands that *khoti* should be abolished and that tenants should get title to the land they cultivated. In this conference, 'touchable' and untouchable farmers threw off the practice of caste discrimination that they had followed for generations, and sat down together to eat. On the other hand, even in a capitalist industrial city like Bombay, where the workers' movement and the workers' level of consciousness had reached a higher level, caste Hindu workers still practised untouchability. In such times, it was a truly historic event that poor caste Hindu and untouchable farmers sat down together for a meal in a backward village in the Konkan. The importance of this revolutionary event lay as a class-based step forward for the removal of untouchability. This was a real beginning of a social and political revolution. It was a scientific and India-wide solution for a disease that afflicted Indian society.

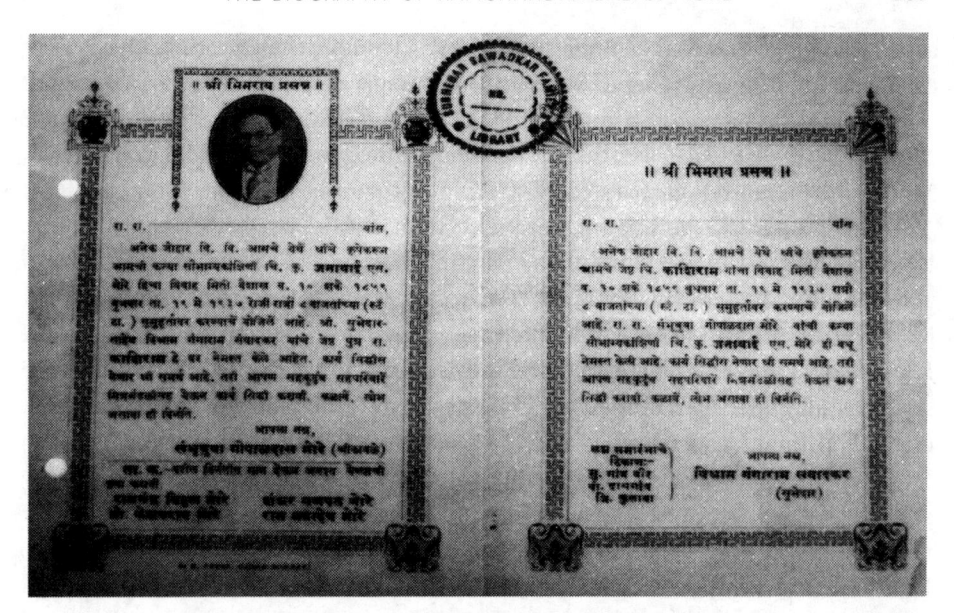

Invitation for Kashinath Sawadkar's wedding. Note the invocation to Ambedkar. Kashinath Sawadkar ran Bharat Bhushan Printing Press, which came to be called the Buddha Bhushan Printing Press after Ambedkar's Buddhist conversion in 1956. His father, Vishram Sawadkar (b. 20 August 1889; d. 1939), designed the wedding invitation. Sawadkar, a close associate of R.B. More's and key organizer of the Mahad *satyagraha* went on to found a Depressed Classes Students Hostel in 1927, and played a leading role in Ambedkar's Independent Labour Party. Vishram's father, Gangaram Bhagoji Sawadkar (b. 15 April 1865) was a *subhedar* in the British Army and died in Turkey during the First World War. For more on the Bharat Bhushan Printing Press, see: https://www.pressreader.com/.
Courtesy of Anil Sawadkar.

The workers' movement of the time had accepted this viewpoint, but did not have the courage to put it into practice. The leadership of the workers' movement was rebellious, but their rebelliousness was of an individual nature. Similarly, the independent movement of the untouchables did not take account of the revolutionary class viewpoint of the working class. Because of this weakness on both sides, there could not be a lasting unity between these two divisions of the movement. In the days to come, there were efforts, largely brought about through More, to bring together the two sides in Maharashtra (the Bombay Presidency of the time). The leaders of both sides formed a temporary kind of accord, but the real need was for a sustained unity, and that was not fulfilled.

After Chiplun, More organized Bahishkrit Conferences together with district farmers' conventions at Khed and Rohe, in the districts of Ratnagiri and Colaba (the present-day Raigad district). But they could not coalesce into permanent organizations; a district-level farmers' association was not formed. To fill this gap, More took the lead in establishing the Colaba District Farmers' Association in 1930, with B.G. Kher as president. More was the first general secretary of this association. (Bal Gangadhar Kher, the first president of the association, later went on to become prime minister in the first Congress ministry in Bombay Presidency.) This association organized a number of agitations during the Civil Disobedience Movement of 1930–31. Later, the government banned this association, and barred More and others from entering the district.

The industrial revolution and a new capitalist social system which were favourable for Babasaheb's movement for the liberation of the untouchables had arrived in India. With this change in one material stratum of life, untouchability had received a jolt. Karl Marx had remarked, when the Hindustan railway was founded, that factories would come up around the railway, and the rural economic system would be shaken up, and the practice of untouchability would also develop cracks.[20] This was realized in actuality even before Babasaheb was born.

Even in Babasaheb's time and a little before that, though society was still shackled by the orthodox thinking of the Vedas and Puranas, some progressive-thinking people were coming forward in society. Among these Anantrao Chitre, Bapu Sahasrabuddhe, Purushottam Prabhakar aka Bapurao Joshi and Tuljaram Mitha deserve special mention here. They were present at the first *satyagraha* conference at Mahad. Later, many more persons from caste Hindu society, like Com. Shamrao Parulekar, Acharya M.V. Donde, P.G. Kanekar, S.C. Joshi, Barrister Samarth, Devrao Naik, D.V. Pradhan, R.D. Kavali, Raghunath Kadrekar, Gupte and Joshi came forward as Babasaheb's followers and took part in his work for the abolition of untouchability. Their background was the Servants of India Society. So they were connected with the peasant movement as well as the movement for the rights of Dalits.

---

[20] It is well known that the Indian railways were financed by private capital with assured rates of profit. As well, railways (like steam shipping) enabled new modes of natural resource extraction and their accelerated global circulation. However, Satyendra More articulates a rather simple view of the relationship between (social) technology and the transformation of social relations, which is challenged by his own account and that of R.B. More. Their narratives suggest that though Dalits embraced new discourses of rights and dignity, they also confronted new forms of untouchability in the city. Moreover, Marx's writings on India are rather complex. On the one hand, he echoes nineteenth century commitments to unilinear progress and the benefits of modern institutions and technologies. At the same time, his analyses underscore the paradoxical ways in which liberal 'freedom' exacerbates social inequality. A small sample of writings about Marx on India (and the colonies) includes: Aijaz Ahmad (ed.), *On the National and Colonial Questions*, Delhi: LeftWord, 2001; Kevin Anderson, *Marx at the Margins: On Nationalism, Ethnicity, and Non-Western Societies*, Chicago: University of Chicago Press, 2010; Harry Harootunian, *Marx After Marx: History and Time in the Expansion of Capitalism*, New York: Columbia University Press, 2015; and Sudipta Kaviraj, 'Marxism in translation: critical reflections on Indian radical thought', in *Political Judgement: Essays for John Dunn*, ed. Richard Bourke and Raymond Geuss, Cambridge: Cambridge University Press, 2017, pp. 172–200.

The Simon Commission

Thus, on the one hand the movement of workers and peasants was deepening throughout the nation, and Socialist-Communist awareness was spreading within it; on the other hand, an independent movement of Dalits was taking shape, aimed at gaining freedom from their social and political slavery. The movement for national independence was gaining strength, and at the same time the process of Hindus and Muslims being organized on communal lines had also begun. It was the policy of the British to divide Hindus and Muslims from each other in order to rule over them. That was why, when they introduced the Morley–Minto reforms in 1909, the Muslims were granted political rights for the first time.[21] Later, the Southborough Committee upheld the terms agreed upon in the Lucknow Pact of 1916, which sought to iron out differences between Hindus and Muslims within the Congress, and approved extended seats for Muslims. Thus, the British created internal enemies for the Congress and continued with their attempts to weaken it.

When the Southborough Committee was sent to India, it had four Indians among its ten members, but not even one Indian was included in the Simon Commission. On 26 November 1927, the ruling Conservative Party announced its policy of granting additional political rights to the Indian people. Stanley Baldwin was prime minister of Britain at the time; he announced the appointment of a Commission headed by Sir John Simon to survey the matter of granting political rights to Indians and to conduct negotiations in this regard.[22] The main intention of this Commission was to make constitutional provisions for self-government of the colony unilaterally. Secondly, following the strategy of divide and rule, the intention was to dangle the carrot of limited franchise before the people, in such a way as to deepen the rifts among them.

To tell the truth, the question of the liberation of the Dalits should have been an issue before the national movement equal in importance to independence. But the British government took advantage of the fact that the leaders of the freedom movement were indifferent or unclear about this issue, and managed to keep the Dalits separate from the movement by posturing as their true benefactors. Ultimately, the British rulers' tactic of granting political rights to the Dalits brought about a transformation in their lives. Unwittingly, the British helped the cause of the Dalits.

The six members appointed to the Simon Commission, besides Sir John

---

[21] Muslims were granted a separate electorate with weightage in 1909 in recognition of their status as a community of 'historic and political importance'.

[22] The expansion of colonial franchise was a response to Indian involvement in the First World War, followed by a wave of political protests which marked British intransigence on the question of self-government.

himself, were all English. That was why the Indian National Congress boycotted the Commission and condemned it. The Muslim League had already announced its opposition to the Commission. The Left forces within the Congress and the Communist Party did not accept the principle of self-government for the colony. Their demand was for full independence. Also, at the time there was a tremendous wave of workers' strikes and general political awakening, which was led by the Communists. Thus, the Communists were in the forefront of the movement opposing the Simon Commission. They had concluded that the Simon Commission was a devious tactic framed by the British to mislead the Indian people.

On 3 February 1928, the members of the Simon Commission alighted from their ship in Bombay harbour. The people of Bombay greeted the Commission with public protest demonstrations carrying black signs. But some Non-Brahmin, Dalit and Muslim leaders welcomed the Simon Commission. There was a lot of criticism of this. Dr. Ambedkar, V.P. Chavan and Sitaram Keshav Bole were condemned as being sycophants.

The untouchable community did not take part in the protests against the Simon Commission because the protesters were fighting for a widening of the scope of their political rights, while the Dalits had no rights. The struggle of the untouchables, who had been denied [the right] to live as human beings for thousands of years, was to gain those rights of humanity. The Simon Commission presented them with an opportunity that they could not afford to miss out on, while the Congress and the Communists did not have a material understanding of the real weakness in the situation of the Dalits. What is more, they had not even given the matter any thought so that some solutions could be worked out. Even so, they had labelled the Dalits as sycophants and puppets of the imperialists. During the 1918 conference for the abolition of untouchability, a Dalit activist Santuji Waghmare had confronted Lokmanya Tilak while addressing the conference and told him, 'Lokmanya Tilak, open up the path of worshipping God to us and allow us entry into the temples.' Tilak listened to what he had to say, but did not express his opinion. Ambedkar decided that it would be foolish to depend on such unreliable national leaders, and so he planned to take advantage of this opportunity.

On 12 October 1928 Dr. Ambedkar deposed before the Simon Commission and placed before it the demand that the Dalits be given 22 seats in the Bombay Provincial Legislative Council. He demanded provincial autonomy and the right to vote for every adult man and woman. Later, on 17 May 1929, according to his earlier announcement, he placed before the Simon Commission his written recommendation on what political rights should be granted to the Bombay Province. More had supported the demands placed by Babasaheb before the Simon Commission through the Mahar Samaj Seva Sangh.

More Joins the Communist Party

The Parel and Poybawadi areas of Bombay, being working-class areas, were naturally the centre of Communist activity and many of the Party offices were located there; at the same time they were also the centre of Dalit mobilization, and Babasaheb's office was in the same area. This was the period around 1927 or 1928. In 1928 a historic strike of mill workers took place, which lasted for six months. More was a witness to this strike and he would occasionally attend the meetings that took place on the Kamgar Maidan, the workers' ground. During this strike many Dalits took part in the meetings as workers, and More began to feel attracted towards the Communists. Secondly, in the manifesto of 18 demands that had been adopted in this strike, there was the demand that Dalits should be allowed to work in the cloth-weaving department where the thread had to be moistened with the worker's saliva while winding it on the shuttle. So More was conscious that the Communists were aware of social issues.

After the strike of 1928, the mill workers' union again called for a strike in 1929. The Communists were in the lead in organizing this strike too. To ensure the success of the strike, the union began picketing at the factory gates. So those workers who did not want to take part in the strike were hustled away from the factory gates. Most of the workers, including a large number of Dalit workers, did not want this strike. These Dalit workers went to meet Babasaheb and asked him to find a way out.

On this occasion, the 29 September 1929 issue of *Bahishkrit Bharat* carried an editorial by Babasaheb criticizing the Communists, with the title 'First the Superstructure, then the Base'. In this he argued that the Indian Communists had not understood Communist philosophy; the article did not say that Communist philosophy was wrong. The central argument was that communism could not take root in India until the struggle against caste discrimination and untouchability was completed. Also, in the 15 September issue of *Bahishkrit Bharat* in that same year, he had stated, 'Even though the objective of the Communists is extreme, we have not said that it is inappropriate.' This encouraged More and he moved closer towards the Communists. It was from 1928–29 that More was drawn towards understanding Marxism. In a way, one could say that Babasaheb himself urged More to understand Communist thinking. From the year 1928/29 onward, More began to attend the meetings on the Kamgar Maidan regularly.

On 23 April 1928, a young mill worker named Parshuram Jadhav was killed in the police firing on a procession of striking mill workers in Sewri. After the strike of 1928 there was a new awakening of consciousness among the workers, and scattered strikes would take place wherever there was a case of injustice. There were about 70 to 80 such occasional strikes. During these strikes, Papa Miya, leader of the Mill Workers' Committee of the Moti Mill, was fired on. This enraged the workers, and an English manager named Davar was killed in the furious attack of the workers. Papa Miya, from Uttar Pradesh (then the United Provinces) and Babu Maruti from Junnar in Maharashtra (then the Bombay Presidency) were tried and found guilty in this case and they were hanged on 18 March 1929. They had been offered a chance to avoid being hanged if they testified that Comrade Dange (then leader of the Communist Party) had instigated them (to murder). But they both chose not to testify and preferred to be executed.

The execution of these two workers resulted in a wave of anger spreading among the workers. Just two days later, on 20 March, in the well-known Meerut Conspiracy Case, 32 Communists were arrested on a charge of conspiring to overthrow the government and sent to Meerut jail.[23] More was impressed to see Dalit and non-Dalit workers, Muslims and Hindus forgetting caste barriers to fight in unison for their rights, and to see the Communist Party, whose declared objective was to establish a secular workers' state free of caste divisions, leading this fight. So he moved even closer to the Communist ideology. To add to the impact of these events, on 8 April 1929 Bhagat Singh threw a bomb and revolutionary leaflets in the Central Legislative Assembly meeting in Delhi while the Public Safety Bill (which would give wide powers to the police against agitators) was being discussed. All the events of that year had a deep influence on More's life and he was drawn to the Communist movement.

More began to attend all the meetings of the Communists. His main objective was to get acquainted with the Communist leadership and to understand the Marxist-Leninist ideology that had helped to establish Socialist state power and build a socialist society in Russia. More personally met Comrades B.T. Ranadive, S.V. Deshpande, Jagannath Adhikari and R.M. Jambhekar, and got them to introduce him to the study of Marxism.

Still, he continued to work for the independent movement for Dalits under the leadership of Dr. Ambedkar. It was his opinion that an independent movement of the untouchables was also a need of the times. But he felt that they needed real liberation on a class basis, and that this was possible only in a society with a socialist state. So More decided on the strategy that the independent movement of the Dalits should be left to grow on parallel lines, and that he would enter the Communist Party and act as a link to see how it could become a part of the struggle

---

[23] This was a case that helped to gain wide support for the still recently formed Communist Party of India. Harkishan Singh Surjeet, a former general secretary of the CPI (Marxist) wrote about the aftermath of the Meerut Conspiracy Case thus: 'A Party with a centralized apparatus, came into being only after the release of the Meerut prisoners, in 1933. The Meerut Conspiracy Case, though launched to suppress the communist movement, provided the opportunity for Communists to propagate their ideas. It came out with its own manifesto and was affiliated to the Communist International in 1934.' (Harkishan Singh Surjeet, '75th Anniversary of the Formation of the Communist Party of India', an article in *The Marxist*, vol. 2, no. 1, January–March 1984.)

of the working class. While he was still with Dr. Ambedkar and working in the peasant movement, Anantrao aka Bhai Chitre had acquainted him with class struggle. This was how More came to decide in his own mind to move towards the Communist movement.

Since Dange and others had been imprisoned in the Meerut Conspiracy Case, it was Comrade B.T. Ranadive and S.V. Deshpande who led the strike of 1929 and functioned as leaders of the Communist Party even though they had joined the Party only that year. Historically this was the first generation of Indian Communists. Those who joined the Party did so with the intention of doing party work; this was a part of their consciousness. In those days, the cost of running the Party was met out of funds raised by middle-class Party members. There were no funds to pay Party workers, and those who came forward as full-time Party workers were mainly young people from wealthy families. Among those who came from the lower middle class, Party workers like Comrade S.V. Deshpande carried on party work side by side with practising their occupations as schoolteachers, etc. Those who came from the working class lacked wealth. They were fed and looked after by the workers themselves, in whom awareness had built up that it was their responsibility to support these activists. Most of these working-class Party workers were unmarried. Most of them were under thirty years of age. More was one among them, a Party worker who had started out with nothing to his name.

But More, unlike the others, was married by then and had one son (the present author, Satyendra). His wife Sitabai came from a family that was quite well off. Her father was a teacher in Dasgaon at the time. The family had some land, and there was a cultured atmosphere in their home. In those times, when women were not educated at all, Sitabai had studied up to the fourth standard. More would bring books for her to read, and so compared to other Dalit women, she was well informed and intelligent. More involved her in all his social and political activities, and treated her as an equal. So More received conscious support from her in his work.

More's mother was alive at the time. She probably lived in their hut in Dasgaon village, and her economic condition was poor. In those days More worked part-time for his livelihood, and from the little he could save from this, he sent some money to his mother from time to time. But since this money did not arrive regularly, she worked for wages in the village to earn a meagre living. More's sister Pithubai had been married at an early age. Her husband Dajjan Hate worked for some time as a teacher and then came to Bombay where he did all kinds of odd jobs for wages. On the whole, the situation was hard. So More worked part-time and devoted the rest of his time to party work like other working-class Party workers.

In those days, the Party leaders were both leaders *and* Party workers doing all kinds of work for the Party. They carried tables and chairs on to the ground for meetings and also made speeches. In those days there was no business with megaphones or microphones. Writing posters, sticking them up, bringing out cyclostyled newspapers, selling them, writing in them, holding workers' meetings, meeting the workers in their homes, educating themselves, educating workers about the class struggle, leading meetings and demonstrations—they carried out all these tasks themselves. These were Communist activists who did not recognize a division between leader and activist, who had live relations with the people. This was the first generation of Communists, fired by the ideal of building a society based on people's power, selfless and soaked in the affection showered on them by the people. And More was one among them.

During 1928–29, More, who was then general secretary of the Mahar Samaj Seva Sangh, used it as a platform to organize speeches on different social and political topics by Comrades S.V. Deshpande, Shamrao Parulekar, Keshav Sitaram Thakre and many such others.[24]

Thus, he was exposed to a world beyond the Dalit movement alone; this was how he tried to build bridges between the Dalit movement and the Communist movement.

In 1930 he read *The Communist Manifesto* and other available books, and became firmly convinced that the liberation not only of the Dalits but of all humanity could be achieved on the basis of Marx's philosophy of people's power. Since he was by nature a sincere and active worker, he plunged himself into the daily work of the Party. The Party took note of this, and towards of the end of 1930, he was given membership of the Communist Party.[25]

In this context, More informed Babasaheb in 1930 that he was joining the Communist Party. On hearing this, Babasaheb was not angry with him, nor did he feel that More had betrayed him; on the contrary, he applauded him. Seeing More's courage and honesty he said, 'I am overwhelmed by your sincerity and dedication. I am proud that I have such a pupil who is of my kind. Not cowardly, but brave. He tells me himself that he is leaving me to join the liberation struggle of the whole of humankind.' Later he said, 'I wonder whether the Communist Party in India, which belongs to Brahmins, will appreciate your dedication and honesty? I am your well-wisher and I hope you will have a bright future. My only wish is that you will be properly appreciated there. I stand for individual freedom and democracy, so I fully accept your leaving me. I will be happy if you take part in the work of running my newspaper even after you go there, but it is up to you. I have no objection at all to your going.' Thus did Babasaheb bid farewell to More in 1930.

As he was leaving More told him,

---

[24] Appendix A gives a list of 19 lectures arranged by the Mahar Samaj Seva Sangh while More was general secretary, between 22 September 1928 and 5 September 1931.—Tr.

[25] The *Communist Manifesto* was translated into Marathi as the *Communist Jahirnama* in 1931 by Gangadhar Adhikari. It is possible More read the *Manifesto* in English before then.

Even though I am setting out to do the work of freeing mankind from all oppression, the struggle for the social and political rights of Dalits in the present framework of capitalist landlordism, which you have started, is also important, and that is the direction of Communist thinking.

But the Communists do not have the social support to build a separate force of Dalits towards this objective, and I am aware that they have these inherent limitations. Similarly, Mahatma Gandhi too will not be able to launch the struggle for the right to be human against untouchability, because he looks at the Dalits as an object of pity. That strength, that leadership resides in you. That is why, even though in the eyes of people I am leaving your fold, still I hold that in my practice I will remain your man on the question of Dalit liberation and I will not desert you.

I have faith that the independent struggle of the Dalits and the workers' struggle for radical revolution can go forward hand in hand. The Communists have never opposed the demand that Dalits must be given their political rights. The only issue is that the Communists do not today have the force to enter the arena of struggle for these rights with the same intensity as you do. This is their weakness today; the Communists admit this and so do I. So today there is a need for an independent Dalit movement as well as a workers' movement.

The First Dalit Communist

Until More joined the Communist Party, not a single Dalit individual from India, let alone Maharashtra, had *with full awareness* become a member of the Party. What was more, none of the activists who had helped to launch Ambedkar's independent movement had ever entered any other political movement, so totally gripped were the Dalits as a community by the independent movement of Dalits. More was in fact one among them.

The prevailing atmosphere was such that for an activist to leave the independent movement to liberate Dalits from a life of social oppression and humiliation, which had been built up for the first time in history, was considered a great insult to the movement. This was the background against which More had joined the Communist Party. Dr. Ambedkar was able to understand how much mental preparation, strength and courage went into this decision. Only a person from the Dalit community could understand this. One who has never had to live the social existence of Dalits would find it difficult even to imagine this. Only a Mahatma Phule could do it. Lokmanya Tilak had been touched by the problem of untouchability, but he did not have the nerve to rebel against it. That is why Tilak has now fallen behind Mahatma Phule in history.

Thus, More was the first person from the Dalit community to join the Party after having been in the forefront of Babasaheb's movement and after consciously attaining an understanding of Marxism-Leninism. Before More, there were many Dalit mill workers or workers from other occupations who were a part of the trade union movement under Communist leadership. Among them was an individual named Piraji Sadhu Bhise from among the mill workers of Bombay; being a *potraj*, he was Dalit by caste. He was not just a member of the union; he was president of the Bombay Mill Workers' Union under the leadership of Dange. But he had nothing to do with the Party. Dalits would join the union, but their loyalty remained with the independent movement of the Dalits. There must have been many such Dalit workers elsewhere in the country who joined unions under Communist leadership, but More was the only one to have been in the forefront of the Dalit movement and who left Babasaheb to join the Party. This was surely something for the Party to be proud of.

It is true that the Party did not at the time realize the strength of Communist consciousness and the courage that was needed for More to become a part of the Communist movement; nor did the Party recognize More's importance for that movement. If it had in fact recognized it, this would have helped the growth of the Party. Even so, today Dalits are joining the Communist Party in large numbers, and for them More is an ideal figure. The Communists do not believe in caste discrimination, but in the world in which we live, religion and caste discrimination do exist. And it cannot be denied that no efforts were made to acquaint Party activists with his thinking, in order to attract Dalits to the Party in the given situation. This injustice was, even if unknowingly, dealt out to More.

More joined the Communist Party at the end of 1930. This means that More was one of the first generation that built the Communist movement in India. This was indeed a matter of pride for the Communist Party. What is more, there were many occasions when More could have gained personal benefit and prominence because of being a Dalit, but he never succumbed to such temptation, neither did he ever turn back from the path he had chosen. If he had remained in the Dalit movement, he would have attained top leadership and would have been eulogized. But More shrugged off these enticements and lived the life of a dedicated Communist.

Having Left Babasaheb's Fold, More Remains Loyal to the Dalit Movement

More joined the Communist Party because he was impressed by Marxism-Leninism's philosophy of radical revolution. In this, he had not revoked Babasaheb and his position that an independent Dalit movement was necessary. He recognized that Babasaheb was the first leader after Mahatma Phule to formulate the Dalit question with such solidity and steadfastness within the framework of a capitalist-feudal society. But while he was working with Babasaheb's independent Dalit movement, More came to hold the firm opinion that ultimate liberation for the Dalits could be brought about only through the Communist movement for radical transformation of society. More was the only one to have left Babasaheb's side while he was still alive and capably building the independent movement of Dalits, and when the Dalits had declared him to be their saviour. To tell the truth this was a rebellious act; but it was a thoughtful rebellion. Many left Babasaheb's fold for selfish reasons and joined the Congress or other bourgeois parties. More did not do so, and that is where his unique importance and his distinctiveness lies.

The reason why Dr. Babasaheb Ambedkar and his independent movement arose was that the Congress party at the time and leaders like Gandhiji were indirectly upholding the feudal social system, and thus, Babasaheb had no alternative but to build an independent movement of Dalits. The Communist Party based on the philosophy of Marxism-Leninism had only just been born. It was aware of these social questions, but it did not possess the inherent organizational strength to tackle them as Babasaheb Ambedkar did, working within the limitations of capitalism. Thus, the independent movement of the Dalits for their liberation was the historical need of the times. More was conscious of this when he joined the Communist Party; and yet he entered the Party. This was because More was convinced that, as long as the independent Dalit movement did not become a part of the wider, basically revolutionary, struggle of the workers and peasants, and as long as the Communist movement did not arrive at an understanding of the social issues of the Dalits, the class struggle would not take root firmly. That was why he took the rather far-sighted view that he should devote the precious years of his life to the Communist movement for radical change, and so he entered the Communist Party and took the position that he would, in Babasaheb's lifetime, become a link between the two movements.

Even though More had left Babasaheb's fold, he still went to meetings and programmes organized by him. He would always be present at all the meetings held by Babasaheb in Bombay. Those others who left Babasaheb before More and after him would never go and sit before the platform at one of his meetings. But More was not one among them; he never took the position: I have left Babasaheb's side and come out of his party, so why should I have anything more to do with him. The thought was constantly in his mind that, if the Communist movement for radical transformation of society was to be made successful, one had to understand the independent movement for the liberation of the Dalits, and see how it could be made part of the Communist movement. That is why, being so much a part of both the Dalit and the Communist movement, he never avoided the meetings and activities organized by Babasaheb in Bombay.

More conducted study circles for young persons from the Dalit community in four *chawls* in Byculla, in Worli–Naigaon, in Agripada–Bombay Central, Delisle Road and many other areas. He taught the basics of Marxism to many of them. In this work he was helped by Comrade S.V. Deshpande Master. In fact, during 1930–

31 More brought the whole contiguous area of Delisle Road, which is now N.M. Joshi Road, on to the Communist Party's map. Chawl No. 14 in this Delisle Road area was his first centre of activity. This *chawl* came to be known as the Red Chawl.

S.R. Gaikwad, who lived in the BDD Chawl, was a friend of More. He used to work in the Films Division as a film editor and artiste. Gaikwad was attracted to More's capacity to think for himself even while he was with Dr. Ambedkar in his independent movement of Dalits. It was the same with Govind Vitthal Tamhankar, Baburao Garud and Bhargav Sonawane, who lived in Chawl No. 14. They were attracted to More's independence of thought and became his friends. They were proud of More in his many roles: as one of the main leaders of the Mahad *satyagraha*, journalist writing for *Bahishkrit Bharat*, editor of *Avhan*, president of the Colaba District Farmers' Association and later a Communist leader.

In those days these young men had a cricket club in Delisle Road. More suggested to them that they should not limit this youth club to cricket alone, but set up a political-social-cultural association. Accordingly, in 1931, with guidance from More, an association called the Friends' Union was established. Through this association More began to spread his ideas among the untouchable people. Through the medium of this association, *jalsas*, plays and festivals and other programmes based on workers' problems and other social questions were organized in the mill precincts of Kala Chowkie and Lal Bagh. The activists of the Young Workers' Association, related to the Communist Party and the Samata Sainik Dal used to stage programmes of the cultural troupe that sprang up from this association. This was the first workers' cultural troupe in the working-class movement of Bombay.[26]

This cultural troupe put up a playlet throwing light on the problem of unemployment in the textile mills. The dialogues in this play were written by More's Communist friend Comrade D.S. Vaidya. S.R. Gaikwad and Baburao Garud had composed the songs. The famous music composer C. Ramchandra (Ramchandra Chitalkar) would often come down to the Friends' Union cultural troupe to give them guidance on music and to write tunes for their songs. He was a friend of Gaikwad and More, and had great respect and affection for More. It is important to note that the Friends' Union cultural troupe was spreading consciousness among the workers even before the Indian People's Theatre Association.

It was from this troupe that composer-singers like Comrade Raghu Kadam and Comrade Sikandar Shaikh emerged, who later joined the cultural troupe of Amar Shaikh and Annabhau Sathe in the movement for a united Maharashtra state and became widely popular. Shahir Raghu Kadam and other artistes were performing the song '*Jagat sukhachi malaki swabale majuranna milanar*' (the

---

[26] The Indian People's Theatre Association (IPTA) was formed in 1943, during the Quit India movement. While this association included many members with a Left or Communist orientation, the Red Flag Cultural Squad was set up in 1944 by Amar Shaikh, Annabhau Sathe and D.N. Gavhankar with a more explicitly Communist agenda.

Annual meeting of 20,000 members of the Samata Sainik Dal, organized by the ILP in Kamgar Maidan, Bombay, on 8 January 1939.
Courtesy of Prakash Vishwasrao, *Dr. Babasahab Ambedkar*.

workers, on their own strength, will come to possess all the joys of this world), set to music by C. Ramchandra, within the movement until recently.

It was through the medium of this same Friends' Union that the first public celebration of Dr. Ambedkar's birthday was undertaken with great enthusiasm on More's initiative, on 14 April 1933 in Chawl No. 14, BDD Chawls. (C.B. Khairmode, biographer of Dr. Babasaheb Ambedkar, has taken note of this birthday celebration in the second volume of his biography of Ambedkar.) In organizing this *jayanti* programme, some activists who had just recently joined the Communist Party took part alongside More. More persuaded Dr. Babasaheb Ambedkar himself to be present for this *jayanti* celebration. On this occasion he praised More for his contribution to the workers' movement. Comrades Raghu Kadam and Baburao Garud personally told the present author that a photograph of the main activists of the Friends' Union was taken with Babasaheb on this occasion.[27]

[27] Baburao Garud and Govind Tamhankar came from military families, who moved to Bombay in the first decades of the twentieth century. Both had grown up in the segregated Saurabh Chawl where Dalits occupied the ground floor, and were not permitted to walk up the floors where the upper castes lived. They moved to the Delisle Road BDD Chawls in 1930.

Tamhankar was politicized by the Mahad *satyagraha*, and joined the Friends' Union together with Garud at the height of the Nashik temple *satyagraha*. The Friends' Union celebrated Ambedkar's first Jayanti (birthday). The Friends' Union also started the first

More also started working for the Party through this Friends' Union and several active members of the Union subscribed to the Party. In those days, More built the first unit of Party members from the Dalit community, in Delisle Road. These included Comrades Govind Tamhankar, Baburao Garud, Bhargav Sonawane, Tukaram Rohekar, Govind Tembe and Hiru Jadhav.

Round Table Conference

At the end of 1928 the Simon Commission was appointed and entrusted with the task of drawing up a constitution for a self-governed Indian colony having Dominion status. In the nation-wide protest against the Simon Commission, in which the Left parties took the position of demanding not Dominion status, but full independence, Lala Lajpat Rai was fatally injured and died soon after. So the Commission had resulted in the loss of a great national leader, though the demand for full independence did not originate with the Congress and Gandhiji. But as a result of this aggressive protest, the 1929 Lahore Conference of the Congress party passed a resolution demanding full independence. Later, in 1930, there were massive protests against British rule all over India. So the Congress was not present for the first Round Table Conference; it had boycotted it. Besides, many Congress leaders were in jail at the time.

On 20 January 1931, the British Prime Minister Ramsay MacDonald announced the holding of the second Round Table Conference. On 26 January Gandhiji and members of the Congress Working Committee were unconditionally released from jail. On 4 March 1931, the Gandhi–Irwin Pact was signed. In the same month, the Congress held a conference at Karachi and in that conference there was a unanimous resolution to agree to a compromise. The Congress decided to set aside the demand for full independence and to hold talks with the British rulers in the Round Table Conference on a unified constitution. In this constitution Indians

---

workers' cultural troupe, the *Mela Kamgar Kalapathak*. Annabhau Sathe, Amar Shaikh, and Gavhankar got their start through this troupe. Garud notes, 'At the time, our thinking was that as workers, we would be one with the Lal Bavtawale [those of the red flag, i.e. the Communists] and we would also join Babasaheb's struggle against untouchability as activists.' Garud attributes his and Tamhankar's entry into Left politics to Comrade R.B. More, and notes that it was More who introduced them to working-class organizations and to the revolutionary message of the Communist Party. R.B. More notes that he had worked with Tamhankar on *Bahishkrit Bharat*, but that Tamhankar associated him with the publications *Avhan*, *Kranti*, and *Railway Mazdoor*. More notes that the Samata Sainik Dal distributed *Avhan* from *chawl* to *chawl*, and thus underlines the significant connections forged between working-class Dalits, Communist ideology, and the Ambedkar movement. See reminiscences by Baburao Garud and R.B. More in *Ek Adarsha Kamgar Karyakarta—Govind Tamhankar: Jeevan, Vichar, Karya*, written to commemorate his first death anniversary, on 17 September 1971, and published by his son, Vasudev Govind Tamhankar, with a foreword by Satyendra More.

would be granted responsibilities, but in their own interest the British authorities would retain certain powers. This was a position of meekly submitting before the British, and so there was wide protest from the Indian people against Gandhiji's going to England for the Round Table Conference. This was a betrayal by Gandhiji.

Dr. Babasaheb Ambedkar's presence at the Round Table Conference had a different significance. The British, within the framework of the Montagu–Chelmsford reforms, and maybe for their own selfish ends, had thought of granting political rights to the Dalits, which Indian society had never done. The Dalits were human beings who had been living a life more humiliating than that of animals for hundreds of years in this society. It would be not just a mistake but great foolishness to imagine that the British were acting as angels in granting them these rights. The British came to India to trade and rob her of her wealth; on top of this they imposed their rule on her residents. The basic socio-economic unit in India was the village; they broke this up and brought the capitalist economy. As they brought a kind of freedom to the poor who were living in bondage in the villages and gave them the opportunity to become workers in the city, so too did the untouchables also gain this freedom. But the British kept the feudal regime as it was. In brief, they transplanted the capitalist system on to the feudal society. So the social system that was imprisoning the Dalits developed at least a few cracks. A new consciousness, a new self-knowledge was born within them. The British had realized, while granting political rights to Muslims in the framework of the Morley–Minto reforms, that in this changed situation they could not afford to neglect their interests. But they did not come to such a realization in the case of the Dalits. Of course, there is no doubt that in granting these rights to Muslims they were seeking to mark them and set them apart (from the majority).

The British did not think of the Dalits in this way because the Dalits had not yet come into existence as a political force, but they perceived the beginnings of such a force. It was so that the Dalits should not prove a threat to them that the untouchables found a place in the Montagu–Chelmsford reforms that followed the Morley–Minto reforms. In carrying out both these (sets of) reforms the British had the selfish objective of pressing on with imposing their rule. The progressives of the time were not wrong in recognizing that this was a policy of divide and rule. But the progressive forces had also largely failed to note that the social, political and economic backgrounds of the Muslims and the Dalits were different. So applying the same criteria to both these groups in this situation showed the faulty understanding of the Communists.

For the Dalits the Montagu–Chelmsford reforms presented an opportunity that had come after hundreds of years. From the point of view of the Dalit question, it would have been wrong to miss it. The progressive thinkers had not understood this. The progressives at the time had neither the organizational strength to deal with the Dalit question, nor a strategy; Babasaheb summed up the situation correctly, and thus, was not wrong to seize the opportunity. Therefore, to say that Ambedkar was a stool pigeon of the British is not to understand the practical reality of the circumstances.

The Simon Commission arrived in India after the aforesaid Montagu–Chelmsford reforms. Babasaheb laid his extensive testimony before the Commission and made a demand for additional political rights for the Dalits. Others had also presented their points of view before the Commission. But nobody was satisfied with the outcome. Thus, almost all the political parties opposed the recommendations of the Simon Commission. All the political leaders in London had taken the same position. The British political leaders suggested that the Indian political parties and these leaders should come together and discuss the matter. So it was decided that Indian and British leaders should hold a 'Round Table' conference.

The major objective of (the British politicians in holding) the Round Table Conference was to defeat the demand for full independence and trap India in the framework of Dominion self-rule. Even so, in the reforms that had been instituted up till then, the right to adult franchise was not included. The rights of *adivasis* were not even mentioned. Dalits' rights had been taken note of and then completely denied. Against this background the eyes of this deprived section of society were on the Round Table Conference as presenting them with a long-awaited opportunity. And even though the Congress had put up the slogan of full independence, it had become amenable to the British position of Dominion self-rule.

In the list of members selected by the government to take part in the Conference in September 1930, there were two representatives of the Dalits: Dr. Ambedkar and [Rettamalai] Srinivasan.[28]

This first Round Table Conference was to begin in London on 17 October 1930. Babasaheb and Srinivasan arrived in London on 18 October 1930 and took part in the Conference. There Babasaheb and Srinivasan first explained the nature of the question of untouchability and how it was distinct. They argued that it was necessary to make special provisions for the Dalits and that the Hindus' and Muslims' viewpoint was a self-interested one. After this, on 31 December 1930, Babasaheb submitted a 15-page written petition enumerating the political demands of the untouchables. The eight main demands[29] in this petition were as follows:

1. For equal citizenship, untouchability must be abolished by law. They cannot accept majority rule in their present state of hereditary bondsmen. Before majority rule is established, their emancipation from the system of untouchability must be an accomplished fact. It must not be left to the will of the majority.

---

[28] Satyendra More refers to R. Srinivasan as 'Srinivas'.
[29] We have translated the eight points of the petition as given by the author.—*Tr.*

2. It must be publicly announced that Dalits have been given equal rights. Anyone who prevents them from passing through their fields, or burns down their house, must be charged with a criminal offence and punished.
3. There must be a Central law against offences based on caste hatred.
4. The untouchables must have adult franchise, separate electorates, and the untouchables must have adequate representation in the Central and Provincial Legislative Councils.
5. Make a constitutional provision for Central and Provincial Public Service Commissions. And appoint untouchables in government service on all kinds of posts.
6. If the powers of Central and Provincial government go into the hands of the 'touchable' Hindus, because of their prejudiced viewpoint they may harm the interests of the untouchables. There should be constitutional provision to prevent this.
7. The constitution should make provision for a special department to put an end to oppression of untouchables and to safeguard their interests.
8. The Emperor must instruct every Governor-General that he must include representatives of the untouchables in his cabinet.

Babasaheb succeeded in bringing up the above topics for discussion in the first Round Table Conference. He managed to secure the agreement of the Conference on the point that the untouchables must be treated differently from the Hindus, and that there should be protective measures to ensure that they would be elected to the Legislative Councils. The question of whether they should be given reserved seats with a united electorate or separate electorates was placed on the agenda of the Conference. The Conference also took note of the seriousness of other issues (concerning the untouchables). In the end, with the sitting of 19 January 1931, the work of the first Round Table Conference was temporarily wound up. After this Babasaheb returned to India and began an agitation to obtain the backing of the untouchables for his political demands.

The question of what kind of constitution India should have was discussed at the first Round Table Conference, but because of the absence of the Congress in this conference no decision was taken. The Congress had boycotted this first conference. To find a way out of this impasse, the government released Congress leaders from jail and convinced Gandhiji to be present at the second Round Table Conference. After this, at the Congress party convention held in Karachi, it was resolved that Gandhiji would go to London as representative of the Congress. So, on 29 August 1931 Gandhiji departed for London on the ship *Rajputana* accompanied by two she-goats, and a few vessels of Ganges water. He arrived in London on 12 September. He took up residence at Kingsley Hall in the East End of London, which was then considered to be an underprivileged district of the city. He was accompanied by Madan Mohan Malaviya, Sarojini Naidu, Sir Prabhashankar Pattani, the Diwan of Bhavnagar, Mahadev Desai, Pyarelal, Devdas, Miraben and Ghanshyam Das Birla. The second Round Table Conference took place from 7 September to 31 December 1931. Dr. Ambedkar and other representatives such as Barrister Sapru, Jinnah, and N.M. Joshi also took part.

On 13 November 1931, speaking before the tenth sitting of the Minorities Committee, Gandhiji said,[30]

> The Congress is the representative of all the minorities.
>
> I am the true supporter and promoter of reforms for the untouchables. I consider their rights to be as precious as my own life. I will not sacrifice the human rights of the untouchables in order to attain independence.
>
> I would not sell the vital interests of the untouchables even for the sake of winning the freedom of India. I claim myself in my own person to represent the interests of the untouchables.
>
> Even if the whole world is promised to me I will not betray the untouchables. Therefore, to follow Dr. Ambedkar's proposal and the provisions of the Minorities Pact to grant them separate political rights would be suicidal for the untouchables. If the untouchables decide to convert to Islam or Christianity I will not oppose them.

He also said that the representatives sent by the Congress for the second Round Table Conference were the true representatives of all castes and religious communities. Ambedkar and others were representatives nominated by the government; they did not represent the people.

Dr. Ambedkar took objection to this. He said that if political power in India passed into the hands of the Hindus and the Muslims, they would continue to ride roughshod over the poor, ignorant and backward people. Ambedkar noted, 'That is why the untouchable people are not fighting for additional political rights for Indians. The untouchable people are struggling, so that, if these additional rights are granted, there must be provision to safeguard the rights of all minority communities and the untouchable community. The Congress desires that the untouchables should place trust in the Congress in the matter of political rights for Indians. But for hundreds of years, the Hindus have treated untouchables as worse than animals.' So he (Ambedkar) refused to give unconditional support to the political demands of the Congress and on 4 November 1931 he submitted a fresh petition incorporating, with some improvements, the demands he had placed before the first Conference.

At the beginning of the Round Table Conference Dr. Babasaheb Ambedkar

---

[30] We have translated the account of Gandhi's testimony before the second Round Table Conference as given by the author.—*Tr.*

had demanded reserved seats and adult franchise in joint electorates, but the untouchables sent him thousands of telegrams asking him to demand separate electorates. Accordingly, he got the demand for separate electorates incorporated in the Minorities Pact. Mahatma Gandhi did not like this and so he incited some anti-Ambedkar Dalits like [M.C.] Rajah, Devrukhkar and P. Baloo (old-time cricketer) to raise a demand for joint electorates. But Ambedkar did not give up his demand for separate electorates. This demand of Babasaheb was supported in the Conference by Sir Tej Bahadur Sapru, Sir P.S. Sivaswami Aiyyar, M.A. Jinnah, Dr. R.P. Paranjpe, Sir A.P. Panze, Sir Henry Gidney, Diwan Bahadur Ramasamy Mudaliar, Diwan Bahadur Ramachandra Rao and Raobahadur A.T. Panniraselvam. Also, Dr. B.S. Moonje (a leader of the Hindu Mahasabha, a fundamentalist Hindu organization) supported him at the time, but did an about turn when he returned to India.

Mahatma Gandhi was in favour of granting separate political rights to Sikhs and Muslims, but he opposed giving the same rights to untouchables. To secure the same opposition from the Muslims, on 7 October 1931, he made a secret pact with the Muslims. Ambedkar says that this information reached his ears through a Muslim representative. Fearing that if Gandhi were to gain support for his position from other minority groups, his demand (for separate electorates) would be defeated; Ambedkar together with his colleagues Raobahadur [Panniraselvam] and R. Srinivasan signed a supplementary petition which was placed before the Round Table Conference. In this petition they demanded that the untouchables be given political rights in proportion to their number in the population. They emphasized the point that provision be made so that the untouchable voters would elect their representative from untouchable electorates. Untouchables should get places in jobs, in local bodies and in Central and Provincial legislatures in proportion to their population.

Mahatma Gandhi's position was that the task of eliminating untouchability fell to the caste Hindus and he would complete it. The untouchables should remain within the Hindu community, then untouchability would be abolished and their representatives would be elected to the legislative bodies.[31] In this way, once untouchability was abolished the road to an overall improvement in the situation of the untouchables would be opened up. While Gandhi was in London, speaking about the political future of the untouchables before the 'Indian Students' Majlis, he said,

---

[31] This sentence reads oddly, but the point Satyendra More is trying to convey is that Gandhi was arguing against separate representation for Dalits and in support of reserved representation, which he believed would achieve the same result, that is, Dalit representation. As we know, Ambedkar's argument was different: he argued for separate representation and against reserved representation on the grounds that when the general (Hindu) electorate elected Dalit representatives from reserved constituencies, they invariably elected representatives who were more palatable to caste Hindus.

The Muslim and Sikh communities have become highly politically conscious and organized. That is not the situation of the untouchables. So to separate them from Hindu society will be harmful to the untouchables. Dr. Ambedkar is the representative of the untouchables. He looks at Hindu society with hostility. The Hindus have treated them (the untouchables) most cruelly and so a hostile feeling has arisen within him. This is a consequence of past events. We are obliged to him that he has not broken our heads out of anger with the Hindus. I have great respect for Dr. Ambedkar. But his demanding separate electorates for the untouchables is a mistake. He may be wanting to make his own fortune through these political rights, but I do not understand what good they are going to do to the interests of the untouchables.

On the contrary Dr. Ambedkar took the view that, if the untouchables dissolved their political existence within the Hindu fold, they would become puppets in the hands of the Hindus, who would then compel them to vote for a candidate put up by the Hindus. The life of untouchables in the villages is subject to the whim of the Hindus. If the untouchables gained separate political rights, they would be able to elect their own representatives, and, because of this separate political existence, they will be able to raise an agitation against the Hindus when they oppress them. This would light the fire of self-awareness within them and the entire untouchable community will become prepared to sacrifice anything for a life of self-respect. They would be liberated from centuries of bone-crushing servitude.

When Gandhiji realized that in all the meetings of minorities he was not able to muster support for his opposition to the demands made by Ambedkar, he called Dr. Ambedkar to meet him and told him, 'Are you willing to revise the demands that you have made for the safeguarding of the interests of the untouchables?' Babasaheb said, 'We are certainly in favour of appropriate revisions.' Then Gandhi put forward his proposition as follows:

> If, in public elections held on the principle of joint electorates, a candidate from the untouchable community fails to get elected, he should lodge a legal complaint and prove before the court that, even though he and the caste Hindu candidate who got elected were in all other respects equally capable, he did not get elected only because of his untouchable caste. If the court is convinced and rules accordingly, the caste Hindu candidate's election will be declared null and void and the untouchable candidate will stand elected.

By proposing this scheme Gandhiji was trying to get the untouchables caught up in legal proceedings. Dr. Ambedkar told Gandhiji then and there that he considered this plan to be impractical and found it completely unacceptable.

At the end of the discussions in the second Round Table Conference, the [composition of] upper and lower houses of the Central legislative body had been decided, as well as the Provincial Legislative Councils. For this, the census of 1931 was taken as the basis. The Southborough Committee and the Simon Commission had granted a handful of seats to the untouchables, and those too were on the basis of nomination. Dr. Ambedkar brought about a modification in these provisions so that the representatives would be elected on the basis of adult franchise, and he also secured a substantial increase in the number of seats (to be reserved for untouchables). In the Central Legislative Council, in the upper house, out of 200 seats 101 were for Hindus, 20 for untouchables and the rest for other minorities. Similarly, in the lower house, out of 300 seats the numbers were 123 and 45 respectively, and in the Bombay Provincial Council they were 88 for Hindus and 28 for untouchables out of a total of 200. The number of seats for untouchables were also increased in the councils for the Provinces of C.P., Madras, Punjab, United Provinces, Assam, Bengal, Bihar and Orissa. So this second Round Table Conference proved to be very favourable from the point of view of Dalits' political rights. *It cannot be denied that the untouchable community had reached such a plane for the first time in history, because they had an independent organization. The thinking put forward by the Communists that the Congress could take care of everything had been proved wrong by history.*

When Dr. Ambedkar left for the Round Table Conference in October 1930, More and the leaders of the Mahar Seva Sangh arranged a public felicitation in Bombay. More also brought out the first issue of the weekly *Avhan* devoted to the Round Table Conference and dedicated it to Dr. Babasaheb Ambedkar. At the time More agreed with the position taken by Dr. Ambedkar in the Round Table Conference, and that was why he took the lead in organizing this felicitation.

POONA PACT

After 1927–28 the workers' movement and the influence of the Communists was growing. That was why, in 1929, Communists were arrested in the 'Meerut Conspiracy' case. On the other hand, the Congress had embarked on their policy of non-cooperation from 1930. It was to dull the edge of this strategy that Gandhiji carried out his salt *satyagraha* as a personal act. But in the end it spread all over the nation.[32] Gandhi did not agree to the demand for an agitation against the salt

---

[32] Gandhi had called off the first non-cooperation movement which had been launched in 1920, after the Chauri Chaura incident of 1922. Chauri Chaura was the infamous incident where Congress volunteers in Gorakhpur district set fire to a police post leading to the death of 22 policemen in response to police firing on a demonstration organized by Congress volunteers during the Non-Cooperation Movement. Civil Disobedience was taken up by the Congress again in 1930. Some critics have argued that Gandhi started the Salt Satyagraha, where protesters made their own salt and refused to pay the Salt Tax imposed by the British, to restore his personal image. Satyendra More is referring to this view here.

tax. He gave an assurance of protection to the *zamindars*. The people did not like this decision, and the fervour of the people's movement intensified. The British regime was shaken. And yet Gandhiji was pursuing a policy of cooperation with the British, and that was why he attended the second Round Table Conference. The British drew up a strategy of exploiting the weakness that had become apparent within the Congress. Here in India the agitations that had begun in 1930 were spreading. Gandhi, by signing the Gandhi–Irwin pact, was in fact taking up a stand of cooperating with the British. But the fury and discontent within the country was catching fire against the British.

Gandhi returned to India at the end of 1931, having concluded the second Round Table Conference. On 4 January 1932 the British made a sudden forceful attack, arrested Gandhiji, and outlawed all associations. In 1930 the Congress was taking an aggressive stance. Now it was being compelled to fight a defensive struggle. Gandhiji put out a command that the struggle against the British should be continued without building underground organizations, and that such an underground struggle was against Congress policy. Further, keeping in mind the experience of Chauri Chaura, where the farmers had launched an agitation against the *zamindars* and the government, a resolution was passed that the landowners would be given protection. Accordingly, it was announced that the Congress would not support any struggle that opposed the interests of the landlords. Thus, he (Gandhi) crushed the people's movements and adopted a policy of cooperating with the British. Gandhiji announced this policy while he was still in jail. Similarly, in the summer of 1932 he put the nationalist movement on hold and concentrated all his attention on the uplift of the Harijans.

It was as a part of this that he raised a new question: that of revising the agreement reached in the Round Table Conference that had granted some concessions to Dalits, and he declared that he would go on a fast unto death for this. In this way he succeeded in diverting the people's attention from the external struggle. He put forward a policy negating reserved seats for Dalits in the Central and Provincial Legislative Councils. He stubbornly insisted that the British should provide for joint electorates in which the untouchables were treated as Hindus. At this time, Gandhiji was imprisoned in Yerawada jail in Pune. Mahatma Gandhi in the month of March immediately sent a notice by way of writing a letter to Sir Samuel Hoare, Secretary of State for India, stating that the untouchables should not be given separate electorates; else he would go on an indefinite fast.

In the end, on 17 August 1932, the British announced their decision.[33] According to this, the untouchables were treated as part of the Hindu community

---

[33] Ramsay MacDonald's Communal Award allowed the Depressed Classes a double vote, as members of an excluded minority and as members of the general Hindu electorate. Gandhi's fast-unto-death was in response to the principle of separation. The Poona Pact compromise granted extra seats (and reserved constituencies) for the Depressed Classes.

and would be able to cast votes on an equal basis as part of the Hindu electorate. Besides this, the untouchables, while remaining part of the Hindu community, could protect their rights and interests by way of a separate constituency. In the present situation, this community required an independent constituency. Wherever backward communities had been granted separate electorates, the common Hindu voter would not be deprived of his franchise. Besides, since the untouchable castes would be included in the Hindu constituencies, a caste Hindu candidate would also require the votes of untouchables in order to get elected. Similarly, an untouchable candidate would need the votes of caste Hindus. On the other hand, because of the communal separate electorates granted to the Muslims, a Muslim would not have the right to vote or to stand for election in a general constituency. But any eligible untouchable voter would be able to cast his vote or even stand as a candidate in a general constituency.

After this, on 18 August 1932, Mahatma Gandhi wrote to the British Prime Minister J. Ramsay MacDonald from Yerawada jail, expressing his opposition to the voting rights granted to the untouchables, and demanding that the scheme of communally determined separate electorates be withdrawn. The representatives of the untouchables should be elected from the general constituencies, and equal voting rights should be granted to all. If the decision was not changed in this way, he (Gandhi) would embark on a fast unto death from the 20th of September.

Dr. Ambedkar felt that Gandhiji did not really want to end untouchability; he just wanted to pose himself as saviour of the untouchables. According to him the social system based on *chaturvarna*, or the hierarchical order of four castes (with untouchables outside and inferior to this order) was an ideal system. Dr. Ambedkar was a sharp critic of this social order, while Gandhi supported it. All the Hindus who claimed to be progressive also viewed this order as ideal; they only said that untouchability should not be practised. That is why social transformation is impossible within the Hindu religion based on caste discrimination. That is why it was Dr. Babasaheb Ambedkar's demand that only if the system of *chaturvarna* were demolished could untouchability be removed. That is why [Dr. Ambedkar] did not accept Gandhiji's pity for the untouchables, his advocacy of a 'change of heart' among caste Hindus and his praise for the efforts made by Hindus. [Babasaheb] wanted to join [the cause of the untouchables] to the political rights ethic brought by the changed capitalist order. That is why he wanted separate electorates and reserved seats. This was unacceptable to Gandhiji. Gandhiji stuck to his position and in the end he announced the start of his fast unto death. The nation was aroused and everyone started to curse Dr. Ambedkar. He received death threats. Senior Congress leaders lined up to press upon Ambedkar.

As decided, Gandhiji began his fast in Yerawada prison on 20 September. Malaviya, Jayakar, Sapru and other leaders went at once to Yerawada to meet him. They sought guidance from him as to what rights should be granted to the untouchables so that he would be satisfied and Dr. Ambedkar too would be agreeable. Accordingly, they placed before Ambedkar a written formulation of suggestions from Gandhiji. After this, on 22 September, they took him along with them to meet Gandhiji. During this meeting Ambedkar suggested that the untouchables should be given 197 seats in all in the Provincial legislatures and that a referendum of the untouchables be held every ten years. Upon which Gandhiji replied, 'What you say is reasonable, but do not demand anything that will separate the untouchables from Hindu society.' On the next day, when talks resumed, Gandhiji said, 'Take what you will: either a five-year validity for the pact, or my life.' After this the time for the meeting was up. It was decided that talks would be continued with [C.] Rajagopalachari, Malaviya and others. It was agreed by all that this issue of a period of five or ten years should be decided mutually in a meeting among the parties. This decision was conveyed to Gandhiji, and he accepted it. Following this, immediately on 25 September 1932, the draft of the Pact was drawn up. Rajagopalachari, along with Birla Shetji and Dr. Ambedkar, went to meet Gandhiji in Yerawada jail and placed the draft before him. Dr. Ambedkar then asked, 'Are you satisfied now at least?'

After the pact had been signed, Babasaheb went to the Assembly Hall in Pune. There he met Raobahadur Chitale from Ahmednagar, who remarked jokingly to Ambedkar that after making so many objections, in the end he had reached a compromise with Gandhiji. Babasaheb answered, 'What could I do? Jayakar was standing behind me holding a dagger and Sapru before me pistol in hand. I had no choice.'

The number of seats granted (to the untouchables) in the Poona Pact was greater than in the communal accord in the Round Table Conference. Instead of separate electorates they had been given joint electorates. In fact, in the first Round Table Conference, Babasaheb had not asked for separate electorates. That was a demand made by the untouchable community and communicated to Babasaheb through telegrams sent to London. Thus, right from the start Ambedkar had adopted a position of readiness to make concessions. And now he was confronted with the grievous choice posed by the staking of Gandhiji's life. That was how the historic Poona Pact was concluded. After the Poona Pact, the Congress took the lead in setting up an organization dedicated to the all-round progress of the untouchables. At first this organization was named 'India Anti-Untouchability League'. Later, it became 'Servants of Anti-Untouchability Society'. In the end, Gandhiji gave it the name of *Harijan Sevak Sangh* ['Association for Service to Untouchables/"children of God"']. Its central committee had nine members from the Congress, while three persons including Dr. Ambedkar were from the untouchable community.

Babasaheb decided to place before Gandhi his ideas on how this association should function. Just then, Dr. Ambedkar's name was included among the selected representatives chosen to take part in the third Round Table Conference, which was to deliberate on the constitution (of the Indian Republic) to be implemented in 1935. So on 7 November 1932 he left for London. Using the time at his disposal in the journey, on 14 November 1932 he wrote a letter containing detailed suggestions on how the Harijan Sevak Sangh should do its work, and posted it from Port Said to Thakkar Bappa. In this letter he expressed the sentiment that the alienation between caste Hindus and untouchables should end and that they should join together. Furthermore, in this letter he conveyed his suggestions as to how the Sangh should work so that Hindu society might become more integrated and strong.

Thakkar Bappa and the Congress threw this letter into the waste basket, and did not even send an acknowledgement. On the contrary, the Congress turned a blind eye to all of these suggestions and embarked on its own, independent programme of service. As a result, relations between the Sangh and Babasaheb did not remain cordial, and Babasaheb tendered his resignation from the Sangh. A few days later, the three other members from the untouchable community, [Rettamalai] Srinivasan, P. Baloo and [M.C.] Rajah also resigned. Because they had withdrawn their support, the Congress labelled them as traitors to the nation and the faith. Not only this; they were called puppets of the imperialists. Because Dr. Ambedkar sought to demand from the British the political rights that the untouchables had been denied for thousands of years, and to secure these rights before independence, he was portrayed as being opposed to the independence struggle. *In short, the Congress too did not understand Babasaheb and did not allow him to come near it politically.*

The Congress continued with its politics of betrayal of the untouchables, and Babasaheb had bitter experience of this in the years that followed, so that he was forced to launch a *satyagraha* to oppose the Poona Pact in 1946.

During the elections to the Bombay Provincial Legislative Council and the Berar Provincial Legislative Council, Dr. Babasaheb Ambedkar's Independent Labour Party had made some gains. This was because the Congress had not put up its own candidates for the reserved seats with full preparation.

Later, when the elections for representatives to be sent to the Provincial Councils took place in March 1946, the non-untouchable voters under Congress influence did not vote for candidates from the Scheduled Castes Federation, and the Federation suffered a humiliating defeat. For the 151 seats reserved (for untouchables) throughout the nation, only Babasaheb was elected from Bengal, and that too from what was then a Muslim constituency. Thus, he could not go as a representative on the committee framing the Indian constitution, because the condition was that a representative should be elected not by the untouchable voters alone, but also by the non-untouchables. The caste Hindu voters gave their votes to the Congress, and so only Congress party members were elected.

Babasaheb's position was that by means of the Poona Pact, Gandhiji had so cheated the untouchables that they had been deprived of their right of vote. The

Congress should now declare the Pact invalid as the British were about to leave.

Dr. Ambedkar now launched a nationwide *satyagraha* movement demanding that the Congress itself should declare the Poona Pact invalid, and he also demanded separate electorates. The *satyagraha* began on 14 July 1946. As a part of this, there was a 'Jail Bharo' agitation in Pune which the Communist Party then supported; many Communist Party members and Party sympathizers from the Dalit community took part in the *satyagraha* and went to jail on this occasion. More's brother-in-law Comrade Vitthal Tukaram Hate, who was then a Party member, was arrested in the *satyagraha* and imprisoned in the Yerawada jail. There the *satyagrahis* received ill-treatment: since they were being served poor food, the jailed *satyagrahis*, following the Communist Party's policy, launched an agitation inside the jail. As a result, Hate was transferred to Visapur jail as a punishment. He and several others spent some time in prison there.

Comrade More's Work in the Trade Union Movement

Even though More had worked with the peasants, he was living in Bombay and his real area of work was with the Bombay working class. At the time the Communist Party did not have any organizational work among the farmers anywhere in Maharashtra. Whatever organization the Party had built was all among the workers. Thus, the Party gave priority to organizing the workers, and the Party cadre had been trained where there were industrial workers. All the Communist activists in Bombay were working among the mill workers and railway workmen.

So, More also began his Communist life organizing these workers. But he also worked with other workers such as construction workers, press workmen, goldsmiths, lift operators and sanitation workers, setting up several small trade unions. In all this work his objective was to arouse the ideology of social power among the workers. He constantly discussed political issues with the workers. His association with them was not confined to the workplace and the union office, as is the case with today's leaders, but he visited their homes and shared in their joys and sorrows. They became his friends, and he brought many of them into the Party, as comrades.

Comrade Lenin used to say 'the Communist is a talking machine', that this was how a Communist should be. More was known for this; he was one of the few in the Party to practise this. His habit of talking constantly drew various other people to him besides workers: he was aware that it was not possible to bring professors, teachers, government servants, insurance employees and middle-class employees of private firms into the Communist trade unions, and so he built groups that could form their own independent unions. In Communist parlance this is called 'fraction work', and he carried this out. On the basis of this work by the Communists of the time, employees of insurance companies, banks, private companies and government servants as well as middle school teachers were formed into associations that were later led by employees with Communist leanings.

Alongside this work, More was also engaged in party-building. The Party in several places in Maharashtra was at the time organized around individuals. Organizational work by the Party existed only in Bombay. The Bombay of the time extended only up to Mahim and Matunga. All areas beyond this were regarded as the suburbs. In order to spread its work to these areas, the Party on 1 and 2 April 1932 organized a Suburban Youth Conference. More played a major role in this. After this, Communist activists were organized in many different suburban areas. In those days Comrade Jagannath Adhikari (Jaggu) lived in Bandra. So his home became a *de facto* Party office. More had a close bond with Adhikari. In those days the process of building the Communist Party had only just begun. Even though the Meerut Conspiracy Case was in the past, the Party was still in its infancy. The Party had two central committees, for Bombay and the rest of the country. The group led by Comrade S.V. Deshpande was known as Deshpande Master's central committee, and the majority of its members were working-class Communists. The party work of this group was mainly confined to Bombay. Comrade B.T. Ranadive and Comrade Gangadhar Adhikari were also working to build the Party in Bombay. More carried on his party-building work under the leadership of Ranadive and Adhikari.

If this was the situation in Bombay and Maharashtra, on the national level a coordination committee had been formed. This committee had also formed its own central committee, which was known as the Central Committee of the Communist Party. It was after the meeting of this Central Committee held in November–December that the Communist Party began organizing as a party on a nationwide scale. The resolutions adopted at this meeting of the Party Central Committee were published in the first issue of the *Communist* as a political manifesto. After this, on 11 May, a draft of the Party constitution was also published. More took part in the internal Party debates that followed. He put forward the view that the independent struggle of the untouchables against untouchability was also a part of the revolutionary liberation movement of the working class and that it was necessary to make efforts towards this end; that the Communist Party needed to work among the untouchable people and take up their problems. Even after he joined the Communist Party, More continued to fight against the injustice suffered by the untouchables.

In 1932, while More was in the Communist Party, the All India Trade Union Congress was dominated by working-class leaders. To break up this influence the 'Red Trade Union Congress' was formed under the leadership of B.T. Ranadive and S.V. Deshpande. In the working committee of the mill workers' union that was formed under this banner, R.M. Jambhekar and R.B. More were also elected.

In the office of the mill workers' union, there were by tradition two *matkas* (mud vessels) of drinking water. One was for the caste Hindu workers and the other for the Dalit workers. Those were times when such practices were common everywhere. Society was so numb to such things that nobody was much troubled by it. In the office of the mill workers' union, the Communist leaders would drink from the vessel meant for Dalits, but other caste Hindu workers did not do so. Even a Dalit leader like Bhise, who was the president of the mill workers' union had to drink water from the *matka* meant for Dalits.

As More had come from Babasaheb Ambedkar's independent movement which taught values of self-respect and a sense of identity, he was disturbed by this. Also, the Dalit comrades from Delisle Road who had joined the Party were disturbed, and the raised the issue in the Party. When More informed Ranadive of the matter he too was perplexed. Upon which More said, 'Keep only one *matka* of water in the office, so anyone who is polluted by caste considerations can go out and drink water from the hotel. This will bring out to people how strict we Communists are in the matter of caste discrimination. It is because we do not fearlessly take such a stand that the Dalits had to raise an independent struggle.' Ranadive and the other Party leaders felt that More's criticism was justified, and from then on the separate *matka* for Dalits in the mill workers' union office was relegated to history.

In fact, it would not be inappropriate to say that this was a contribution made by Dr. Babasaheb's independent movement to the Communist movement. In those days, in the BDD *chawls*, the Cement *chawls* and the BIT *chawls* in Bombay, there were separate taps for Dalits in the working-class colony. More also took the lead in an agitation to demand that this practice of separate taps should end, and all workers should be given equal treatment.

While More's struggle on these various issues was going on, in 1933 the mill owners drew up a plan to instal new machinery and to dismiss workers. The Communist leaders organized protest marches against this, and when these demonstrations were banned, they defied the ban and had to literally engage in hand-to-hand combat with the police. It was in one such battle that More was arrested for the first time. It is probable that Comrade Srinivas Sardesai was with him on this occasion. More broke the law. Because he had entered into a fight with the police, the court sentenced him to rigorous imprisonment and sent him to the Arthur Road jail. At the time, the present author was four or five years old. He had gone with his mother to meet More (his father) in prison. More was brought to the place of meeting in handcuffs; our meeting took place with him in that condition.

In 1933, after he was released from prison, More resumed his work with the mill workers. Later, in the All India Mill Workers' Convention held in Bombay on 29 January 1934, a call was given for a nationwide strike of mill workers. It was decided to form strike committees under the leadership of the Red Flag Mill Workers' Union of Bombay, to prepare for the strike all over India. More played a leading role in organizing this strike. The police kept a watch on him. Even so, More brought together the workers and held a demonstration in Girangaon where it was announced that a meeting would be held in Kombadi Galli in Lal Bagh. The police banned the demonstration, and the meeting, but the workers under More's leadership defied the ban. The police in a *lathi* charge on the demonstration and meeting held in defiance of the ban, beat up the workers severely. More was in the vanguard of the march. A gun-wielding policeman tried to push him back, and hit him hard on the chest with the butt of his rifle. More collapsed on the ground. The police put him in their van, took him to the K.E.M. Hospital and once there, told him that he had been arrested. The police mounted a standing guard around More's hospital cot on that occasion. But even in this situation More evaded the police guard and escaped from the hospital to go underground, and continued to prepare for the strike.

The main demands of the strike were: a minimum wage of 45 rupees, 25 rupees a month as unemployment benefit, free housing and an eight-hour working day. The strike took place in Bombay, Nagpur and Solapur. In Bombay the strike was one hundred per cent successful. Even though meetings and demonstrations were banned, the strike lasted for two months. After the strike ended, the mill owners made an across-the-board cut of 25 per cent in the workers' dearness allowance. But the ten-hour working day was brought down to nine hours.

After the success of the strike More came up from his underground sojourn. But the police still kept a watch on his movements. The Communist Party had also been banned. The police suspected that the Communist Party was handing out illegal secret pamphlets inciting the people to fight against the British government. They put forward this justification for acting under the Trade Disputes Act to surround the homes of B.T. Ranadive and six other Communist leaders and raid them.

More was living in the BIT Chawl in Byculla. The police launched a raid there too at 2 to 3 a.m. Mounting a strong police guard around the *chawl*, they proceeded to search the whole house. They left no corner of the house untouched; they even overturned the coal bin. But they did not find any secret pamphlets. So they confiscated all the pamphlets and Communist literature they could find and left the house at seven or eight in the morning.

When More started his work in the trade union, his earlier history in the Ambedkar movement came in very useful. The Dalit people looked to him with respect as the main organizer of the Mahad *satyagraha*. Also, even though the Dalit people were politically aligned with Dr. Ambedkar, as members of a class they had no alternative to the trade unions run by the Communist Party. They felt close to More because he was of their caste and also proud of him because he had been one of those who helped to establish Babasaheb's independent movement. This was More's strongest point in those days.

More had also taken on himself the task of spreading the ideas of Marxism-Leninism among the Dalits. Up to that time the Communist Party did not have any organizational work among the Dalits, nor did they have a presence in any

Dalit neighbourhood. It was almost as if the Party's image was that of being a party of caste Hindus.

Until he started the Independent Labour Party, Dr. Ambedkar had no work in the area of trade unions.[34] So the field was wide open for More. This benefited More in his party work; wherever he went among Dalit workers or in Dalit colonies, he was always looked to with respect. There was no resistance to hearing what he and his Communist Party had to say. For those who showed greater keenness, More held study camps to explain and make them understand what Marxism meant.

More was also a leader of the railway workers. He was secretary in what was then known as the G.I.P. (Greater Indian Peninsular) Railway Union and is now called the National Railway Workers' Union in the Central Railway. Among the railway workers there were a large number of Dalits. The typical Dalit railway worker was a member of the Communist-led AITUC, but would steer clear of the Communist Party. His politics was that of the Ambedkar movement. But, seeing More, many Dalit worker-activists were drawn towards him. More then bonded them with the Party. Among those whom More brought into the Party were railway workers from Matunga Com. K.M. Patil, Kachru Gangurde, J.G. More (Sayagaonkar), Hari Sakpal and K.D. Khavale, engine driver T.A. Gaikwad from Daund, Baburao Jadhav (son of Dr. Ambedkar's security chief), worker leader from Badnera, Com. Meshram, and many Dalit railway workers from Manmad, Igatpuri, Daund and Nashik Road. More also brought Com. Govind Mahadik from the Western Railway and the famous North Indian Dalit composer and poet Com. Shankar Shailendra, who worked in the Lower Parel Rail Workshop, into the Party. He also brought the Rokade brothers, Bhole and Gaikwad of the Nashik Security Press into the Party. Many of these had to serve terms in jail after they joined the Party and took up organizational and agitational work.

Com. D.B. aka Dinkar Bhosle of the Bombay Electric Supply and Transport Company (BEST, the company running Bombay's bus service) came into the Party. Later he became a member of the Bombay Committee of the Communist Party.

---

[34] The Independent Labour Party (ILP) was a political organization formed under the leadership of B.R. Ambedkar on 15 August 1936. The formation of the ILP was not welcomed or supported by Communist leaders, who argued that it would lead to a split in the working-class votes. Ambedkar replied that Communist leaders were working for workers' rights but not for the human rights of Dalit workers. The ILP secured 14 of the 17 seats they contested in the 1937 Provincial elections. This included 11 of the 13 contested seats in reserved constituencies for the Scheduled Castes. In 1938, the ILP organized a march of 20,000 tenants from Bombay's Konkan region with the support of the Congress Socialists and some Communist Party members demanding the abolition of the *khoti* system. This was the largest pre-Independence peasant mobilization in the region, and included Dalits and other lower castes. In the same year, the ILP joined with Communists to organize Bombay textile labourers in opposition to a bill intended to control strikes. The ILP also opposed this Bill in the Bombay Legislative Assembly.

He and his wife Vimaltai, together with their one-year-old daughter, spent some days in jail. Mill workers G.T. Suryavanshi and Baburao Garud, and activists like Dalpat Koli who organized the sanitation workers in Mazgaon, also joined the Party because of More. All these came from Dr. Ambedkar's independent Dalit movement, and not only did they attain Party membership, but they also made tremendous sacrifices for the Party.

It was a notable characteristic of More's work that he remained in the background playing an important role in building Party branches and independent trade associations of teachers in Bombay's municipal schools, and sanitation workers in the municipal corporation. In this he was greatly helped by Uddhav Lakshman Karandikar Guruji, father-in-law of author Arjun Dangle, Ankush Guruji and others. It would not be inappropriate to say that among the few Party comrades who took the initiative in many such endeavours and also kept up live associations with people from different sections of society, More was one of the foremost.

More organized the sanitation workers in Matunga Labour Camp, Mazgaon, Mahalakshmi–Arthur Road and Khar. And so in the conventions of sanitation workers organized under Party leadership in Nagpur, Jhansi and Vijapur, More was present as chief guest or chairman. During these conventions, he drew connections between the social issues of the Dalit people and their class rights as workers, and took the lead in building a strong working-class movement. In this way he joined the class artery of the Party with the social movement. Thus, he had attained a proximity to the Dalit people and the Ambedkar movement.

The Communist Party considered trade unions to be schools for nurturing class consciousness, and More, like the other cadres, carried out his work from this point of view. That was the spirit of the times. The opportunist trade unions of today that have fallen prey to economism did not exist in that situation. Today's union leaders treat the workers to cups of tea; in those days a worker would invite a union leader for tea and give him one or two rupees extra for his travelling expenses. The union leaders of those days, for their part, would not accept money just because a worker was proffering it, and if he did accept, it would be only to the tune of his actual fare. The leaders were honest and dedicated; they would have thought it wrong to travel by first class when the workers went third class.

Those times were different; trade union activists were fired with integrity and revolutionary to the core. More was a trade union activist, but no one had appointed him. He would just go where the workers were and organize them; this was the nature and direction of the Party's work. Thus, More built trade unions of all the kinds of workers he came across: liftmen, pressmen, watchmen. In those days one did not build a union by sitting at a table in the union office. The union leaders would meet the workers not only in the factory, but also at home. They would share meals with them and become a part of their joys and sorrows.

In this way, when the Reserve Bank of India building was being constructed

K.M. Salvi, to whom R.B. More dedicated his autobiography.
Courtesy of Subodh More.

in 1933, More out of his own awareness and on his own initiative organized the construction workers working on that site. In this he met a militant activist named Comrade K.M. Salvi, who later came to prominence as a leader of the construction workers' union. The surprising thing was that, like More, he was a product of the Ambedkar movement but in its second stage; he was one of the foremost leaders in organizing the Kalaram Mandir *satyagraha* in Nashik. After the *satyagraha* began and the District Collector ordered all four doors to the temple to be closed, Kachru Mathuji Salvi or Comrade K.M. Salvi was one of the leaders of the squad of *satyagrahis* that stood firm before all the doors. He was chief of the team of *satyagrahis* at the eastern door of the Kalaram Temple. Babasaheb himself and the main organizer of the *satyagraha*, Bhaurao aka Dadasaheb Gaikwad, selected Salvi for this role.

Salvi, like More, was honest to the bone, and he also had the capability of thinking independently. More gave him *The Communist Manifesto* and other available literature to read. After some discussion, he too was convinced that the Communist movement was, indeed, complementary to the Ambedkar movement. After this he developed a strong attachment to More. More then, after Delisle Road, began to visit the labour camp at the site of the Lokmanya Tilak Hospital. This was the labour camp now known as the Matunga Labour Camp, which was later transferred to Dharavi.

The Kalaram Mandir *Satyagraha* at Nashik

Even though the temple entry *satyagraha* at Amaravati (in 1927) had not opened the doors of the orthodox Hindus' minds, the untouchables organized a *satyagraha* at the Parvati Temple in 1929. Here, too, the experience of Amaravati was repeated. Even so, the Dalits and the progressive-minded non-Dalits decided to continue the temple entry movement. The untouchables of Nashik district accordingly went to Bombay in October 1929 to discuss the matter with Dr. Ambedkar. They decided to enter the Kalaram Mandir and stage a *satyagraha* if they were opposed. Babasaheb took up this decision for action. While the decision about the Nashik Kalaram Mandir *satyagraha* was being taken, the activists from Bombay felt that if this temple entry agitation was to succeed, the Bombay cadre should take the lead since Bombay was a large developed capitalist city in which untouchability had been somewhat diluted. But since it would have been difficult to sustain the movement in Bombay and Nashik at the same time, Dr. Ambedkar decided that they would concentrate on Nashik alone. Accordingly, the Nashik Kalaram Mandir *satyagraha* committee was set up under the chairmanship of Bhaurao Krishnaji Gaikwad aka Karmaveer Dadasaheb Gaikwad. Dadasaheb was also elected secretary of this committee, and it was he who issued a notice to the temple *panch*. But the Kalaram Mandir *panch* proved that it was no different from those at the Amaravati and Parvati temples by not replying to the notice. After waiting five months for a reply, it was announced on 3 March 1930 that the *satyagraha* would continue until entry to the temple was obtained.

To lead this *satyagraha*, it was decided that four persons would be stationed at the four doors of the temple. The leader chosen for the east door was Kachru Mathuji Salvi, at the north it was Patit Pavandas, at the south door Pandurang Nathuji Rajbhoj, and at the west door Shankardas Narayan Das was the chosen leader.

When the Nashik temple entry *satyagraha* began, More was carrying on his work as a Communist activist, building the Party organization and workers' associations. But even though More had joined the Communist Party he had not separated from the struggle of the Dalits for democratic rights. In those days More had started a newspaper named *Avhan* which he edited himself, and which took up the cause of workers, peasants and untouchables. He held several meetings in support of the Nashik temple *satyagraha*, using this newspaper as a propaganda sheet. He also collected funds to help the cause of the *satyagraha*, and sent a group of comrades from the Delisle Road Party unit to take part in the *satyagraha*. This group was led by Comrade Baburao Garud.

In order to defeat the *satyagraha*, the temple *panch* at first closed all the doors to the temple, denying entry to everyone including Hindus. But later they began to allow entry to caste Hindus using a hidden door. When the untouchables opposed this, they stopped it, and in an attempt to end the *satyagraha*, the government imposed Section 144 of the Indian Penal Code, whereby a magistrate can declare any assembly of five or more persons as unlawful. What is more, the police showed their casteist face by beating up several untouchable demonstrators and sending them to jail. But the *satyagrahis* did not budge. The Dalits kept up the *satyagraha* for five and a half years. When the Dalit leaders sent a letter to Babasaheb seeking guidance on how long to continue the *satyagraha*, he replied as follows in a letter to Dadasaheb Gaikwad written on 3 March 1934:

> The objective of this temple entry *satyagraha* which I initiated was not that after the untouchables attain entry to the temple, they sit around doing *puja* in the belief that this will bring them *moksha*. This was never my understanding. Neither do I believe that temple entry will secure a place, a respected place, in Hindu society for the untouchables. My intention was that the untouchables should become aware of their human rights and there should arise in them a readiness to fight constantly against those who oppose them in this. I have achieved this objective. Because of this *satyagraha*, the confidence and the tendency to fight for their human rights has been awakened in the untouchables of Maharashtra and Hindustan. The next step is to make all efforts for the education of the untouchables and for their political rights; and when the untouchables have been enriched by education and empowered with political rights, then they will become an excellent part of Hindu society. But to achieve this final objective, the Hindu society, Hindu religion and Hindu religious texts will have to be revised from top to bottom, and the untouchables will have to go on struggling to induce the caste Hindus to do this.

After this, there was no organized movement for temple entry anywhere in India. This *satyagraha* too was called off by Dr. Ambedkar in 1935. And it was in 1935 that he made the public statement at Yeola in Nashik district: 'Although I was

15 November 1931 issue of *Avhan*.
Courtesy of Anil Sawadkar.

Page 6 of the above mentioned issue of *Avhan*.
Courtesy of Anil Sawadkar.

born a Hindu, I will not die a Hindu.' By this statement Babasaheb gave a call for religious conversion, which caused a stir throughout the nation.

More Becomes Active Again in the Peasant Association

Even after More came into the Communist Party, he maintained contact with Anantrao Chitre from the Ambedkar movement, who held a class viewpoint, and other members of the Colaba District Peasants' Association. While he was a part of the independent Ambedkar movement together with Chitre and Narayan Nagu Patil, More worked for the Colaba District Peasants' Association. Even after he entered the Communist Party, More kept contact with the association and continued his work among the farmers. During the non-cooperation movement of 1930–31, the British government declared the association illegal and banished More from Colaba district. Even so, More continued his work secretly; at the same time, he was active among the workers in Bombay.

Even though Bhai Chitre and Narayan Nagu Patil were a part of Babasaheb Ambedkar's social movement, they were also trying to weave together the farmers' movement with the Ambedkar movement. Thus, Babasaheb too was always a part of the farmers' struggles in Maharashtra. In 1934 the government lifted the ban on the Colaba District Peasants' Association. Taking advantage of this, on 16 December 1934, Narayan Nagu Patil organized a farmers' convention at Chari in the Alibag *tehsil* of Colaba district, with Dr. Ambedkar presiding. More was present at this convention.

After it was over, he took Comrade Mhatre, who had only recently joined the Communist Party, and some other activists along with him to raise awareness among tenants against the landowning *khots* and the *khoti* system of tenant farming. More had studied the *khoti* system under Dr. Babasaheb Ambedkar. Using this knowledge More drew up a petition of demands of the conscious militant tenants to send to the government. Then, in 1937–38, More, Narayan Nagu Patil and Shamrao Parulekar led the tenants of Chari in a campaign to not cultivate the land belonging to the *khots*, much as workers conduct strikes in Bombay. This put the *khots* in a fix. They made many attempts to break the strike, but these farming tenants were under the influence of the Bombay working-class and the Communists, and they held out. In 1937, according to a law passed in 1935, a council of ministers from the Congress party was in power in the Provincial assembly. The chief minister was then called prime minister. Balasaheb Kher was the prime minister of that Assembly. This government was in fact on the side of the *khots*, but the government too was rendered helpless by the strike, and the then agriculture minister Morarji Desai went personally to negotiate with the striking tenants, and on 4 February 1939 the Assembly enacted an ordinance giving protection to the tenants. After this the strike was called off.

More had contacts with the farmers' movement in Maharashtra, especially in the Konkan, even before he joined the Communist Party. In those days, the Communist Party mainly worked with the working class. There were efforts to build an independent peasant movement under Party leadership, but in Maharashtra an independent farmers' movement did not come up under the Party. Thus, More, who had brought the legacy of the Ambedkar movement to the farmers, was always active in the Colaba district farmers' struggle. Thus, when an all-India farmers' convention was held in Lucknow in 1936 under Communist leadership to establish an all-India farmers' front (*Akhil Bharatiya Kisan Sabha*), More was present as a representative of the Colaba district. Thus, More was a part of the founding of the Akhil Bharatiya Kisan Sabha.

DEDICATED DALIT COMRADES IN THE COMMUNIST PARTY

A number of activists from Delisle Road worked with More in the mill workers' strike of 1934. These activists were likewise more active in the work of the Young Workers' Association and the Unemployed Labourers' Forum, which had been started by the Party, and of which More was secretary.

Later on, Vishram Jadhav, Krishna Khere Kudikkar, Bhikaji Tambebuva, Ramchandra Nandgaonkar, Mahadev Bhoir also joined these associations. Besides them, Dagadu Shirke, Dhanaji Mhatre, Shahir Raghu Kadam, Shahir Sikandar Shaikh, Kamlakar Kuvekar, Baloo Pawar, Arjun Surve, Bhargav Mohite, Hiru Jadhav, Vishram Kamble, Narayan Mohite, Sadashiv Shirke, S.K. Pawar, Harishchandra Shirke, Pedamkar, Nana Ovhal and others were also added.

In 1948, the Second Congress of the Communist Party was held in Calcutta, in which the strategy and tactics for revolution as based on people's power were spelled out. Around the same time, armed struggle was being carried out under the Party's leadership in Telangana. Comrade B.T. Ranadive was leading the Party as its general secretary. The Calcutta Congress gave a call for intense struggles by the toiling people all over the country. On 9 March 1949 the Party had begun preparations for an all-India strike of railway workers, and it had been decided that the mill workers of Bombay would stage a one-day symbolic strike in support of the railway workers. At the time the Party organizer of the Delisle Road area, Comrade (Dr.) A.B. Sawant was working from underground together with More. So, the two of them together with Party workers from Delisle Road and the vice-president of the Mill Workers' Association, Comrade Baburao Garud, organized a secret meeting of leading comrades on the night of 8 March 1949 at the home of Comrade Bhiku Kuvekar, a Party member who lived in the Red Municipal Chawl on Arthur Road.

The Congress government had been shaken by the announcement of this strike. They imposed Section 144 of the Criminal Procedure Code (which allows anticipatory action to be taken 'to prevent a disturbance of the public tranquillity or a riot or an affray. In such circumstances private rights must give way') and started a round of repression. Anyone considered suspicious was being arrested. The police and the army had been put on standby ready to act against workers and the people. But the above-mentioned meeting had been organized in spite of this situation, defying the repression that had been unleashed. Besides the leading comrades mentioned above, Professor G.K. Joshi and Comrade Madan Phadnis were present.

After the meeting was over some comrades left, and, since it was quite late, some were still sitting there holding a discussion. Suddenly, at three a.m., the police surrounded the *chawl*. Some persons had already left. Those who remained, i.e. Govind Tamhankar, G.K. Joshi, Bhargav Sonawane, Arjun Surve, Kamlakar Kuvekar, Yashwant Gurav, Kashinath Mhatre, Ramchandra Nandgaonkar, Dagadu Shirke, Baloo Pawar and Baburao Garud were arrested under this preventive Act and sent off to jail. During the railway strike of 9 March 1949 about twenty-five thousand activists were arrested, including those named above and the Delisle Road Party unit.

The next day the news was flashed in all the newspapers that while the Communists were preparing to blow up the railway with bombs, guns, pistols, knives and other weapons, the police had arrested the lot with their weapons and saved the lives of citizens of Bombay. In fact this was all false. That was the first time I experienced how the police can spread false propaganda.

After all these comrades had served a year in jail, they were served notices of banishment from the city precincts. So all of them came to stay in Thane. This meant loss of their jobs and a crisis for their families. Yet they held fast and went on doing party work as before.

Later, on 8 November 1949, a huge contingent of workers led by the famous cine artiste Comrade Balraj Sahni, Com. Bhiku Kuvekar, Com. Belose and Com. Gavhankar demonstrated against police tyranny by marching from Lal Bagh to the Delisle Road police station. The police answered with a brutal *lathi* charge and firing. In this, Comrade Bhiku Kuvekar was killed, and Balraj Sahni was severely thrashed and taken to jail.

Just as More had built the Delisle Road Party unit and the surrounding neighbourhood as a fortress of Communist influence, so, with the help of Com. K.M. Salvi, did he build the Matunga Labour Camp as another such fortress. Here, the Communist leader B.T. Ranadive himself went along with More to take study classes. Among those who came close to the Party because of the influence of More and Com. Salvi were singers, composers, poets and writers like Annabhau Sathe, Baburao Bagul, Hari Jadhav, Tukaram Sartape, Shahir (poet) Majnu Indori, Kashinath Rokade, Vishram Gangurde, Umaji Dhengale, Shankar Narayan Pagare, Sopan Waghmare, Hiraman Samant, Murlidhar Gaikwad, Sandipan Dethe, Dajiba

Bhagwandas, Dolraj, Rocky Faro, Sukhdev Nikam, Bhurelal Hazari, Bihari Fakira, Jagaram Hazari, Balkubuva Sartape, Kashinath Ahire, G.B. Gaikwad, Khairmode Master, Godabai Dethe, Najabai Sartape and others. Many of these lost their jobs and had to serve time in prison. Besides this, they were arrested and punished in many other struggles, and they also took part in the *satyagraha* movement for independence of Goa (from the Portuguese, in 1961). They were in the forefront in the struggle for a united Maharashtra state. Because of all this, they lost their jobs and many of them dedicated their lives to the Communist movement. Later, Hari Jadhav visited Moscow and several other places abroad as representative of the youth front of the Communist Party. Like Hari Jadhav, Com. K.G. More from the Parel Railway Workshop also lost his job and became a Party full-timer. Later, he worked with the Kisan Sabha in Raigad district.

Thus, innumerable activists from the Dalit community came close to the Communist Party under More's influence when Babasaheb was still alive. Among them were Bajirao Kamble and S.T. Gaikwad from Pune, Raoba A. Chikane from Thane. Like Delisle Road and Matunga Labour Camp in Bombay, in Nagpur the Dalit colonies of Bezan Bagh and Indora were also centres of Communist activity. Mainly untouchable railway workers, sanitation workers and mill workers from these areas became active workers in Communist organizations. Some of the neighbourhoods there were known as 'Red Square' because of the influence of the Communists. Among the persons active in the movement in these areas were Com. Maruti Meshram, Com. Kashinath Bansod, Com. Balwantkumar Meshram, Com. Bhojraj Ramteke, Com. Chauthmal, Com. Bhaiyalal Samudre and Com. Damayanti Balwantkumar Meshram.

It was these comrades who took the lead in organizing a convention of sanitation workers from Central Provinces and Berar in Nagpur in April 1946 and invited Com. More to preside over the convention. After this convention there was a successful strike of sanitation workers in which the above mentioned comrades played an active role. Com. Balwantkumar Meshram gave over his house to be used as the office of the South-Eastern Railway Union. Senior Communist leaders like Com. A.B. Bardhan also stayed at his house when they were underground. (His son Com. Biplab is even today an active worker of the Communist Party of India (Marxist).) Many of the comrades from this region were in contact with More as well as with Com. S.Y. Kolhatkar and with one of the founder leaders of the Communist Party, Muzaffar Ahmed from West Bengal, and all these activists were influenced by them. Similarly, Com. Bhaskar Jadhav, who studied in Siddharth College in Bombay with the present author, and later became full-timer, general secretary and finally a great leader of the Lal Nishan Party, also used to meet More and Annabhau Sathe in the Matunga Labour Camp in his youth. He had great respect for More and was impressed by his organizational work. He too felt that Com. More's biography should be published. All these comrades from the Dalit community shared the feeling that the Ambedkar movement was doing work that was complementary to the Communist movement.

Several Dalit activists came into the Communist Party because of More's influence, even in Babasaheb's lifetime. Many of them lost their jobs, spent time in jail, and suffered all kinds of hardships. But the people in Babasaheb's independent Dalit movement did not have the capacity to understand these Dalit activists, who joined the Communist Party even while they believed in Babasaheb's cause. There were among them some who were of a criminal tendency and believed themselves to be the true supporters of Babasaheb. Because they had also not understood Babasaheb properly, they boycotted the Dalit Communists and even made murderous attacks on them. In spite of this, these Communists from the Dalit community stuck to the Party.

The reason for this is that a person who joins the Communist Party is already prepared to leave the beaten track, and has the inborn qualities to rebel against the establishment in pursuit of his cause. Also, he has to be honest to the bone. And if such a person's thoughts are shaped by Marxism and Leninism, then there is born in him an immovable dedication to building the socialist society of tomorrow based on people's power. Once such a person enters the Communist Party he does not look back, or go back. If he is not made of such stuff then he usually does not join the Party; or if one joins the Party by mistake, he leaves it of his own accord, it is not necessary to remove him. And if he remains in the Party with his capitalist-feudal faults, he leaves a little later, or the Party has to throw him out. This is the criterion that distinguishes the true Communist: not just of his own mettle, but of his having assimilated the principles of Marxism and Leninism. Of such stuff was More made, and also the Dalit activists he brought into the Party!

On one occasion, in Maharashtra, some anti-Communists who considered themselves faithful followers of Babasaheb launched attacks on Communists from the Dalit community. In Bombay these took place mainly in Delisle Road, Matunga Labour Camp and, to a lesser extent, in the BDD *chawls* at Naigaon. This also spread to Nashik and other places. At first Communists from the Mahar caste were attacked. Then they widened the scope to include Matangs, and Mehtars. Heads were broken and blood was spilt. What is more, Communists from the Mahar community were boycotted. Kinship relations within the caste were cut off, and nobody attended their marriages, funerals and other joyful or sorrowful family occasions. In Chandori in Nashik district, Shankar Narayan Pagare, great-uncle of author Arjun Dangle, was viciously attacked because he had become a member of the Communist Party. In Nashik there were fights at places where Dalits filled water. In the Cement Chawl in Delisle Road many Party members had their heads smashed. At the Matunga Labour Camp, Communists were dragged out of their homes and beaten. A staunch Communist like Hari Jadhav was tied to an electric pole and beaten up. When Party members from the Valmik community including

Chandori Valmiki, Bhagwan Chaudhari, Bhurelal Jagaram Hazari and Bihari Fakira were beaten up, women Party comrades Bhagawati and Shija ran to help, and they were also beaten up.

Then those who had been beaten up told More what had happened and asked him to meet Babasaheb about it. So More met Babasaheb and told him about the beatings. Babasaheb expressed great grief on hearing this, and he called together his party's main leaders and activists and chastised them. Those who had carried out the attacks were made to apologize. After this the beatings stopped and the boycotts also were relaxed to some extent.

In those days More used many different tactics to increase the scope of the Party's work. In 1945 the third convention of the Scheduled Castes Federation was to be held in Bombay. More posted a prominent news feature about this convention before it started in the Communist weekly paper *Lokyuddh* ['People's War'], and also gave the convention publicity by writing a special feature about the convention which appeared with a large photograph of Babasaheb and the huge crowd of people who attended. This helped to draw activists from the Dalit community towards the Party.

Many of the Bombay-based activists of the Scheduled Castes Federation had become fellow-travellers of the Communists. S.B. Jadhav, secretary of the Scheduled Castes Federation, resigned from his party and joined the Communist Party. When he heard that the chief of the Samata Sainik Dal, Captain Sasalekar, was on the point of joining the Communist Party, Babasaheb of course had to step forward to save his party. It was in this context that Babasaheb, in a meeting held at the Nare Park grounds in 1945 or 1946, had criticized the Communists saying, 'The Communists are ants sticking to molasses.' Here he had used 'molasses' as a simile for the Dalit people; his words were true then, and remain true even today. Because the Communist Party is basically a party of the oppressed, the working class, peasants and the Dalit workers. Babasaheb had recognized this innate relationship of the Communist Party with the oppressed of society, and so his statement was in no way wrong. He had made this statement in an attempt to stem the outflow from his party, the Scheduled Castes Federation. But this did not mean that he was an enemy of the Communists. But his devious middle-class followers made opportunistic use of this statement of Babasaheb's to keep the Dalit people away from the Communists, and finally took resort to the Congress party. They conveniently forgot that Babasaheb had remarked about the Congress party that the Congress was a burning house. Among those who thus joined the Congress is a long list of names, from R.D. Bhandare to S.M. Kamble.

Thus, these Communists from the Dalit community were at the same time activists of the movement run by Babasaheb to fight for the socio-political rights of the Dalits, and activists of the Communist movement. Those like More believed firmly that a fundamental transformation of society could not come

स्वतंत्र मजूर पक्ष, मुंबई.

वार्षिक सर्वसाधारण सभा

स्वतंत्र मजूर पक्षाच्या मुंबई शाखेची पहिली वार्षिक सर्व साधारण सभा रविवार ता. २७ मार्च सन १९३८ रोजी रात्रौ ९ वाजतां पक्षाचे अध्यक्ष डॉ. बाबासाहेब आंबेडकर यांचे अध्यक्षतेखालीं नायगांव बी. प्लॉट वरील पटांगणांत भरणार आहे. तरी सर्व सभासदांस सभेस हजर रहाण्याची आग्रह- पूर्वक विनंती आहे.

सभेंत गेल्या वर्षांतील कामाचा अहवाल मंजूर करणें, कार्यकारी मंडळा- वरील सभासदांची संख्या वाढविणें, वगैरे कामें होतील. मुंबई शहर किंवा उपनगरें येथील जे गृहस्थ आठ आणे वर्गणी भरून पक्षाचे सभासद झाले असतील त्यानांच सभेच्या कामांत भाग घेता येईल. तरी सभेस येतांना प्रत्येक सभासदानें आप- आपली पावती घेऊन येणें जरूर आहे.

वाहेदिना मेन्शन
पोयबावडी, परळ
मुंबई नं. १२
ता. १५-३-३८

आपले नम्र,
के. व्ही. चित्रे
एस. ए. उपशाम
चिटणीस, स्व. म. प.
मुंबई.

भारत भूषण प्रिं. प्रेस, दादर-मुंबई.

For the annual meeting of the Independent Labour Party,
Bombay Branch, 27 March 1938.
Courtesy of Eleanor Zelliot,
from the collection of Anupama Rao.

about without the Communist movement, and that there was no alternative to this movement. They, like More, were at the same time attentive to the weaknesses of the Communist movement. They also understood that Babasaheb was trying to obtain more benefits for the Dalits within the framework of a capitalist social system, and they knew the limitations of this undertaking. But it would have been foolish to discuss this openly and make it a target of criticism. Because Babasaheb was not just leader of the Dalits but he was also their identity. These Communists from the Dalit community understood the emotional side of the question and they had considerable political maturity. And More was able to build such a generation of class-conscious, communist-thinking Dalits because he had only given up Babasaheb's platform, he had not given up the ground he stood on.

Independent Labour Party

The objective of Babasaheb's movement was to secure social equality, political rights and economic equity for the Dalits. To this end, in 1923, thinking in tune with the times, he had established an organization called the 'Bahishkrit Hitakarini Sabha', or Association for the Welfare of Outcastes. While forming this organization he had not kept non-Dalits from joining. Because his ultimate objective was to integrate with Indian society and to try and solve problems like untouchability and social problems related to it as a part of Indian society as a whole. It would not do to consider this a problem for the untouchables alone; it was Babasaheb's position right from the outset that untouchables and caste Hindus should come together to solve it.

In the circumstances in which the Bahishkrit Hitakarini Sabha had been formed, its historical task was to make the movement for social transformation universal. Similarly, the 'Samaj Samata Sangh' or Association for Equality in Society had been formed with the objective of broad equality. In this were included various struggles, from the Mahad *satyagraha*, the Bahishkrit conventions, farmers' conventions, the fight against the *khoti* system right up to the temple entry *satyagraha* at the Kalaram Mandir in Nashik. These struggles, through the joint efforts of untouchables and caste Hindus, stirred up society so thoroughly that the Chavdar reservoir in Mahad was opened up for the public. Gradually, temples also opened up, almost unperceived. But those who had borne in their hearts the hope that once temples were opened up, untouchability would disappear, found that this did not happen. The next struggle was for political rights and to attain economic prosperity for Dalits.

With this aim, Babasaheb started the Independent Labour Party as a broader version of the Bahishkrit Hitakarini Sabha. And this too was organized together with Dalits and non-Dalits. Babasaheb had this broad political vision. Because they have not understood this, some have said that some of Babasaheb's friends

For the Delisle Road Dalit women's condolence meeting
on 26 November 1938 for two labourers killed in police firing
on 7 November 1938.
Courtesy of Eleanor Zelliot,
from the collection of Anupama Rao.

suggested to him that he should form a wider organization, so that these friends could be put up for election to general (non-reserved) seats, and thus, participate in the party. And elsewhere we find the analysis that the Independent Labour Party had been formed as an opposition party on the lines of the Labour Party in England, and to secure the votes of non-Dalits for candidates put up for the reserved seats. Both these opinions have been put forward by non-Dalit intellectuals. Both these opinions are imaginary and do injustice to Babasaheb. On the contrary, the senior thinker Raosaheb Kasbe says that Babasaheb's Independent Labour Party was the first attempt at unity between the untouchables and like-thinking non-Dalits.

It is my opinion that the class of Dalits consists mainly of workers, farmers and agricultural labourers. It is possible to bring about their economic advancement through bringing them together with their non-Dalit class fellows. Thus, Babasaheb also took a class point of view when he started the Independent Labour Party.

He announced the formation of this party on 15 August 1936. In the manifesto that he published on this occasion, he announced a policy of starting a land mortgage bank for the benefit of farmers, and setting up a network of cooperative marketing societies for agricultural produce. He promised to bring a ban on the fragmentation of holding and to give protection to tenants under the *talukdari* and *khoti* systems of farming. A programme for people's welfare was put forward in which were included the restructuring of heavy industries, a support for technical education, compulsory primary schooling, adult education and a restructuring of the education system. Keeping the Dalits in mind, the manifesto proposed to abolish the *watandari* system (whereby the Mahars worked as village servants in return for the grant of rights to land) which was responsible for the low status of the Mahars, and replace it by a system of salaried jobs. *What is more, the colour of the party's flag was red.*

This was the programme that Babasaheb took up. On 11 November 1936, in an interview with *The Times of India* he said that the Congress was a party of the capitalists and landlords and that it was contributing to the exploitation of the people. If the Independent Labour Party were voted to power, it would enact laws in the legislature that would put limits on the exploitation of the people. Those who believed in this noble objective could join this labour party. The party was open to persons of all faiths and castes. At the same time he announced the names of six caste Hindus: C.T. Ranadive (brother of B.T. Ranadive), Anantrao Chitre, Shamrao Parulekar, Surbanana Tipnis, A.V. Gadkari and B.V. Pradhan as candidates from the unreserved seats in the (Bombay) Legislative Assembly.

In fact, the advocate A. Vinayakrao Gadkari was elected from Pune (East), Shamrao Vishnu Parulekar from Ratnagiri, and Anantrao V. Chitre from Ratnagiri (North). And in all ten persons including Babasaheb were elected from reserved seats.

The Congress had fielded the cricketer Palwankar Baloo against Babasaheb in the Parel–Byculla constituency. Babasaheb got 13,245 votes while Palwankar

स्वतंत्र मजूर पक्ष मुंबई
शेतकऱ्यांचा मोर्चा

महाराष्ट्रांतील शेतकऱ्यांच्या आज्च्या नाडलेल्या परिस्थितीची योग्य ती जाणीव मुंबईच्या लेजिस्लेटिव्ह असेंब्लीस करून देण्याकरितां सोमवार ता. १० जानेवारी १९३८ रोजीं महाराष्ट्रांतील शेतकऱ्यांची जंगी मिरवणूक निघणार आहे. ही मिरवणूक निरनिराळ्या संस्था व पक्षांकडून स्थापन करण्यांत आलेल्या 'किसान मार्च कमेटी' तर्फे काढण्यांत येणार आहे. ह्या कमेटींत ज्याप्रमाणें इतर संस्थांनीं भाग घेतला आहे, त्याच प्रमाणें स्वतंत्र मजूर पक्षानें घेतला असून, पक्षाचे तीन सभासद ह्या कमेटीवर आहेत. तरी स्वतंत्र मजूर पक्षाच्या सभासदांनीं व अनुयायांनीं ही मिरवणूक यशस्वी करून दाखविणें हें त्यांचे कर्तव्य आहे. म्हणून सर्व कामकरी व शेतकरी जनतेनें सोमवार ता. १० जानेवारी १९३८ रोजीं भाकरी खाऊन सकाळीं ९ वाजतां मोठ्या जमावानें परळ येथील कामगार मैदानावर जमावें. तेथून मिरवणूक कोटांत आझाद मैदानावर जाईल. कोंकणांतून येणारे शेतकरी आझाद मैदानावर जमा होतील. ह्या मैदानावर सभा भरविण्यांत येईल व तेथून असेंब्लीच्या हॉलकडे (काळ्या घोड्या जवळ) मिरवणूक निघेल. तरी सर्व कामकरी शेतकरी जनतेनें बरोबर सकाळीं ९ वाजतां कामगार मैदानावर (पोयबावडी) जमा व्हावे.

शेतकऱ्यांचा विजय असो !
कामकऱ्यांचा विजय असो !
स्वतंत्र मजूर पक्षाचा विजय असो !

स्वतंत्र मजूर पक्षाची कचेरी
वाहेदिना मेन्शन,
पोयबावडी, परळ,
मुंबई नं. १२.

आर. आर. भोळे एम्. एल्. ए.
डी. व्ही. प्रधान
गणपत महादेव जाधव उर्फ मडके बुवा

For a peasants' procession from Kamgar Maidan, Parel, to the Assembly Hall by the ILP, 10 January 1938. Courtesy of Eleanor Zelliot, from the collection of Anupama Rao.

got 11,225 votes and was defeated. What was surprising was that P.N. Rajbhoj and Devrukhkar, who had always gone about claiming to be Babasaheb's followers, also stood against him. They got 205 and 437 votes respectively and were also defeated. Another of Babasaheb's close followers, Rankhambe, joined the Congress because he was not given an election ticket. There was always a swarm of such selfish followers in the circle around Babasaheb. Besides Bombay, the Independent Labour Party fought this election in the Berar Province also.

So a Congress government came to power in the Bombay Provincial Council. Since the Independent Labour Party was the second largest party, it played the role of an opposition party. At the time the Congress tabled a bill banning strikes and lockouts that purported to be in the interest of the workers, but though the ban on lockouts was made out to be the aim, it was really intended to remove the workers' right to strike. On 2 September 1938, after Balasaheb Kher tabled this Bill in the Bombay Provincial Council, Shamrao Parulekar and others launched a scathing criticism of the Bill. On 5 September 1938, Babasaheb also criticized the Bill severely. Comrade Dange's speech on the Bill was also much talked about. Babasaheb announced that there would be a one-day general strike protesting against the Bill on 17 October. Later there were some difficulties, and finally, 7 November 1938 was declared as the day of the general strike. The Communist Party and the Independent Labour Party came together for the strike and Dr. Ambedkar, Dange, Ranadive and Shamrao Parulekar held joint meetings.

The strike of the Independent Labour Party was successful. The working class came out on the streets in large numbers. There was stone throwing on Delisle Road. The police resorted to firing and added to the workers' rage. Home Minister [K.M.] Munshi's car had its windows smashed. In the police firing at the *chawl* near the David Sassoon Mill a worker named Bhairu Raoji Chavan was killed and a Dalit worker, Bhagoji Waghmare, was severely injured and later died. In this way Ambedkar carried out a strike together with the Communists and expressed the desire to unite for struggle in the future.

Just as Dr. Ambedkar was fighting for the workers, he was fighting for the cause of farmers too. He and his Independent Labour Party tabled a bill to abolish the *khoti* system and an amendment bill seeking to reform the *watan* system of service by the Mahars. He held farmers' conventions to organize the peasantry. On 10 January 1938, a protest march of 20,000 farmers under Babasaheb's leadership was held on the Azad Maidan. More, though he was underground at the time, helped in many ways to organize this demonstration. Communist leaders Com. S.S. Mirajkar and Com. Lalji Pendse, together with their cadre, took part, and promised on behalf of their party always to cooperate with the Independent Labour Party and Babasaheb. The Communist Party declared that there was a need to further strengthen this class unity in the future.

More Turns Down the Offer of an Election Ticket

At that time, most of the Dalit people stayed with Dr. Ambedkar in his independent movement for the abolition of untouchability. But the more articulate among his followers wanted to secure their own advancement together with Dalit liberation. Among these was Ganesh Abaji Gavai from Berar, who had been a part of the movement to end untouchability that had been launched by non-Dalits even before Babasaheb's independent movement. Later he joined Babasaheb but finally left him and tilted in the direction of Hindutva politics. Another was Raobahadur M.C. Rajah, who was sometimes with Babasaheb and sometimes opposed him. His politics was one of competition with Babasaheb. A third such was P.N. Rajbhoj, who even though he was with Babasaheb from the beginning, still sometimes joined hands with the Congress, and tried to outmanoeuvre Babasaheb. But in the end he embraced the Buddhist faith as a follower of Babasaheb.

A fourth example was Sitaram Shivtarkar, who in fact was in Babasaheb's movement right from the start. After Babasaheb denied him an election ticket in 1937 he left Babasaheb, went straight off and joined the Congress party. A fifth was Balkrishna Janoji Devrukhkar, who left Babasaheb to work for some time in Communist trade unions. Later he left even that and joined the Congress party, where he passed no opportunity to oppose Babasaheb. Then finally, he returned to Babasaheb's fold and was elected to the Bombay Municipal Corporation. Later, he was brutally murdered as a follower of Babasaheb. For all his twists and turns, he will go down in history as a follower of Babasaheb. A sixth example is that of Amritrao Rankhambe of Nashik, who was a wealthy gentleman who took a leading part in the Kalaram Mandir *satyagraha*. When Babasaheb denied him candidacy in the election of 1937, he moved away from him and joined the Congress party.

R.B. More, on the other hand, began his work as a social activist in collaboration with Babasaheb, but never held the hope of becoming a leader. He did not join the Congress party as many others did. He joined the Communist Party within Babasaheb's lifetime because he was deeply dedicated to the cause, but he treasured his close association with Babasaheb to the end, and had deep respect for him. Babasaheb never felt that More had left him. That was why, when elections to the Bombay Provincial Council were announced following the law of 1935,[35] Babasaheb denied tickets to Shivtarkar and Rankhambe. But on the other hand, even though More was openly a Communist, he requested him to stand for election from the Independent Labour Party. More turned him down with thanks; upon which Babasaheb told him, 'I am ready to field you as a candidate even if you do not leave your party.' But More turned down this offer also.

There is a similar incident pertaining to the election of 1946. At the time

---

[35] Satyendra More is referring to the Government of India Act, 1935, commonly referred to as India's first Constitution.

Babasaheb was labour minister in the government. His special railway carriage (Minister's Car) used to stop at Bombay Central station. D.G. Jadhav, then the Labour Commissioner in the Central government had come there to meet him. More was then living in the Municipal Workers' Chawl in the Calcuttawalla Estate near Bombay Central. Babasaheb sent Jadhav there to bring More to him. More came to meet Babasaheb as soon as he received the message. Babasaheb again suggested to More that he stand for election from his party. Since More was a staunch Communist, and did not have any bourgeois ideas about becoming a Member of the Assembly in his head, he turned the offer down. More was of a very gentle disposition. Because he never fell prey to individual ambition, he again gently turned down Babasaheb's request because he was true to his party's class politics. This was the difference between More and Babasaheb's other followers!

In his autobiographical narrative, *Atmashodh* ['Awareness of Self'], R.B. More's Party colleague Datta Kelkar, relates the following story:

> One evening, as we were sitting in front of the Dalvi Building, More put his hand on my shoulder and said, 'Comrade, you're not busy with anything special just now? Dr. Babasaheb Ambedkar is holding a meeting at the Kamgar Maidan. Let's go there.' We set off. As we were on our way, More said, 'We can stand on the pavement outside, that way it'll be easier for us to walk out afterwards.' We chose a spot on the pavement that was a hundred feet or so from the stage. We reached there just as Madkebuva's introductory speech was ending, and he requested Babasaheb to guide the audience. Babasaheb was at the time a member of the Viceroy's Executive Council, which is equivalent to what would be a government minister's post today. But security for ministers was in those days very slight. Babasaheb stood up to give his speech. As was his habit, he cast a glance all around, over the entire audience. He did not fail to notice R.B. More standing on the pavement. He shouted out loudly, 'Hey More Saheb, your place is not on the sidewalk, come up here.' More folded his hands in a *namaste*, remained where he stood, and gestured to say, 'No, I am better over here where I am.' Babasaheb declared in a commanding voice, 'Go and get that More up on to the stage.' A dozen campaigners who knew More ran up to him and he had perforce to go up on the stage. As he arrived Babasaheb again thundered, 'This R.B. More is a great man. More here is one of the few persons through whose efforts I entered politics!'[36]

---

[36] This paragraph has been added at the request of Subodh More as it was omitted from the first edition of the Marathi text.

The Second World War—Congress and the Communists

On 3 September 1939, Great Britain declared war against Germany. There were then Congress cabinets in power in the Provincial assemblies, according to the 1935 law. Britain had not consulted the Congress before starting the war. This was an insult to the Indian people and to the Congress party in power. So, on 14 September 1939, the Congress Working Committee protested against the British government in a public petition. The petition demanded that Britain should declare its intentions regarding democracy and imperialism in this war. Did Britain's objectives include ending imperialism and relating to India as an independent nation? Would India's policy in this war be decided according to the wishes of the Indian people?

In short, the petition reminded Britain that the movement for independence was not over. It did not vehemently oppose the war or demand that the war be ended. The British government gave a substantively negative reply to this straightforward petition from the Congress, insisting again on colonial self-government rather than independence. So in October 1939, the Congress ministers all resigned.

The Communists, on the other hand, opposed what they saw as an imperialist war, and clearly declared this position. On 2 October 1939, the workers of Bombay conducted a political strike against the war and against imperialist oppression. The Communist Party had already been banned before this. Dange and Ranadive were arrested, while More and other activists went underground.

The Congress position at the time was different from that of the Communists. They wanted to use the opportunity presented by the war to wrest some concrete concessions from the British. Theirs was a pragmatic policy, while the Communist stand was on based on principles, keeping the international interests of the working class in mind.

Even though the Congress had resigned from the council of ministers, in 1940 they gave conditional support to the British. Their only demand was that the British government should accept Indian independence and immediately establish an interim national government at the centre. The British turned a blind eye to this demand and so the Congress in October 1940 started not a collective, but an individual *satyagraha* under Gandhiji's leadership. And after this a policy of symbolic individual *satyagraha* after obtaining Gandhiji's permission was announced. But the people ignored this and *satyagrahas* were held all over the country, and several arrests were made.

When the Soviet Union was attacked by Fascist Germany in June 1941, the nature of the war was transformed. It became a war between Fascism and Socialism in the world. All anti-Fascist countries, imperialist and Socialist, formed a united front in this war. Nehru welcomed this united front, but the British did not welcome it as they should have.

In December 1941, the Congress announced its position of cooperating with

'Harijans and the Coming War: "How We Feel About It"', *The Bombay Chronicle*, 26 May 1939. Courtesy of Anupama Rao, Maharashtra State Archives.

the Allied nations, with Britain in the fight against the Fascist countries. The only condition was that a situation be brought about wherein the Indian people would be systematically united under the leadership of a national government. Some of the Allied governments also brought pressure to bear on Britain. The Australian Foreign Minister said that while the war was on, the Indian people should be given the right to form their own government. Accordingly, in December 1941 the main Congress leaders were released from jail and the British prepared the grounds to hold talks with them. The Soviet Union was the epitome of world working-class power. Now that the war had acquired a new significance as a war for the defeat of Fascism and the defence of society built on people's power, the Communists declared it to be a People's War. As a result, on 22 July the ban on the Communist Party was lifted, and arrested Communists were released.

More too came out from underground in July 1942, when the warrant against him was withdrawn. This was also the time when the Party entrusted the Delisle Road Party organization to him. Besides this, More was also working independently to organize the workers. The Party's policy at the time was to join the Congress party's voluntary organizations to gain paramilitary training to fight for the nation. The Party carried out a critique of bureaucratic practice and called on Party organizations and its sympathizers to come forward and take part in civilian defence squads. Accordingly, More set up several civilian defence squads. Some, including Com. Balwantkumar Meshram from Nagpur even joined the military forces.

After this, the Congress party executive under Gandhi's leadership held a meeting at Gowalia Tank in which the historic 'Quit India' call was adopted in a resolution. Thousands were arrested. Around 940 persons were killed in firing by the police and the army. As the Communist Party had at the time taken a position against the 'Quit India' movement, Party workers distributing the weekly *People's War* were attacked in Delisle Road, Worli, Matunga, Dadar, Naigaon, Sewri, Girgaon, Byculla, Grant Road and several other parts of Bombay. The Party was at that time isolated from the people. All Party workers, from the top leadership down to ordinary activists, considered it a revolutionary act to sell copies of the Party's organ *People's War*, and everyone came out on to the streets. Com. Gangadhar Adhikari's wife Com. Vimal Adhikari and Com. Sitabai More would go out together to raise slogans and sell the journal. Those who sold more than a hundred copies were awarded a red badge. Sitabai, working as a Party member on the women's front, won a badge too.

This writer, just a young boy at the time, was also active on the women's front. He also took the lead to form a children's organization under the name *Pioneer Squad*, together with his sister Kamal, Com. Parvatibai Bhor's son Shivaji, Com. Salvi's son Madhukar and daughter Parubai, Com. Dange's daughter Roza, the poet/singer Com. Annabhau Sathe's daughter Shakuntala, Com. Suman Mokashi

अस्पृश्य जनतेस जाहीर विनंती

काँग्रेस मंत्रीमंडळाच्या गेल्या २॥ वर्षांच्या अमदानींत मुंबई व इतर प्रांतांत अस्पृश्यांची स्थिति मुसलमानांपेक्षाही अत्यंत शोचनीय झाली होती. आपली स्वाभिमानाची व स्वावलंबी चळवळ नामोहरम करण्याचा काँग्रेस सरकारनें आटोकाट प्रयत्न केला. इतकेंच नव्हें तर अधिकाराच्या जाणिवेनें चढेल झालेल्या काँग्रेस अनुयायांकडून व इतरांकडून अस्पृश्यांवर होत असलेल्या जाचास कोणत्याही प्रकारें आळा न घालतां तो जाच काँग्रेस सरकारनें वाढीस लाविला. निरनिराळ्या प्रांतांतून अस्पृश्यांवर झालेल्या जुलुमाच्या अनेक प्रकारच्या तक्रारी आमच्या कानांवर येत आहेत.

अशा परिस्थितींत काँग्रेस सरकार अधिकारच्युत झालें याबद्दल अस्पृश्य जनतेस हर्ष से वाटले. मुसलमानांचीही तशीच स्थिति झाली असल्यामुळें, त्यांचे पुढारी बॅ. जीना यांनी गुरुवार ता. २२ डिसेंबर १९३९ रोजीं ' मुक्तता दिन ' पाळण्याचें ठरविलें आहे व त्याकरितां त्याच दिवशीं महमदअल्लीरोडवर रात्री ९ वाजतां सभा भरविण्याचें ठरविलें आहे. मि. जीना यांनी या कार्यक्रमांत भाग घेण्यास सर्व ३ स्पर्शसंख्यांकांना निमंत्रण केलें आहे. तरी या वेळीं सर्व अस्पृश्य बांधवांनीं एक होऊन या कार्यक्रमांत भाग घेऊन, आपल्यावर काँग्रेसकडून झालेल्या छळमारांची चौकशी रॉयल कमिशन मार्फत व्हावी अशी एकमुखानें मागणी करणें जरूर आहे. म्हणून सर्व अस्पृश्य जनतेस अशी आग्रहाची विनंती आहे कीं, त्यांनी ता. २२-१२-३९ रोजीं ' मुक्तता दिना ' निमित्त होणाऱ्या सभेंत अवश्य भाग घ्यावा. मी स्वतः या सभेला हजर राहून भाषण करणार आहे, व छोंचे.

राजगृह, मुंबई
ता. २१-१२-३९

आपला,
भिमराव. रामजी. आंबेडकर.

भारत भूषण प्रिं प्रेस दादर-मुंबई

For the Deliverance Day meeting on 22 December 1939. Dr. Ambedkar too addressed the meeting.
Courtesy of Eleanor Zelliot, from the collection of Anupama Rao.

(Sanzgiri), Com. Shripat Ghag, Com. Mirajkar's son Prabhakar and Com. Kopikar's niece among others. This was later renamed the *Bal Sangh* or Children's Front, and many other children of Party members also joined a little later. The Children's Front sold Party journals and organized cultural programmes to propagate the Party's ideology.

The first all-India Congress of the Communist Party was held in Bombay in 1943. The present author and Roza Deshpande were chosen to make speeches at this conference. But since he was of a shy disposition he avoided making a public speech in front of so many Party members, and it was Roza who spoke. Also, the present author's sister Kamal and Roza sang a song at this Congress. In short, Com. R.B. More in those difficult circumstances not only worked single-mindedly for the Party, but also involved his whole family in the Communist movement. And he took the Party to the Dalits and the oppressed in a real sense. The Party leadership took note of his devotion and his selfless service to the Party, and in this first Party Congress the More family was felicitated before the assembled members as 'Red Family'. A photograph of the family together with Party representatives was taken and displayed in the exhibition set up there. This was the only family to be working for the Party.

The Stafford Cripps Mission and the Establishment of the Scheduled Castes Federation

The changed international situation after the Second World War and the rapid progress of the Soviet Union pushed the British to think about India's independence. It was during this period of war that the British government announced the formation of the Stafford Cripps Mission. On 23 March 1942, the Mission announced that it had agreed to the formation of a Council for drawing up a constitution for India. According to the Stafford Cripps plan, the elected members of the Provincial Legislative Assemblies would be on this Constitution Committee. The Congress did not agree with the position that India would be given Dominion status after the end of the World War. It wanted a national government to be established while the war was still on. The British government did not agree to this and the talks broke down.

When Congress leaders met the Stafford Cripps Mission, Dr. Ambedkar also met with the Mission as a representative of the Dalits. He asked what arrangements had been made for the Dalits. Instead of answering his question, the response was given that since you are a leader of the Independent Labour Party, you have no right to make demands on issues of the Dalits. If you wish, you can place your petition through a separate caste organization. The Congress party also has a majority of Hindus, so there could be negotiations with them on the welfare of the untouchables as a part of the Hindu community.

REPORT

OF

DEPRESSED CLASS CONFERENCES

NAGPUR SESSIONS

ALL-INDIA DEPRESSED CLASSES CONFERENCE

THIRD SESSION

★

ALL-INDIA DEPRESSED CLASSES WOMEN'S CONFERENCE

★

SAMATA SAINIK DAL CONFERENCE

held on July 18, 19 and 20
1942

Report of the Depressed Classes Conference session, 18–19 July 1942.
Courtesy of Anupama Rao, from the collection of the late Vasant Moon.

Dr. Ambedkar realized that in order to gain the right to speak about the welfare of the untouchables in this Hindu nation, he would have to establish a separate organization of the Dalits.

It was with these circumstances in mind that Dr. Ambedkar founded a new party, The All India Scheduled Castes Federation in July 1942, during the third all-India Conference of the Depressed Classes which was held in Nagpur from 18 to 19 July 1942. The resolution to establish this Federation was passed in the Conference, and sent to the British government together with four other resolutions.

The Conference announced through its first Resolution that the constitutional changes suggested by Stafford Cripps were entirely unacceptable to the untouchable class. On 8 August 1940, the Viceroy, while announcing a policy position on behalf of the British government, had said that any constitutional change that was not acceptable to the untouchables would be considered a betrayal, and no such change would be imposed on them. Through its second Resolution the Conference declared that the criterion of acceptance by the untouchables should be imposed on the Constitution Committee to be set up for the new national government to be brought into power with the consent of the British government. Similarly, instead of considering the untouchables to be part of the Hindus, their separate national existence should be recognized, and provision for their security and their development should be made in the constitution. The third Resolution made demands regarding provision for the security of Dalits, budgetary provision for their economic welfare, positions in the Public Service Commissions, and provision for positions of authority in legislative bodies and local self-government bodies. The fourth Resolution asked for independent settlements for the untouchables, for which a Settlements Commissioner was to be appointed and government land granted.

These were just demands in light of the rights of Dalits. Ambedkar later gave up the demand for independent settlements, but at the time the Communist Party had backed even this demand. It was Babasaheb's policy to make sure that the interests of the Dalits were met within the existing framework of capitalism and *zamindari*. There was no reason for the Communists to oppose this. In short, Ambedkar adhered to the principle that the so-called democracy within the capitalist system was in the interest of the Dalits and of all Indians.

At the time of the India visit of the Stafford Cripps Mission, Ambedkar was a member of the Governor-General's Executive Council. On 9 July 1942, the Governor-General appointed him labour minister. If we consider the circumstances as a whole, even though Ambedkar was the sole representative of the untouchable community, the leaders of the Congress party and other capitalist parties regarded him as an agent of the imperialists. At that time, after Ambedkar adopted a policy of reconciliation with the British, an intense struggle began between the Congress party and the Scheduled Castes Federation.

In those days Gandhiji considered himself the sole well-wisher of the Dalits. And in 1944 he went on a fast in Worli in Bombay to press for the interests of the untouchables. The Dalit public at the time felt that Gandhi's fast was hypocritical. The Dalits, led by R.D. Bhandare protested at the site of the fast with black flags. Caste Hindus under Congress influence then beat up the Dalit protesters, and attacked Dalits in other colonies also. Intense fights broke out in several places between activists of the Scheduled Castes Federation and the Congress party. On this occasion, the Communist Party stood firmly with the Scheduled Castes Federation and took on the responsibility of ensuring the security of the Dalit people. More took the initiative in involving both caste Hindu and Dalit activists of the Party in this. As a result, the Communist Party's influence among the Dalits increased, and many activists from the Dalits joined the Communist movement.

The Communist Party regarded Ambedkar's conciliatory policy towards the British with a realistic perspective and with sympathy. Communist intellectuals were of the view that the British had sown the seeds of dissension by granting special concessions to the Muslims. By granting concessions to the untouchables, they were looking to widen the rift and to weaken the Congress. Even if this were true, when we keep in mind the dealings of the Congress with the Dalits, we see that it would not have been wise for them, knowing the actual weakness of their struggles, to have given up the chance to get some political concessions. So we should not have misconceptions about Babasaheb's politics, the formation of the Scheduled Castes Federation, and the movement for independence.

More's Selection for the International Workers' Conference

Even though More had separated from Babasaheb, he had an affectionate relationship right until Babasaheb's *Mahaparinirvana*. The relation between the two was like that of a father and son with different opinions. From 1930, when More joined the Communist Party, except for the eight-and-a-half to nine years when he was underground, there was never a year till 1956 when More did not meet Ambedkar when he came to Bombay. And they did not meet just to inquire about each other's health; Babasaheb did not have time for that. They met because Ambedkar wanted to discuss with More the criticisms he had regarding the Communist position on various national and international questions. It is characteristic of More, like other Communists, that they were always well up with national and international politics. More was well-read and competent on these matters; one could say he was a Party intellectual. So these conversations were always lively. It is true that the Party was not aware of More's abilities or about Ambedkar's movement. But Ambedkar was conscious of the importance of the Communist movement and so when More went to meet him he would send all his followers out and parley with More.

More's endeavour was to convince Babasaheb of the Communist view, and to act as a bridge between the Communist movement and the independent movement of Dalits. This was not work assigned to him by the Party. He was a true Communist who always worked in this fashion; he kept up links not only with Babasaheb but with the Dalit people in general.

In every meeting with Babasaheb, More never failed to give him the available publications of the Communist Party and other Party literature. Babasaheb always paid promptly for whatever material More gave him. He knew that More lived in abject poverty. So he was careful not to put any burden on him. When anybody in his party misappropriated funds, Babasaheb would not spare them; he denounced them in front of other activists and often pointed to More as an example. He had great affection and respect for More.

Many of those who left Ambedkar to join the Congress did so for selfish reasons, not out of ideological conviction. More joined the Communists because he was taken by its ideology, and out of total commitment. Babasaheb knew that Communists do not live for individual profit. That was another reason for his love for More. He had the nagging feeling that he should do something for his benefit. In 1937 there was an opportunity to put up More as a candidate for election, but More refused on principle. But in 1942 Ambedkar had been appointed minister for labour in the British regime. He used his position for More's benefit, without informing him. In 1945, the final list of delegates to be sent to Paris for the 27th session of the International Labour Conference was sent to him for approval. He looked for More's name in the list sent by the All India Trade Union Congress (AITUC), but N.M. Joshi's name was there as the representative of the Indian working class, while S.S. Mirajkar, Abdul Momin, R.A. Khedgikar and P.L.K. Sharma were listed as advisors. The government had the authority to amend this list or to make any additions. He used his authority to add R.B. More's name as an advisor at the end of the list which was sent back to the AITUC.

Both More and the Party were surprised to see his name there. From the Party's point of view it was a matter of satisfaction that another representative had been included in the delegation. What had happened was that Babasaheb, from behind the scenes, had procured for More the chance to visit Paris as a member of a workers' delegation. Besides More, Ambedkar also sent another of his colleagues, D.G. Jadhav as advisor to the government, after first appointing him Regional Labour Commissioner. Babasaheb had this way of helping deserving persons from the Dalit community. He knew that More was as concerned about the freedom and development of Dalits as he was, and that was why he selected him as a delegate to this convention. More was felicitated in the *chawls* in his neighbourhood before he left for Paris.

In those days More and his family lived in a 10' by 10' room in a municipal workers' *chawl* in the Bombay Central area known as the Calcuttawalla Estate, rented for them by the Bombay secretary of the Scheduled Castes Federation, S.B. Jadhav, who had a job in the Bombay Municipal Corporation. It was from here that he made preparations for the trip to Paris, including getting a passport. The Communist Party entrusted the task of taking More to the airport to a dynamic young leader, Com. G.L. Reddy. The airport we see at Santa Cruz today did not exist then. Flights took off from the runway now used by pilots in training. The plane was to depart at six in the morning, so Com. Reddy arrived at More's home in a jeep together with seven or eight other activists at 3 a.m. More and his family had been awake all night, packing and collecting documents.

We left by jeep at four-thirty and reached the airport by five o'clock. We had hardly finished checking all the documents when, at 5.45, a small aeroplane landed at a distance of hundred feet from where we were sitting. As More walked up the steps to the plane carrying a small bag, we waved to him. The only travellers in that small aeroplane flying to Paris via Karachi were More, government delegate D.G. Jadhav and businessmen delegates Lakshmi Niwas Birla, S.P. Ogale, Muhammad Husain and Rahimulla Chenoy.

Com. Mirajkar and the other AITUC delegates had already left for Paris. So More was left alone. Among those at the airport to see him off were the present author and the whole family, More's friend Sakharam Sawant, P.L. Wadawalkar, and the late Ghanshyam Talwatkar, former secretary of the People's Education Society and chairman of the Konkan Buddhist Council. Talwatkar was then a student and an ardent admirer of More.

Working-class representative N.M. Joshi and More, his advisor, reached Paris in October 1945. N.M. Joshi was genuinely happy at More's selection. He nominated More to participate in a discussion on the petition to be drawn up by the employment committee. In his speech More talked about how untouchables were not treated equally even as workers. He made history for the ILO and the Communist movement by explaining for the first time how untouchables were not allowed in the textile section of mills in Bombay, and how the government too was indifferent to this unequal treatment. He also moved a resolution that provision should be made for untouchables to be given posts in the government administration. More suggested that the resolution be passed forthwith and that the International Labour Office should submit a petition after studying the issue carefully. He also asked that a review of progress made should be taken in the next, the 28th, convention.

After the convention, More's speech and the related resolution were sent to the newspapers and later published. Babasaheb read this news and conveyed his congratulations to More through N.M. Joshi. Later, when he met him, he patted his back.

Arrangements for More's stay in Paris had been made in the hotel where N.M. Joshi was staying. One day, Joshi called More to his room and told him that there was a message from Dr. Ambedkar that More should not make haste to return home. He should stay in Europe at the government's expense and complete the Labour Advisor's training course. Then, on returning to India, he would be able to work as a Labour Advisor and serve the workers at the same time. More thanked Babasaheb but refused the offer. But Babasaheb did not stop there. He knew from what his own activists had told him that More and his family lived in the deepest poverty, and he went on trying even after More refused.

R.S. Nimbkar was a veteran Communist leader who had been jailed in the Meerut Conspiracy Case of 1929, and who was a contemporary of S.A. Dange. Dange and Nimbkar were a pair famous in the working class, but in the end Nimbkar left the Party and became Labour Advisor to the government. Seeing that More was not willing to accept his offer, Ambedkar requested Nimbkar to write to More setting an example to him as a senior Communist, and asking him to reconsider. But More still refused. In his opinion, Nimbkar left the Party and became a Labour Advisor because his commitment to Marxism was only skin deep. Babasaheb was not angered by More's refusal; it deepened his respect for him. He would cite More's example when talking to his Dalit followers as one who belonged to the same caste but was untouched by temptation. More too felt the same affection and respect for Babasaheb.

When More went to Paris for the ILO convention, international youth organizations under Communist leadership organized youth rallies against Fascism in many places. More took part in these rallies as a representative of the Communist Party of India. After this, he returned to India. Thus, the Party also honoured More by giving him the opportunity to participate in these campaigns as a Party representative.

After More's return from the Paris convention, the Communist Party jointly with the Scheduled Castes Federation organized meetings to felicitate him. When, during the historic mill workers' strike of 1929, the Communists had raised the demand that Dalits should be given jobs in the weaving section, the mill owners had turned it down under pressure from orthodox workers. Since workers in the weaving section have to take the thread into their mouths, untouchable workers were only employed in the traction section.

The caste Hindu workers did not mind if Muslim or Christian workers were taken on in the weaving section, but untouchables were unacceptable. So Dalits were left out of the weaving section. This was untouchability being practised among the workers. So this was a struggle against untouchability, to which the Communist Party was committed. But the Party had not really taken up this demand with much energy. More knew that Ambedkar often referred to this when he was pointing out the defects of the Communists. Since More had been born in a Dalit family, he felt a natural anger about this issue. Many Communists had attended International Labour Conventions before More. But since they were from 'touchable' castes, they had little awareness or feeling on this question, and they did not speak about it. But More made full use of the opportunity of speaking at the convention, and he brought up the demand, which the Communists had put on the table in 1928. The Party too praised him for this. But sadly, there were some half-baked Marxists in the Party then who criticized More, unhappy that he had to take up an issue relating to his caste even in an international convention! Such half-baked Communists are a danger to the Party, but this cannot be helped. The enemy will always use such issues to damage the reputation of the Party; we must always be alert about this.

After More had raised this issue in the Paris convention, it was taken up for discussion in the Indian Mill Workers' Federation held at Kanpur from 4 to 6 July 1947. A resolution was passed that all mill workers should fight intensely against untouchability. A similar resolution was also passed in the Calcutta convention of the AITUC in 1947.

Dalits Elect Com. Dange to the Legislative Assembly

In 1946, the Communist Party had nominated Com. S.A. Dange for the election to the seat in the Legislative Assembly reserved for a representative of the working class. Dr. Ambedkar did not put up any candidate from his party, nor did he support anyone else. The Congress party had then begun some work among the industrial workers of Bombay. Under the leadership of Com. P.B. Donde and Com. D.B. Bhosle, the Communist Party had built a union in the Bombay Electric Supply & Transport (BEST). The Congress attempted to split this union by bringing in Abid Ali Jafferbhai. The Congress had also spread its tentacles among the mill workers. To build on this base and taking advantage of its leadership of the freedom movement, the Congress had put up Barrister Nuri for the workers' seat in the Legislative Assembly election. It is a sad truth that, although the Communist Party had played a major role in the independence movement, within the public at large and even among the workers it was the capitalist Congress that was influential.

The Communist movement is a class movement, and this consciousness comes to the Communists only through class struggle. It is not the same with bourgeois parties; they can be elected on a 'wave'. The Communists never get swept in by a wave. In 1946, when Com. Dange stood for election, the influence of the Communist Party was at its peak, throughout the nation and among the Bombay working class.

When the government lifted the ban on the Party in 1942, a favourable atmosphere was created for it to work in the trade unions. There was a ban on the Party from 1934 to 1942. Once the ban was lifted, the number of trade unions in the country went up from 182 to 608, and their membership from 337,695 to

726,000. The number of strikes and lockouts went up from 359 to 1,811, with the number of worker participants increasing from 291,054 to 1,840,784. The number of man-days lost in disputes went up from 2,330,503 to 16,562,666. From the available figures on membership of the Communist Party, the number was 4,000 in 1942. It went up to 15,000 after the first Party Congress was held in May 1943. The numbers were 30,000 in 1944 and 53,000 in 1946. The separate figures for Bombay are not available, but it too showed a rising trend.

Even so, it was difficult for Dange to be elected in competition with the Congress party candidate. In the end the worker who was with the Communists in the factory would align with one or another bourgeois party at home. The Dalit workers were under the influence of Dr. Ambedkar's Scheduled Castes Federation. But during this time and a little earlier, many Dalits joined the Communist Party because of More's efforts.

The Party could not rely only on its trade union work in order to win this election for Dange. It called on its activists working among the Dalit community in the Party offices at Delisle Road, Matunga Labour Camp, Naigaon, Worli and Sewri to put all their efforts into this campaign. The Party's Dalit comrades literally combed the Dalit settlements for voters. On the day of the election crowds of Dalit workers were brought to the voting booth and they waited their turn standing in orderly lines shoulder-to-shoulder with the Communists.

One cannot say what would have happened in this election if Dr. Ambedkar had taken a different position. It was his firm position that Dalits should not vote for the Congress party in elections. There is no doubt that Dange benefited from this; if Dange had not got the votes of Dalit workers, Barrister Nuri would surely have been elected. So did the Dalit working class secure victory and send Dange to the Bombay Provincial Legislative Assembly.

All this was work carried out by More. He had always nurtured his relationship with the Dalit people. It cannot be denied that the Dalit workers voted for Dange because they were influenced by the Party's working-class politics.

More's Underground Life

When the Second World War started in 1939, rising prices began to stretch the wages of workers in the mills and factories of Bombay. Since manufactured goods were being supplied to the war front, there were shortages and increases in market prices. The AITUC and the Communists, for the first time in India, called for a general strike of workers demanding dearness allowance. So strikes and rallies took place in all the mills. The British rulers took a grim view of this agitation led by the Communist Party.

From March–April 1940, the government began a wave of arrests of activists from the Communist, Socialist and other left-wing parties. In Bombay, Com.

Dange, Com. Ranadive, Com. Jambhekar and other leaders were arrested. More too was on the government's blacklist because of his activity in the workers' movement. The police had their eye on him, and there were warrants for his arrest; but he escaped their notice and went underground. At the time, D.S. Vaidya and More were the only two leading Party activists who stayed out of jail and carried the responsibility of continuing the Party's work. This was More's second experience of going underground. He was known in the Party as an experienced comrade. It was he who set up the network of dens and organized the distribution of secret pamphlets. Later, D.S. Vaidya was also arrested. After this More was solely responsible for the Party's activities, right until the warrants were lifted in 1942.

It was during this 'underground' period that More brought together Party activists to organize anti-war demonstrations. During the meeting of the All-India Congress Committee held in Bombay in September, he sent all the activists to try and press for an anti-war resolution. He activated all Party branches for anti-war efforts. He also sent representatives from Bombay to the conference of the Party's student wing, the All India Students' Federation. This was a time when much was happening in the country. The anti-war movement was strong. On 26 January 1941, Subhas Chandra Bose left the country to go first to Germany and then to Japan, to try and gain an advantage for the independence struggle from the war. There was seething discontent all over the country. In May 1941, twenty thousand persons had been jailed, including members of the Congress and the Communist Party. Those were difficult times for the Party, but More and other underground comrades ably organized the open work of the Party.

In 1940, More was in charge of the underground 'dens' or shelters. Chief among the Party members who worked with him was Com. Shivram Soma Jadhav (who later married Yashoda, More's sister-in-law). In 1941, he and another activist working as a courier, Com. Raghu Kadam, were arrested. They were tortured continuously for a fortnight in police lock-up: they were beaten on the soles of their feet, made to sleep on ice, their private parts were put in a vice. They were not allowed to sleep, but still they did not budge. Com. Jadhav had information about all the Party's underground shelters, but he did not let a word slip. Their ideal in those days was Julius Fučík.[37] After the fruitless police torture, the government sent them to jail for a year and a half. They lost their jobs as a result, and their families suffered greatly. We need to take note of such Dalit Communist activists who stood by the Communist movement in the face of such great injustice.

The families of More and activists like these were barely surviving, but even so, More was absorbed in party work and kept the Party office going. Those with whom he took shelter in his underground period were mainly Dalits and working-class activists. He lived with them in their huts. An activist from the Ambedkar

---

[37] Julius Fučík (1903–1943), was a Czech journalist and leader in the forefront of the anti-Nazi resistance.—*Tr.*

movement, Shirke, who later joined the Communist Party, made arrangements for More's stay in the then undeveloped Bombay suburbs of Pali and Khar, in the Mahar colony there which was called Chuim–Shirley. Of course, he never stayed in one place, and those who escorted him did not know all his hiding-places. He took care so that all the 'dens' would not be exposed if one of his escorts was caught by the police. That is how he remained out of the clutches of the police till the end.

During More's underground existence, leaders of the Ambedkar movement like Dadasaheb Rupavate, Ghanshyam Talwatkar, the famous cinematographer Ram Aurangabadkar and others gave him a lot of help. Not only did they accommodate him in their relatives' homes, but they also worked as couriers passing messages and notes in the underground organization. Rupavate's sister's husband lived in the servants' quarters in Charni Road Gymkhana. More stayed there with his family at times and, since Rupavate was a friend and admirer, he often couriered for him. What is more, on More's request he asked Com. Samuel Augustine, leader of the Naval Workers' Union, to provide shelter for him in the Siddharth College students' hostel at Charni Road, and Augustine also paid for his meals. Rupavate was then rector of the Siddharth College hostel.

Even though Rupavate, Talwatkar and Aurangabadkar were sympathizers of the Communist Party, their main allegiance was to the Ambedkar movement. But they had great affection for More, and More was always close to activists of the Ambedkar movement.

Although More was imprisoned during the mill workers' strike of 1933, after this he evaded prison and remained active underground. During 1934 and 1938 and even up to 1948, he was underground for eight-and-a-half to nine years. During this time he organized several strikes and ran the Party's 'den' machinery. He was completely devoted to the cause. Once Com. R.K. Bhogle, an old mill workers' organizer and Party leader, asked him, 'Why don't you go to prison and get some respite rather than working continuously underground?' To which More replied, 'Communists should avoid imprisonment as far as possible and keep on working. It is true that to go to prison is a sacrifice, but we should not forget that party work suffers when comrades are in jail.'

Hardships of Life in the Movement

While working for the liberation of Dalits and workers, More and his family members had to undergo all kinds of hardships, starvation, pain, indebtedness and poverty. Some prominent incidences of this are recounted in the letters More sent to his colleagues. The present author too was witness to some experiences. I give below some memories and selected letters found among More's effects.

Dear Dadasaheb,[38]

I have worked up the courage to write this somewhat strange letter to you, when I have not written to you about our good health, and so I first express my apologies.

Since I am in debt, and since, not having any employment, I am not able to make repayment from time to time, I have to suffer all kinds of insults. Orders are ready to requisition my property for some one or two larger debts, and the smaller loans make the food taste bitter in my mouth. This indebtedness is affecting my bodily health, my mind and my intellect. I cannot think what to do, I am as if crazed. All kinds of thoughts come to my mind. So, instead of taking some rash step, I have decided to tell my friends of my situation and to ask you for two hundred rupees. I have exhausted all options. So, please forgive me for this untoward behaviour. To say yes or no is your prerogative. Do not be sorry if this is not possible, and do not hold back if it is possible. As it is, I cannot repay my earlier obligations to you; so if you hold out your hand to this drowning man you will be truly blessed. So be it. It is not the time to write anything more. If you can rescue me from a dozen moneylenders and take me into your bosom, you will be a true friend. I promise to repay the amount before I die, and if I do die, forgive one who was a sinner when he lived.

I meant to write just two lines but this unnecessary content has written itself. I have said enough to explain the situation; I will not show off my penmanship by writing more. You are an understanding person. I await your reply at the address below. I salute all my elders. A kiss to little Babu. Do not be disturbed by my letter. I hope it will not cause estrangement between us.

Your disaster-stricken friend,
Ramchandra Babaji More

Sri R.B. More
Neighbourhood House School, New Nagpada,
Bellassis Road, Bombay
18 July 1930

---

[38] The Dadasaheb to whom this letter is addressed may be either Dadasaheb aka Sambhaji Tukaram Gaikwad of the Dalit movement in the Konkan, or More's relative from Dasgaon, Dadasaheb aka Namdeo Vitthal Joshi.—*Tr.*

> BIT Chawl No. 2, Room No. 41,
> Clark Road, Jacob Circle, Bombay.
> 24-9-30

To My Dear Friend Sri Pandurang Babaji Jadhav[39]

I salute you

Efforts are on to build our caste *panchayat* of people from the Konkan. We have convinced all our people in Bombay to join the Mahar Social Service Sangh. We have trained 500 soldier-volunteers for Dr. Ambedkar's Seva Dal. The remarkable strength of the Sangh has now come to Babasaheb's notice. On the occasion of immersion of the public Ganapati idol, a procession of seven to eight thousand went through the working-class districts to Mahim. Since then, everyone is in awe of the Sangh. Babasaheb is going to England for the Round Table Conference. There is a plan in the Sangh to present him with a purse and a certificate. Because of this public activity I have not been able to eat or sleep regularly for two months. To give you an idea of the work that is being done, I am sending you some of our pamphlets along with this letter. We have decided on 2/10/30 (Dussehra) as the date for presenting the purse and the certificate. I have no doubt that this occasion will be extremely gratifying. On 4 October Babasaheb will board the ship 'Viceroy of India' for his journey to London. Since the Congress does not support the Round Table Conference, there may be some commotion then. Most of the Mahar community is united. But there are some idiots from the J. State who are not yet in line. Try and come if you can. I will not write more now. The boarding arrangements are being taken care of by Baba. We are all well here. . . .

> Awaiting your reply,
> Your poor friend,
> Ramchandra Babaji More

More was arrested and imprisoned for the first time in 1933 when he was an organizer of the working-class movement. Here is an incident from then:

While More was in prison, Com. B.T. Ranadive and Com. Suhasini Nambiar (later Jambhekar) came to meet his wife Sitabai in the dimly lit room in a dilapidated *chawl* where More had been staying. There was not a grain of food in the house. The present author and Sitabai had not eaten since the previous day. Com. Suhasini

---

[39] There is a footnote in the original Marathi here, which is as follows:
- Pandurang Babaji Jadhav, from the princely state of Murud-Janjira, a leading activist in Ambedkar's movement and in the Mahar Samaj Seva Sangh.
- J. State: the princely state of Murud-Janjira, in the Konkan.
- Sangh: Mahar Samaj Seva Sangh.

Party card of Sitabai More.
Courtesy of Subodh More.

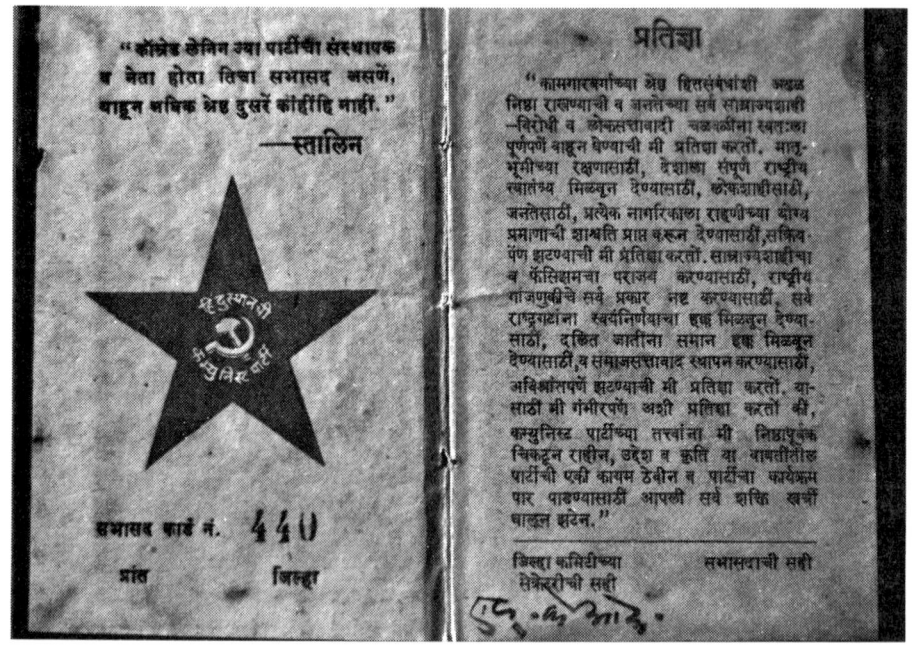

Party card with pledge.
Courtesy of Subodh More.

asked the present author, 'Have you eaten?' The present author, being then four years old, answered truthfully: 'No, I have not.' When she again asked, 'Do you want to eat?' he answered yes and then she called for a meal to be ordered from a restaurant. Four plates of *dal* and rice were ordered from a nearby Irani restaurant. On seeing four plates, B.T. Ranadive asked, 'Four plates for whom?' To which the present author replied, 'Two for you, two for us.' Ranadive made much of the child for his innocent answer.

At this time, while More was in prison, his Dalit neighbours were so impressed with his self-sacrificing way of life that they would send cooked food over to his family, knowing their dire straits. What is more, activists Latekar and Jatekar, of the Marine Lines Mahar Konkan Residents' Panchayat, on Babasaheb's instructions, gave a call for people of the Dalit community to collect funds for More's family. But this was the time when B.T. Ranadive met Sitabai and took the initiative to give her help from Party funds. After this, Sitabai asked Babasaheb and the Dalit activists to stop collecting funds, and told More about what had happened when she went to meet him. More was happy to hear that Sitabai had asked for the collection to be stopped, and told her that he was proud of her.

Ranadive not only helped More out of Party funds, but he also informed Shamrao Parulekar, then working with Babasaheb, about the situation. Parulekar promptly met Sitabai and purchased grain and other foodstuffs. After this, Parulekar became a regular visitor to Sitabai's home. Parulekar's first wife Malatibai and Sitabai had soon become good friends. Malatibai continued to help Sitabai with food, money and other assistance, right through More's imprisonment and even after. During the Diwali festival, she would send over large tins of sweetmeats. Parulekar and Malatibai considered More's family to be part of their own.

In 1938 More's circumstances were so bad that he could not hold on to the room in Rajanbhai Building, Parel, which he rented for three rupees a month. Because he could not pay the rent, a repossession order was issued by the court. But the bailiff had a problem deciding what he could seize from that room. A tin trunk with four base metal pots, some old worn clothes—that was the sum of the family's possessions. In the end, the bailiff drove More, his wife Sitabai and daughter Kamal as well as the present author out of the house, put a lock on the door and returned empty-handed. After this More and his family, with the trunk and a bundle of clothes, went to the place of a relative who lived in the one-storey *chawl* near what was then Governor's Gate.

In 1940, while More was underground, he once more had to face the distress of eviction. In those days More lived in the Dadabhai Chawl in Parel. His family had to leave that room too because the rent had not been paid in a long time. Then Sitabai took her family and went to live with her sister Yamuna Tipnis in her Dadar house. This place actually belonged to the Tipnises' friend Mr. Deshpande, and this Deshpande was also living with them. He was not happy about Sitabai taking shelter in his home. When he said so explicitly, Sitabai took her children and left the place at 1 a.m. At the time Sitabai's condition could be compared to a cat trying to find a safe place for her kittens.

The family then went for shelter under the Elphinstone Bridge, where a distant cousin from Loner lived the life of a beggar-cum-labourer, and had set up house in a corner under the bridge. It was summer, so he placed an old folding cot on the road for Sitabai and Kamal, while the present author slept on a patchwork quilt spread on the ground. They spent the night like this, and the next day Sitabai went to meet Shivram Soma Jadhav, an activist who worked as a courier for the Party. Com. Jadhav then informed More about the situation. More sent Jadhav to his friend Nadgaonkar Tambe, who lived in Worli. Tambe arranged for the family to stay in a room in the BDD Chawl No. 4 in Worli. The present author then started attending the school being run in Chawl No. 54, and his sister Kamal went to the municipal school. But since they could not buy books and notebooks, there was no studying to be done. Sitabai did some tailoring and other odd jobs to support her family's needs.

More's family had settled down in Worli. But there were many daily problems. It was during this time that Sitabai once fell ill and there was nobody to take care of her medical treatment. But a sympathizer of the Party and of More, Dr. Kopikar, who had a clinic in Matunga, was prepared to treat her. But Sitabai's condition was such that it was not possible to take her to the clinic in Matunga. So the present author went to Dr. Kopikar's clinic in Matunga and told the doctor about his mother's illness. Dr. Kopikar had great respect and affection for More, and he welcomed the opportunity to do something for his family. He jokingly asked the present author, 'But how will we get to Worli?' To which the twelve-year-old boy quickly replied, 'We will go up to the *Bharatmata* cinema house by tram and then take a bus up to Worli.' He was impressed by this, and, bag in hand, he accompanied the present author to Chawl No. 4 by the above-mentioned route.

He examined Sitabai, gave her an injection, and wrote out a prescription for some tablets. He handed the paper to the present author and asked, 'Do you have money to buy the medicines?' The reply was, 'There is no money,' but Sitabai immediately added, 'We will see about getting the medicines.' The doctor said, 'Why answer me like a stranger? I just asked Satyendra out of fun. If I did not have affection for More and his family, I would not have come all the way here. I have come because it is my duty to do so. I am giving you fifty rupees to buy medicine and fruits. Please accept it.' He handed the money to the present author, who took it at once. Sitabai had no alternative but to accept, but her face fell. She thanked the doctor in a choked voice.

Another incident from this time is from when the present author had a younger brother, Subhash, who was a year and a half old. He was a lovely child and everyone in the *chawl* was fond of him. My sister Kamal was then eight or nine years old. She went to pick up a cooking vessel from the stove while she was carrying Subhash when she lost her balance and the stove fell on the child. He was quite badly burned. The people from the *chawl* took him at once to Wadia Hospital. But he succumbed to his injuries after two days.

Sitabai did not have a single *paisa* at the time. More was not there to comfort her for her loss. There was a warrant out for More so he was underground. Some Party comrades told him the sad news. His eyes filled with tears but he could not go and see his son for the last time. He sent some money for Sitabai with some comrades. Then Subhash's last rites were performed in the presence of some relatives and Party comrades. About nine months later, while More was still underground, the present author's four-year-old brother Sadanand also died from a measles epidemic, when he could not get medical help in time. Sitabai faced both these sad events with fortitude. She did not lose her dedication to the movement in these trying times.

The Party later asked More to leave the room in Worli to take up residence in the Dalvi Building in Worli where a Party office was also located. More brought his family to live there. Once they were living there, the Party stipends being paid to More, Com. Parab and Com. Shivankar were pooled to pay for their meals. Later, a mess was started there for Party full-timers, and More's family was able to have meals there. The present author and his sister Kamal went to school from here. A little later the Party informed More that the place where he was staying was required for the office of the engineering workers, and he had to move out again. The Party then gave More a room in the Manakeshwar Building where the curtains and set props used by the cultural organization IPTA (Indian People's Theatre Association) were stored. More and his family spent some days in the inconvenient dwelling. Later, the Party needed this place too for some other purpose, and More moved out again without any bitterness. He then moved his household to an Israeli friend's room in Parel. After this they went to another rented room in Parel. After a few days, they had to leave this room also because of unpaid rent, and once again take shelter below the Elphinstone Bridge.

More's friend and colleague in the Communist and trade union movement, Com. Datta Kelkar, has recorded a memory of those days in his autobiography *Atmashodh* ('Awareness of Self'). He writes:

> One day D.S. Vaidya and I were walking from the Dalvi Building to the railway station, on our way to Victoria Terminus. The road passes by the side of the Elphinstone Bridge towards the station. The road beside the station goes from the C.M.E. office via the railway employees' quarters to the railway workshop. When that road was in sight, Vaidya asked me, 'Is not the woman sitting under the bridge the wife of R.B. More?' I know R.B. More very well. But I had never met his wife or seen her. Several beggars used to take shelter under that bridge. Why should R.B. More's wife be sitting there? As I was thinking thus, Vaidya

cried out in a concerned tone, 'Hey, it is she.' We both approached her. Next to her there were two or three tin boxes, a sack with cooking pots, and a little boy. The lady told us, 'We had not paid the rent, had we? So the bailiff from the court threw us out. My husband has gone to look for another room. Until then I will wait here.' Vaidya could not hide the tears that came to his eyes.

. . . After a few minutes Vaidya said, 'Things had come to such a pass, and you didn't let us know?' More answered, 'If everyone were to bring their personal troubles to the Party, it could not function as a party any more!' Vaidya was silent for a moment, then said, 'You could have told me as a friend, not as a member of the Party.' More merely answered that he did not want to burden the secretary of the Bombay Committee of the Party with any more problems. Our conversation ended here, as we had reached Krishna Nagar. The More family hardly stayed a week in my rooms.

Defeat of Babasaheb in the Elections of 1952

Following the provisions of the Constitution of India adopted in 1950, the first general elections in independent India were held in 1952. Both the elections to Parliament and to the State Legislative Assemblies were held together. The peculiarity of these elections was that, for the reserved seats (reserved for Scheduled Castes and Scheduled Tribes), there was provision to put up Dalit candidates. But alongside this, there was provision to put up a 'general category' candidate also. For the unreserved seats, only one person was to be elected.

In brief, for the reserved seats the voter had to cast one vote in the ballot box for the reserved candidate and a second vote in the box for the general candidate. This pattern of double voting was implemented for the first time in the elections of 1952. The election in Bombay was held on 3 January 1952. For the parliamentary seat, in the reserved category, Dr. Ambedkar stood from the Peasants and Workers Party, while Narayan Kajrolkar of the Congress stood against him. For the same seat, the candidates from the general category were Com. S.A. Dange of the Communist Party, Asoka Mehta from the Socialists, and Vitthal Balkrishna Gandhi of the Congress party.

When the build-up to the elections began in 1951, the Communist Party approved the names of Com. S.A. Dange from the general category, and Com. S.S. Mirajkar as his 'dummy'. Also, it had been announced that Dr. Ambedkar would be contesting the reserved seat.

The Communist Party, according to the strategy that had been worked out, had decided to support Dange for the general seat and Ambedkar as his counterpart in the reserved category. The Communist Party could not even consider giving support to the Congress, which was a party of the capitalist and landlord classes. And, since the Party's theoretical position was that Ambedkar and the Dalit class that followed him were true and firm allies of the Communists, the policy of supporting Ambedkar for the second vote had been decided on. More conveyed this to Ambedkar. Ambedkar heard him out and replied, 'First I will publish my election manifesto, then we will see.'

On 6 October 1951 the Scheduled Castes Federation published its election manifesto. After this, Ambedkar made an alliance agreement with the Socialists, and clearly announced that his party had decided not to cooperate with the Communists and with casteist parties. 'If the Congress had come forward for an alliance, I would have pointed to their faults and demanded that they be improved on' (Source: *Navashakti*, Saturday 20-11-1951).

In short, Ambedkar was ready to ally with the Congress, but had put the Communists and casteist parties into the same ideological category. Even though this was Ambedkar's thinking, the Communist Party considered the Dalit masses to be its natural allies. Thus, the Party continued its efforts for an alliance with Ambedkar right up to the day of the elections, but Babasaheb did not respond to these efforts.

In Ambedkar's view, the Socialist Party, which had originally been a part of the Congress as the Congress Socialist Party, but disassociated itself from the Congress in 1948, had the potential to become a large party of the people in future. So an alliance with this party would help in building a strong opposition party. This was his understanding at the time, on the basis of which he formed an alliance with the Congress Socialist Party. The equations he had formed in his mind held the Communist Party to be a weak force. That was why he completely overlooked the Communist Party.

The Congress had put up Vitthal Balkrishna Gandhi as its general candidate, and Narayan Kajrolkar as its reserved category candidate. The Socialist–PWP alliance had put up Asoka Mehta and Dr. Ambedkar respectively. The Communist Party had put up Com. Dange for the general category and was trying to persuade Dr. Ambedkar with respect to the reserved category candidacy. But it had decided not to vote for the Congress candidate Kajrolkar in any case.

Dr. Ambedkar, however, had turned his back on the Communists and did not intend to break the alliance he had made with the Socialists under any circumstance. On the other hand the Socialists and the Communists had no truck with each other, and the Socialists had a policy of isolating the Communists. Babasaheb had created a dilemma by allying with the Socialists.

There was daily discussion on this dilemma within the Communist Party, and as there was no other way out, it was decided not to vote for Kajrolkar, the reserved category candidate of the Congress, but since Ambedkar was not ready for an alliance, Party voters were asked to cast only one vote, in favour of Dange in the general category. This meant that no reserved-category vote was to be cast, it was to be 'wasted'. Many within the Communist Party opposed this, saying that Dr. Ambedkar should be seen not as an individual, but as the identity of the independent movement of Dalits. More and others argued within the Party that the Dalit people were the Party's allies in its revolutionary struggle. They argued that the policy of wasting votes should be dropped, since after all this was an election to one parliamentary seat in an election held on capitalist-democratic lines. The present author had also written a letter to Com. Dange to this effect. But the Party did not accept these arguments and took a majority decision.

In this election, Dr. Ambedkar won 123,576 votes while Kajrolkar of the Congress got 138,137. Ambedkar was defeated by 14,561 votes. In the general category, V.B. Gandhi got 149,138 votes while Asoka Mehta got 139,741 and Dange 96,755. The vote-wasting policy cost 39,000 votes, which, if they had been cast in favour of Ambedkar, would have certainly ensured his victory. Also, if the Communists had allied with Ambedkar, Dange might also have been elected.[40]

In the State legislature elections, B.C. Kamble of the Scheduled Castes Federation did get elected, but the Socialists betrayed Ambedkar by not casting nearly 3,000 votes. In Sewri, Kala Chowkie, Naigaon and Wadala constituencies the Socialists brought about the defeat of the SCF candidate R.D. Bhandare. The Socialist candidate M.G. Mane got 23,593 votes, while Bhandare got 19,337. The difference between the two was only 4,000 odd votes, while the Congress reserved candidate Shivtarkar who stood against Bhandare won 19,890 votes. This means that the Socialists either wasted 4,251 votes or they voted for the Congress. Even in the parliamentary election, the figures show that the Socialists wasted 16,135 votes, or else gave them to the Congress, as they won 139,741 votes, and so Ambedkar should have received the same number. Kajrolkar was elected even though he got 138,137 votes, or 1,604 less than Asoka Mehta. This picture of treacherous behaviour by the Socialists became clear once the election results were announced.

After the elections, there was rethinking within the Communist Party and it was accepted that a strategic mistake had been made. A resolution was passed to this effect. What is unfortunate is that the Dalit people never considered the fact that Ambedkar had also made a mistake in playing the politics of allying with Asoka Mehta, and the Dalit leaders kept them in the dark about the actuality. Middle-class Dalit leaders have firmly convinced their working-class followers that Ambedkar was defeated because of the Communists. This hurt the Dalit people. The Communist Party later admitted that, even though Ambedkar had refused their offer of an alliance, it should have instructed its people to vote unilaterally for

---

[40] The point is that both Ambedkar and the Communists lost out because of Ambedkar's view that the Communist Party was a weak force and therefore not an ally to be preferred, and the Communists' reaction to this decision even though they believed that Ambedkar's party was a better potential ally. The details of this 1952 election have been a source of mistrust between Ambedkarites and Communists ever since.

Ambedkar in the larger interest. Still, one cannot deny that this was a display of immaturity on the part of the Communist leadership.

What is more, during the campaign for this election Comrade Dange published a booklet entitled *What is the Stand of the Ambedkar–Asoka Mehta Alliance?*, which became part of the Communist Party's official position. In it he says of Ambedkar, 'The Mahar Platoon fought on the side of the British in the battle of Koregaon and he (Ambedkar) is proud of that history. I swear that nowhere, at no time did he oppose the British during the nationalist movement, even in his dreams.' This sharp criticism is proof that Dange did not understand the content of the social liberation movement of the untouchables. Comrade Dange was trying to say that the Dalits should regard the coming of Peshwa rule, a regime that tied clay pots around their necks, as independence for them (because it was not rule by foreigners). In fact several comrades expressed their difference of opinion and opposition to this. This author himself wrote a letter about this, and Dange told me that I was very young and that my Marxism was still raw.

Fortunately, just after this controversial election, there were elections to the Ahmednagar District Local Board. In this election the Communist Party and the SC Federation corrected their earlier mistake and fought together. Babasaheb's SC Federation candidate and the Communist candidate both got elected. After this, Ambedkar learned from experience that the Communist Party and not the Socialists had come to occupy the position of principal opposition party. So there was nothing wrong in making election alliances with the Communists, while allying with the Socialists would be against his party's interests. Similarly, the Communists realized that their policy of wasting votes had jolted the Dalit people's sense of identity. The Party later expressed its regret over this.

After the controversial Bombay elections, R.D. Bhandare, who was then considered to be one of Babasaheb's most dedicated activists, left him to join the Congress fold. Earlier, he organized a huge public meeting in Worli to ask the Communists to answer for the stand they had taken. He invited More on to the stage and challenged him as a representative of the Party. More explained the Party's position. He expressed heartfelt regret that Babasaheb had been defeated and made a plea that both sides should try and understand each other in future. He said that the Socialists had failed everywhere to bring socialism, and that in the end they serve the interests of the capitalist class. More gave examples to support his argument: in 1938, the Socialists had brought an anti-working-class law in the Bombay Provincial Legislative Assembly, and Ambedkar had opposed them on that occasion. He added that the Dalits would not gain ultimate liberation unless they allied with the Communists, whose politics was based on Marx's scientific ideas of Socialist power, rather than with the utopian socialists. More wound up his speech by stating that he and his party were saddened by Ambedkar losing the election. Babasaheb Ambedkar came specially to hear More's speech on this occasion. He parked his car at a distance so that no one would notice. When he met More later, he congratulated him for his speech.

Conversion to Buddhism

Babasaheb had declared at Yeola in 1935 that he would change his religion, and he carried out that intention by taking on the Buddhist faith on 14 October 1956 in Nagpur, together with a large number of his followers. Babasaheb was not an individual, he was a collective figure. He wanted to embrace this change of religion taking with him the Dalit people, who were living their lives with all their weaknesses. Also, he studied the history and geography of these people, in order that they would fit in with this step that he was taking. And he did not want to go from the frying pan into the fire, to be caught up in the idea of a God; so he rejected the Muslim, Christian and Sikh faiths and in the end decided to embrace Buddhism as taught by Gautam Buddha. Here too, he went back to the original form of Buddhism, without the later additions brought by the Mahayana and Hinayana sects.[41] To this end, in the 22 principles that he laid down for the Dalit people, his emphasis was on denying the existence of a God and the soul, and on freeing the Dalits from funeral rites and other naive beliefs. His endeavour was to free the Dalit people from superstition and blind faith, and to give them the strength to live their lives on the basis of independent thought.

When Babasaheb accepted the Buddhist faith, Rahul Sankrityayan, a great thinker who was once a Buddhist *bhikku*, or mendicant, and who later gave up Buddhism and as the next step joined the Communist Party, remarked, 'By taking on the Buddhist faith Babasaheb has shown great cleverness.' Since the Buddhist religion negates the concepts of God and the soul, the Dalit people will in the future find it easy to understand Marxism. This was consistent with what Rahul Sankrityayan believed. In his view, the conversion was a progressive step for Ambedkar and for the Dalit people.

Comrade More used to say that Babasaheb's conversion to Buddhism was a step towards all kinds of liberation for the Dalit people. He welcomed Babasaheb's conversion. He says in an article published in Amar Shaikh's *Yugadip*:

> It must be said that, after Charvak and excepting the Communists, Dr. Babasaheb Ambedkar was the first great man who openly placed the principle of atheism before the people, with great firmness and without any beating about the bush. Ideas about God take humanity away from reality and into the mystical; they kill humanity's efforts and their sense of manhood. It is no small thing that lakhs (hundreds of thousands), nay crores (tens of millions)

---

[41] It is interesting that Satyendra More considers Navayana Buddhism a return to Buddhism's origins.

of toiling people came forward on the path of Dr. Babasaheb Ambedkar's teachings to tell the world that there is no God. This has added to the strength of the Socialist forces supporting a materialist philosophy, and the strength of the enemies of the people has been reduced.

After the Dalits had converted to Buddhism, some anti-social foxes weighed down by Hinduism tried to continue despising the Dalit people by referring to them as 'neo-Buddhists'. Since More, in spite of being a true Communist, was truly one of the heirs to Babasaheb's legacy, he decided to raise a voice against this trend. He contacted his old Communist friend D.K. Bedekar, who was one of the directors of the Gokhale Institute of Politics and Economics in Pune, and requested him to organize a seminar on the topic 'Problems of the Newly-Converted Buddhists'. Accordingly, Bedekar took the initiative and invited More to present a paper along with intellectuals of the time from Maharashtra, including G.B. Sardar, Justice Gajendragadkar, Laxmanshastri Joshi, Shankarrao Kharat and Professor Sumant Muranjan. More asserted in his paper that Dalits who had recently converted to Buddhism should straightforwardly be called Buddhists. But, so that they should not be denied the benefits due to them because of their backwardness, one could call them 'newly-converted Buddhists'. To call them neo-Buddhists is an expression of contempt. More's suggestion was accepted by all those present, and it was decided to implement it in official government procedures. In this way More remained a part of the independent movement of Dalits, even after Babasaheb's death.

It was with the objective of abolishing untouchability and social inequality from Indian society that Babasaheb turned to Buddhism, as a means to an end. In Kathmandu he compared it (Buddhism) to Marxism.

He placed before the untouchables of India this path to ending the caste system. Following him, almost all Mahars in Maharashtra converted to Buddhism. However, people from other untouchable communities in Maharashtra did not rebel as the Mahars did. They felt this would lead them to be counted as Mahars. So they were not able to free themselves from the social structure of Hinduism based on four *varnas*, nor from their superstitious beliefs.

Even though the non-Mahar untouchable castes of Maharashtra did not embrace Buddhism, in other states of the country the Chamars and other untouchable communities have recently started, albeit in small numbers here and there, to rebel against the Hindu religion and accept Buddhism.

BABASAHEB'S COLLEAGUES ALSO JOIN THE COMMUNIST PARTY

When More was working in the Mahad *satyagraha* agitation with Anant Vinayak Chitre aka Bhai Chitre's Dalit liberation movement, he was drawn to the farmers' movement as well. While Chitre was working with Ambedkar for the liberation of

Dalits, he was primarily a believer in class struggle. So, when Raobahadur S.K. Bole started the Konkan Province Farmers' Association, he took part in that as well. He also brought Babasaheb into this association.

More had been initiated by Chitre into the movement for abolition of untouchability, as well as the struggles of farmers against moneylenders and the *khoti* system and working-class struggles; in short, into class struggles. While working to expand the farmers' movement in Colaba district, Chitre would bring together untouchable and 'touchable' farmers to fight in unison against the *khots*, the moneylenders and the landlords. His overall endeavour was to go outside caste and bring class consciousness to the peasants. More had been influenced by this too. Chitre was happy that he had joined the Communist Party in Bombay and would continue to involve More in the farmers' movement.

Chitre's effort was to bring other activists of Babasaheb's independent movement for the abolition of untouchability besides More, like Shankarrao Wadawalkar and C.N. Mohite, into the farmers' movement. Chitre and Sahasrabuddhe were also activists of the Servants of India Society [a social service organization founded by G.K. Gokhale (1866–1915), a prominent member of the Indian National Congress]. Devrao Naik, D.V. Pradhan and Bhaskarrao Kendrekar were also activists of the Servants of India Society, while they worked with Babasaheb in his movement against untouchability. D.V. Pradhan was president of Ambedkar's *Mumbai Samaj Seva Sangh* ('Bombay Social Service Association'). When Chitre organized a farmers' convention at Khed on 17 May 1931, he purposely invited More to be a speaker. Later, More threw himself wholeheartedly into the farmers' movement in Colaba district with Chitre. Although he was also active among the workers of Bombay at the time, he was elected secretary of the Colaba District Farmers' Association.

While More was working with the Communist Party, Chitre's political journey took him from the *Hindi Rashtriya Sabha* to Ambedkar's Independent Labour Party and then to the Peasants and Workers Party. Just as More had kept up contact with Babasaheb even after he joined the Communist Party, so did he with Chitre. Chitre had taken up the cause known as the Dabhade Project with the Peasants and Workers Party, but later on the leader of that movement, Shankarrao More, left the Peasants and Workers Party to join the Congress. Chitre was disturbed to see the gap between the party's philosophical base and its actual functioning. He discussed this at length with More, who called on him to join the Communist Party. This was just what Chitre wanted. Then More placed Chitre's name on the Communist Party's list of candidate members, with a recommendation. In 1954 he became a Party member. In this way More brought into the Communist Party his senior colleague from the Mahad *satyagraha*, a leader who had always directed the movement towards class struggle.

On 26 January 1959 Com. Anantrao Chitre, More's mentor, passed away. The

Party gave him a last *lal salaam* ('red salute') and More paid his respects by writing an article on his life's work in the Party organ *Yugantar*. More was a pupil who brought his teacher along with him into the Communist Party.

More had close relations from 1930 with another of Babasaheb's co-workers from his independent movement and a leader of the Independent Labour Party, Com. Shamrao Parulekar. He too about ten years later left Ambedkar to join the Communist Party. For a total of about 38 years he was in the vanguard of first the united Communist Party and then the Communist Party of India (Marxist). In his youth, he took up the causes of the wretched lives of Dalits and women's subordination, and fought with fire and intensity. As soon as he acquired his M.A. and LL.B. degrees, while he was still young he accepted life membership of the Servants of India Society and began his life work in social service. Like Chitre, he first worked in the Social Service League of the Servants of India Society. Later he began work in the trade union section of this Society, under the leadership of N.M. Joshi. He worked with Bakhle, and often clashed with him because Bakhle was a reformist trade unionist and opposed militant trade union struggles.[42]

Between 1926 and 1929 Parulekar led several strikes and struggles. Even though Dange was the leader of the historic 1928 strike of textile mill workers, Shamrao Parulekar was secretary of the strike committee that ran the strike from day to day. While he worked with the industrial workers, he also organized the peasants. In 1929, because of the economic crisis, struggles of the workers and peasants were becoming intense. The farmers of the Konkan began agitations against the *khoti* system and against bonded labour. Parulekar was there to give them leadership. He also organized strikes like those in the Swadeshi Mill at Kurla, at the Hattersley Mill in Ghatkopar, and in the match factory at Ambarnath, during 1937 and 1938. During the Ambarnath mill strike the police used all kinds of repression. Helping Parulekar run this strike were Com. More and Com. Siddiq Bakshi from Madanpura in Bombay. These leaders had become so popular among the workers that they composed a poem about them. This was published by the then public prosecutor J.V. Rajadhyaksh after he retired from service, in the Marathi literary magazine *Mauj*.

---

[42] The All India Trade Union Congress (AITUC) was founded on 31 October 1920 and was influenced by the social democratic ideas of the British Labour Party. It was led by moderates like N.M. Joshi and R.R. Bakhle, but also had more left-leaning leaders like S.A. Dange and R.S. Nimbkar, among others. In 1929, AITUC was divided into two groups: the Reformers, called the Geneva Amsterdam Group, which wanted affiliation with the International Federation of Trade Unions; the other was the Revolutionary or Moscovite Group which wanted affiliation with the Red Labour Union (RITU). AITUC was affiliated with the Pan-Pacific Secretariat and to the Third (Communist) International. In protest against this open alliance with global Communist organizations, N.M. Joshi withdrew and formed the All India Trade Union Federation in 1929. V.V. Giri was its first president.

O Brothers! O let us go and join the strike
Parulekar is the friend of toilers
Phadkesaheb gives us fortitude
Bakshisaheb fires away ahead
Brother More gives us lectures
O Brothers! O let us go and join the strike

It was the policy of the Servants of India Society to build Ambedkar's independent movement for the abolition of untouchability side by side with the farmers' movement. Thus, Chitre, Sahasrabuddhe and, later, Parulekar came in contact with Babasaheb. In 1930, Chitre and Parulekar organized a farmers' convention against the *khoti* system and bonded labour, at Chiplun in the Konkan. They requested Dr. Babasaheb Ambedkar to chair the convention. Untouchable and 'touchable' peasants were sitting together in the audience in large numbers. This also impressed More and helped move him in the direction of the Communist Party later.

Parulekar took part in all the farmers' conventions then organized in Pen, Khed, Rohe, and at Chari in the Alibag *tehsil*. The convention at Rohe was particularly successful. More had already joined the Party and he had started working in the Young Workers' Association. He suggested that five members of this association be sent to Rohe for the convention, and accordingly the Party sent five young worker delegates. Thus, More joined the workers to the pulse of the farmers' movement, for the first time. More chaired the welcome committee for this function, while Balasaheb Kher presided over the convention. More was becoming closer to Parulekar, who was delighted that More, who came from the Dalit community, had entered the Communist Party even while he was working with Dr. Ambedkar.

Later More moved further away from Dr. Ambedkar, while Parulekar had become very close to him (Ambedkar). He then started to work in Ambedkar's Independent Labour Party. In the elections of 1937 he was voted to the Bombay Provincial Legislative Assembly as a leader of the Independent Labour Party. At the time, the Independent Labour Party was the largest opposition party. So, Ambedkar was the leader of the opposition, while Parulekar was deputy leader. Here, together with Ambedkar, he brought a farmers' bill against the *khoti* system. Also, Ambedkar and Parulekar opposed the anti-worker bill that the government had tabled. What is more, they joined the Communists in organizing a strike and a massive agitation on this issue.

Meanwhile, More's relationship with Parulekar was becoming stronger by the day. Just as Ambedkar used to hold discussions with More about the Communist movement, so did More and Parulekar have long discussions. Parulekar had close ties with the Communists' trade union movement, which led him to study communist philosophy. He admired the fact that More had left Ambedkar's reformist movement behind to take up the revolutionary struggle of the

Communists. More would use every opportunity to bring about meetings between Parulekar and other Communist leaders, and he would give him Party literature to read. For seven or eight years the relationship between Parulekar and Communist More grew steadily deeper.

On 3 September 1939 the Second World War began. The Party organized a one-day strike of Bombay industrial workers to protest against this imperialist war. Parulekar was a labour leader and he was in agreement with the Communists on this protest strike. Later, when the war caused rapid inflation, the Communists through the leadership of the All India Trade Union Congress (AITUC) gave a call for a strike demanding dearness allowances. Parulekar went along with this call, and was in the vanguard of the strike together with other workers' leaders. He was arrested, and in prison came into close contact with the Communists.

Parulekar was released in 1940 and on his release he took membership of the Communist Party. Godutai Parulekar, Shantabai Bhalerao and Kamal Wagle also joined the Party with Parulekar and permanently broke off their ties with the Servants of India Society, to devote themselves to the revolutionary movement.

Thus, Shamrao Parulekar, who was, like Chitre, one of the prominent leaders of Ambedkar's independent movement, joined the Communist Party 14 years before Chitre. More felt great pride at this. Com. Shamrao Parulekar became a member of the Party's Central Committee and president of the All India Kisan Sabha (Peasants' Association). He died in 1965 while in prison, because the Indian government did not provide him with timely medical attention. More wrote an article on his life and work in the Communist Party of India (Marxist)'s Marathi journal *Jivan Marg*.

The Ambedkar College at Mahad and More's Work in Education

In Mahad, where the *satyagraha* at the Chavdar reservoir took place under Ambedkar's leadership and laid the foundation for social equality, and where Ambedkar's distinct individuality took shape, there was no memorial to Ambedkar after his death. More intensely wished that a memorial be erected, not in the form of a statue, but a living tribute to his memory. He approached Ghanshyam Talwatkar and Kashinath Vishram Sawadkar, secretaries of the People's Education Society, to discuss the matter of a memorial to Ambedkar at Mahad, and suggested that the People's Education Society come forward to start a college named after Ambedkar in Mahad.

Both men, who were from the Raigad district and were admirers of More, liked his suggestion and got to work at once. Later, a Babasaheb Ambedkar Memorial Committee was set up in Mahad with More and several prominent persons from the vicinity of Mahad. This committee, under the People's Education Society's guidance, started building the college at an appropriate point on the Bombay–Goa highway, and from June 1961, the Dr. Babasaheb Ambedkar College, Mahad, began to take students. Many young people from the Konkan region benefited from this, and Babasaheb's dream of educating Dalit students also took form here.

Like this college, More's native village Dasgaon is also at a distance of some five or six miles from Mahad. This is where More grew up and where he went to school. His old school building was falling into ruin. More, together with his fellow villagers, through their *shramdaan*, or donations of labour, rebuilt the Marathi school at Dasgaon. He received the cooperation of Nanasaheb Kunte, Narayan Nagu Patil, Com. G.L. Reddy, Com. Sitaram Jagtap and others in this task. The school was inaugurated in 1962, on the insistence of the villagers, by the state chief minister, Yashwantrao Chavan, who happened to be touring the area at the time. Present on this occasion was Barrister Abdul Rahman Antulay, then a youth leader of the Congress party who later became chief minister of Maharashtra. Since Antulay belonged to the Raigad district, he had great respect for More. Chavan spoke of More in his inauguration speech: 'More's actions in building this school have demonstrated to me that a Communist revolutionary who is constantly engaged in struggle can also do substantial constructive work. All Communists should treat him as an ideal.' He heaped great praise on More while making a few backhand thrusts against Communism, and said that this school was a memorial to More put up in his lifetime, and that the villagers of Dasgaon should cherish it into the future.

After the primary Marathi-medium school was constructed in Dasgaon, More called a public meeting of Dasgaon natives in Bombay, to discuss with them the matter of starting a high school in the village. With this objective, he set up in 1962 an association of persons hailing from Dasgaon and its environs who then lived in Bombay, the *Dasgaon Janata Pragatishil Sangh* ['Dasgaon People's Progressive Association'], with himself as president. This association then started a high school starting from the eighth standard in a villager's house, the *Pragatik Madhyamik Vidyalay*, or 'Progressive Middle School', of Dasgaon. The entire cost of this venture was borne by wage workers who came from Dasgaon and its vicinity to Bombay for a living. The government had not recognized this school. The school expanded year by year to reach the eleventh, or matriculation, class. The society then took a building on rent, and the present author, after he was elected to the Legislative Assembly, secured government funding for the teachers' salaries, rent and other facilities.

When this school was started the Association was not in a position even to pay salaries to the teachers. A young man named Madhavrao, the graduate son of More's friend Ramji Babaji Potdar, came forward to take on the responsibility of teaching without any pay. By giving two or three years of his life, he helped More and the villagers establish this school.

Old building of the R.B. More Primary and Secondary School, Dasgaon.
Courtesy of D.P. Kshirsagar, who arranged for photograph to be taken by
S. Kumar's Cyber Cafe, Mahad.

Photograph of the newly constructed R.B. More Primary and Secondary
School, which was inaugurated on R.B. More's death anniversary in 2007.
Courtesy of D.P. Kshirsagar, who arranged for photograph to be taken by
S. Kumar's Cyber Cafe, Mahad.

More had another progressive-thinking friend, J. Sawant from the village of Sape, whose son Nilkanth aka Bhai Sawant, an industrialist, also came forward to help the school. The Association made him head of the 'School Education Committee'. Over the next twenty years or so, Bhai Sawant involved himself completely in the affairs of the school, supplied funds and helped this Middle School stand on its own feet. Later, Sawant joined the Peasants and Workers Party, which, like More, leaned in the direction of Marxist-Leninist thought. He was elected as a member of the Maharashtra Legislative Assembly. All those who helped More in his educational work were progressive thinkers.

The Pragatik Madhyamik Vidyalay started by the association established by More has been running successfully for the last 36 years. Today, about 450 children from Dasgaon and its vicinity attend this school. It now has classes from the fifth standard up to the Secondary School Certificate class, thanks to More. There is no home in Dasgaon and its vicinity today whose children do not go to this school. Many of them have gone on to graduate from the Ambedkar College at Mahad after obtaining their school certificate. Some of them have become doctors and engineers; some are in high positions in India and abroad.

Unfortunately, the school building which was taken on rent in 1970 when the school expanded up to the Secondary School Certificate class has in the last few years fallen into ruin.[43] The present author, in his position as secretary of the Association, called on the villagers and other institutions to provide funds for building a new sturdy school house, but managed, with difficulty, to collect about a million rupees. Five rooms have been constructed on a cement-concrete base. These five rooms are insufficient, but the work has stopped due to lack of funds. Most other schools collect funds by taking substantial donations when appointing teachers; the teachers are made to sign receipts for more pay than they actually receive; and donations are taken from the pupils also. But the Dasgaon Janata Pragatishil Sangh, the association established by R.B. More, does not engage in any such corrupt practices. It is the only association in Raigad district that abides by the values that More lived for. This school needs generous donations.

More's Journalism

Newspapers have an important part to play in any socio-political movement. More, having started his political career writing for journals of Babasaheb Ambedkar's independent movement like *Bahishkrit Bharat*, understood the importance of newspapers. In *Bahishkrit Bharat*, More did all kinds of work, from writing, editing, preparing news stories, columns, and reports; also correcting proofs, preparing

---

[43] A site for a new school building was identified and building work started there. In 2000, some classes were shifted to the new location. In 2003, More's birth centenary year, the school was given R.B. More's name. The two-storey school building was completed in 2007.

dummies and other tasks. He thus gained experience in all aspects of the day-to-day running of a newspaper. His thinking had also deepened. He had passed the old matriculation examination and he was fluent in both Marathi and English. He competently translated material from English into Marathi. More had a penchant for writing. In those days he even wrote poetry. Besides *Bahishkrit Bharat*, he wrote for the Communist *Kranti*, or 'Revolution', for the railway workers' *Rail Worker*, *Asprushya Nivarak* ['Shelter-Giver to the Untouchable'], *Mumbai Kamgar* ['Bombay Worker'], *Kaivari* ['Champion (of the poor or oppressed)'] and other journals and weeklies.

In *Bahishkrit Bharat* he found that there was a shortfall of material on the struggles of the working class and the peasants, the struggle against capitalism and imperialism and the Communist movement. On the other hand, the Communists' *Kranti* did not take proper note of the struggles against social injustice which were taking place under the leadership of Ambedkar and others.

In short, he began to feel the need for a weekly newspaper that would look at the issues confronting workers and peasants, or untouchables, and which would give voice to them and throw light on all aspects of their situation. From this point of view, on 4 October 1930 he started a tabloid newspaper, *Avhan*, or 'The Challenge'. He printed the newspaper's motto in bold letters on the front page: 'A weekly paper that will destroy discrimination based on caste, *varna*, nationality or religion; that will awaken class consciousness among the workers and peasants.'

In an advertisement on the front page he announced, 'Workers! Farmers! Untouchables! Subscribe to *Avhan*, the newspaper that fights capitalists and the employing class on your behalf. Help by increasing its circulation!' It is clear from this whom the newspaper was for. At the time two thousand copies were printed and sold in Satara, Sangli, Kolhapur, Pune and Solapur in western Maharashtra, Akola, Amaravati, right up to Nagpur in Vidarbha and Colaba, Ratnagiri in the Konkan and even in Belgaon. In Bombay, activists from the Young Workers' Association, the Samata Sainik Dal, and the Mahar Samaj Seva Sangh subscribed to *Avhan* and there were also many subscribers from outside Bombay.

The first issue of *Avhan* was published when Babasaheb Ambedkar left for the Round Table Conference in London, and it was dedicated to him. Later issues of *Avhan* carried news about Ambedkar's actions at the Round Table Conference, articles, and news of the peasants' movement in Colaba, the struggle against *khoti*, the non-cooperation movement of 1930 demanding independence, workers' struggles led by the Communists, strikes and so on. There were expansive news stories on the Kalaram Mandir *satyagraha* in Nashik, and other campaigns by the untouchables. Prominent leaders of the Communist and the Dalit movement like Dadasaheb Gaikwad also wrote in *Avhan*. Meetings organized by *Avhan* in support of the Nashik *satyagraha* and on other issues gave force to the socio-political struggles and helped to spread the movement.

The impact of *Avhan* in stirring discontent among the people began to irk the British, and it was banned in 1931, after twelve issues had come out. We may note that the Communists' *Kranti* was also banned at this time. More was barred from entering Colaba district and a prohibitory order was passed on him. It is sad that, while the foreign British rulers took note of the impact made by *Avhan*, R.K. Lele, late reporter of the *Maharashtra Times*, did not see fit to even mention it in his book on the history of Marathi newspapers. Even the book on Dalit newspapers written by Appasaheb Ranpise does not mention *Avhan*. The saddest thing is that of the twelve issues of *Avhan* that appeared, only a photocopy of the eleventh issue is now extant with our family. (The original issue no. 11 of *Avhan* is available in the office of Anil Sawadkar, collector of rare documents of the Dalit movement.)

Because of his prolonged underground existence and the straitened circumstances of Com. More's life, he was not able to buy an ordinary house for many years. He was always moving from one place to another, carrying his family and his possessions on his back like a scorpion. So, he could not make a collection of issues of *Avhan*, his articles in various journals, his books and other documents of the movement, however much he may have wished to do so. More has written for Ambedkar's journals *Bahishkrit Bharat*, *Samata*, and *Janata*. He was on the editorial board of *Bahishkrit Bharat* even when he was openly a Communist. He was a prolific writer on social and political matters in various magazines and weeklies like *Mashal* ['Torch'], *Lokyuddh* ['People's War'], *Lokyug* ['Age of the People'], *Yugantar* ['Epoch-Change'], *Yugadip* ['Light of the Age'], *Lokmanya* ['Respected by the People'], *Soviet Varta* ['Soviet News'], *Prabuddha Bharat* ['Enlightened India'], and the daily papers *Maratha* and *Krishiwal* ['Agrarian'].

In the evening of his life, in 1965, More started a new progressive weekly magazine from his rented room in Siddharth Nagar in Goregaon. As editor, he stated his position on caste and class in the pamphlet published to advertise the launch of this new weekly. He says,

> Friends, this is the epoch of social evolution, when we can bring fundamental change in our society, whose fabric has been worn threadbare by caste and class differences; to build a new society free of caste and class, built on a base of social and economic equality. In such a time, we have realized the need for a newspaper like *Jivan Marg* so that Dalits, workers and the ordinary poor people can raise their voice against the enemies of their interests, to organize their struggle and to attain the goal of a happy and prosperous life of equity. So, even in these unfavourable circumstances, we are resolved, with full confidence, to start this paper.

More published the first issue of this tabloid newspaper on 14 April 1965, that is, on Ambedkar's birth anniversary. He paid his respects by carrying a large

An issue of *Jivan Marg*, 14 April 1965.
Courtesy of Subodh More.

photograph of Babasaheb on the front page. So, from the very first issue, he expressed his affection and respect for Babasaheb and for the movement of the Dalits and the toiling people. In this issue, Ghanshyam Talwatkar, then a leader of the Dalit movement, wrote an article on the question of untouchability. There were also articles by More's old friend from the Peasants and Workers Party, D.B. Patil, and Communist Party leader, journalist Com. R.M. Jambhekar, among others. More was supported by several friends and colleagues from the Communist and Dalit movements in starting *Jivan Marg*. These persons also became subscribers. Even so, More first held discussions with the leadership of the CPI (M), especially Com. S.Y. Kolhatkar. Thus, this newspaper later became the official organ of the CPI (M) in Maharashtra, and remains so even today. More's name is inscribed as its founder. More gave voice to many problems facing the Dalits and the oppressed through this newspaper.

More and the Cultural World

Because More was widely known as a journalist and social activist, he came in contact with many renowned persons and institutions in the socio-cultural world. His colleagues in the Dalit movement often invited him to speak. He would be asked to speak at important social functions in Siddharth College, Dr. Babasaheb Ambedkar College, Siddharth Hostel at Wadala, the auditorium of the *Bauddhajan Panchayat Samiti* in Bhoiwada, etc. He was also in close contact with young literary writers from the Dalit community. He would have regular discussions in Siddharth College with writers like Ghanshyam Talwatkar, Baburao Bagul, Daya Pawar, Dinesh Lakhmapurkar, Chokha Kamble, Bandhu Madhav, Bhausaheb Adsul and others who were active in the Siddharth Literary Association, the Maharashtra Dalit Literary Association, and the Buddhist Literary Council. He was a part of the first Dalit Literary Convention that was held in 1958. Acharya Atre, satirical writer and leader of the movement for a Marathi-speaking Maharashtra state in the 1950s, was to inaugurate the convention, but since he was unavailable at the last moment, the senior progressive writer and poet Com. Annabhau Sathe was asked to inaugurate. In his historic speech he said, 'The earth is balanced, not on the head of the great snake Sesha, but on the palms of Dalits.'

It was on the advice of More and Baburao Bagul that Talwatkar invited Annabhau Sathe to inaugurate the convention. More, as part of the movement, had worked for a long time to encourage the artistic and literary talents of Annabhau Sathe, just as he had encouraged young writers to set up the Friends' Union, a cultural organization at Delisle Road. It was More and Com. Salvi who motivated Annabhau, with the help of the poet Gavhankar, to start the *Lal Bavta Kala Pathak*, or 'Red Flag Art Troupe'. He published many of Annabhau's early stories in special editions of the Communist Party's magazines and weeklies like *Mashal, Lokyuddh* and *Lokyug*. Further, More asked Annabhau to write accounts of atrocities on Dalits or on the terrible drought of that time in these Party journals. Some of these accounts by Annabhau became the subject of intense interest at the time. Few are aware of Annabhau Sathe's role as a Party journalist. Com. More and Com. Salvi had a large role in his development as comrade, poet and writer. Annabhau's brother has acknowledged this in his book, *Majha Bhau Annabhau*, or 'My Brother Annabhau'. Of course, Annabhau's second wife Jaiwantabai also played an important role in making Annabhau continue to write. Taking inspiration from Annabhau's work, Com. Hari Jadhav initiated the *Navjivan Kala Mandal* ('New Life Art Group') in the Matunga Labour Camp and later a separate Dadar Art Troupe, in which Pushpa Kothare, Visu Jadhav, Usha Urdhvareshe, Pralhad Dethe, Janardan Panchal and others took part.

As More himself had an interest in plays, songs and *jalsas*, he was always encouraging young artists and had close relations with them. Govind Mhashilkar and Shrawan Yashwante, folk artists and singers from the Ambedkar movement, and Dinkar Bhosle, writer-composer of *jalsas*, were close friends of More. Bhosle later became a Communist Party activist and leader of the BEST (Bombay Electric Supply and Transport company) union. The playwright Moreshwar Tambe, who wrote the play *Maharachi Soon urph Prem Pratap* ('The Mahar's Daughter-in-law or the Exploits of Love') which supported inter-caste marriage, and who was the first Dalit playwright from the Konkan region, was also a supporter of More. When he lived in Khar and More was underground, he often helped him. Several artistes from the Konkan, like Ghanshyam Talwatkar, Bhai Narendra More, Dhotre and others acted in this play. Babasaheb attended a performance of this play. More also organized shows to raise money to help schools and boarding for untouchable children.

The critic Dr. Acharya Madhav Potdar, who wrote a thesis on Shahir Amar Shaikh, was also impressed by More's work. More also encouraged his nephew, the writer B.S. Hate, and published his work in the Party's *Yugantar* and other progressive journals. Later, B.S. Hate and More's second son, the late Jagdish More, started *Sambodhi* ['Enlightenment'], an association dedicated to the service of progressive literature and drama in Goregaon. The association was nurtured and expanded through the efforts of Ramesh Shinde, collector of Ambedkarite literature, and others like Mohan Waghmare, Bhimsen Dethe, Daya Pawar, Pramod Sartape, Shirish Hate, Mohan Amberkar, Datta Thakkar, Vasant Kamble and Harishchandra Kamble.

Sambodhi was instrumental in putting up dramas and one-act plays on social issues, and later in organizing the Dalit *Natya Sammelan*, or 'Dramatic Convention'. The first book published by Sambodhi was B.S. Hate's *Jithe Pani Petle*, or 'Where Water Took Flame', written to commemorate the Chavdar reservoir *satyagraha* at Mahad on its fiftieth anniversary (in 1977, sometime after R.B. More's death).

Later, many Dalit and progressive writers like Bhimsen Dethe, Urmila Pawar, Premanand Gajvi, Datta Bhagat, Dr. Sada Karhade, Manohar Ranpise, Madhukar Aarkade, Ankush Guruji and Dr. V.S. Jog published books and established their own identity as writers.

The contribution of Sambodhi to Dalit literature was acknowledged in 1991, when, in its special issue brought out on the occasion of Ambedkar's birth centenary, the *Maharashtra Times* published a special interview with Jagdish More. Many luminaries like Com. Godavari Parulekar, (literary critic) P.S. Nerurkar, (working-class poet) Narayan Surve, (Dalit poet and anthologist) Arjun Dangle, (left-wing playwright and novelist) Anil Barve, (Dalit poet) Keshav Meshram, (activist among tribals) Com. Kumar Shiralkar, playwright Manohar Wakode and others have taken part in functions organized by Sambodhi.

To sum up, Com. More's legacy in the progressive cultural movement was kept alive by his second son also. Such was More's involvement in the world of culture. Leading progressive figures of the world of film and the stage, like Shahir Amar Shaikh, Annabhau Sathe, Balraj Sahni, Kaifi Azmi, Khwaja Ahmad Abbas, Dina Pathak and others had great respect for him. Annabhau Sathe in his last days lived next door to More in Goregaon, and they met and had discussions regularly.

The Communist Evaluation of the Caste Question

Within the Communist Party, More always pressed for a Marxist-Leninist evaluation of the Ambedkar movement and the Communist movement, as he felt this was necessary if a people's democratic revolution, Dalit liberation and the establishment of Socialist power were to be achieved in India. In this context, I give below the policy on agriculture that the Party announced in 1930.

> As a result of British imperialism, even today hundreds of thousands of people in our country are slaves, and ten times that many untouchable toilers are living a life under social boycott. They are deprived of all rights. British imperialism, the *zamindari* system, the reactionary caste system, religious fraud and all the traditions of slavery in the country are coming in the way of the people's liberation. The total effect of all these is that, even in the twentieth century, the untouchables cannot mix with their countrymen. They cannot drink water from communal wells; they cannot be educated with everyone in common schools. Instead of wiping away this stain on the Indian people, Gandhi and the Congress are supporting this caste system which is responsible for the social boycott of the untouchables . . .
>
> . . . Only the complete and uncompromising elimination of the caste system, even the 'reformed' caste system of Gandhi, together with a revolution in agrarian relations, can bring about the social, economic, cultural and legal

liberation of the boycotted workers and the untouchables. The Communist Party calls on all untouchables together with the workers to join a united revolutionary front against the imperialist power and *zamindari*. Working-class untouchables should not fall prey to the tactics of the British and the reactionary forces to divide the workers and make them fight among themselves. This too is what the Communist Party calls for . . .

The Communist Party is fighting to eliminate completely the caste system, caste inequality and all forms of slavery. The Communist Party is fighting for complete and unconditional equality for industrial workers, untouchables, and all toiling people in the country. . . .

On More's suggestion the Party organized study classes to explain Marxist philosophy to Dalit activists who joined the Party during this time. Before its Second Party Congress, the Party brought out a special document, organized discussions and worked out policy on how to work in Dalit colonies and among workers. Thus, an awareness of how the Ambedkar movement and the Communist movement were closely tied grew within the Party.

Even so, the Party showed weaknesses in taking an objective view of Dr. Ambedkar and his independent movement. Before British rule was established, during the Peshwa regime, the human rights of the untouchables had been denied. In comparison, the untouchables found the coming of the British a welcome transition. The untouchables only wanted liberation, recognition as human beings and equality. The National Congress and Gandhi gave them sympathy, while looking to preserve the *varna* system and caste. If Ambedkar did not have faith in them, how was that wrong? The Communist Party had taken up the issue of untouchability on principle, but the Communists did not succeed in taking up that question within the capitalist-*zamindari* system and organizing the Dalits. Thus, it was the need of the time to awaken their sense of identity and to organize them separately.

Earlier, in 1909, when the British implemented the Morley–Minto reforms and introduced separate electorates for Muslims, the Congress welcomed this. They further supported separate electorates for Muslims in 1916 when they signed the Lucknow Pact on the composition of Indian self-government. In this situation, the British had used their politics of concessions and reserved seats in order to draw the Dalits towards them. What would have happened if they had said, we don't want your concessions, we will remain under the Congress flag and obtain these concessions from them? It cannot be denied that the Communists, in taking the position that this question be resolved under the leadership of the Congress, betrayed a failure to think it through seriously.

Remember that this was a time when the Muslims and other non-Dalit people enjoyed social equality, even though they were slaves of the British. In the feudal structure of power, these people were given at least limited political and economic rights. But in this structure, the voices of Dalits were completely gagged. They could not speak out for themselves. They had been crippled by the slavery imposed on them for centuries. They were denied the most basic human rights and were deprived of all social, political and economic rights. The Dalit people gained some opportunities because of capitalism and the industrial revolution that the British brought with them.

The Communists did not fully understand that it was a big mistake to compare such a people with the Muslim section of society. The untouchables needed a party that would awaken them from hundreds of years of mental slavery and subjugation, and would create self-awareness and self-respect among them. Where was the party that would do this? The Communist Party had just been formed; it was in its infancy. So, it too did not have this organizational capacity. Mahatma Phule was the only leader who was capable of this; after him there was a vacuum. Where was the party or individual who could competently handle the favourable situation for attainment of human rights which had arisen for the Dalits, even if from the 'divide and rule' politics of the British?

From this point of view, Dr. Babasaheb Ambedkar met the need of the times. Rather than thinking of him thus, he is said to have wanted British rule to continue, so that he could get concessions for the Dalits. It is implied that this was Babasaheb's selfish view of the British: that he was not for independence of the nation. In reality, Babasaheb was aware of the craftiness of the British, and he knew that a favourable outcome for the Dalits could only come about in an independent nation. He publicly stated this point of view in his presidential address at the convention of the All India Depressed Classes Conference held in 1930:

> I think that the British favour a hue and cry being made about your unfortunate situation, not with the intention of improving it, but because it gives them a good excuse to bring obstacles in the way of Hindustan's political progress.... Before the British came, you were not allowed to draw water from the village well. Have the British secured rights over these wells for you? Before the British came, you were not allowed to enter temples. Can you enter them now? Before the British came you were not given jobs in the police force. Does the British government give you jobs in the police? Before the British you were barred from the military. Is that profession open for you now? Gentlemen, you cannot answer 'yes' to any of my questions. A regime that has ruled over the nation for such a long time is bound to have done some little good to the people, but there is no doubt that there is no fundamental improvement in your condition. In your case, the British have accepted the previous order.
>
> A Chinese tailor was asked to stitch a new coat and he was given an old coat as a model. That tailor proudly produced a new coat exactly like the old

one: complete with holes, patches and all. So have the British kept the old social system as it is. The injustices you suffer have remained as they were, they have not been eliminated.

Nobody will be able to overcome your suffering like you yourselves can. And as long as you do not have political power in your hands, you will not be able to overcome that suffering. As long as the British regime lasts, you will never get your share in political power. Unless you have political power you will not be able to liberate your people, and it is only in *swaraj* (independence) that there is a possibility of that power coming into your hands.

In spite of this, the Communist Party could not make an appropriate evaluation of Ambedkar and his independent movement, nor of the limitations of its own strength. In this context, we are reproducing verbatim the resolution on untouchability adopted at the Second Party Congress held at Calcutta in 1948.

Sixty million untouchables are the most exploited and oppressed of our people. This is a formidable reserve force in the struggle for a democratic revolution. As the control of the Congress party is mainly in the hands of upper-caste capitalist leaders, the party has always refused to press for the welfare of the untouchable masses, or to consider the struggle for freedom from social and economic serfdom of the untouchables as an integral part of the struggle for independence. That is why it was possible for reformist and separatist politicians like Ambedkar to keep the untouchable masses away from the broader democratic movement and to foster the illusion that one could put faith in the imperialist regime for improving their situation.

The Communist Party has before it the tasks of bringing the untouchable masses into the democratic front, of removing the caste prejudices of upper-caste workers and peasants, of bringing about unity of the common people of all castes against our common enemies. This can be achieved only by fighting determinedly against the upper-caste capitalists and also against the opportunistic and divisive leaders among the untouchables themselves. We must expose the true nature of these leaders, remove the authority that they have over the untouchable masses, and convince these masses that their interests lie only in uniting with other sections of the exploited people, and that their social weakness and slavery will be eliminated when the democratic revolution is victorious. Every injustice committed against the untouchables is a tactic by the capitalists to sustain the divisions among the people. We must assume this and so oppose these injustices, and fight for every just demand of the untouchables as a part of the struggle being waged for the people's rights.[44]

---

[44] This text is taken from the English original, rather than being re-translated from More's Marathi version.

More did not accept this position of the Party with regard to Ambedkar. He expressed his dissent within the Party through a special memorandum written in 1953. In this he points out how the Party had neglected the caste question, how the above analysis with respect to Ambedkar was inappropriate, and how Ambedkar had made a valuable contribution in this area, and expresses his resentment. He also says that instead of looking at this question according to Marxist principles, the Party was taking the mechanistic position that the problem of caste would be solved once economic reforms took place. And he demands that the Party should immediately take up a campaign against caste. He said this not in order to criticize the Party, but in a constructive spirit, so that the Party's collective awareness should increase. He did what was his duty as a Communist.

The distinction between a Communist party and all other parties is this, that when differences of opinion arise, their members only talk about resolving those differences within the party, but in reality they criticize the party outside. These other parties are capitalist parties, and they fall prey to capitalistic individualism. Their members want to assert themselves as individuals, blow their own trumpet. This is not the case with Communists. Communists are serious about the questions that they raise. They make whatever criticisms they wish to make, within the party. Because there is great democratic freedom within the party, what has to be said should not be said outside the party. Because there can be no revolution without a revolutionary party of the working class, the responsibility of keeping the party strong rests not just with its leaders but also ordinary party members. This is a cadre-based party of soldiers. In other, capitalist, parties, members are made through taking subscriptions, and they are not what the Communists refer to as party cadre. The activists of other parties glorify their undisciplined behaviour in the name of inner-party democracy. The Communist Party does not have this kind of democracy. Keeping inner-party discussions alive from one Party Congress to the next, the Party tries to state its ideas in as scientific a manner as possible. That is why Com. More never publicly declared his differences with the Party on the question of caste.

More sent the above note to E.M.S. Namboodiripad, who was then Party leader, on 23 December 1953. Namboodiripad himself acknowledged the receipt of this letter on 23 February 1954. At the end of his note More had demanded that the next Party Central Committee, due to be elected at the Third Party Congress at Madurai during 27 December 1954 to 2 January 1955, should direct the Party to form a special committee to study the actual existence of untouchability as it was still practised in different provinces of the country. This committee should then submit the report of its study to the Party. Accordingly, the Politburo in memorandum no. 7/54 dated 1 March 1954, sent More's note in its entirety to all Party branches in the Provinces for discussion and to gauge opinion within the Party before the December Congress.

The Party took note of More's memorandum. But he still felt that it was incomplete, and so he handed over a revised version dated 16/12/1957 to Party General Secretary Com. Ajoy Ghosh in person when he came to Bombay. Ajoy Ghosh placed it before the Party and sent a telegram to invite More to the Party Congress at Amritsar to be held from 6 to 13 April 1958. However, More could not attend because he was unwell. He was not satisfied with the discussion on the caste issue that took place in the Amritsar Congress and in 1964 he sent another revised version of his note to E.M.S. Namboodiripad for the next Party Congress.

The visible impact of these three memoranda can be seen after More's death, after a gap of some 15 years, in Com. B.T. Ranadive's article on 'Caste, Class and Property Relations', and in Namboodiripad's article 'The Growing Unity of Democratic Forces against Caste Conflict'. Com. Sanzgiri,[45] in his 1999 article 'Dr. Babasaheb Ambedkar, a Marxist Evaluation', published in the Party's theoretical journal *The Marxist*, has picked up many of the arguments made by More. He later published a booklet with the same title, in which there is considerable self-criticism, an evaluation of past events and a Marxist analysis of the contemporary situation on caste.

Explaining how the Congress party had hurt Dr. Ambedkar on the question of caste, he says,

> In 1928 the Congress party's working committee had called an all-party meeting to discuss the outlines of a constitution for independent India. This conference formed the Motilal Nehru Committee with the task of preparing a draft of the constitution. The Congress had invited representatives of religious minorities like the Muslims, Sikhs and Christians to this conference. But no organization of Dalits was invited, not even the organizations led by Dr. Ambedkar. The Motilal Nehru Committee proposed reserved seats for Muslims, but not for the untouchables. It was not surprising that Dr. Ambedkar was distanced from the Congress by this conscious neglect of the Dalit class and their right to get protection.

Sanzgiri quotes a part of Dr. Ambedkar's speech at the Round Table Conference in his booklet and points out how pertinent his words are:

> Before the British came our position regarding untouchability was repugnant. . . . The social system that the British found among us was accepted by them

---

[45] Prabhakar Sanzgiri (d. 9 March 2009), Central Committee member of the CPI (M), was a Communist politician, trade union organizer and newspaper editor based in Mumbai. He served as secretary of the Maharashtra State Committee of the CPI (M), vice-president of the Centre of Indian Trade Unions, Maharashtra State Committee president of CITU and editor of the Marathi Party organ *Jivan Marg*.—Tr.

just as it was. And they have nurtured that social system with great sincerity. We want a government that . . . will not hesitate to bring in those reforms in social and economic life for which there is the greatest need from the point of view of justice and the changing times. The government of the British will never be able to play this role. Only a government of the people, by the people and for the people will be able to do it.

He made these remarks face-to-face with the British at the Conference. There was a frequently-made accusation that Ambedkar was a stooge of the imperialists. Com. Sanzgiri takes issue with this, citing Gandhi's views on the rulers of princely states: 'We do not have the right to tell the princes what they should and should not do within their state.' Ambedkar was severely critical of this position: 'The representatives of the princely states should be elected by the people of those states, not nominated by the princes.' Com. Sanzgiri goes on to say in his booklet:

He (Ambedkar) vigorously opposed such a compromising attitude to the question of national leadership. Just because he took such an opposing stand it does not mean that we can think of Ambedkar as a puppet of imperialism. Dr. Ambedkar believed in a parliamentary method of work and a parliamentary approach to reforms. And he opposed the struggles started by Gandhi, but at the same time he organized the Dalit community to fight for their human rights. . . . Gandhiji did not want the Dalit masses to become organized and fight against oppression. We can understand Ambedkar's opposition to the Congress, but we regret that his position regarding the Communists was not a welcoming one.

Giving the reasons for this he says,

Basically, his inclination was towards taking the constitutional and reformist path to attain his objectives, and so he was opposed to the radical revolutionary methods used by the Communists. Even so, the Communists should have taken up a special action programme to gain the confidence of this section of the people, as a part of their overall strategy.

Further, he expresses his regret that when Ambedkar on various occasions took the position that he was opposed to the Communists, and would even cooperate with the Congress, the Party did not try and understand him, though they supported whatever appropriate steps he took. Sanzgiri says that the fact that the Indian Constitution was given a secular base can be attributed to the perspective and the influence of Ambedkar. He states this firmly as the position of the Party.

The above exposition of views by Sanzgiri is the official position of the

Communist Party. More had stated almost the same views in his memoranda. The Party, albeit some considerable time after More had sent his observations to them, has now developed a very comprehensive position on the question of untouchability. It is possible that some lacunae still remain, but the Party will work incessantly to remove them, with changes corresponding to changes in the contemporary situation. One of More's memoranda is given in the appendix to this book.

More's Activities in the Last Stage

The Second Party Congress of the Communist Party was held in Calcutta from 28 February to 6 March 1948. In the Resolution adopted at this Congress the Party gave a call for militant struggles of the workers and peasants. As a result, the Congress government led by Nehru imposed a ban on the Communist Party. Com. B.T. Ranadive was elected Party general secretary while many leaders were being arrested, and many leaders and comrades went underground.[46] More also went underground.

In 1951 the Party announced that it had changed the above policy, and the ban was lifted. More came out from the underground, while a struggle was going on within the Party on basic policy issues. There were two views in the Party on the class nature of the Indian state, which threatened the unity of the Party. More was at that time a full-time activist. The Party was paying him and his family one hundred rupees a month. As soon as the present writer found a job, More ceased taking money from the Party. This was also the time when the new Party committee for Bombay was elected. Members of both factions in the Party: those who had supported the policy statement of 1951, and those who had opposed it, were elected to this committee. But More felt that the Party leadership's policy of encouraging dissent within the Party was harmful for the growth of Party organization and contrary to Marxist principles. So, he resigned from membership of the Bombay committee, took up residence in his native town Dasgaon and devoted himself to the work of party building.

Besides this developing inner-party strife, the motivating factor behind More's shift to Dasgaon was the fact that he had to leave his residence once again. Com. S.B. Jadhav, with whom he had been staying, retired from his service in the Municipality and More had to leave his quarters; if he had not done so, Jadhav would have had problems in claiming his Provident Fund. More could possibly have found another room, but he then decided to leave Bombay and start party work at the district level.

---

[46] Satyendra More is coy about noting the historic nature of the Calcutta Congress which saw the adoption of the Ranadive thesis of armed insurrection, and a sidelining of the P.C. Joshi line on support for working within a constitutional Communist Party framework. As Satyendra More notes, this inaugurated intense internecine conflict within the CPI.

More had returned to Dasgaon with his wife and children; the present author barely managed to send him sixty or seventy rupees a month. When More went to Dasgaon the government had to appoint a policeman to watch over him. Whenever More came to the bus station, this man would enquire where he was going. If he answered, 'Alibag', he would ask a lorry driver headed in that direction to take him there. So, the policeman in fact helped him. When he went to Alibag or any other place where there were Party activists, they would give him meals and his return bus fare. It was a way of life with More never to take more than his bus fare and a rupee or so more. In these difficult circumstances, he built a group of activists sympathetic to the Party's ideology.

He also developed close relations with workers of the Peasants and Workers Party (PWP), which had adopted the 'Dabhade thesis'; but the cadre was still unfamiliar with Marxism.[47] They found discussions with More very fruitful. So, persons like Bhai Shetye, visually challenged member of the State Legislative Assembly, and D.B. Patil, leader of the PWP, soon became close friends with More. More also wrote for the daily newspaper *Krishiwal* which came out from Alibag, and for other local papers.

It was during More's stay in rural Konkan that the movement for freedom of Goa from Portuguese rule and the movement for a Marathi-speaking state were going on. He sent three squads of activists to the Goa freedom movement. Everybody knew More's name as a Communist Party leader in Raigad district, especially when a campaign was being organized. He got senior leaders like Com. Srinivas Sardesai to join in the conferences he organized: for example, a discussion on socialism in China where historian Prof. N.R. Pathak was invited to speak. In this way More worked to propagate socialist thinking.

More was trying to start work with the Kisan Sabha, the Party's front for farmers, but because of his poverty and his working-class background, he found it difficult to set up an office and collect funds. The Party was not in a position to finance these efforts, and More too did not think it appropriate to appeal to the Party. In 1957 More returned to Bombay and began writing for the Party weekly *Yugantar*.

There was inner-party conflict from 1951. The main point of disagreement was class struggle versus class conciliation. When India went to war with China, the Nehru government attacked that faction which was for solving the dispute through conciliation, and arrested those Party members on 7 November 1962. As the Communist Party did not immediately protest, others were arrested on 21 November. One group accepted the position that China had an expansionist policy and was attacking India. More, who believed in proletarian internationalism, was

---

[47] The Peasants and Workers Party of India was founded in 1947. The Dabhade project or Dabhade thesis was the proposal that the party should formally accept Marxist ideology. This was put into effect in 1948.

strongly of the opinion that a Socialist nation could not be expansionist and try to subjugate other nations, and so opposed the war following Marxist-Leninist principles. In the convention of the All India Trade Union Congress (AITUC, the nation-wide trade union organization of the Communist Party) held in Hyderabad in 1963, some representatives wanted to pass a resolution demanding release of those comrades who had been arrested during the India–China border conflict. Dange was infuriated by this and declared, 'The sky will not fall if these champions remain in jail.' This statement opened the eyes of many working-class comrades. More had in any case opposed the Party's policy (of supporting the war against China).

Even so, efforts were on to bring together the two factions. On 4 July 1964, the leaders of the national committee held talks with the opposing faction. But the majority on the national committee insisted that a resolution was possible only if the opposing faction ceded to the Party position. Later, at the Tenali conference, the assembled comrades called for convening the 7th Congress of the Party. Accordingly, in November 1964, the opposing faction held what it called the 7th Congress of the Party, and the Communist Party of India (Marxist) was formed. As More accepted the policies of the CPI (Marxist), he left the Communist Party of India and the Party organ *Yugantar*. He then began working for the new Party in Bombay.

When the Communist Party of India (Marxist) was formed, many Party comrades were in jail and many were underground. More was a guide for many of these who entered the new Party. Among these were Advocate Jayant Pradhan, Com. Patekar, and Comrades Vichare, Gopalan, Krishnan, K.L. Bajaj, Nambiar, K. Ramchandra and others. Among these, Jayant Pradhan and others played a leading role in spreading the Dalit Panther movement and in campaigning for the Dalit Panthers through Anil Barve's weekly *Ranangan* ('Battlefield'). (Jayant Pradhan in his book *Comrades Lal Salaam* has said that it was More who first made him aware of the oppression suffered by women and Dalits.) Com. S.Y. Kolhatkar was underground at the time, and More was in constant contact with him. More, who had experience in journalism, concentrated his efforts on starting a newspaper for the Party, and the weekly *Jivan Marg* was launched in 1965.

The End and Last Respects

From 1966 to 1967 More's health deteriorated and he was always ill. He still remained active as a member of the Bombay committee of the Party. When the all-India Congress of the Party was held in Cochin in 1969, More was specially invited and his work in the Communist movement was lauded.

During 1971–72, More's health became much worse; he was frequently in hospital, and his old asthma also troubled him. He died in Goregaon in Bombay on 11 May 1972, at almost 69 years of age.

R.B. More with family.
Courtesy of Subodh More.

Following More's wishes and his thinking, no religious rites were performed for him after his death. His mortal remains were lit by Bombay Party Secretary Com. P.K. Kurne and Com. L.S. Karkhanis, secretary of the Communist Party of India. The present author deliberately avoided lighting the fire even though I was his son. More had believed that one's true heirs are those who are working to further one's ideology, and so it was leaders of both the Communist parties who lit the funeral pyre.

When More was alive he used to say, 'When I die, I am not going to become a crow or anything according to the Hindu scriptures; neither am I going to attain *nirvana* by people touching each other and performing a water ritual according to Buddhism; so, nobody should feel obliged to perform any religious rituals.' More's family followed his wishes, and, as they too were materialist in their thinking, they did not bring home his ashes from the burning ground or conduct any funeral ceremony. Many other famous Communists and progressives had families who held rigid religious views and performed funeral rites after their death; this did not happen in More's case. Just as he had lived his life according to his beliefs, so did his family respect his wishes after his death. Thus did More's life end; and what is left behind are memories and the work he did, which still goes on and

S.R. More with wife.
Courtesy of Subodh More.

which will continue in the future, as new generations of young people join the Communist Party.

On hearing of More's death, Com. B.T. Ranadive, senior Politburo member of the Communist Party of India (Marxist), expressed his sorrow by sending a telegram. He and Com. Vimal Ranadive later wrote letters to the More family expressing their grief. Obituaries were written in the all-India Party weekly *People's Democracy*, *Swadhinata* and *Jivan Marg*. The Party's trade union organization, Centre of Indian Trade Unions (CITU), passed a condolence resolution in its state conference. Many renowned persons in the social sphere expressed their grief.

More kept in touch with the Dalit and working people until the very end. So, after his death, even though More was a leader of the Communist Party and had broken political ties with Ambedkar, the leaders of the Dalit movement, through the Bombay Buddhist People's Panchayat Samiti, organized a condolence meeting for More in Parel in Bombay on 30 July 1972. Presiding over the meeting was Babasaheb Ambedkar's son Yashwantrao aka Bhaiyasaheb Ambedkar. Among the main speakers were ex-mayor of Bombay Dr. P.T. Borale, Ghanshyam Talwatkar, S.A. Upsham Guruji, C.N. Mohite Guruji, P.L. Lokhande, Bhaskar Kadrekar, R.G. Ruke, Sumant Gaikwad, U.L. Karandikar Guruji and other Dalit leaders from

Bombay, as well as Bombay secretary of the Party [CPI], Com. Dr. A.B. Sawant, and Com. D.B. Bhosle. Most speakers talked about More's difficult life, his sacrifice, his dedication to his ideals and his honesty, and praised him. They all said that even though More was a Communist, Babasaheb had great love and affection for him, and that one of Babasaheb's dearest followers had now passed from us.

GLOSSARY OF PEOPLE AND TERMS

People

There are many names mentioned across both the parts of this text, and this is not a comprehensive Glossary. Neither do we provide detailed biographical information about individuals. Some prominent names are covered below. Anupama Rao's Introduction and footnotes provide more comprehensive details about many people who appear in this Glossary as well as some who do not.

ADHIKARI, JAGANNATH (JAGGU), AND GANGADHAR: Brothers, both active workers of the CPI; Gangadhar's translation of the *Communist Manifesto* into Marathi was published in 1931. He was also one of those jailed in the Meerut Conspiracy Case.

ADREKAR, KESHAVRAO GOVIND: Founder of the Mahar Samaj Seva Sangh in Bombay.

ATRE, PRALHAD KESHAV (1898–1969): Popularly known as Acharya (teacher or mentor), Atre, playwright, editor of the influential newspaper *Maratha*, and prominent leader of the Samyukta Maharashtra movement for the formation of Maharashtra state through the consolidation of Marathi-speaking areas from the Bombay and C.P. and Berar Provinces, and the princely state of Hyderabad.

BHALERAO, SHANTABAI (BORN 1914): Daughter of Dagduji Bhavji Shinde, who worked as driver to the Viceroy Lord Chelmsford. He was a close associate of Ambedkar and, being relatively well off, also gave financial support to the movement. Shantabai was a young girl at the time of the *satyagraha*, and read out a short speech. She later became an activist in the Ambedkar movement.

BOLE, SITARAM KESHAV (1869–1961): Born in a well-off Bhandari (toddy tapper) caste family in Bombay. Later, he became a follower of Satyashodhak ideology. He was thus one of the prominent supporters of Ambedkar from a non-Dalit, non-upper-caste background (the section of society referred to by Jotiba Phule as *shudras* and classified as Other Backward Castes after Independence). Bole was elected to the Bombay Legislative Council from the Non-Brahmin Party in 1920. In 1923, he passed a resolution in the Bombay Legislative Council to open public lakes, wells and *dharamshalas* to all citizens.

CHANDAVARKAR, SIR NARAYAN GANESH (1855–1923): Early leader of the Indian National Congress. He was a member of the Saraswat Brahmin community of south Konkan (now in Karnataka state). In 1900 he was elected president of the current session of the Congress. He also served as a Judge of the Bombay High Court. He was a follower of the Prarthana Samaj, and worked for reforms within the Hindu community.

CHANDORKAR, RAMCHANDRA: A resident of Goregaon, near Mahad, he was one of those who jumped in the reservoir during the Mahad *satyagraha* and was beaten up. Later worked with N.M. Joshi.

CHITRE, ANANTRAO: A close associate of Dr. B.R. Ambedkar from the Chandraseniya Kayastha Prabhu caste. Active in the Mahad *satyagraha*, he was elected as MLA from the Independent Labour party and later joined the Communist Party.

DANGE, S.A. (1892–1991): One of the founders of the Communist Party of India. Among the main accused in the Meerut Conspiracy Case.

DESHPANDE, S.V.: A prominent Communist trade union leader. In the 1930s, he organized several front organizations (e.g. the Marxist Students' Club) to continue the Party's work when the British had declared all Communist activity illegal.

GAIKWAD, BHAURAO KRISHNAJI AKA KARMAVEER DADASAHEB GAIKWAD (1902–1971): Led the Kalaram Mandir *satyagraha* in Nashik in 1930. After Ambedkar's death, he led a mass agitation of landless labourers from the Dalit and other lower castes to fight for better wages, common grazing lands (*gayraan*), and other rights in 1959.

GAIKWAD, SAMBHAJI TUKARAM (1864–1949): A resident of Colaba district, he trained as a motor mechanic in Bombay and earned a good salary. He was one of the main organizers of the March *satyagraha* at Mahad in 1927. He was elected chairman of the reception committee.

GARUD, BABURAO: Communist Party member; close associate of R.B. More.

JADHAV, BHASKARRAO VITHOJIRAO (1897–1950): Was an important Non-Brahmin leader who served in Kolhapur State between 1895 and 1921 under Shahu Chhatrapati, and as Minister of Health and Education (1923) and Minister of Agriculture and Excise (1928) in the Bombay government. Jadhav also served as the president of the Satyashodhak Samaj between 1911 and 1930, and was deeply involved in supporting Maratha educational and social reform, in addition to playing a key role in supporting political Non-Brahminism. For instance, Jadhav demanded separate representation for the Marathas at the Southborough Committee. Jadhav also played an important role in promoting Non-Brahmin leaders such as Arjun Alwe, and G.N. Kasle for important positions in the Girni Kamgar Union, and in challenging the Brahmin leadership of the trade union movement while he was in the Bombay government.

JADHAV, S.B.: Secretary of the Scheduled Castes Federation in Bombay.

JOSHI, NARAYAN MALHAR (1875–1955): Born in Colaba district of Maharashtra in 1875 and was educated at Pune and Bombay. In 1909, he joined Servants of India Society. He was instrumental in the founding of the Social Service League in 1911 for improving the condition of the common masses. He was also associated with several labour organizations and in 1921 he joined the All India Trade Union Congress. In 1931, N.M. Joshi broke away from the AITUC and formed the All India Trade Union Federation. He was responsible for several enactments on labour welfare. In 1947, he became a member of the Central Pay Commission.

KADAM, SHAHIR RAGHU: Communist Party member and singer; contemporary of Satyendra More.

KAMBLE, SHIVRAM JANBA (BORN 1875): An important anti-caste activist who founded the newspaper *Somavanshiya Mitra*, led the Parvati Satyagraha, and petitioned the British government for Mahars' re-entry into the Army.

KELKAR, COMRADE DATTA: Member of the CPI, trade union leader, and a friend of R.B. More. He has recounted memories of the latter in his book *Atmashodh* ('Awareness of Self').

KHAIRMODE, CHANGDEO B.: Author of a 13-volume biography of Dr. B.R. Ambedkar.

KHER, BALASAHEB (1882–1957): The first prime minister of Bombay Province; he took office in 1937. He worked with Ambedkar and was a member of the board of the Bahishkrit Hitakarini Sabha founded by Ambedkar in 1924.

KUVEKAR, KAMLAKAR: Known as Bhiku Kuvekar; Communist activist who was killed during a textile mill strike.

LOKHANDE, NARAYAN MEGHAJI (1848–1897): Pioneer of the labour movement among textile mill workers in 19th-century Bombay, founder of the Bombay Mill-Hands Association (1890) and editor of *Dinabandhu*. He raised the issue of discrimination against Dalit workers on the basis of their 'untouchability'.

MHATRE, KASHINATH: Belonged to the Agari caste of salt producers, settled in coastal

Maharashtra. Communist activist; took part in the anti-*khot* agitation.

MR. PALYEYASHASTRI: A Sanskrit scholar consulted by Ambedkar regarding the Mahad reservoir case.

NAMBIAR, SUHASINI: Sister of Sarojini Naidu; the first woman member of the Communist Party of India.

PARULEKAR, GODUTAI, OR GODAVARI PARULEKAR (1907–1996): A freedom fighter, writer, and social activist. She was married to Shamrao Parulekar, another freedom fighter and activist. Both joined the Communist Party of India, and after the split in the Party Godutai worked with the CPI (Marxist). She devoted the latter part of her life to working for the rights of the Warli tribals in Thane district in Maharashtra.

PARULEKAR, SHAMRAO: Member of the Communist Party; raised Dalit issues within the Party. He and his wife Godutai Parulekar were jailed twice for their political activities; in the 1940s and in the 1960s while fighting for a separate state for Marathi speakers. They then devoted their life to working for the *adivasis*, or tribals, of Thane district. Shamrao died in jail in 1965.

PATIL, NARAYAN NAGU (1906–1976): Supporter of Ambedkar in the anti-*khot* movement. Later joined the Peasants and Workers Party.

PHULE, JOTIBA (1827–1891): Founder of the Satyashodak Samaj (1873), creator of a new history and identity for the Dalit and labouring castes which challenged the enduring power of Brahminism in all walks of life, and among the most important anti-caste thinkers that the subcontinent has produced.

PRABHAKAR, PURUSHOTTAM AKA BAPURAO JOSHI: Resident of Mahad who took part in the *satyagraha*.

RANADE, JUSTICE MAHADEV GOVIND (1842–1901): An Indian scholar, social reformer and author. He was a founding member of the Indian National Congress and held several designations as member of the Bombay Legislative Council, member of the finance committee at the centre, and judge of the Bombay High Court.

RANADIVE, B.T. (1904–1990): Active in the CPI and in its trade union federation the All India Trade Union Congress. He took the lead when the Party split in 1964 and became a major leader of the CPI (Marxist).

RISLEY, SIR HERBERT HOPE (1851–1911): A British ethnographer and colonial administrator.

A member of the Indian Civil Service, he conducted extensive studies on the tribes and castes of the Bengal Presidency. He is known for implementing the caste-wise enumeration in the 1901 Census of British India.

Rupavate, Dadasaheb (born 1925): Edited *Prabuddha Bharat* after Ambedkar's death. After Independence, he held important posts in the Maharashtra cabinet and worked for the welfare of Dalits and the downtrodden.

Sahasrabuddhe, G.N.: A member of the Chitpavan Brahmin community, who burned the *Manusmriti* at the Mahad *satyagraha* of 25 December 1927. He later worked as editor of Ambedkar's journal *Janata*.

Salvi, Kachru Mathuji or Comrade K.M. Salvi: Worked as an activist in the Matunga Labour Camp, and played a key role in the Kalaram Mandir temple entry agitation. R.B. More dedicated his autobiography to Salvi.

Sathe, Annabhau or Tukaram Bhaurao Sathe (1920–1969): A social reformer, Communist folk poet, and writer. Sathe was a Dalit born into the untouchable Mang community, and his upbringing and identity were central to his writing and political activism. He wrote novels apart from composing and performing ballads and traditional heroic songs. Sathe was also one of the founders of the Indian People's Theatre Association which was active from the 1940s.

Shinde, Vitthal Ramji (1873–1944): Important religious and social reformer of Maharashtra, working with the Prarthana Samaj. In 1906 he established the Depressed Classes Mission. Between 1918 and 1920 he organized conferences for the removal of untouchability and worked with Gandhi, the Maharaja Sayajirao Gaikwad of Baroda, and B.R. Ambedkar. He gave evidence before the Southborough Franchise Committee in 1919, and demanded political representation for untouchables. However, he had disagreements with Ambedkar over the forms of representation to be demanded.

Talwatkar, Ghanshyam: A participant in the Mahad *satyagraha*, he later led a faction of the Republican Party of India. Secretary of the Peoples' Education Society.

Tamhankar, Govind: Member of the CPI; conducted classes in Delisle Road, Bombay together with R.B. More and other comrades.

Thakre (or Thackeray), Keshav Sitaram (1885–1973): Also known as Prabodhankar Thackeray, was a writer and social reformer who took up several causes such as the fight against untouchability, child marriage and dowry. Born into the Chandraseniya Kayastha Prabhu caste, his writing is polemical and sharply critical of Brahminical practices in contemporary Hinduism. His son, Bal Thackeray, founded the right-wing Shiv Sena in 1966 which targeted South Indians, Dalits, and Muslims as 'outsiders' disabling the economic progress of the Marathi *manus*, or the ordinary Marathi man.

TIPNIS, SURENDRANATH GOVIND OR SURBANANA TIPNIS: Another member of the Chandraseniya Kayastha Prabhu caste who served as chairman of the Mahad Municipality and played an important role in the Mahad *satyagraha*. He also took part in the anti-*khot* agitation led by Ambedkar, in spite of being a landlord himself. He served as M.L.S. in the Independent Labour Party.

VAIDYA, COMRADE D.S.: Communist leader. When B.T. Ranadive and others were in jail, Vaidya, together with Telangana leader P. Sundarayya, E.M.S. Namboodiripad from Kerala, and P.C. Joshi, all outside jail, favoured carrying on the struggle against British rule even while Britain was allied with the Soviet Union in fighting the Nazis.

WADAWALKAR, SHANKAR: A singer in the Ambedkari *jalsas*; Ambedkar's biographer C.B. Khairmode says that he and R.B. More helped in Khairmode's research on the origins of Ambedkar Jayanti celebrations.

WALANGKAR, GOPAL BABA (C. 1840–1900): An early anti-caste activist from the Mahar caste. He was born in Raodhal, near Mahad. He served in the Army and settled at Dapoli. He published a booklet called *Vital-Vidhwansak* ('Destruction of Brahminical Pollution'). He was appointed to the local *tehsil* board of Mahad in 1895.

WARERKAR, B.V. AKA MAMA (1883–1964): A Marathi writer of novels, plays and short stories particularly depicting the lives of labourers, and also sympathetic to women in a male-dominated society.

TERMS

Some Marathi terms have been explained in the text itself, or they have very specific contexts for their use. These are not included in the brief Glossary that is provided below.—Tr.

akhada: a gymnasium, or a place where wrestling is practised

anna: one-sixteenth of a rupee

babhali: a thorny bush, *acacia Arabica/acacia nilotica*

bahurupi: a kind of folk artist in Maharashtra who takes on the form of various characters for entertainment bhajan: a devotional song

bhakari: flat bread made of different kinds of millet flour or sometimes rice flour; staple food across rural Maharashtra

bidi: a cheap cigarette made of unprocessed tobacco, wrapped in leaves

chatni: a relish made from pounded chillies; in parts of rural Maharashtra it can mean any vegetable accompaniment to the *bhakar/bhakari*, or staple flat millet bread

chawl: a long and narrow building divided into many separate tenements, offering cheap, basic accommodation to labourers

chhabina: a guard of horsemen (around a camp or fort, preceding an army on march, accompanying a king or an idol in procession, etc.)

dakshina: in Buddhist, Hindu, Sikh and Jain literature it may mean any donation, fees or honorarium given to a cause, monastery, temple, spiritual guide, or after a ritual

darshan: an opportunity to see or the occasion of seeing a holy person or the image of a deity; Hindus attach great importance to a *darshan*, or view, of a saint or holy man

desi: of this country, indigenous

dharamshala: a simple lodging built for travellers

dhoti: a garment worn by male Hindus, consisting of a piece of material tied around the waist and extending to cover most of the legs

hamam: a public bath

handa: a cooking pot, or more generally a wide-mouthed vessel

jalsa: a session or performance, often referring to performances of street art

janava: the sacred thread worn by Brahmin males, and sometimes by men and boys of the other 'twice-born' castes

jatak: the *Jātaka* tales are a voluminous body of literature native to India concerning the previous births of Gautama Buddha in both human and animal form. The future Buddha may appear as a king, an outcast, a god, an elephant—but, in whatever form, he exhibits some virtue that the tale thereby inculcates. The reference on p. 51 is to a jocular use of the term, which compares Ramchandra's tastes to that of a mongoose.

jatra: a periodical festival in honour of a local deity, where pilgrims gather

jayanti: birth anniversary

jogtin: a girl dedicated to serve and worship a deity; see also 'murali'

joshi: an astrologer; this is a common surname among Brahmins in Maharashtra

kadelot: precipitation from a precipice (of a criminal, or of one's self in propitiation of a god)

kamgat: it means work to be done, a task; the precise meaning in this context is explained by the author

karkhanis: the officer appointed to a *karkhana*, or any business or industrial establishment, to keep accounts, etc.

khot: a landlord in the Konkan, the coastal region of Maharashtra. These landowners also collected taxes for the British. The *khoti* system was severely exploitative of the farmers of the Konkan, who had to give up 75 per cent of their output as rent, tax or interest on loans. Ambedkar led a movement against the *khoti* system from 1933 to 1939.

kirtana: a celebration or praise of God through music and singing; it also refers to a genre of religious performance arts, connoting a musical form of narration or shared recitation, particularly of spiritual or religious ideas

lathi: a baton

lungi: garment similar to a *sarong*, wrapped around the waist and extending to the ankles

maadiwalla: the meaning of 'maadi' is given in the text (p. 111); so 'maadiwalla' is the owner of a two-storey house

maidan: any plain, level tract of ground

malkhamb: a wrestler's pillar

mama: maternal uncle, mother's brother

mamlatdar/mamledar: a stipendiary revenue officer at the *taluka*, or sub-district level, who also exercises judicial functions

mandap: a temporary platform set up for weddings and religious ceremonies

mann: a measure of weight, sometimes called a maund, ranging from 11 to 70 kilograms

matka: a mud vessel, often used for storing drinking water

mukadam: a title given to the managing authority of a village; more generally, the chief of a body or caste of public labourers

murali: a girl dedicated to the god Khandoba

nanduki: nanduki, or nandruk tree, *ficus microcarpia*

paan: betel leaves prepared and used as a stimulant

panch: a person or institution that judges and settles a quarrel between two other people or groups

Peshwa: the chief minister of a Maratha prince; under Shivaji he was the head of an advisory council, but after his death the council broke up and the post became hereditary and was held by Brahmins

pujari: a Hindu priest, one who performs *puja*

pheriwalla: a pedlar

Puranas: the eighteen sacred poetical works that form the body of Hindu theology

qawwali: a style of Muslim devotional music now associated particularly with Sufis

raiyat: 'Raiyat means a person who, by virtue of Section 44 or otherwise has acquired a right to hold land directly under the Government mainly for the purpose of cultivating it by himself or by members of his family or by, or with the aid of, servants or labourers or with the aid of partners or bargadars, and includes also the successors-in-interest of persons who have acquired such a right'. (Section 82(2) of the State Acquisition and Tenancy Act, 1950)

samadhi: here, a tomb

sardar: a person of high rank (such as a hereditary noble)

satyagraha: 'holding onto truth' or truth-force, a concept introduced in the early 20th century by Mahatma Gandhi to designate a determined but non-violent resistance to subjugation; Gandhi's *satyagraha* became a major tool in the Indian struggle against British imperialism, and Ambedkar also referred to many of his protests as *satyagrahas*

sutra: a section, or literally 'thread', of a Hindu religious text

tamasha: a traditional form of Marathi theatre, often with singing and dancing, widely performed by local or travelling theatre groups across the state of Maharashtra

varna: type, order, colour or class; the term refers to social classes in the Dharmashastra literature such as the *Manusmriti*. Hindu literature classified society in principle into four *varnas* though there is also an elaborate description of new castes that are formed through caste mixing (forced and voluntary), which suggests the caste order was more fluid than the textual prescription would suggest. Sanskrit prescriptive texts order the castes in the following hierarchy: Brahmins (priests, scholars and teachers); Kshatriyas (rulers, warriors and administrators); Vaishyas (merchants and traders); and the Shudras (manual labourers and agriculturalists). The Dalits, or *atishudras*, fall outside the *varna* system and were considered untouchable.

wada: the word means either a palatial edifice, or a part of a village, a colony or settlement; it is often preceded by the name of a caste, e.g. *Kumbharwada*, potters' colony, or *Maharwada*, to indicate a caste-based colony within a village

watan: an *inam*, or the grant of tax-free land from a ruler to a subject for service. During the pre-colonial period certain lands were given to particular persons for services rendered to rulers, to the community or to both. (The British extended this practice in some instances.) These lands are called 'watan lands'. Mahars were also granted *watan* lands which often rotated between families, and were held in return for the performance of village labour, e.g. the removal of dead cattle, carrying messages between villages, and so forth.

APPENDICES

Appendix A

Details of the Lecture Series organized by the Mahar Seva Sangh with R.B. More as general secretary.

S. No.	Date	Topic	Speaker
1.	22/1/28	The Present-Day Tasks before Untouchable Women	Mrs. Manoramabai Pradhan Mrs. Devakibai Satamkar
2.	7/9/29	Brahminical Religion	Mr. Devram Vishnu Naik
3.	8/9/29	Discourse	Mr. Keshav Sitaram Thakre
4.	9/9/29	Contemporary Religion	Mr. Dattatray Vitthal Khandke
5.	10/9/30	Caste Associations	Mr. Narhari Vitthal Khandke
6.	11/9/31	Untouchability	Mr. Gangadhar Sahasrabuddhe
7.	12/9/31	Principles of the Satyashodhaks	Mr. Shivram Khatavkar
8.	13/9/31	Duties of Women	Mrs. Ramabai Gangadhar Sahasrabuddhe Mrs. Devakibai Satamkar
9.	14/9/31	The Revolt in the Puranas	Mr. Konddev Kholwadikar
10.	15/9/31	The Present Conditions of the Untouchables	Mr. Changdeo Narayan Mohite
11.	17/8/30	Questions Facing the Untouchable Class	Mr. D.V. Naik/Mr. Kadrekar
12.	28/8/30	Women's *Dharma*, Making Gold out of Mud	Mrs. Yamunabai Ghodekar Mrs. Manoramabai Pradhan Mrs. Kamalabai Prabhu Miss Krishnabai Khare
13.	31/8/30	The Congress (party) and the Untouchable Class	Dr. G.Y. Chitnis Mr. R.D. Kavali
14.	31/8/30	The Working-Class Movement and the Untouchable Class	Mr. S.V. Parulekar Com. S.V. Deshpande
15.	1/9/30	The Present Situation and the Duties of Women	Mrs. Avantikabai Gokhale Mrs. Padmavati Asaikar
16.	1/9/30	History of Untouchability	Mr. Achyut B. Kolhatkar Mr. Sambhaji T. Gaikwad

17.	2/9/30	The Secret of Revolution	Mr. K.S. Thakre
18.	4/9/30	Our *Dharma*	Mr. Shetye/S.G. Jadhav
			Mr. Changdeo N. Mohite
19.	5/9/31	The Future of the Outcastes	Mr. D.V. Pradhan/Mr. Gupte

(*Source*: Annual Report of the Mahar Seva Sangh, ed. R.V. Ruke.)

Appendix B

Revised note sent to the Communist Party by Com. R.B. More in 1964, on the question of untouchability and the caste system.

On Untouchability and Caste System

The problem of five crores of our proletarian untouchable countrymen is a major problem before our Party. This problem by its very nature has a character of a fundamental problem. The Party must make all serious efforts to solve this problem if the Party has to carry out a people's democratic revolution against imperialism and feudalism, successfully.

The Party has never correctly analysed this problem from the Marxist-Leninist point of view and, subsequently, the Party had to suffer gravely. Not only this, but the Indian revolution too received a definite setback.

We have looked at this problem of untouchability with an outlook based on 'Economism'. We have always been so overwhelmed by this outlook that we have almost revised and vulgarized Marxism. We have formulated an over-simplified theory that a change in an economic environment automatically brings about a change in the consciousness. We fail to understand that the change in the consciousness does not and cannot come automatically, but there is always a necessity to fight for it. No wonder, therefore, that all our efforts to understand and solve this problem were mechanical, sectarian and based on the wrong outlook of 'Economism'. This must be rooted out, if at all our Party is to become the real revolutionary party of the working class.

It must be frankly admitted that the problem of untouchability which is peculiar to India has been mainly a problem of social and religious slavery which has resulted into a political and economic slavery. To anslyse the phenomenon of untouchability as a feudal phenomenon is, therefore, not enough. We must concretely examine this problem which is the natural outcome of the caste system created by the ruling classes of ancient times for their own interest and which was given religious sanction.

The caste system is interpreted by some as a division of labour. The fact is it is not only a division of labour but it is a division of labourers; and it is not only a division of labourers but a gradation of divisions of labourers.

Untouchability and caste system have always been the main disruptive factor of our working class and people's unity. It can be safely said that the foreign imperialist powers have always utilized untouchability and caste system to enforce their domination and slavery on the Indian people. The whole course of Indian history proves this beyond doubt.

Our Party in a real revolutionary sense is fast becoming an All-India party and it is, therefore, all the more necessary for our Party to study this problem of untouchability which is an all-India problem in all its aspects and to evolve correct slogans to eradicate this medieval monstrosity. The origin of untouchability lies obviously in the practices of ruling classes who created untouchability to enforce and perpetuate their class domination over conquered slaves. The number of these untouchable slaves increased as all those who violated the rules, customs, and discipline of the caste system began to be treated as untouchables even though they belonged to the conquering tribes. Thus millions and millions became untouchables in India. According to the first census report the population of untouchables in South India was one third of the total population. We also know that the vast numbers of human beings, men and women, were not only untouchables but treated as unseeables in South India not in the very distant past.

If we care to understand the class character of these five crores of untouchables (the figure accepted by Comrade Zukov in his article 'Manoeuvres of British Imperialism in India') we can immediately see that 99% of these untouchables are the urban or rural proletariat and a small number of them belong to the class of poor peasants.

It will not be out of place if I just state how the untouchable landless labourer lives in a village. He is a bonded slave of a village. The caste Hindu population of a village controls his entire life. He must do any work that he may be ordered to, it may be a government job or a private one. He simply cannot refuse. He cannot leave his village without the permission of a village Patil (the Chief of a village). He has no choice regarding his possessions. He must live in a village and do the job allotted to him. He cannot complain about his wages. He cannot leave his village to find a better means of subsistence even though he is practically starving in his village. He has to carry away the dead cattle belonging to the caste Hindu, has to skin them, has to play music in marriage and other religious ceremonies. He is not allowed to build his house in the village proper where caste Hindus have their houses. He cannot take water from public watering places nor can he use public places for cultural functions such as marriages, etc.

Let us now see his private life. He cannot open a shop in a village. He cannot trade. He cannot freely mix in a caste Hindu crowd. Though he belongs to the Hindu religion and observes Hindu customs, Hindu priests do not give him religious services. This is the life of a landless untouchable labourer in a village. He is a slave of a slave. He cannot be touched and if he dares to move his fingers, he can be socially ostracized and economically strangled. No wonder these five crores of human beings refuse to live the life of medieval slaves in the 20th century and demand a complete overthrow of the domination of the ruling classes. This overthrow has become the necessity for their very existence. They do not want to live by the old ways and do want to live normally like their caste Hindu countrymen.

This section of the proletariat is important not only for its quantitative aspect but for its qualitative aspect too. The qualitative aspect of it will be clear if refer to the following quotation of Stalin. He says:

> I think that the proletariat as a class may be divided into three sections.
>
> One section is the basic mass of the proletariat, its core, its permanent part, the mass of 'pure-blooded' proletarians, who have long broken off connections with the capitalist class. This section of the proletariat is the most reliable bulwark of Marxism.
>
> The second section consists of newcomers from non-proletarian classes—from the peasantry, the petty bourgeois or the intelligentsia. These are newcomers from other classes who have only recently merged with the proletariat and have brought with them into the working class their customs, their habits, their waverings and their vacillations. This section constitutes the most favourable soil for all sorts of anarchist, semi-anarchist and 'ultra-Left' groups.
>
> The third section, lastly, consists of the labour aristocracy, the upper crust of the working class, the most well-to-do segment of the proletariat, with its propensity for compromise with the bourgeoisie, its predominant inclination to adapt itself to the powers that be, and its anxiety to 'get on' in life. This section constitutes the most favourable soil for outright reformists and opportunists.
>
> ('Once More On the Social-Democratic Deviation', pp. 17–18)

There is no doubt that the untouchables belong to that section of the proletariat which Stalin calls 'the most reliable bulwark of Marxism'. We have, however, failed to strengthen this bulwark because of our failure to organize and unify the untouchables with the touchable proletariat. We have refused to recognize the fact that untouchability is the main cause of this failure to organize and create solidarity amongst the Indian proletariat.

A section or these untouchables belong to the modern industrial working class. More than 50% of our industrial proletariat belong to castes that are deemed to be untouchable. In the Textile Industry, their percentage is as follows in various places: Bombay, 40%; Ahmedabad, 50%; Nagpur, 75%. In tea gardens the percentage of untouchables is 80%, in Mining Industry, it is 90%. In Railways and Docks, in Engineering and Chemical Industry, the percentage of untouchables is not less than 40%. In sanitary departments, untouchables are, of course, 100%.

Such is the picture of different industries in our country. Such is the picture of our working class whose vanguard we claim to be, though hardly have we even noticed this glaring objective reality that nearly 50% of our proletariat are untouchables.

Why this refusal to recognize so glaring an objective reality? The reason is not far to be sought. Our understanding of Marxism is mechanical and exclusively based on economism. Otherwise, it should not have been difficult for us to analyse and find out which section of the Indian working class we are organizing in our trade unions and *kisan sabhas*, which sections have remained out of these organizations and why they have remained so. When we can do this, then alone can we build class unity and class solidarity.

We have led many class battles in the past. We have also built many class organizations. Then why have we not yet succeeded in bringing about class solidarity among untouchables and caste Hindu workers on political problems? The reason is obvious. We have not even recognized the necessity of fighting the old medieval Hindu consciousness of the caste Hindu proletariat. A caste Hindu worker still thinks that he is a member of his caste first and a 'worker' afterwards. *Caste consciousness is more powerful than class consciousness. This caste consciousness is the great obstruction that is hindering the growth of the proletariat class consciousness in our working class.* We must understand that our proletariat is an Indian proletariat and, therefore, must inherit all Indian culture. We must take into consideration all the peculiarities of Indian Society and must fight ruthlessly against all backward modes of our ideological as well as political weakness. Our class organizations have also remained weak and our Party did not grow as much as it should have, in spite of the favourable International situation.

With the advent of British Imperialism in India came the bourgeois social order. This new social order could not eradicate the old caste system and untouchability because the British Imperialists did not want everything old to go, but they wanted to preserve it whenever it was in their interest. It must be, however, understood that the old caste system and untouchability had formerly received a powerful blow from Buddhism but it is still struggling hard for its survival because the reactionary religious and social forces led by Shankaracharya were strong enough to defeat Buddhism and strengthen the old caste system and untouchability. The British brought about new class relationships in India and created the conditions for the overthrow of the relics of the old social order, yet the caste system and untouchability could not be abolished; they are still alive. These relics will not die smoothly. They are bound to resist. Their roots have gone deep in the Hindu mind and hence the necessity of a ruthless struggle against them.

Along with British Raj come the bourgeois ideology in our country and it began to fight the old reactionary feudal ideology. Stalwarts such as Raja Ram Mohan Rai [sic], Mahatma Fule [sic], Ranade, Agarkar, Mahatma Gandhi and some others had this ideology to some extent. But so far as the struggle against untouchability and caste system is concerned Dr. Ambedkar's role was most militant and uncompromising. He alone pointed out that the root cause of untouchability is the *varna vyavastha* and the caste system which must be wiped out lock, stock and barrel. He attacked all old Hindu scriptures ruthlessly and mercilessly and no wonder became the greatest Emancipator of the most downtrodden masses of the untouchables. It is true that Dr. Ambedkar did not give prominence to the economic side of the problem. Yet it must be said that his approach was more objective and dealt with the problem fundamentally and his methods were absolutely free from any tinge of humanitarian sentimentalism. He roused the untouchable mass, he created in them a feeling of self-respect and taught them to fight for their human rights and social equality. He shifted the problem of removal of untouchability from the plane of begging and appeals to the plane of assertion and struggle.

What is the position of the untouchable mass of workers today? We as communists must not fail to take cognizance of the new phase that is being brought about in the life of the untouchables by the movement of conversion to Buddhism. This is a new development in the history of the untouchables and is going to play a very important role in the process of the transformation of the entire Society. Since Dr. Ambedkar's conversion, in October 1956, about a crore of people have gone over to Buddhism and the number of converts in increasing. This movement has made a revolution in the minds of the untouchables. They have now begun to feel that they are no more untouchables and that they have freed themselves from the humiliating and enslaving fold of Hindu casteism. But at the same time they have also begun to realize that for the common uplift of the whole Indian Society of peasants and workers, united efforts of all the progressive people is a necessity. This conviction that unity amongst all the downtrodden sections of the Indian masses is a necessity has transformed the old 'Scheduled Castes Federation' into the new Republican Party of India. All the converts are being politically organized under the banner of this new party. It is not, however, restricted to these converts only. The party has thrown its doors open to all.

What is going to be our attitude towards this organization?

In determining our attitude we must note the fact that just as change of religion was Dr. Ambedkar's own decision, the foundation of the Republican Party of India was also his own move. Dr. Ambedkar realized that the untouchables could not progress in any way unless they came out of the Hindu fold. He, therefore, took them out of the Hindu fold and made clear their way to progress. He chose Buddhism mainly because it is the strongest enemy of the *varna vyavastha* and casteism, and also because it is a materialistic and atheistic religion giving full freedom of thought to everyone. In this connection we should remember that Marx himself regarded Buddhism as the most progressive force in the religious movements of the world.

If we review the development of the political movement of the untouchables it will be seen that Dr. Ambedkar had come to the conclusion of founding the Republican Party because he was convinced that the further progress of the new Buddhist converts and the untouchables was impossible without the cooperation of other progressive forces in the country.

The Republican Party has now been founded and the party has created a collective leadership in the form of a Presidium the members of which come from all over India.

It will be quite clear from this that both the moves of Dr. Ambedkar, religious and political, are of great historical significance from the point of view of the development of the progressive movements in the country.

In the light of these observations our Party should immediately decide the policy regarding the Buddhistic movement as well as the Republican Party of India.

I do not want to waste any time in stating as to what we have done so far about the problem of untouchability. An objective self-critical review will tell us that we have done nothing at all. We have not attacked untouchability even as intensely as Agarkar and Mahatma Fule and obviously Dr. Ambedkar stands head and shoulders above us in this respect. However, no amount of breast-beating is going to change the past. Let us now at least earnestly see what we can do in future. In the first place, we must begin our ideological struggle against the caste Hindu reaction, particularly against the *varna vyavastha* and the caste system.

We are a communist party and must become the vanguard of the whole working class. It is a fact that vast sections of the working class and the landless labourers and poor peasants who are untouchables and Buddhists are not under our influence. Where such sections are under our influence, we have to examine self-critically as to what we have done to create a feeling of self-respect in these sections. It would be realized that without this section of the proletariat we cannot strengthen and develop our Party so as to be able to capture political power.

Some comrades think that the Party should support all struggles started against untouchability but should not start any independent struggle on its own. Some comrades who are still under the influence of 'Economism' think that the achievement of Socialism will solve the problem of untouchability. Both these conceptions are seriously wrong and are capable of doing serious damage to the Party and the revolutionary movement. This must be ruthlessly fought and defeated. The Communist Party must struggle against untouchability independently.

The Party cannot connive at the problem of the Caste System also which is at the root of untouchability and which is the cause of such deep-rooted conflicts as are conspicuously marked in states like Tamilnad [*sic*]. We must not be under the wrong impression that caste system exists no more. The political and economic struggles in India have not been able to annihilate caste consciousness. Though the caste system appears to have been abolished in public life yet it peeps out everywhere and is strong enough to influence even the political life of our nation.

The urgency of the problem can best be realized if we just try to understand the reasons of our strength in provinces where there is no untouchability in an acute form such as Tripura or where the major '*avarna*' section has come under the influence of the Party such as Kerala. This will show how we have gathered strength wherever a section of the untouchable mass has been attracted to our Party, and caste consciousness has been empowered by class consciousness as well as political consciousness.

It will be agreed that in order to build the democratic front of progressive forces in the country a thorough investigation into the problem is an urgent necessity. I, therefore, appeal to this Congress, as I had appealed to the Third Party Congress in 1953, to appoint a Commission to study this problem concretely and submit a thorough report to the Party within a specific period.

An Addition to the note 'On Untouchability and Caste System'

I think that this additional note is necessitated on account of the fact that a serious thought to the problem of casteism has never been given and no direct and conscientious efforts have been made by the [Communist Party of India] to uproot the monstrous evil of casteism, which is the root cause of untouchability and of the prevention of the mighty unity of the Indian people.

In the note it has been made clear that caste consciousness is a hindrance in the way of class consciousness. This has always worked against the really strong and comprehensive unity of the working class and other toiling masses during this period when the people are rising to struggle for their fundamental democratic rights. Such a unity is the prime necessity for the achievement of the stage of the Indian revolution which we strive for. The unity that we see today is only superfluous and not at all genuine, according to Marxist-Leninist principles of class organization.

It is generally agreed that caste distinctions are fast disappearing and that in some cases they have already disappeared. It is also said that nowadays nobody believes in caste and that caste system in the Hindu Society is outmoded. Even many political workers, including some communists, are found to support these arguments. These arguments, however, are a self-deception and deception of others made knowingly or unknowingly. To say that nobody believes in caste and at the same time observe caste in caste-ridden society is inconsistent and contradictory. Every individual belonging to a particular caste has to follow (though it may be against his own conscience) the customs and practices that are imposed upon him by his own caste. He cannot behave [sic] against them and has no courage to defy them. Here the pertinent question that arises is: How can a person, who behaves [sic] against his own conscience be called a progressive? And if he cannot be called a progressive, how can he be helpful for the revolutionary change in the society?

It must be noted, therefore, that casteism cannot be eradicated by simply saying that nobody believes in caste. Casteism, in fact, is deeply rooted in the minds of the people. So the real nature of caste must be thoroughly understood.

Caste in Hindu Society is by nature anti-social and anti-democratic. The caste distinction does not give freedom to the individual for his personal development and for the fulfilment of his duty towards Society. This is because caste does not give any importance to the personality of an individual, who is supposed to be a slave of his own caste. Caste has always played a very ugly role in the political life of the country, particularly when there are strikes, demonstrations, elections, etc. This clearly shows that the caste system is not only thoroughly useless for the progress of society in any direction but on the contrary it hampers the progress immensely.

It is beyond doubt and dispute that the caste system is the basis of untouchability, the must vulgar form of slavery. It is really a matter of the greatest concern that such an unnatural and disgraceful form of social structure should be treated on par with religion, sex, race and nationality. To treat the caste system on par with religion means nothing but to allow it to perpetuate.

The problem of untouchability and the caste system is not an academic problem as many may think. The problem is connected with the life of the crores of people in India. It is more atrocious than the racial problem in Africa. The caste system is a hideous form of hypocrisy of which a revolutionary party like the Communist Party must take cognizance and its hideousness must be thoroughly and unhesitatingly exposed.

The Communist Party, the party of the Indian proletariat must take bold steps to openly denounce and annihilate casteism, which is a powerful remnant of feudalism. Every Party member should disown his caste in which he is born. There should be no doubt that such a gesture will be a model to all the progressive elements in the country and it will be a guarantee for the task of annihilating this medieval monstrosity.

INDEX

Aarkade, Madhukar 248
Abbas, Khwaja Ahmad 248
Adhikari, Gangadhar 185, 211
   Communist Jahirnama 33, 166
Adhikari, Jagannath 164, 185, 261
Adhikari, Vimal 211
Adrekar, Keshavrao Govind 141, 158, 261
Adsul, Bhausaheb 246
Agarkar, Gopal Ganesh 114, 144, 275
   Sudharak (periodical) 54, 115
Agavane, Maruti 101, 139
Ahire, Kashinath 198
Ahmed, Muzaffar 43, 198
Aiyyar, P.S. Sivaswami 177
Akhil Bharatiya Kisan Sabha 196, 198, 239, 256
Alegaonkar brothers
   night school started by 86
All India Depressed Classes Conference (1930)
   Ambedkar's speech at 250
All India Mill Workers' Convention (1934) 186
All-India Outcaste Community Conference
   first conference 137
All India Trade Union Congress 102, 185, 188, 217–18, 220–21, 237–39, 257, 263–64
All India Trade Union Federation 237, 263
Ambedkar, Balaram Ramji 92, 103–04, 125, 127–28, 145
   death of 149
Ambedkar, B.R. 21, 24–28, 30, 39–47, 54, 56, 64, 75, 87, 92, 95–98, 101–3, 109–10, 113–17, 122, 124–34, 136–40, 143–60, 162–79, 181–84, 186–92, 195–96, 198–200, 206–8, 212–13, 215–21, 223, 225, 227, 230–40, 242–44, 246–54, 259–66, 268, 270, 276
   stance on resisting untouchability 131, 178, 181, 202, 235, 250

   being christened 'Babasaheb' 148
   conversion to Buddhism 234
      More on Ambedkar's 234, 276–77
   deposition to the Southborough Committee 133
   deserters from movement led by 207
   engagement with the CPI 43–44, 163, 206, 231–34
   felicitation in 1917 at Family Lines of 127–28
   friendship with Tilak's sons 155
   Mooknayak (periodical) 146, 156
      founding of 136
   More's association with 202
   on Marx 39–41, 45
   return to India as barrister 137
   'The Caste System in India' 130
   The Problem of the Rupee 138
   view of the DCM 133–34
Ambedkar Seva Dal 150
Ambedkar, Subhedar Ramji 56
Ambedkar, Yashwantrao aka Bhaiyasaheb 259
Amberkar, Mohan 247
American Civil War 28, 29
Antulay, Abdul Rahman 240
Asagikar, Ramji 139
Asaikar, Padmavati 271
Asprushya Nivarak (periodical) 243
Atre, Acharya 246, 261
Atre, Pralhad Keshav. *See* Atre, Acharya
Augustine, Samuel 223
Aurangabadkar, Ram 223
Avhan (periodical) 27, 170, 172, 179, 192–94, 244
   founding of 243
Azmi, Kaifi 248

Baba Padamji 114
Bagul, Baburao 39, 197, 246

Maran Svast Hot Ahe 33
Bahishkrit Bharat (periodical) 25–27, 146–50, 152, 163, 170, 172, 242, 244
Bahishkrit Hitakarini Sabha 37, 105, 137–39, 142, 154, 202, 263
    More's role in the 25
Bajaj, K.L. 257
Baldwin, Stanley 161
Baloo, P. *See* Palwankar, Baloo
Bansod, Kashinath 198
Bardhan, A.B. 198
Barve, Anil 248
    Ranangan (periodical) 257
Bauddhajan Panchayat Samiti 246
Bedekar, D.K. 235
Bhadekaru Sangh ('Tenant Union') 37
Bhagat, Datta 248
Bhagwandas, Dajiba 197
Bhalerao, Shantabai 239, 261
Bhandare, R.D. 200, 216, 232–33
Bhatankar, Subhedar Bahadur Gangaram Krishnaji 113–14, 117–22
    anecdotes of fighting untouchability 118
    help given to untouchables 118
Bhise, Piraji Sadhu 168, 186
Bhogle, R.K. 223
Bhoir, Mahadev 196
Bhosle, D.B. 220, 260
Bhosle, Dinkar 188, 247
Birla, Ghanshyam Das 176, 182
Birla, Lakshmi Niwas 218
Bole, S.K. 87, 98, 131, 162, 261
    Bill to open reservoirs to untouchables 101, 116, 138, 142
    Konkan Province Farmers' Association 236
Bombay 21, 24–30, 32, 34–39, 41, 43–45, 47, 52–53, 56, 60–63, 69, 74–75, 77–83, 85, 87, 89–94, 101–5, 107, 109–10, 114, 116, 122–25, 127–29, 131, 133, 136–47, 149–50, 154–60, 162–65, 168–71, 179, 183–89, 191, 195–201, 206–11, 213, 216–18, 220–23, 225, 230, 233, 236–40, 243, 247, 253, 255–65, 274
    19th century migration to 29
    1896 epidemic in 35
    Batatyachi Chawl 78–79

BDD Chawl 170, 228
BDD *chawls* 31, 36–37, 39, 45, 186, 199
BIT Chawl 187, 225
Cement Chawl 39, 45, 92, 128, 199
Chawl No. 14 on Delisle Road. *See* Bombay: Lal Chawl
chawls 31, 34, 36–39, 45, 60, 79, 137, 150, 169, 186, 199, 217
cotton production in (the Province of) 28
Dadabhai Chawl 227
Dalit life in 27, 30, 32, 186
Dalit politics in 26, 37
Family Lines 60, 75–76, 82, 90, 92, 127
    More's life in 75
history of settlement in 34–36
Kamgar Maidan 44, 163, 171, 205, 208
Lal Chawl 37, 170–71, 196
migration of Dalits to 29
More's first visit to 30, 60
More's life in 27, 31, 32, 75
Municipal Workers' Chawl 208
Red Municipal Chawl 196
Saurabh Chawl 171
slum life in 34
theatre in 39, 78–80
the working class in 28, 30, 32, 34–36, 170
working-class movement in 37, 163
Bombay City Improvement Trust 34–36
Bombay Development Directorate 31, 34, 36–37, 39, 45, 170–71, 186, 199, 228
Bombay Electric Supply & Transport company 188, 220, 247
Bombay Mill-Hands Association 37, 114, 263
Bombay Mill Workers' Union 168
Bombay Theatre 80
Borale, P.T. 259
Bose, Subhas Chandra 222
Brigade Panchayat 127
British Army 22, 29, 113, 118, 122, 159
    expulsion of Dalits from 29
    untouchables in the 54, 110
Buddhist Literary Council 246

caste
    Ambedkar's view of 129–30
    More's challenge to 64

resistance to 21–22, 112–22
   Ambedkar's view on the 131
   Communists and the 25
   importance of Mahad in the 96
   Left politics and the 21, 25–26
   More's role in the 26, 63, 67–66, 107–8, 219–20
Centre of Indian Trade Unions 253, 259
Chandavarkar, Rajnarayan 36
Chandavarkar, Sir Narayan Ganesh 131, 262
Chandorkar, Ramchandra 142–43, 262
Chapadekar, Jamadar 139
Chaudhari, Bhagwan 200
Chauri Chaura 179–80
Chavan, Dr. V.P. 138, 162
Chavan, Yashwantrao 240
Chavdar lake 24, 64–65, 98, 112, 138, 143, 145–47, 149, 151, 153, 202, 239, 247
   satyagraha at 17
      More's role in the 17
chawl life 36–37
Chawl No. 14, Delisle Road. *See* Bombay: Lal Chawl
Chenoy, Rahimulla 218
Chikane, Raoba A. 198
Chitale, Raobahadur 182
Chitalkar, Ramchandra 170–71
Chitnis, G.Y. 271
Chitre, Anantrao Vinayakrao aka Bhai 44, 64, 102, 138–40, 143–45, 157–58, 160, 165, 195, 204, 235–36, 238, 262
   death of 236
   marriage of daughter to Dalit youth 157
Chitre, Bhai. *See* Chitre, Anantrao Vinayakrao aka Bhai
Chitre, Dattatray Mahadev 145
Chitre, Kamlakant 138, 140
Civil Disobedience Movement 160
Colaba District Bahishkrit Parishad. *See* Colaba District Outcastes' Association
Colaba District Depressed Class Conference. *See* Colaba District Outcastes' Association.
Colaba District Farmers' Association 159, 170, 195, 236
Colaba District Outcastes' Association 102, 104, 137, 142–43

conference in Mahad of 149
   Ambedkar's decision to attend 144
   1924 decision to hold a 102
   More's role in organizing the 102–5, 144
Colaba District Peasants' Association. *See* Colaba District Farmers' Association
Com. Chauthmal 198
Communist movement 164–66, 168–69, 186, 191, 198–200, 202, 213, 216–18, 220, 222, 238, 243, 248–49, 257
Communist Party of India 21, 25–28, 31, 41, 43–44, 46–47, 132, 162–72, 184–85, 187–89, 192, 195–96, 198–200, 206–7, 209, 211, 213, 215–23, 230–39, 243–44, 246–52, 255–59, 262–64, 272
   1938 joint strike with ILP 206
   All India Students' Federation 222
   Ambedkar and the 39, 43–44, 163, 200
   and the caste question 26, 162, 219–20, 233, 248–49, 251–52
      More's critique of 27, 46, 252, 272–79
   Communist (periodical) 185
   Dalits and the 46, 167, 169
   Dalits in the 31, 188–89, 198–200
   Fifth (Amritsar) Congress of 253
   First Congress of 213
   in Bombay 185
   life of activists of 165, 189
   lifting of the ban on 211, 220
   Lokyuddh (periodical) 200, 244, 246
   More's early association with the 25–27
   opposition to the Poona Pact 184
   opposition to the Simon Commission 162
   people drawn by More into the 197
   People's War (periodical) 211
   policy on agriculture (1930) 248
   relations with Ambedkarites 44–45, 199
   role in the 1949 railway strike 196–97
   Second Congress of 196, 249, 255
      resolution on untouchability at 251–52
   Seventh Congress of 257
   Third Congress of 252
   untouchability within the 186
   Yugantar (periodical) 27, 237, 244, 247, 256–57

Communist Party of India (Marxist) 27, 198, 237, 239, 246, 253, 257, 259, 264
 and the caste question 253–54
 'Eighth' Congress of 257
 evaluation of Ambedkar 254
 formation of 257
 Jivan Marg (periodical) 239, 244–46, 253, 257, 259
  More on the launch of 244
 People's Democracy (periodical) 259
 Swadhinata (periodical) 259
 The Marxist (periodical) 253
Com. Patekar 257
Comrade R.B. More: A Powerful Link between the Dalit and the Communist Movement 15
 compiling of 27–28
Comrade Vichare 257
Congress Socialist Party 37, 43, 188, 231
cotton farming 28

Dabhade Project 236, 256
Dalit Panthers 26, 41, 257
Dalits 21–22, 24–33, 37, 39, 41, 43–47, 55, 110, 112–17, 126–27, 129, 132, 134, 136, 140, 142, 146, 150, 154, 156–58, 162–69, 172–73, 177, 184, 186–89, 192, 196, 198–200, 202–4, 206–7, 216–17, 219, 221–22, 224, 227, 230–35, 238, 240, 243–44, 246–50, 253–54, 257, 259
 and Bombay city 21, 39
 and the British Army 29
 cultural life of 25, 39, 247
 movement of the 39, 46–47, 112, 134, 157–58, 166–69, 189, 191, 199, 202, 224, 243–44, 246, 259
  temple entry struggles 37, 101, 148–49, 190–92, 202, 207, 243, 262, 265
 under British rule 122–26, 173
  politics of the 161, 173
 writings of 26, 247–48
Dange, S.A. 41, 43, 164–65, 168, 206, 209, 211, 219–22, 230–33, 237, 257, 262
 What is the Stand of the Ambedkar–Asoka Mehta Alliance? 233
Dangle, Arjun 189, 199, 248
Dapoli 22, 53–54, 56, 110, 113, 142, 156, 266

Dalit community in 22
Dasgaon 22, 30, 32, 49, 51–54, 56–64, 68–69, 72–75, 77–78, 80–82, 87, 89, 92–94, 110–12, 125–26, 128, 142–43, 150–51, 165, 224, 240–42, 255–56
 importance in Konkan of 53
 Mahar school in 58, 112
 retired Mahar soldiers in 56
 school started by More in 240, 242
Das, Shankardas Narayan 191
Deccan Riots of 1877 29
Delisle Road Friends' Union 37, 170–72, 246
 celebrating Ambedkar's 1933 birthday 171
 setting up of the 170
Depressed Classes Mission 37, 122, 132–33, 136, 265
 Ambedkar's criticism of the 133
Desai, Mahadev 176
Desai, Morarji 195
Deshmukh, Dr. Punjabrao 149
Deshpande, Roza 213
Deshpande, S.V. 39, 164–66, 169, 185, 262, 271
Dethe, Bhimsen 247–48
Dethe, Godabai 198
Dethe, Pralhad 247
Dethe, Sandipan 197
Devrukhkar, Balkrishna Janoji 177, 206–7
Dhengale, Umaji 197
Dhodapkar, Ramchandra 'Bhikoba' 63–64
Dinabandhu (periodical) 54, 114, 263
Dolas, Devji Dagduji 145
Dolraj 198
Donde, Acharya M.V. 160
Donde, P.B. 220
Dulbhya Subhedar 113, 114. *See also* Bhatankar, Subhedar Bahadur Gangaram Krishnaji

Fakira, Bihari 198, 200
Faro, Rocky 198
Fučík, Julius 222

Gadkari, A.V. 204
Gaikwad, Bhikaji Sambhaji 141, 146
Gaikwad, Karmaveer Dadasaheb aka Bhaurao

INDEX

Krishnaji 41, 141, 150, 191–92, 243, 262
Gaikwad, G.B. 198
Gaikwad, Murlidhar 197
Gaikwad, Sambhaji Tukaram 103, 138–39, 141, 145, 150, 155, 158, 224, 262
    Bahishkrit Aikya-Samvardhak Mahar Samaj Seva Sangh 141
Gaikwad, Sayajirao 127, 131, 265
Gaikwad, Shivram Sambhaji 102
Gaikwad, S.R. 170
Gaikwad, S.T. 198
Gaikwad, Sumant 259
Gaikwad, T.A. 188
Gaikwad, Wakhrikar 145
Gajendragadkar, Justice P.B. 235
Gajvi, Premanand 248
Gandhi, Devdas 176
Gandhi–Irwin Pact 172
Gandhi, M.K. 43, 128, 131, 155, 167, 177, 270, 275
    opposition to separate electorates 180–81
    fast in 181
Gandhi, Vitthal Balkrishna 230–31
Gangurde, Kachru 188
Gangurde, Vishram 197
Garud, Baburao 39, 170–72, 189, 192, 196–97, 262
Gavai, Ganesh Abaji 207
Gavhankar, D.N. 170
Geddes, Patrick 36
Ghatge, Subhedar Radhoram 153
Ghodekar, Yamunabai 271
Ghosh, Ajoy 253
Gidney, Sir Henry 177
Girni Kamgar Union 43–44, 263
Godbole, Bapu Hari 116
Gokhale, Avantikabai 271
Gokhale, Gopal Krishna 103, 236
Gokhale Institute of Politics and Economics 26, 235
    More's address at 26
Gokhale, Jayashree 39, 41
Goldenweiser, Dr. A.A. 130
Gopalan, A.K. 257
Gudekar, Tanaji Mahadev 141, 158
Gurav, Yashwant 197

Guruji, Ankush 189, 248
Guruji, S.A. Upsham 259

Harijans 180, 210
Hate, B.S. 112, 247
    Jithe Pani Petle 247
    Yugavidhan 112
Hate, Jayaram Vitthal 57, 126
Hate, Namdeo Vitthal. *See* Namdeodada
Hate, Shirish 247
Hate, Sitaram Kalu 145
Hate, Vitthal. *See* Hate, Vitthal Anand
Hate, Vitthal Anand 22, 53, 56–57, 110–12, 126, 224
    house in Dasgaon of 111
Hate, Vitthal Tukaram 184
Hazari, Bhurelal 198, 200
Hazari, Jagaram 198, 200
Hindi Rashtriya Sabha 236
Hindu Mahasabha 177
Hindutva 207
Hoare, Sir Samuel 180
Husain, Muhammad 218

Independent Labour Party 41, 44, 118, 159, 171, 183, 188, 201–2, 204–7, 213, 236–38, 266
    and the 1937 Bombay Provincial elections 204
    and the unity of Dalits and non-Dalits 204
    colour of party flag 204
Indian National Congress 39, 41, 43–44, 46, 114, 131–34, 160–62, 169, 172, 174–76, 179–80, 182–83, 195, 200, 204, 207, 209, 211, 213, 215–17, 220–21, 225, 230–33, 236, 240, 248–49, 251, 253–54, 262, 264, 271
    All-India Congress Committee 222
    Ambedkar's view of the 200
    Congress Working Committee 172, 209
    Harijan Sevak Sangh 182–83
    relations with Dalit leaders of the 183
Indian People's Theatre Association 170, 229, 265
Indori, Majnu 197
International Federation of Trade Unions 237
International Labour Conference (1945) 217

More's speech at the 218
International Labour Organization 218, 219

Jadhav, Baburao 188
Jadhav, Bhaskar 198
Jadhav, Bhaskarrao Vithoji 67, 262
Jadhav, D.G. 157, 208, 217–18
Jadhav, Ganpat Mahadev 145, 208
Jadhav, Hiru 172, 196
Jadhav, Nivrutti 138
Jadhav, Pandurang Babaji 150, 225
Jadhav, S.B. 200, 218, 255, 263
Jadhav, Shivram Gopal 158
Jadhav, Shivram Soma 222, 228
Jadhav, Vishram 196
Jadhav, Visu 247
Jafferbhai, Abid Ali 220
Jagtap, Sitaram 240
Jambhekar, R.M. 164, 185, 222, 246
Janata (periodical) 244
Jawalkar, Dinkarrao 153
Jayakar, M.R. 131, 181–82
Jedhe, Keshavrao 153
Jeenwalla, Nissim Rustumji 138
Jinnah, M.A. 176–77
Jog, V.S. 248
Joshi, G.K. 197
Joshi, Laxmanshastri 235
Joshi, Narayan Malhar 102, 138, 140, 142, 170, 176, 217–18, 237, 262–63
Joshi, Purushottam Prabhakar aka Bapurao 160, 264
Joshi, S.C. 160
Joshi, Vitthal. *See* Hate, Vitthal Anand
Joshi, Vitthal Hate. *See* Hate, Vitthal Anand
Joshi, Tukaram Vitthal Hate 56, 57

Kaatkari, Chandrya, the robber 73
Kadam, Raghu 170–71, 196, 222, 263
Kadrekar, Bhaskar 259
Kadrekar, Raghunath 160
Kaivari (periodical) 243
Kajrolkar, Narayan 230–32
Kamble, Bajirao 198
Kamble, B.C. 41, 232
Kamble, Bhanudas 141, 146

Kamble, Chokha 246
Kamble, Harishchandra 247
Kamble, Mahadev Ambaji 138
Kamble, Shivram Janba 113–15, 117, 121–22, 263
  contributions to social reform of 114–15, 116–17, 122
  second Somavanshiya Parishad (1910) 122
  Shri Satchidanand Vachangriha (public library for Dalits) 116
  Shri Shankar Prasadik Somavanshiya Hitachintak Mitra Samaj 116
  Somavanshiya Mitra (periodical) 117
    closing down by Mahars of 117
  Suchipatra 116
Kamble, S.M. 200
Kamble, Vasant 247
Kamble, Vishram 196
Kamleshwar Drama Company 78
  Manovijay
    More's role in 79
    More's role in staging play called 79
Kanekar, P.G. 160
Karandikar Guruji, Uddhav Lakshman 189
Karandikar, U.L. 259
Karhade, Sada 248
Kasbe, Raosaheb 41, 204
  Ambedkar Ani Marx 41
Kavalapurkar, Shivasambha 79
Kavali, R.D. 160, 271
Kelkar, Datta 31, 208, 229, 263
  Atmashodh
    episode from 31, 208, 229–30
Kendrekar, Bhaskarrao 236
Khairmode, Changdeo B. 148, 171, 263, 266
Khandke, Dattatray Vitthal 271
Khandke, Narhari Vitthal 271
Khaparde, G.S. 131, 133
Kharat, Shankarrao 235
Khare, Krishnabai 271
Khare, Ramchandra Keshav 57, 126
Khatavkar, Shivram 271
Khavale, K.D. 188
Khedgikar, R.A. 217
Kher, Bal Gangadhar 138, 160, 195, 206, 238,

263
Kholwadikar, Konddev 271
Kinjalolikar, Krishnabuva 139
Kolhatkar, Achyut B. 271
Kolhatkar, S.Y. 198, 246, 257
Koli, Dalpat 189
Konkan 22, 52–54, 57, 84, 102, 110, 112, 118, 126, 141–43, 145, 150, 156, 196, 218, 224–25, 227, 240, 243, 247, 256, 262, 268
    anti-*khot* agitation of 44, 87, 158, 188, 195, 202, 204, 206, 236–38, 243, 268
    education for Dalits in 52, 56
    epidemic of cholera in 93, 126–27
    migration of Dalits from 30
    More's role in struggles in 24
    religious life in 49
    untouchability in 52, 54
Konkan Buddhist Council 218
Kothare, Pushpa 247
Krishiwal (periodical) 244, 256
Kudikkar, Krishna Khere 196
Kunte, Nanasaheb 240
Kuvekar, Bhiku 196, 263
    police killing of 197
Kuvekar, Kamlakar 196–97, 263

Lakhmapurkar, Dinesh 246
Lal Bavta Kala Pathak 246
Lalit Kaladarsh. *See* Patankar Theatre Company
Lal Nishan Party 198
Lele, R.K. 244
Lenin, V.I. 41, 43, 184
Lokhande, N.M. 37, 263
Lokhande, P.L. 259
Lokhitavadi (Gopal Hari Deshmukh) 114
Lokmanya (periodical) 157, 244
Lokyuddh (periodical) 200, 244, 246
Lokyug (periodical) 244, 247
Lucknow Pact 161, 249

MacDonald, Ramsay 172, 180–81
Madhavan, T.K. 148–49
Madhav, Bandhu 246
Madkebuva. *See* Jadhav, Ganpat Mahadev
Mahad 22–24, 26, 37, 44, 49, 51, 54, 56, 61–68, 72–74, 78, 87–88, 93–103, 105, 107–12, 114, 124–26, 128–29, 136–51, 154, 156–60, 170–71, 187, 202, 235–36, 239–42, 247, 262, 264–66
    drinking water crisis at 65–66
        solving the 66, 138
    satyagraha at 24, 26, 44, 98, 102, 109, 116, 118, 129, 141, 142, 144, 148–49, 156–57, 159–60, 170–71, 187, 202, 235–36, 262, 265–66
        Ambedkar's speech (26 December) at the second 153
        Ambedkar's speech at the second 152
        calling off the second 152–53
        immediate reaction to the 146
        More's role in 144–46
    the tea shop/restaurant for Mahars at 66–67, 96–98, 100–1, 138
Mahadik, Govind 188
Mahad Municipal Council 56, 114, 140
Maharaja of Baroda. *See* Gaikwad, Sayajirao
Maharashtra Dalit Literary Association 246
Maharashtra Times (periodical) 244, 248
Mahars 22, 25, 29, 37, 53–54, 56–61, 65–67, 69, 72–74, 77, 87, 92, 94, 96–98, 100–1, 103, 109–10, 115, 118, 120, 122–23, 126, 129, 132, 139, 141–43, 145–46, 150, 154–55, 162, 166, 179, 199, 223, 225, 227, 233, 235, 243, 247, 261, 266, 271–72
    cultural life of 50
    disbanding of 111th Mahar regiment 96, 132
    gods of the 50
    in Dasgaon 53, 56
        education among Mahars 110, 126
    in Mauritius 110
    More on the rise of 100
    story of Rainak 61
    tradition of carrying a stick among 145
Mahar Samaj Seva Sangh 25, 37, 118, 141–43, 146, 150, 155, 162, 166, 225, 243, 261
    lecture series in Bombay 142, 271–72
    More's role in the 25
Malaviya, Madan Mohan 176, 181–82
Manusmriti 52, 144, 149, 151–52, 265, 270
Maratha (periodical) 244

Maratha Dinabandhu (periodical) 114
Maruti, Babu 164
Marwadi, Samant Nanaji 138
Marx, Karl 25-27, 39, 41, 44-47, 130, 160, 233
   The Communist Manifesto 166, 191
Marxism 21, 25-28, 33, 37, 43-46, 48, 73, 160, 163-64, 168-69, 187-88, 199, 219, 233-35, 256, 272, 274
   Ambedkar on 39, 41
   indigenization of 26-28, 33, 39, 45
   More's attraction to 163
Mashal (periodical) 244, 246
Matunga Labour Camp 35, 37, 39, 45, 189, 191, 197-99, 221, 247, 265
Mauj (periodical) 237
Meerut Conspiracy Case 43-44, 164-65, 185, 219, 261-62
Mehta, Asoka 230-33
Menon, Keshav 149
Meshram, Balwantkumar 198, 211
Meshram, Damayanti Balwantkumar 198
Meshram, Keshav 248
Meshram, Madhavrao Govind 149
Meshram, Maruti 198
Mhashilkar, Govind 247
Mhatre, Dhanaji 196
Mhatre, Kashinath 197, 263
Miraben 176
Mirajkar, S.S. 43, 206, 213, 217-18, 230
Mitha, Tuljaram 160
Miya, Papa 163
   execution of 164
Mohite, Bhargav 196
Mohite, Changdeo Narayan 141, 158, 236, 259, 271-72
Mohite, Narayan 196
Mohoprekar (Joshi) 66
Momin, Abdul 217
Montagu-Chelmsford reforms 98, 132, 134, 173-74
   Communists' view of 134
Moonje, B.S. 177
More, Babu 139
More, Bhai Narendra 247
More, Jagdish
   Sambodhi 247

More, Kamal 211, 213, 228-29
More, K.G. 198
More, Ramchandra Babaji 21, 22, 25-28, 31, 39, 44-49, 52, 71, 74, 97-98, 101, 103, 105-6, 109, 111, 113, 142, 154, 156, 158-60, 172, 185, 190, 207-8, 213, 217, 224, 229, 241-42, 247, 258, 263, 265-66, 271-72
   as a Communist activist 184-85
      conducting study circles in *chawls* 169
      first arrest 186
      going underground 187, 209, 255
      life and party work after 222-23
      harassment by police 187
      setting up civilian defence squads 211
   as a Dalit Communist 28, 41, 47, 157-58, 164, 169, 187-88, 192, 219-20, 233, 259
      Ambedkar on More 47, 166
   as a member of the CPI (M) 257
   autobiography of 15, 26, 46
   Dasgaon
      ancestors' arrival in 110
      implementing the S.K. Bole resolution in 143
      the Pragatik Madhyamik Vidyalay in 240, 242
   death of 258-60
   death of son Sadanand 229
   death of son Subhash 229
   deprivation of family of 31, 225-29
   dire straits of mother of 68-69, 77, 93, 165
   early life 22-24
      acquaintance with a robber 73
      'Akka' in Family Lines 82, 90
         relationship with 75-78, 81
      appearing for high school scholarship exam 57-60
      being a reckless youngster 90-91
      being homeless 31, 83
      birth of 22, 49, 109, 126
      childhood 51, 63
      early activism 24, 66, 88
         becoming a committed activist 101
         first speech in Bombay 104
      education at Mahad 67-68
      experience of untouchability 24, 56-57, 59-60, 62, 65-66, 72

finding work at the docks 77–78, 90–91
first conviction 69
first visit to Bombay 30, 60
in Khadki
  life and work 83–89
  education 86, 88
job as a seamen's cashier in Bombay 75–76
joining Tilak's funeral procession 30, 89–90
leaving Bombay 80–83
life after return to Dasgaon 73–74
life as labourer 30–32, 90–91
marriage 70–72
  decision for 69–70
missing recruitment to Army 74
mixing with the wrong crowd 76–77
moving to Ladawali 60–61
participating in cultural activities 73, 78–80
political activism 37–39
relations with his uncles 58, 61–62, 68–70, 77, 80, 93
schooling in Dasgaon 52, 56–57, 126
second return to Dasgaon 92
  teaching job after 92–93
second trip to Bombay 74–75
spurning job offer of Forest Ranger 94–95
the English school at Mahad
  admission to 63
  denial of admission to 127
  experience of 64–65
  on getting scholarship for 62–61
  return to 95, 96
the tea shop/restaurant at Mahad
  role in setting up 66, 138
  state of affairs after return to Mahad of 96–98, 100–1
third arrival in Bombay 90
establishing the Colaba District Farmers' Association 159
family link with Mauritius 109–10
family of 22
  education in 52, 54, 112

father of
  birth of 111
  death of 51, 58–59
  unfair imprisonment of 111
gaining respect among the Mahar community 100–1
getting acquainted with Marxism-Leninism 164, 166
hardships faced by 224–25
in the 1929 Bahishkrit Parishad at Chiplun 158
in the Greater Indian Peninsular Railway Union 188
leaving Bombay 255
leaving the CPI 257
observations on life in the Konkan 57
observations on caste 50, 54, 98
observations on oppression 50, 96
on his father's wealth 51
on his grandmother 51
  her death in epidemic of cholera 93
on his teachers 57
on the inner-party conflict in CPI after 1962 257
organizing the Colaba District Outcastes' Association conference 102–5, 139–40, 144
Red Family of 213
relationship with Ambedkar 147–49, 166–67, 207, 216–19, 233
  explanation for joining CPI 167
return to Bombay in 1957 256
role in cultural sphere of 25, 246–48
sister Pithu aka Pithubai 89, 126, 165
S.R. More's biography of 27, 46–47
the Dasgaon Janata Pragatishil Sangh 240, 242
Two Historic Conferences at Mahad 134
understanding the systemic oppression of Mahars 97–98
untouchability
  observations on 53, 92, 95, 98–100
  acknowledging role of British in alleviating 98
visit to Paris 218–19
working among sanitation workers 189

More, Raya 139
More, Satyendra R. 13, 15, 17, 25–27, 31, 39, 44, 46–47, 49, 74, 92, 98, 109, 122, 160, 165, 172, 174, 177, 179, 207, 228, 234, 255, 262–63
   forming the Bal Sangh 211–13
   praise for More 146, 168–69, 189, 208
   resentment against More 18
More (Sayagaonkar), J.G. 188
More, Shankarrao 236
More, Sitabai 71, 165, 211, 225–29
More, Subodh 13–14, 27–28, 71, 97, 106–7, 190, 208, 226, 245, 258–59
Morley–Minto Reforms 132, 161, 173, 249
Mudaliar, Diwan Bahadur Ramasamy 177
Mukunda, Govind Wullud 115–16
Mumbai Kamgar (periodical) 243
Mumbai Samaj Seva Sangh 236
Municipal Kamgar Sangh 41
Munshi, K.M. 206
Muranjan, Sumant 235
Musadkar, Shivrambuva 158
Muslim League 162

Naidu, Sarojini 176, 264
Naik, D.V. 154, 160, 271
Nambiar, Suhasini 225, 264
Namboodiripad, E.M.S. 46, 252–53, 266
Namdeodada 59, 60, 62, 126
Nandgaonkar, Ramchandra 196–97
Naoroji, Dadabhai 133
Nariman, G.K. 138
Nashik *satyagraha* 41, 243
National Railway Workers' Union 188
Natya Sammelan 247
Naval Workers' Union 223
Navjivan Kala Mandal 247
Nayar, Madhavan 149
Nayar, Velappan 149
Nehru, Jawaharlal 43
Nerurkar, P.S. 248
Nikam, Sukhdev 198
Nimbkar, R.S. 219, 237
Non-Brahmin Party 87, 261
Nuri, Barrister 220, 221

Ogale, S.P. 218
O'Hanlon, Rosalind 112
Omvedt, Gail 39, 41
Ostekar, Dharmabuva 150
Ovhal, Nana 196

Pagare, Shankar Narayan 197, 199
Pal, Bipin Chandra 131
Palwankar, Baloo 129, 177, 183, 204
Palyeyashastri, Mr. 154, 264
Panchal, Janardan 247
Panniraselvam, Raobahadur A.T. 177
Pant, Shridhar 155
Panze, A.P. Sir 177
Paranjpe, Dr. R.P. 138, 177
Parulekar, Godavari 239, 248, 264
Parulekar, S.V. 44, 106, 158, 160, 166, 195, 204, 206, 227, 237–39, 264, 271
Patankar Theatre Company 80
Patel, Vitthalbhai 131
Pathak, Dina 248
Pathak, N.R. 256
Patil, Dadasaheb 149
Patil, D.B. 246, 256
Patil, K.M. 188
Patil, Narayan Nagu 158, 195, 240, 264
Patil of Charai, Putalya Mahar 72–73
Pattani, Prabhashankar 176
Pattherao, Bapu 79
Pawar, Baloo 196–97
Pawar, Daya 246–47
Pawar, S.K. 196
Pawar, Urmila 248
Peasants and Workers Party 41, 158, 230, 236, 242, 246, 256
Pendse, Lalji 206
People's Education Society 218, 239
Periyar 149
Phadnis, Madan 197
Phule, Jotirao 56, 88, 112, 114, 116, 122, 156, 167–68, 250, 261, 275
   Dashavatar Pradipika of 88
   Gulamgiri of 88
Phule, Savitribai 122
Poona Pact (1932) 43, 179–80, 182–84
   result of the 183

Potdar, Acharya Madhav 247
Potdar, Ramji Babaji 143, 240
Prabhu, Kamalabai 271
Prabuddha Bharat (periodical) 244, 265
Pradhan, B.V. 154, 204
Pradhan, D.V. 160, 236, 272
Pradhan, Jayant
   Comrades Lal Salaam 257
Pradhan, Manoramabai 271
Praja Socialist Party 41
Prarthana Samaj 37, 123, 262, 265
Pune
   More's life in 30, 32
Pyarelal 176

Quit India movement 170, 211

Raigad district
   colonial administration in 52
Rai, Lala Lajpat 102, 129
   death of 172
Rail Worker (periodical) 243
Rajadhyaksh, J.V. 237
Rajagopalachari, C. 182
Rajah, Raobahadur M.C. 177, 183, 207
Rajbhoj, P.N. 141, 145–46, 151, 191, 206–7
Ramasamy Naicker. *See* Periyar
Ramchandra, K. 257
Ramteke, Bhojraj 198
Ranade, Justice Mahadev Govind 114, 264, 275
Ranadive, B.T. 46, 164–65, 185–87, 196–97, 204, 206, 209, 222, 225, 227, 253, 255, 259, 264, 266
Ranadive, C.T. 204
Ranadive, Vimal 259
Rancière, Jacques 30
Rankhambe, Amritrao 206, 207
Ranpise, Appasaheb 244
Ranpise, Manohar 248
Rao, Diwan Bahadur Ramachandra 177
Rathod, Zinabhai Moolji 138
Red Chawl (or Red Tenement). *See* Bombay: Lal Chawl
Reddy, G.L. 218, 240
Red Flag Mill Workers' Union 186

Red Trade Union Congress 185
Republican Party of India 41, 265, 276–77
Risley, Sir Herbert 114, 264
Rohekar, Tukaram 172
Rokade, Kashinath 197
Round Table Conference
   British objective of 174
   the First 174–75
      Ambedkar's petition at 174–75
   the Second 172, 176–78, 180
      Ambedkar and Gandhi's fight at 176–78
      Ambedkar's demand at 177
         support for 177
      Gandhiji's betrayal at 173
      Gandhi on reform for untouchables at 176
      impact on Dalit political rights of 179
      Minorities Committee at 176
   the Third 182
Ruke, R.G. 259
Rupavate, Dadasaheb 223, 265

Sahasrabuddhe, G.N. 138, 143–45, 151, 160, 236, 238, 265, 271
Sahasrabuddhe, Ramabai Gangadhar 271
Sahni, Balraj 197, 248
Sakpal, Hari 188
Salve, Pandoba 158
Salvi, K.M. 39, 190–91, 197, 246, 265
   friendship with More of 191
Salvi, Pandurang Mahadev 141
Samaj Samata Sangh 154–57, 202
   Samata (periodical) 154, 244
Samant, Hiraman 197
Samata Sainik Dal 150–51, 171–72, 200, 243
Samudre, Bhaiyalal 198
Samyukta Maharashtra Samiti 41
Sankrityayan, Rahul 234
Sanzgiri, Prabhakar 253
Sapru, Tej Bahadur 176–77, 181–82
Sardar, G.B. 235
Sardesai, Srinivas 188, 256
Sartape, Balkubuva 198
Sartape, Najabai 198
Sartape, Pramod 247

Sartape, Tukaram 197
Sasalekar, Captain 200
Satamkar, Devakibai 271
Sathe, Annabhau 39, 170, 172, 197–98, 211, 246–48, 265
   Majha Bhau Annabhau (book by his brother) 247
Satya Prakash (Marathi periodical) 24, 88
Satyashodhak Samaj 102, 114, 116, 155, 262
Sawadkar, Anil 13–14, 99, 118–19, 151, 159, 193–94, 244
Sawadkar, Kashinath Vishram 239
Sawadkar, Subhedar Vishram G. 56, 140, 118, 159, 239
Sawant, A.B. 196, 260
Sawant, J. 242
Sawant, Nilkanth aka Bhai 242
Sawant, Sakharam 218
Scheduled Castes Federation 44, 183, 200, 213, 215–16, 218–19, 221, 231–32, 263, 276
   founding of 215
   struggle with the INC 215–16
Seligman, Edwin Robert Anderson 130
Servants of India Society 102–3, 138, 160, 236–37, 239, 263
Setalvad, Dr. Sir Chimanlal Harilal 138
Shahu Maharaj, Chhatrapati 116, 122, 129, 134–37, 146
   death of 137
Shaikh, Amar 170, 172, 234, 247–48
   Yugadip (periodical) 234, 244
Shaikh, Sikandar 170, 196
Shailendra, Shankar 188
Sharma, P.L.K. 217
Shastri, Rajaram 114
Shetkari Kamgar Paksha 41
Shetye, Bhai 256
Shinde, Ramesh 247
Shinde, Vitthal Ramji 131–32, 136, 265
   betrayal of untouchables by 122
Shiralkar, Kumar 248
Shirgavkar, Ramji 139
Shirke, Dagadu 196–97
Shirke, Harishchandra 196
Shirke, Sadashiv 196
Shivaji, Chhatrapati 61

Shiv Sena 43, 63, 266
Shivtarkar, Sitaram 207
Shivtarkar, Sitaram Namdeo 138, 145
Siddharth College 105, 198, 223, 246
Siddharth Literary Association 246
Simon Commission 43, 161–62, 172, 174, 179
   Ambedkar's deposition before the 162, 174
Simon, Sir John 161
Singh, Bhagat 164
Socialist Party 231–32
Social Service League 102–3, 138–39, 144, 237, 263
   background of 103
   Damodar Hall (in Parel) 102–5, 138–40, 156
   Sahakari Manoranjan Theatre Company 104, 139
Sonawane, Bhargav 39, 170, 172, 197
Southborough Committee 122, 129, 132–34, 136, 161, 179, 262
   Ambedkar's deposition to the 133
South-Eastern Railway Union 198
Soviet Union 209, 211, 213, 266
Soviet Varta (periodical) 244
Srinivasan, Rettamalai 174, 177, 183
Stafford Cripps Mission 213, 215
Strathern, Marilyn 21
Surve, Arjun 196–97
Surve, Narayan 13, 248
Suryavanshi, G.T. 189

Tagore, Rabindranath 131
Talwatkar, Ghanshyam 218, 223, 239, 246–47, 259, 265
Tambebuva, Bhikaji 196
Tambe, Moreshwar 247
   Maharachi Soon urph Prem Pratap 247
Tambe, Nadgaonkar 228
Tamhankar, Govind 39, 171–72, 197, 265
Tamhankar, Govind Vitthal 170
Teltumbde, Anand 43
Tembe, Govind 172
Thackeray, Bal 63, 266
Thackeray, Prabodhankar 63, 156–57, 166, 265, 271–72

solemnizing More's sister-in-law's marriage 156
Thakkar Bappa 183
Thakkar, Datta 247
Thakre, Keshav Sitaram. *See* Thackeray, Prabodhankar
the Peshwas 16
The Times of India (periodical) 204
third all-India Conference of the Depressed Classes (1942) 215
   Resolutions on the Cripps Mission 215
Tilak, Lokmanya Bal Gangadhar 30, 86, 115–16, 131–32, 148, 155–56, 162, 167, 191
   death of 89–90
   Kesari (periodical) 115, 132
   neglecting Dalit issues 115, 132, 156
Tipnis, Govind Gopal 64
Tipnis, Kamalakar Kashinath
   marriage of More's sister-in-law to 156
Tipnis, Nanasaheb 158
Tipnis, Shantaram 145
Tipnis, Surbanana 140, 145, 204, 266
Tipnis, Surendranath Govind. *See* Tipnis, Surbanana
Tipnis, Yashwant Narayan 64

Urdhvareshe, Usha 247

Vaidya, D.S. 170, 222, 229, 266
Valmiki, Chandori 200

Wadawalkar, P.L. 218
Wadawalkar, Shankar Lakshman 141, 148, 156–57, 236, 266
Waghmare, Mohan 247
Waghmare, Santuji 162
Waghmare, Sopan 197
Wakode, Manohar 248
Walangkar, Gopal Baba 22–23, 30, 54, 56, 69, 96, 110, 112–14, 116–18, 132, 145, 266
   Anarya Dosh Parihar Mandal 113–14, 116
   contribution to social reform of 54, 112–14
   Destruction of Caste Pollution 112
   meeting Jotiba Phule 112
   More's relation to 22, 30
   relations with More's family 56
Warerkar, B.V. aka Mama 154, 156, 266
   Duniya (periodical) 155
Wargharkar, Tukaram 139

Yashwante, Shrawan 247
Young Workers' Association 170, 196, 238, 243